D0913200

D0913200

Wagner Androgyne

PRINCETON STUDIES IN OPERA

Reading Opera, edited by Arthur Groos and Roger Parker (1988)

Puccini's "Turandot": The End of the Great Tradition by William Ashbrook and Harold Powers (1991)

Unsung Voices: Opera and Musical Narrative in the Nineteenth Century by Carolyn Abbate (1991)

Wagner Androgyne: A Study in Interpretation by Jean-Jacques Nattiez, translated by Stewart Spencer (1993)

Wagner Androgyne

A STUDY IN INTERPRETATION

Jean-Jacques Nattiez

TRANSLATED BY
STEWART SPENCER

PRINCETON UNIVERSITY PRESS
PRINCETON, NEW JERSEY

Published by Princeton University Press, 41 William Street,
Princeton, New Jersey 08540
In the United Kingdom: Princeton University Press,
Chichester, West Sussex

Library of Congress Cataloging-in-Publication Data

Nattiez, Jean-Jacques.
[Wagner androgyne: a study in interpretation /
Jean-Jacques Nattiez; translated by Stewart Spencer.
p. cm.
Includes bibliographical references and index.
ISBN 0-691-09141-2
1. Wagner, Richard, 1813–1883—Criticism and interpretation.
I. Title.
ML410.W13N3513 1993
782.1'092—dc20 92-23250

This book has been composed in Linotron Galliard

Princeton University Press books are printed on acid-free paper and meet the guidelines for permanence and durability of the Committee on Production Guidelines for Book Longevity of the Council on Library Resources

Printed in the United States of America

1 3 5 7 9 10 8 6 4 2

To Carolyn Abbate

Culture and art, too, could be perfect
only if a product of the act of suspending the
divided unity of male and female.

—Richard Wagner

CONTENTS

Part Three. *Wagner and Androgynous Hermeneutics*

PREFACE

IN ACT II of Wagner's *Siegfried*, the hero stretches out on the forest floor beneath the speading branches of a lime tree and, to the accompaniment of the Forest Murmurs, starts to reflect on his parentage. He begins by congratulating himself that Mime, the loathsome dwarf who has brought him up, is not his real father, and then goes on to ask himself:

Wie sah mein Vater wohl aus?	What must my father have looked like?
Ha! gewiß, wie ich selbst!	Ha! Of course, like myself!

(*GS* 6.133)[1]

His thoughts then turn to his mother:

Aber—wie sah meine Mutter wohl aus?—	But—what must my mother have looked like?—
. . . .	. . . .
Ach, möcht' ich Sohn meine Mutter sehen!— Meine Mutter— ein Menschenweib!—	Ah, might I, her son, see my mother!— My mother— a mortal woman!—

(*GS* 6.134)

Later, the Wood Bird tells him that he will find a wondrous woman, the Valkyrie Brünnhilde, asleep on a rock, sunk in deepest slumber as a punishment for having transgressed her father's will: only a man who has never known fear will pass through the circle of fire that shields her. Only a hero such as he will be able to set her free.

And when, in the final scene of all, Siegfried finds himself in the presence of the sleeping Brünnhilde, the entire action hinges on the question of sexual confusion. Brünnhilde lies "in a deep sleep, in full shining armor, a helmet on her head and covered with a long shield," according to Wagner's stage direction (*GS* 6.164). "Ha! In armor, a man!" Siegfried exclaims; and, even before removing the warrior's helmet and seeing his hair, "What rapture his likeness recalls!" Taking out his sword, he removes the coat of mail and discovers Brünnhilde in her woman's clothing: "It's not a man!" (*GS* 6.164). Shocked, surprised, and filled with dismay, Siegfried cries out for help: "Mother! Mother! Remember me!" (ibid.).

Through womankind, Siegfried learns the meaning of fear:

Wie end' ich die Furcht?	How can I put an end to my fear?
Wie fass' ich Muth?	How can I summon up courage?
Daß ich selbst erwache,	That I myself may wake,
muß die Maid ich erwecken!—	the maid I must awaken!—

(*GS* 6.166)

And he wakes her by kissing her: "He sinks, as though dying, on the sleeping woman and, his eyes closed, presses his lips to her mouth." (This stage direction appears only in the full score.)

There now begins one of the great love duets in the history of music. Brünnhilde greets the sun, renewing her links with the Earth and the sky, and telling Siegfried she has always loved him. He asks:

So starb nicht meine Mutter?	So my mother did not die?
schlief die minnige nur?	Was the lovely woman only sleeping?

(*GS* 6.167)

To which Brünnhilde replies:

Deine Mutter kehrt dir nicht wieder.	Your mother will not return to you.
Du selbst bin ich,	Your own self am I
wenn du mich Selige liebst.—	if you but love me, blessed that I am.

(*GS* 6.168)

"Du selbst bin ich": in her love for Siegfried, Brünnhilde is the first to describe herself as androgynous.

She, too, feels for the first time what it is like to wake up to her own sexuality. As Patrice Chéreau has rightly pointed out, the Valkyries have known only dead men until now:

Er erbrach mir Brünne und Helm:	He broke open my breastplate and helmet:
Brünnhilde bin ich nicht mehr!	Brünnhilde am I no more!

(*GS* 6.171)

She, too, feels afraid, and Siegfried presses her to act as a woman:

Liebe dich,	Love yourself
und lasse von mir:	and let me be:
vernichte dein Eigen nicht!	do not destroy what is yours!

(*GS* 6.173)

To which Siegfried replies:

Dich lieb' ich:	It is you whom I love:
. . . .	. . . .
Nicht hab' ich mehr mich.	I no longer possess myself.

(Ibid.)

Thus Siegfried, in turn, lurches toward sexual ambivalence.

The scene culminates in the lovers' androgynous embrace, an embrace instinct with death:

lachend lass' uns verderben, lachend, zu Grunde geh'n!	laughing let us perish, laughing go to our doom!

(*GS* 6.175)

And:

Erb' und Eigen, ein' und all'! Leuchtende Liebe, lachender Tod!	My heritage and own, my one and all! Light-bringing love and laughing death!

(*GS* 6.176)

In his study *Wagner l'enchanteur*, Jean Matter writes:

> The all-consuming need for *unity* that is at the heart of the Wagnerian oeuvre derives from extremely deep-seated causes, which we must attempt to define before proceeding any further. And this need for unity, which is nothing more nor less than the love defined by Aristophanes in Plato's *Symposium*, is associated here with the figure of Wagner, so much so, indeed, that it is tempting to refer to that race of androgynous beings, described in the same speech, from which Wagner himself, like so many other creative artists of his caliber, almost seems to be descended. We may claim, in this context, that the existence of *bisexuality* was glimpsed by Wagner well before it came to preoccupy the thoughts of those masters of modern psychoanalysis of whom we are so proud. . . . Space, alas, does not allow us to expand on a subject that would fill a book of its own. (1968, 29)

This is the book that I myself have attempted to write, albeit from a different standpoint.

Although it has never been the subject of any specific study, the idea of Wagner's androgyny has occurred from time to time in writings on the composer. One thinks, for example, of Anne-Marie Matter's *Richard Wagner éducateur* (1959, 145–50), which in many ways anticipates Robert Donington's Jungian interpretation of the *Ring* (1963); of Jean Azouvi's article "Siegfried ou la quête de l'unité" (1977), in which

Azouvi discovers the Platonic myth of androgyny in the relationship between Siegfried and Brünnhilde; of Jean-Pierre Juliard's study "Le Tondichter et l'androgyne" (1979), in which Wagnerian androgyny is illustrated by an examination of the libretto; and, finally, Serge Gut's 1981 article, in which the author believes he can detect an androgynous element in the Tristan Chord.

The idea, then, is not new. Indeed, it would be surprising if it had not already been broached by earlier writers in some hidden corner of a bibliography so immense that no single scholar can claim to have read all around it.[2] At least this proves that if the data on which I rest my case are not the ones most often discussed in dealing with Wagner, they are nonetheless sufficiently self-evident to have caught the attention of observers well known for the seriousness of their approach.

But, if there is no doubting the androgynous dimension to Wagner's thought and works, the same is not true of the way in which that dimension may be interpreted. Faced with such a subject, the straitjacket of psychoanalytic exegesis—be it Freudian or Jungian—never seems far away. But is this really what we need? Is it enough to say, as Thomas Mann did when describing the confusion between mother and wife in *Siegfried*, that the hero's appeal to his mother is "pure Freud, pure psychoanalysis" (Mann 1933, 98)?

It may be thought surprising that a musicologist with an interest in semiology (Nattiez 1990) whose writings have been devoted, in part, to purely musical analysis should now take an interest in psychoanalysis, even though he has no firsthand experience of it, either as patient or as practitioner. I would counter the objection, however, by pointing out that if musicology does not concern itself with psychoanalysis, psychoanalysis will concern itself, sooner or later, with musicology, as is clear from the writings of Reik, Michel, and, more recently, Salomon. In a wider context, too, an entire area of my thinking, more in evidence here than in my previous writings, relates to the links between the semiotics of music and hermeneutics.[3] It was only to be expected, in approaching a subject such as Wagner and androgyny, that we would have recourse to the hermeneutics of the *symbol*, which represents a different area of reflection and activity but whose semiological character is difficult to deny.

It should be clear, therefore, what is at stake here. An opera is a complex semiological reality in which libretto, musical composition, and stage action are interrelated. Moreover, no other composer has left so many autobiographical traces as Wagner: some forty volumes of correspondence,[4] ten volumes of prose writings, and an autobiography. What is the significance of androgyny in Wagner's works and theoretical writings when seen within the context of the texts, the composer's life, and the age in which he lived? This is the question to which I hope to provide an answer.

The search for an answer will lead me to attempt to demonstrate two different theses, both of which ascribe a central role to androgyny: first, that the myth around which the *Ring* revolves may be read as a metaphorical reenactment of Wagner's conception of the history of music; and second, that throughout his life, Wagner's theory of the relationship between poetry and music is reflected, in his music dramas, in the relations between man and woman. But how is such a demonstration best undertaken? On the epistemological plane, Paul Veyne's concept of "plot"[5] is at the very heart of our investigations. In discussing the data with which the historian works, Veyne writes:

> Facts do not exist in isolation, in the sense that the fabric of history is what we shall call a plot, a very human and not very "scientific" mixture of material causes, aims, and chances—a slice of life, in short, that the historian cuts as he wills and in which facts have their objective connections and relative importance. . . . The word plot has the advantage of reminding us that what the historian studies is as human as a play or a novel, *War and Peace* or *Antony and Cleopatra*; . . . then what are the facts worthy of rousing the interest of the historian? All depends on the plot chosen; a fact is neither interesting nor uninteresting; . . . in history as in the theater, to show everything is impossible—not because it would require too many pages, but because there is no elementary historical fact, no eventworthy atom. If one ceases to see events in their plots, one is sucked into the abyss of the infinitesimal. (1971, 32–33)

The situation of someone seeking to understand and analyze an opera is not fundamentally different from that of the historian. We can attempt to explain the presence of androgyny in Wagner's works in terms of the Freudian or Jungian "plot" but also by applying the methodology of genetic history and asking ourselves where Wagner first encountered the idea of androgyny. How does that idea tie in with his own life? And if, as we shall see, Wagner's androgyny is closely bound up with his conception of the links between music and poetry, who shall we say is right—those in whose view music and poetry alternated in importance throughout his life or those for whom, Wagner's own hesitations notwithstanding, music remained his quintessential preoccupation? Can one say that all these plots are of equal validity and that there is no single and exclusive Wagnerian truth? At a time when the siren song of deconstruction continues to exercise its powerful sway, the epistemological stakes are clearly considerable: can I say anything definitive, anything at all reasonable about what I am studying? I shall attempt to discover the answer to this question by examining Wagner's androgyny in all its complex symbolism.

• • •

Parts of this study were originally the subject of a seminar first held in the Faculty of Music at the University of Montreal in 1976–77 and repeated on subsequent occasions. Certain of the ideas advanced here were also presented at conferences at Columbia University, the University of Maryland, the University of Michigan, the Universities of Montreal and McGill, the Toronto Semiotic Circle, the Banff Fine Arts Center, the Hebrew University of Jerusalem, the Porter Institute of the University of Tel Aviv, the Sorbonne, the Université Laval (Quebec), the University of Melbourne, and the University of Queensland (Brisbane). It is impossible to mention by name all the students and colleagues, most of whom remained anonymous, whom I met in the course of my travels, but their questions often encouraged me to think more deeply about the subject. To all of them I owe my thanks.

I must, however, list the names of those who invited me to present these papers: Judith Becker, Jan Finlay, Marike Finlay, Margareth Kartomi, Carol Robertson, Kay Shelemay, Paul Bouissac, Étienne Darbellay, Itamar Evenzohar, Mantle Hood, Jean-Rémy Julien, David Mendelson, and Gordon Spearritt. I am additionally grateful to those who spontaneously provided me with information or who took the trouble to reply to specific requests: Danièle Pistone, Ruth Solie, James Boon, Eric Domville, Andrew Gray, Lawrence Kramer, Georges Leroux, Jean Le Tourneux, Pierre-Michel Menger, Charles Rosen, Alexander Ringer, and Heinz Zednik; also to Carolyn Abbate, John Deathridge, and Jean Molino, who kindly agreed to cast a critical eye over earlier versions of the manuscript. But for the lengthy and detailed conversations that I had with the latter, this study would have had a different structure, while the epistemological orientation of the concluding chapters would not be as pronounced. My final debt of thanks is to Herr Günter Fischer for the welcome he gave me at the Nationalarchiv der Richard-Wagner-Stiftung in Bayreuth.

It must be emphasized that although it was begun more than ten years ago, this study would not have been completed if the University of Montreal had not accorded me leave of absence. My warmest thanks, finally, are due to Céline Pagé-Laniel, who proved equal to the task of deciphering an often difficult manuscript and to Lise Durocher for preparing the musical examples.

Jean-Jacques Nattiez
September 1989

NOTE TO THE ENGLISH EDITION

THE PRESENT STUDY is essentially a translation of the volume published in French in 1990 under the title *Wagner androgyne*. I have taken the opportunity to correct a number of errors in the French edition, and in Chapter Six I have added a note on the significance of androgyny in *Tristan und Isolde* and commented on the intellectual relationship between Nietzsche and Wagner. With my agreement, the system of references used to cite Wagner's writings has been altered from the numerical system adopted in the French edition and brought into line with the chronological approach employed elsewhere in this volume.

BIBLIOGRAPHICAL NOTE

THIS STUDY contains many references. Because the date of publication bears heavily on the line of argument, it is important that all such dates be readily accessible. Hence the following conventions:

1. In the case of Wagner's theoretical writings, be they books or articles, all references are to the chronological Catalog of Writings included at the back of the volume. References to the ten-volume *Gesammelte Schriften und Dichtungen* (*GS*) are to the second and subsequent editions (Leipzig: E.W. Fritzsch, 1887–88); for the later volumes, the sixteen-volume *Sämtliche Schriften und Dichtungen* (*SS*) has been preferred (Leipzig: Breitkopf und Härtel, 1911–16). The first number refers to the relevant volumes; that following the period refers to the page. Since Wagner's prose has been translated afresh for the present volume, it was not considered useful to include textual references to William Ashton Ellis's eight-volume translation of Wagner's prose works (London: Kegan Paul, Trench, Trubner, 1892–99; reprint, 1972).
2. *ML* represents Wagner's autobiography, *Mein Leben*, the first unexpurgated edition of which was published by List Verlag of Munich in 1963. References are also made to the English translation by Andrew Gray, edited by Mary Whittall and published by Cambridge University Press in 1983.
3. Wagner's libretti are quoted from the *Gesammelte Schriften* edition, modified, where necessary, to take account of changes that Wagner made to the published text while working on the musical setting. All these texts have been newly translated for the present purposes, although existing translations by Newman, Jameson, and Porter have occasionally been consulted.
4. Drafts of unfinished operas, including *Die Bergwerke von Falun* (The mines of Falun), *Achilleus*, *Jesus von Nazareth*, *Wieland der Schmied* (Wieland the smith), and *Die Sieger* (The victors), are cited from the *Gesammelte* or *Sämtliche Schriften*.
5. *SB* represents *Sämtliche Briefe*, Wagner's collected correspondence, currently being published by the Deutscher Verlag für Musik, Leipzig. Of a projected forty volumes, only seven have appeared to date, covering the period up to July 1857. For the later period, the following editions have been used:

   Familienbriefe *Familienbriefe von Richard Wagner (1832–1874)*. Ed. Carl Friedrich Glasenapp. Berlin: Alexander Duncker, 1907.

   Freunde und Zeitgenossen *Richard Wagner an Freunde und Zeitgenossen*. Ed. Erich Kloss. Berlin and Leipzig: Schuster und Loeffler, 1909.

Liszt-Briefe *Franz Liszt–Richard Wagner: Briefwechsel*. Ed. Hanjo Kesting. Frankfurt am Main: Insel Verlag, 1988.

Nietzsche-Briefe *Nietzsche: Briefwechsel. Kritische Gesamtausgabe*. Ed. Giorgio Colli and Mazzino Montinari. Berlin and New York: Walter de Gruyter, 1975–.

Röckel-Briefe *Briefe an August Röckel von Richard Wagner*. Ed. La Mara [Marie Lipsius]. Leipzig: Breitkopf und Härtel, 1894.

Wesendonck-Briefe *Richard Wagner an Mathilde Wesendonk: Tagebuchblätter und Briefe 1853–1871*, 44th ed. Ed. Wolfgang Golther. Leipzig: Breitkopf und Härtel, 1914.

Wille-Briefe *Fünfzehn Briefe Richard Wagners mit Erinnerungen und Erläuterungen von Eliza Wille geb. Sloman*. Munich, Berlin, and Zurich: C. F. Meyer, 1935; reprint, 1982.

6. *CT* represents Cosima Wagner's diaries, translated by Geoffrey Skelton (London and New York: Collins, 1978–80), and is cited according to the date of the relevant entry (e.g., *CT*, 1 January 1869).
7. *WWV* represents *Wagner Werk-Verzeichnis*, ed. John Deathridge, Martin Geck, and Egon Voss (Mainz: Schott, 1986).
8. All other references are indicated by the author's name followed by the year of publication. Page references are either to the original edition or, in the case of an existing translation, to the latter. Full details are included in the alphabetical bibliography at the back of this volume.

PART ONE

Androgyny and the *Ring*: From Theory to Practice

MYTHIC NARRATIVE, THEORETICAL DISCOURSE

The Story of the Ring

Because we shall be concerned essentially with the four parts of the *Ring*, it seems sensible to preface the following remarks with a summary of its plot, reduced, so far as possible, to a neutral account of the action on stage. This, in turn, may help to make the subsequent interpretation more readily intelligible.[1]

Das Rheingold [The Rhine gold]

Scene 1. On the bed of the Rhine. An orchestral prelude describes the surging floodwaters, in which the three Rhine daughters—Woglinde, Wellgunde, and Floßhilde—frolic and play, watched by the Nibelung Alberich, who tries in vain to seduce them. His gaze is arrested by a ray of light that catches the gold in the Rhine daughters' care. They commit the folly of telling him that only the man who renounces love will be able to forge a ring from the gold and thus acquire universal power. Alberich does not hesitate: he curses love and makes off with the gold.

Scene 2. On the banks of the Rhine, with Valhalla in the distance. Fricka has been asleep beside her husband, Wotan. On waking up, she discovers Valhalla, the gods' new home, which Wotan, their chief, has prevailed on two giants, Fasolt and Fafner, to build. Fricka reminds him that as their reward, he has promised the giants Freia, the goddess of youth and beauty. It is Freia's golden apples that grant the gods their eternal youth. Despite the treaties engraved on his spear, Wotan assures his wife that he never intended to hand over Freia to pay the giants: he is counting on Loge, the god of fire, to save her with his cunning. The giants now enter to claim their due, but of Loge there is no sign. Wotan begins to temporize, showing reluctance to keep his word. The giants prepare to carry off Freia, but Donner, the god of thunder, threatens them with his hammer. Loge arrives and reports the theft of the gold, describing the virtues of the ring. The giants express an interest in it and Loge proposes that he and Wotan should go and steal the gold from the thief, claiming that such an action would not be a crime. The giants accept this new proposal but keep Freia as a hostage, while Wotan and Loge descend into Nibelheim, Alberich's subterranean home.

Scene 3. In Nibelheim. Alberich belabors his brother, Mime, snatching away the Tarnhelm, a magic helm that permits its wearer to turn himself into any shape he chooses. He tries it on and, rendered invisible by its power, proceeds to whip his brother with an equally invisible scourge. Alberich tells the Nibelungs that they are now his slaves. Wotan and Loge enter and listen to Mime's litany of woe. Alberich returns, driving before him an army of Nibelungs weighted down with gold and silver. Seeing Wotan and Loge, he holds out the ring, striking terror into the Nibelung horde and ordering them to return to the mines and bring out yet more gold. He reveals his desire for universal power but Loge flatters him and, to demonstrate his skill, the dwarf turns himself first into an enormous serpent and then into a toad. Wotan and Loge seize him and, having bound him, lead him away with them.

Scene 4. Beneath the walls of Valhalla, as in scene 2. Alberich asks the price of his freedom. The others demand his treasure. He summons the Nibelungs, who enter with the gold. Loge also demands the Tarnhelm. Wotan tears the ring from Alberich's finger, provoking the latter into laying a curse on it. The giants return with Freia and decide to pile up the gold until she is hidden from view. The Nibelung gold having proved insufficient to cover her completely, they demand the Tarnhelm and then the ring, which Wotan feels constrained to give up following Erda's intervention. The giants argue over the gold and Fafner kills his brother, thus furnishing proof of the power of Alberich's curse. He carries off the treasure, having handed Freia back to the gods. Fricka looks forward to settling down in Valhalla, but Wotan is sunk in somber thoughts. Passing over a rainbow bridge created by Donner, the gods enter Valhalla, while Loge predicts their downfall and the Rhine daughters sing of their stolen gold, demanding its return.

Die Walküre (The Valkyrie)

Act I. Inside Hunding's hut. Sieglinde, unaware that she is Wotan's daughter, has been forced into marriage with Hunding. As the drama opens, Siegmund, fleeing his enemies, stumbles into Hunding's hut and, exhausted, begs a drink of water from Sieglinde, who is awaiting her husband's return. A bond of love develops between them, and Siegmund decides to wait for Hunding. The latter is struck by the similarity between his wife and Siegmund. At Hunding's bidding, Siegmund tells the story of his life. Without revealing his name, he recalls how one day he returned from hunting with his father to find his mother murdered and his twin sister snatched away. He then goes on to tell of a desperate struggle in the course of which he killed some of Hunding's kinsmen, blood relatives of the very man with whom he has now sought refuge. Hunding offers him a night's hospitality but challenges him to single combat the following morning. After Hunding has left, Sieglinde returns. She explains to Siegmund that an old man (in reality Wotan) had entered the room and thrust his sword into the trunk of the ash tree that grows through the floor of the house. The sword, he had said, would belong to the man who succeeded in drawing it out. Siegmund and Sieglinde yield to their mutual love. The door flies open, allowing the springtime night to enter the room and suborn the lovers with its spell. The moon grows ever brighter. Conscious of what they are to each other, brother and sister embrace. Siegmund draws the sword from the tree and names it Nothung. He draws his sister into his arms and she abandons herself to his embrace.

Act II. A wild and rocky mountain landscape. Wotan has summoned Brünnhilde, his Valkyrie daughter by Erda, and bids her side with Siegmund in his impending fight with Hunding. Fricka enters, the guardian of wedlock's sacred bonds. She expresses her revulsion at the carnal union between brother and sister and demands that Wotan reverse his decision. At the end of a long and difficult altercation, he yields to his wife's entreaties and now has to justify his change of heart to his daughter. Wotan renounces godly splendor and senses that Alberich's power is growing. He orders Brünnhilde to do as Fricka wishes. The lovers enter. Sieglinde, exhausted by their long flight, collapses in a faint, while Siegmund settles down to wait for Hunding. Brünnhilde enters to tell him that he is destined to die. Armed with Nothung, Siegmund refuses to believe her and even threatens to take Sieglinde's life. Brünnhilde is shaken by his show of love and determines to disobey her father, promising Siegmund protection in his fight with Hunding. The latter enters and the two men do battle. Siegmund is at the point of killing his rival when Wotan intervenes, and it is Siegmund who is killed. Brünnhilde snatches Sieglinde away. In his despair, Wotan takes his son's body in his arms and, with a wave of his hand, consigns Hunding to oblivion. Rising to his feet, he sets off in pursuit of his dissident daughter.

Act III. On the summit of a wild and rocky mountain. The act opens with the famous "Ride of the Valkyries." Brünnhilde enters, fleeing her father's wrath and telling Sieglinde that she will give birth to the hero, Siegfried. Sieglinde makes her escape, taking with her Nothung's shattered fragments and seeking refuge in the forest, not far from the cave where Fafner, transformed into a dragon, guards the golden hoard. Wotan enters. Brünnhilde begs his forgiveness, reminding him that she had only wanted to carry out her father's innermost wishes. But Wotan remains inflexible: he will put her to sleep on a rock, prey to whoever happens to wake her. But she begs that the rock be surrounded by fire, so that only a hero can win her. Wotan yields to her entreaties. Kissing away her godhead, he puts his daughter to sleep, covering her with her shield, and summoning Loge. He disappears behind the wall of fire.

Siegfried

Act I. Mime's forge in the depths of the forest. Sieglinde has died giving birth to Siegfried, who has been brought up by Mime, not without ulterior motives: with Siegfried's help, Mime hopes to win the ring and the hoard that Fafner guards not far from his cave. The curtain rises on Mime, whom Siegfried has ordered to forge a sword for him; but all the dwarf's labors are unavailing and Siegfried shatters his latest effort on the anvil. Siegfried attempts to discover the names of his parents; Mime replies by showing him Nothung's fragments, which Siegfried orders him to reforge. He then runs off into the forest. Wotan has renounced all power and wanders the face of the earth in the guise of the "Wanderer." He enters Mime's smithy, and a long game of question and answer, summarizing the previous action, develops between the two characters. Wotan leaves Mime, telling him that only the man who does not know the meaning of fear will succeed in reforging Nothung and that Mime will perish at his hands. Siegfried returns and asks if Mime has forged the sword. Faced with the dwarf's incompetence, Siegfried sets to work himself. Throughout all this, Mime tries in vain to teach him the meaning of fear. Siegfried reforges Nothung and, to Mime's horror, splits the anvil in two with it.

Act II. In the depths of the forest. Alberich and Wotan are prowling around outside the cave in which Fafner guards not only the Rhinegold but, far more important, the ring. Wotan rouses Fafner and announces Siegfried's impending arrival. Mime tries to discourage his charge from attacking the dragon, but Siegfried's courage is all the more whetted. Left alone, Siegfried begins to muse on his past and wonders, wistfully, who his mother was. He hears a forest bird and attempts to imitate its singing, but in vain. Taking up his horn, he wakens Fafner, who emerges from his lair. A fight ensues, at the end of which Siegfried drives Nothung into the dragon's heart. He tastes its blood and suddenly finds he can understand the language of the forest birds. The Wood Bird tells him to enter the cave in search of the Nibelung treasure. Mime and Alberich emerge from their place of concealment and quarrel over the treasure even before they have Siegfried in their power. The latter now returns from the cave, wearing the ring and carrying the Tarnhelm. Invincible, he is able to understand Mime's innermost thoughts and discovers that the dwarf is planning to poison him. When Mime tries to make him drink the potion that he has brewed, Siegfried strikes him dead with his sword. Once again he hears the voice of the Wood Bird, inviting him to waken Brünnhilde.

Act III. Disturbed by the course that events are taking, Wotan consults the Earth goddess, Erda, but she has no new suggestions to make. Even though he is powerless to prevent the fate of the world from passing from the hands of the gods into those of humankind, he attempts to bar Siegfried's way as the latter repairs to Brünnhilde's rock. But Siegfried shatters Wotan's spear. There follows Brünnhilde's awakening and the love duet described in the preceding pages here.

Götterdämmerung (The twilight of the gods)

Prelude. On the Valkyries' rock, the three Norns weave the rope of fate. They embody the past, the present, and the future. The rope breaks in the hands of the third of them: the end of the gods is approaching. A musical interlude follows, describing dawn. Siegfried and Brünnhilde enter. She is wearing the ring that he has given her as a token of his feelings. They swear eternal love. The orchestra describes Siegfried's journey along the Rhine in search of new adventures.

Act I. The curtain rises on the Hall of the Gibichungs, situated on the banks of the Rhine. Hagen, Alberich's son, dreams of possessing the ring. Gunther and

Gutrune, brother and sister, would like to marry. Hagen suggests that Gunther might succeed in winning Brünnhilde with the help of Siegfried, intimating that a magic potion would ensure that the latter fell in love with Gutrune. His plot is put into practice. Siegfried comes ashore. Replying to their questions, he naïvely shows them the Tarnhelm. He drinks the potion that Gutrune offers him and immediately falls in love with her. In order to obtain Gutrune from her brother, Siegfried offers to win Brünnhilde for Gunther and the two men swear an oath of blood-brotherhood to that effect.

The scene returns to the Valkyries' rock, where Brünnhilde waits for Siegfried's return. Waltraute, one of her Valkyrie sisters, comes to plead with her, asking her to give up the ring and free the race of gods from the curse that lies upon it. Seeing in it only a token of Siegfried's love, Brünnhilde refuses to do so. She hears his horn but Siegfried, wearing the Tarnhelm, enters in the shape of Gunther. He seizes the ring and places his sword between the two of them in order to keep the oath of loyalty that he swore with Gunther.

Act II. In front of the Hall of the Gibichungs. Alberich presses his sleeping son to murder Siegfried and regain the ring. Hagen replies that his plan will be crowned with success. Alberich leaves and Hagen summons the vassals to celebrate the double wedding of Siegfried and Gutrune, and Gunther and Brünnhilde. Brünnhilde cannot believe her own eyes, whereas Siegfried remains in total self-control. She sees the ring on his finger and realizes that it was he who passed himself off as Gunther. Hagen seizes his chance. On the point of Hagen's spear, Siegfried swears his innocence, while Brünnhilde vows to avenge the man who betrayed her. Left alone, Hagen persuades Gunther to connive with Brünnhilde at Siegfried's death. She reveals that his back is vulnerable. Hagen suggests that they make his death appear the result of a hunting accident.

Act III. A wild and wooded valley along the Rhine. The Rhine daughters attempt to persuade Siegfried to give them the ring but, in spite of their prophecy that he is shortly to die, he refuses to do so. Hagen and Gunther enter with a group of vassals. Siegfried tells them the story of his life. Before he reaches his meeting with Brünnhilde, Hagen offers him a drink, which restores the tender memories that he has of her. The vassals are dumbstruck by these revelations and Hagen seizes his chance to plunge his spear into Siegfried's back. A funeral march accompanies the body's return to the Hall of the Gibichungs. Ignorant of the plot to murder her husband, Gutrune anxiously awaits his return. Confronted by his body, she accuses Gunther of murdering him, but the latter points the finger of blame at Hagen. Hagen claims the ring. Gunther refuses to hand it over and Hagen kills him. As Hagen attempts to remove the ring, Siegfried raises his arm in a threatening gesture. Brünnhilde enters: wisdom has now been vouchsafed to her. It is she who will put an end to the curse that has weighed on the gods since Wotan committed the very first crime. Through her actions, she will usher in an era of human love. She places the ring on her finger, gives orders for a funeral pyre to be built around Siegfried's body, and finally sets it alight. She spurs her horse into the flames as the Rhine overflows its banks, bearing with it the Rhine daughters, who claim the ring as their own. Hagen plunges into the floodwaters, trying to snatch the ring back from them, but is dragged down into the depths. The flames seize hold of Valhalla, which falls in ruins. Dusk falls on the gods.

The action is complex, certainly, and only the basic outline has been retained in the present retelling; yet the plot is perfectly logical. But caution is called for: one narrative can always conceal another . . .

Interlocking Texts

In his "Letter to M. Villot," written in 1860 and more familiar under the title of *"Zukunftsmusik,"* Wagner writes:

> It would be truer to say that the most daring of my conclusions concerning the form of the music drama that I was seeking to render feasible forced themselves upon my attention precisely because, even then, I was already toying with the idea of my great Nibelung drama, part of which I had already written, realizing my plan in such a way that my theory was virtually little more than an abstract expression of the artistic and creative process then at work within me. (1860c, *GS* 7.118)

This text can be understood in one of two different ways:

1. the *Ring* is the work in which Wagner offers the best illustration of the dramaturgical principles that he discusses in theory elsewhere (the cycle has already been analyzed a thousand times over from this particular point of view); or
2. it is not only the *form* of the *Ring* that reflects its author's dramaturgical ideas but its *content*, too—in other words, the story that it tells.

In opting for the second of these two interpretations, we may be able to read into certain aspects of the *Ring* a work *on* music drama, a *metaphor*, both fictional and narrative, of more abstract ideas expressed in the theoretical writings on which Wagner worked between 1848 and 1853, that is, at the very time when the libretti of the *Ring* were gestating in his thoughts.

I am well aware that such an approach represents a certain reversal of the normal way of interpreting Wagner's writings. Carl Dahlhaus, the leading German Wagner scholar, concludes his study of Wagner's theoretical writings by arguing that "Wagner varied the philosophical, aesthetic and political theories he proclaimed in his writings entirely for the sake of his musical dramas, which in the last analysis were the only thing that truly possessed him. The works are the key to the writings, not vice versa" (Deathridge and Dahlhaus 1984, 87). To the extent that Wagner did not set out to elaborate a philosophical and aesthetic system that, once and for all, would be illustrated by his dramatic works as the practical counterpart of an a priori theoretical position, Dahlhaus is right to argue as he does. Certainly, Wagner published numerous justifications, all of which were subject to the influences of the moment, his 1854 conversion from Feuerbachian "optimism" to Schopenhauerian "pessimism" being not only the best-known example of this dramatic volte-face but also, no doubt, the most fundamental change of outlook of his entire development. Nonetheless, it remains the case that Wagner's most important writings were committed to paper at the very time when his head was filled with ideas concerning the conception and composition of the music dramas themselves. It would be surprising, therefore, if there were not a profound semantic relationship between the two types of text, so that the abstract discourse casts light on the contents of the aesthetic undertaking.

A detailed examination of the chronology of the period under review shows clearly how imaginative works and theoretical writings were inextricably interlinked in their creator's mind:

4 October 1848. Wagner completes prose draft of *Die Nibelungensage (Mythus)* (The Nibelung legend [Myth]) (1848g), later retitled *Der Nibelungen-Mythus. Als Entwurf zu einem Drama* (The Nibelung myth. As draft for a drama) and published in *GS* 2.156–66.

20 October 1848. Completes prose draft of *Siegfrieds Tod* (Siegfried's death), the earliest version of *Götterdämmerung. Siegfrieds Tod* versified 12–28 November 1848.

Late 1848 or early 1849. *Die Wibelungen: Weltgeschichte aus der Sage* (The Wibelungs: world history from legend) (1849a).[2]

January 1849. Drafts *Jesus von Nazareth*, a drama probably intended for the spoken theater.

10 February 1849. "Der Mensch und die bestehende Gesellschaft" (Man and existing society), an article published in August Röckel's *Volksblätter* (1849f).

18 April 1849. "Die Revolution," an article published in the *Volksblätter* (1849g).

End of July 1849. Completes *Die Kunst und die Revolution* (Art and revolution) (1849h).

First half of September 1849. Revised version of *The Wibelungs*.

4 November 1849. Completes *Das Kunstwerk der Zukunft* (The art-work of the future) (1849m).

End of 1849. Beginning of interest in *Wieland der Schmied* (Wieland the smith).

12–28 January 1850. First prose draft of an opera scenario, *Wieland der Schmied*.

23 February 1850. Begins "Kunst und Klima" (Art and climate) (1850a).

11 March 1850. Completes second draft of *Wieland der Schmied.*

Before 3 June 1850. Writes (unpublished) preface for *Siegfrieds Tod* (1850b).

Between 27 July and 12 August 1850. Two sets of musical sketches for *Siegfrieds Tod.*

After 22 August 1850. Completes "Das Judenthum in der Musik" (Judaism in music) (1850c).

10 January 1851. Completes *Oper und Drama* (Opera and drama) (1851a).

17 April 1851. Completes "Ein Theater in Zürich" (A theater in Zurich) (1851f).

Between 3 and 10 May 1851. First prose sketch of *Der junge Siegfried*, the forerunner of *Siegfried.*

24 May–1 June 1851. Extended prose draft of *Der junge Siegfried.*

3–24 June 1851. Versification of *Der junge Siegfried.*

Between 9 and 15 July 1851. Begins *Eine Mittheilung an meine Freunde* (A communication to my friends) (1851h).

Mid-August 1851. Completes *Eine Mittheilung an meine Freunde.*

Between 3(?) and 11(?) November 1851. First prose sketch for *Das Rheingold.*

Between 11(?) and 20(?) November 1851. First prose sketch for *Die Walküre.*

Late 1851 and early 1852. Additional prose sketches for *Das Rheingold* and *Die Walküre.*

23–31 March 1852. Extended prose draft for *Das Rheingold.*

17–26 May 1852. Extended prose draft for *Die Walküre.*

1 June–1 July 1852. Versification of *Die Walküre.*

23 August 1852. Completes *Über die Aufführung des "Tannhäuser"* (On performing *Tannhäuser*) (1852e).

15 September–3 November 1852. Versification of *Das Rheingold.*

15 December 1852. Completes revisions to *Der junge Siegfried* and *Siegfrieds Tod.*

22 December 1852. Completes *Bemerkungen zur Aufführung der Oper "Der fliegende Holländer"* (Remarks on performing the opera *The Flying Dutchman*) (1852h).

Mid-February 1853. Publication of poem of *Der Ring des Nibelungen* in a privately printed edition.

1 November 1853. Begins musical composition of *Das Rheingold.*

If the foregoing summary differs from those that are generally found in accounts of the genesis of the *Ring*,[3] it is because I have included not only Wagner's theoretical writings but also *Wieland der Schmied* and *Jesus von Nazareth*. The reason for their inclusion will become clear shortly.

But in attempting to find correspondences between two types of textual reality—theoretical writings on the one hand and a theatrical work on the other—we still have to account for the logical steps that allow us to find in the *Ring* something of the theory that accompanies it. And this is true even if they were conceived by one and the same person over a relatively short period of time.

The link between them is provided by the symbolic figure of androgyny—a figure that, as we have seen, is present at least in the duet between Siegfried and Brünnhilde but that, as the following chapter will show, also underpins the composer's conception of the relationship between poetry and music as expounded in the theoretical writings of 1849 to 1851.

Chapter One

THE THEORETICAL ESSAYS OF 1849 TO 1851

HARDLY HAD WAGNER completed the full score of *Lohengrin* on 28 April 1848 when a whole new series of ideas began to clamor for his attention—*The Nibelung Legend*, the prose draft of *Siegfrieds Tod*, an article on the Wibelungs, the prose draft of *Wieland der Schmied*, the essays. As we saw in the Introduction, theoretical reflections and plans for dramatic works went hand in hand at this crucial moment in the life of a man whose mind was teeming with a thousand simultaneous projects, as he glimpsed the creative opportunities for the whole of the rest of his life even if, for the present, he lacked the maturity needed to bring them to fruition. In fact, the *Ring* was not completed until 1874. Even the music was not started until 1 November 1853, by which date Wagner had already written a long series of essays, to the chief among which we must now turn our attention: *Art and Revolution* (1849h), *The Art-Work of the Future* (1849m), "Judaism in Music" (1850c), *Opera and Drama* (1851a), and *A Communication to My Friends* (1851h).[1]

This whole series of essays is typical of Wagner's creative style: *Art and Revolution* is the length of an average article (33 pages in Wagner's collected works). Scarcely had he completed it when he began a much more elaborate work, *The Art-Work of the Future* (135 pages), which takes up and develops ideas contained in the earlier piece. But already he was planning a multipart sequel, originally called "The Artists of the Future," "The Men Who Will Build the Art of the Future," and "The Essence of Opera." Conceived as a single article, it quickly grew into a full-scale work and was published, in two separate volumes, under the title *Opera and Drama* (327 pages). Even while *Art and Revolution* was still in press, Wagner was already announcing *The Art-Work of the Future*, while what was later to become *Opera and Drama* was explicitly presented as the *conclusion* of the earlier essay.[2]

Each essay, in fact, amplifies its predecessor, taking us from the abstract to the concrete. In *Art and Revolution* Wagner traces the rough outlines of a development leading from the original, unified art of the Greeks to the art of the future, which, he argues, will not be viable until *after* the coming revolution. This development is described in greater detail in *The Art-Work of the Future*, where Wagner looks more closely at the component parts not only of Greek tragedy but also of the musical drama in which he places all his hopes. *Opera and Drama* attempts a more historical approach and takes as its essential theme the relationship between poetry and music throughout the evolution of opera as a genre.

It is this that enables us to approach these three texts as a single entity, a unified whole into which other shorter but no less important texts such as "Art and Climate" and, above all, "Judaism in Music" can readily be inserted and which Wagner worked on over a period of only eighteen months. Anyone other than Wagner would perhaps have combined the contents of all these essays and made them the subject of a single work. But scarcely had he committed one idea to paper when he felt the need to see it in print, trying to make himself understood by those who did not understand him (in other words, the entire world), even if it meant starting all over again the following month.

These works have an underlying thematic unity. And because each of them takes up the ideas of the preceding piece, developing and transforming them, the paradigmatic method seems best suited to taking full account of them. What is meant by the paradigmatic method is a technique that consists, in this case, of superimposing the four main essays so that their common thematic axes emerge as though, at bottom, we were dealing with only a single text. This does not mean that we shall ignore the differences between them. Quite the opposite. The paradigmatic perspective allows us to show that precisely the same function is fulfilled by Apollo in the one essay, by Christ in a second, and by Siegfried in a third. But beyond the disparities that they contain, all four essays tell a single story: when the art of drama was still in its infancy, among the ancient Greeks, unity reigned supreme; then, beneath the destructive pressures of the Romans and Christianization, this pristine unity fell apart; a new age will come, however, when unity will be restored.

Original Unity

Greek Tragedy as a Unifying Rite

In the beginning were the Greeks: "If we consider the matter closely, we shall admit the impossibility of taking even a single step in present-day art without noticing the way in which it is bound up with the *art of the Greeks*. For, in point of fact, our present-day art is but a link in the chain of development of the whole of European art; and this development started out from the Greeks" (1849h, *GS* 3.9). What Wagner is struck by, above all, is the existence of an elevated artistic genre—tragedy—whose creation and execution reveal an underlying *unity* of god, populace, poet, and theater: "Having placed the *beautiful, strong, and free human being* at the very pinnacle of religious consciousness, the Greek spirit . . . found its fullest expression in *Apollo*. . . . It was this Apollo who fulfilled the will of

Zeus upon the Grecian earth; who was, in fact, the Grecian people" (ibid., 3.10). This being, who embodied both man, the people, and god, was a familiar figure to Aeschylus, "the tragic poet who, inspired by Dionysus, joined the bond of speech, the supreme poetic intent, to all the elements of those disparate arts that had sprung unbidden, of themselves, and as the result of inner necessity, from the fairest human life, concentrating them into a single focus in order to produce the highest conceivable work of art, the *drama*" (ibid., 3.10–11). The theatrical celebration was, therefore, nothing more nor less than a "divine festival" in which the whole of society communed with itself, and "the poet, as its high priest, was reified and embodied in his work of art. . . . Such was the Greek work of art; such their god Apollo, incarnate in actual, living art; such was the people of Greece in its highest truth and beauty" (ibid., 3.11). And what did the populace do, in amphitheaters built to seat thirty thousand people? They flocked to see the *Prometheia*, each member of the audience "finding inner harmony before this mightiest of works of art, gaining self-understanding, fathoming the meaning of his private actions, and merging in intimate oneness with the essence of all that was Greek, with his community, and with his god" (ibid.).

In *The Art-Work of the Future* Wagner insists on the ritual character of the Hellenes' theatrical ceremony: "Lyric and dramatic works of art were a *religious* act. . . . Tragedy was thus a religious ceremony raised to the level of a *work of art*" (1849m, *GS* 3.132).

Wagner's insistence on the fusion of the constituent parts of Greek society, united in the theatrical mystery, must not be underestimated. Greek tragedy was unity *embodied*, unity *enacted*.

Unified Society

It was necessary, however, for society itself to be unified if tragedy was to fulfill this function. The unity of the populace, the creative artist, and art itself presupposed a *harmonious relationship between man and nature*:

> The free Greek, who placed himself at the head of nature, could create art from man's delight in himself. . . . Art is the highest form of activity on the part of each and every individual who has developed his physical beauty in harmony with himself and with nature; man must derive supreme delight from the world of the senses before he can create the instruments of his art from it; for only in the world of the senses can he find the will to create the work of art. (1849h, *GS* 3.15)

Nonetheless, this harmonious union of man and nature does not signify a state of equality. After all, Wagner insists that man places himself "at the head of nature," the better to dominate her:

> It was left to the Hellenes to develop the purely human work of art and, of their own accord, to extend it to the point where it represented nature. They could not be ready for this human work of art, however, until they had triumphed over nature in the sense in which it presented itself to the Asiatic peoples and until they had placed man at the head of nature, imagining those individual forces of nature as gods who, fully anthropomorphized, bore themselves with the beauty of human beings. (1849m, *GS* 3.124)

Wagner returns to this theme in his article "Art and Climate": "The progress made by the human race in developing its innate ability to wrest from nature the satisfaction of those needs that increased as its own activities increased is synonymous with the *history of culture*. . . . Only the man who, by dint of individual activity, gains his *independence from nature* is the *historical* individual, and *only historical man*—not primitive man, who is dependent on nature—has summoned *art* into life" (1850a, *GS* 3.208–9).

The union of creative man and nature presupposes *societal unity*: "Tragedy flourished for only so long as it was inspired by the spirit of the people and so long as this spirit was truly popular, in other words, a *communal* spirit" (1849m, *GS* 3.105). Greek tragedy, therefore, was less the work of an individual artist than of a community of artists: "In tragedy he [the Greek] rediscovered himself, finding there the noblest part of his own nature united with the noblest parts of that common nature shared by the nation as a whole" (1849h, *GS* 3.12). Not even the "greatest minds" can create "the one, true, great work of art: we, too, must help them to produce it. The tragedies of Aeschylus and Sophocles were the work of Athens" (ibid.).

This collective achievement was due to men whose intellectual qualities were equaled only by the physical qualities of the *holistic* human being: "thus the Greek was himself actor, singer, and dancer" (ibid., 3.24). The spectator was indistinguishable from the performer: "In chorus and protagonists Greek tragedy brought audience and work of art together. . . . The drama developed into a work of art only when the chorus's clarifying judgment found such irrefutable expression in the actions of the protagonists that the chorus could retire from the stage and mingle with the audience and thus become useful as a participant in the action, enlivening that action and helping to bring it about" (1851a, *GS* 3.268).

The Unifying Components of Tragedy

When god, the people, the poet, and drama are united, and when man is united with nature and with the rest of the social body, tragedy itself is bound to be an expression of unity. In *Art and Revolution* there is only one reference to the arts as three sisters engaged in a round dance (1849h,

GS 3.20), but the image returns as the central symbol of *The Art-Work of the Future* in keeping with Wagner's typical procedure of amplifying former ideas: "*Dance*, *Music*, and *Poetry* are the names of the three primeval sisters whom we see entwining their measures the moment that the conditions necessary for the manifestation of art arise" (1849m, *GS* 3.67). Although Wagner does not refer to the Greeks here, they are evidently in his thoughts since, a few pages later, he alludes to the fate of these "three graceful Hellenic sisters" (ibid., 3.71). The three artistic genres originally formed a single entity since they were a product of the people: "Wherever the *people* made poetry, . . . the poetic intent entered into life on the shoulders of dance and music, as the *head* of the full-fledged human being" (ibid., 3.103). The *mousike* of the Greeks, of course, was not only music but a kind of lyric poetry intoned or sung.

In *Opera and Drama* Wagner refers briefly to the unity of text, gesture, and music that had constituted the framework of *The Art-Work of the Future*:

> The lyric and dramatic work of art was a spiritualized form of physical movement, a process made possible by language, while monumental visual art was its unconcealed deification. The Greeks felt impelled to develop music only to the extent that it had to serve to underline gesture, whose meaning was already expressed, melodically, by language. In accompanying dance movements with the melodious language of words, that language acquired so fixed a prosodic meter that . . . the natural speech accent . . . often took second place. (1851a, *GS* 4.104)

The thinking behind *Opera and Drama*, however, is no longer ternary but binary, and although the three Hellenic sisters have not been entirely forgotten, the author is now concerned with rather more recent history in the form of the history of opera. By the same token, the manifestation of ancient unity that serves as Wagner's point of departure in this third of his major essays is no longer Greek tragedy, with its synthesis of dance, poetry, and music, but the folk song, with its combination of language and music. "Here poetry and music [*Wort- und Tondichtung*] are as one. It never occurs to the common people to sing their songs without a text; there would be no tune for them without the words. Just as the tune changes with the passage of time and with the different degrees of kinship to the common tribe, so the words change, too: it is impossible to imagine them being separated in any way, since both belong together like man and wife" (ibid., 3.249). A little later, Wagner returns to the sexual metaphor, which is even more explicit this time: "When the *common people* invented tunes, they did so in the manner of natural human beings, who beget and give birth to other human beings in the spontaneous act of sexual congress" (ibid., 3.309).

Primal unity rests on an act of physical union that, in the case of Wagner's three sisters in *The Art-Work of the Future*, is possible only when love and liberty reign supreme.

Liberty and Love

> As we gaze upon this entrancing measure of the artist's truest and noblest muses, we now perceive all three of them, each with her arm affectionately entwined about her sister's neck; then, now this one and now that frees herself from the others' embrace in order to show them her beauteous form in full independence, merely brushing the others' hands with the tips of her fingers; now one of them, entranced by the sight of her sisters' tight embrace, bowing down gently before their twin beauty; then two of them, transported by the charm of the third, greeting her with tender homage; until at last all three are tightly clasped, breast on breast and limb to limb, melting together with the fervor of love's kiss to create a single, wondrously living human form.—Such is the love and life, the wooing and winning of art, the one true art whose several parts, ever for themselves and ever for one another, diverge to create the richest contrast and reunite in blissful harmony. This is art that is free. The sweet and forceful impulse in the sisters' dance is the *yearning for freedom*; the kiss of love as their arms entwine is *the joy of newfound freedom*. The *lonely man is not free*, because, in the absence of love, he is fettered and dependent; *the sociable man is free*, because, unfettered, he is made independent by love. (1849m, *GS* 3.67–68)

I have quoted this passage in extenso partly because I shall have more to say about it shortly and partly because it offers a clear formulation of Wagner's belief that the constituent parts of the total work of art are essentially interdependent—a belief that he underlines in his somewhat bombastic manner (although Wagner's amphigorical style is not of any concern to us here), arguing that if dance, music, and poetry freely combine, it is in the name of love:

> Knowledge through love is freedom, the freedom of human abilities or *universal ability*. Only the art that reflects this universal ability is free, therefore, not the individual kind of art that issues from only a single human ability. On their own, dance, music, and poetry are limited. . . . The very act of grasping the hand held out by her sister art lifts her above the barrier that divides them; . . . and, when every barrier has been destroyed in this way, neither the individual varieties of art nor the barriers themselves will exist any longer, for what will emerge will be art itself, communal, unrestricted art. (Ibid., 3.69–70)

What, then, was the subject matter of Greek tragedy? "Until now, genuine drama could issue only from the Greek view of the world. Its subject matter was *myth*, and only on the basis of the latter's innermost nature can we understand the supreme work of Greek art, the very form of which so fascinates us. . . . Greek tragedy is the artistic realization of the content and spirit of Greek myth" (1851a, *GS* 4.31–33). It is the modern poet's task to rediscover man's essential purity in a unified whole: "It was the tragic poet who offered the most convincing and intelligible account of the content and substance of myth, and tragedy is nothing more nor less than the artistic culmination of myth, while myth itself is the poetical expression of a common view of life" (ibid., 4.34). The common people or *Volk* rediscovers its corporate identity in the unity of myth, since myth expresses "the common people's common poetical vein" (ibid., 4.31). Thus the poet of Greek tragedy was none other than the people themselves: and thus the argument comes full circle.

The system underlying Wagner's thinking is straightforward. At the beginning is a state of primal unity, the unity of the god (Apollo), the poet-priest (Aeschylus and Sophocles), the common people, and drama. The unity of society reflects the union of man and nature. Unity forges a link between the constituent parts of tragedy (dance, music, and poetry) and of its parameters (gesture, prosody, music). None of this was possible without freedom and love. The scenery had been set up, but then, with the arrival of the barbarian hordes and the expansion of Christianity, humanity would be plunged into darkness for two thousand years. The paradigmatic axes of the opening act would remain the same, but Wagner inverts the signs.

Lost Unity

Humanity was lost in the wilderness from the end of the Hellenic period to the time when Wagner arrived on the scene. "It is to *philosophy*, not to art, that the two thousand years belong that have passed between the decline of Greek tragedy and our own day" (1849h, *GS* 3.13). Only a handful of isolated beacons penetrate this period of gloom. "Here and there, art's dazzling beams lit up the night of discontented thought, of humanity's brooding madness" (ibid.). These were the rays of light cast by Shakespeare, Bach, Goethe, Schiller, and Beethoven:

> For centuries, the greatest and most noble minds—before whom Aeschylus and Sophocles would have bowed their heads in brotherly joy—raised their voices in the wilderness. . . . Of what avail, then, is the fame of these noble minds? Of what avail that *Shakespeare*, like a second Creator, revealed to us the infinite wealth of genuine human nature? Of what avail that *Beethoven* gave to music the independent, manly strength of poetry? . . . What is your art now, what is your drama? (Ibid., 3.22–23).

The original state of unity has been lost and, with it, the tragedy that embodies that unity. Wagner goes on to identify the stages in this process of disintegration in order to give a clearer idea of the way in which unity can be restored.

The Causes of Disintegration

The decay to which Greek tragedy fell prey was a reflection of political decay:

> Hand in hand with the dissolution of the Athenian state went the decline of tragedy. Just as the spirit of the community was fragmented in a thousand egotistical ways, so that great work of total art that is tragedy disintegrated into the individual components that it contained: on the ruins of tragedy, the writer of comedies, Aristophanes, wept in demented laughter, and all impulse to create art finally stagnated in the face of philosophy's gloomy broodings as it pondered the reasons for the transience of human beauty and strength. (1849h, *GS* 3.12)

Two new ideas are found here, replacing Wagner's earlier themes. In place of collective communion and love—qualities characteristic of the Hellenic age—come individual egoisms, while tragedy gives way first to comedy and then not to any artistic creation but to philosophical speculation.

First came the Romans, who replaced the festival of art, essentially religious in nature, with gladiatorial games: "they did not open up their great popular theater to the gods and heroes of myth nor to the free dancers and singers of the sacred chorus. No! Wild beasts, lions, panthers, and elephants were forced to tear themselves to pieces in the amphitheater in order to glut the Roman eye, while gladiators, slaves who were trained to be strong and skillful, were obliged to delight the Roman ear with their final agonized screams" (ibid., 3.13). In such a world, it was "self-contempt, existential loathing, horror of the generality of mankind" that gained the upper hand (ibid., 3.14). Art could not flourish in such a climate, where only Christianity thrived.

Wagner's paradigmatic coherency is particularly apparent here. For the Greeks, art and religion had conjoined to form a single entity—tragedy. Art had disappeared, and a new religion taken its place. It is important, however, to bear in mind that, for Wagner, there were two types of Christianity. First, there was early Christianity, with Christ's authentic message and its magnificent response to the barbarousness of Roman civilization. Christ, for Wagner, was the successor to the Greek Apollo, and it was to him that Wagner devoted his dramatic fragment *Jesus von Nazareth*, sketched out in the early part of 1849, some six months before he set to work on *Art and Revolution*:

> Thus *Jesus* would have shown us that we are all equal, that we are all brothers, while *Apollo* would have stamped this great bond of brotherhood with the seal of strength and beauty, leading mankind from doubt in his own intrinsic worth to awareness of his highest godlike might. Let us, then, erect the altar of the future, in life as in living art, to the two sublimest teachers of mankind: *to Jesus, who suffered for all mankind, and to Apollo, who raised them to their joyous dignity.* (Ibid., 3.41)

But Christianity, historically, was not the word of Christ. "It justifies man's dishonorable, useless, pitiful existence on earth by appealing to the wondrous love of a God who certainly did not create mankind . . . for a joyful, self-conscious life on Earth" (ibid., 3.14). Christian thought—or, as we would say nowadays, Christian practice—turned its back on the Greek world, rejecting physical beauty as a manifestation of the Devil (ibid., 3.16). Whereas the Greek had gone to the amphitheater, the Christian shut himself away in a cloister, replacing "honest democracy" with "hypocritical absolutism" (ibid.).

Christianity could produce nothing of merit on the aesthetic front: "Christianity was neither art itself nor could it ever bring forth true, living art from within itself" (ibid., 3.15). Elsewhere, Wagner denounces the "Christian lisping of the stereotyped word, eternally repeated to the point of utter thoughtlessness" (1849m, *GS* 3.90).

And so we come to the modern age, when "art sold itself, body and soul, to a far worse mistress, *industry*" (1849h, *GS* 3.18); and it was Christianity that was responsible, inasmuch as it "located man's goal entirely outside his earthly existence, a goal that was centered in an absolute, nonhuman God, so that life could remain the object of man's care only in respect of his most unavoidable needs; . . . and so it is with horror that we see the spirit of modern Christianity embodied in present-day cotton mills: for the benefit of the rich, God has become our industry" (ibid., 3.25).

Here, too, there is paradigmatic continuity. In discussing the Greeks, Wagner had briefly evoked the positive figure of Hermes: "He was Zeus's thoughts incarnate; in winged flight he swept down from the heights to the depths, proclaiming the sovereign god's almighty power" (ibid., 3.18). The Romans replaced him with Mercury: "But with them his winged mission assumed a more practical aspect, inasmuch as it signified the restless activity of those haggling, profiteering merchants" (ibid.). He is now "the god of the modern world, the sacred, aristocratic god of 5 percent, who organizes our art and acts as its master of ceremonies. . . . Behold Mercury and his docile handmaid, Modern Art" (ibid., 3.19). And it is clearly Italian opera that is associated in Wagner's mind with the figure of Mercury: "You see him incarnate in the bigoted English banker, whose daughter married a ruined Knight of the Garter and who engages the leading singers from the Italian opera to sing for him in his own drawing room rather than in the theater (though never on the day of rest), since he will have the glory of paying more for them here than there" (ibid., 3.19).

> Opera became a chaos of sensuous elements that, jostling each other without rhyme or reason, encouraged each spectator to select whatever took his fancy—here a ballerina's dainty leap, there a singer's bravura display, here the set-painter's brilliant effect, there the amazing eruption of an orchestral volcano. Or does one not read nowadays that this and that new opera is a masterpiece since it contains so many beautiful arias and duets, because the instrumentation is so brilliant, and so on? (Ibid., 3.20)

The way in which nineteenth-century society was dominated by money and the resultant mercantilization of art are denounced by Wagner ad nauseam. The merest mention of present-day art provokes a tirade of invective: "Its true nature is industry, its moral purpose the acquisition of money, its aesthetic aim the entertainment of those who are bored" (ibid., 3.19). "Our God is money, our religion the acquisition of money" (ibid., 3.28). The result is an art that is a source of only frivolity and amusement: "When a prince arrives at the theater from a tiring lunch, the banker from a fatiguing financial deal, the workman from a wearying day of toil, he wants to rest, to relax, and to be entertained; he does not want further exertion and renewed excitement: . . . for this end everything possible has to be done, except to employ the body and soul of art" (ibid., 3.21). The artist thus achieves an illusory reputation thanks to money and public acclaim (ibid., 3.22).

Everything bound up with art has been perverted: it is no longer the common people who attend performances but the monied classes; social culture has been replaced by social barbarism (ibid., 3.24). It is no longer a question of promoting a thoughtful education but of encouraging thoughtless teaching aimed at obtaining industrial profits (ibid., 3.25). Where actors, singers, and dancers once collaborated on a single spectacle, mercantilism now reigns triumphant. It is no longer art that is practiced but artisanship pure and simple (ibid.). Invention has been replaced by mechanization (1849m, *GS* 3.58), the artistic by the artificial (ibid., 3.57), nature by fashion. "Fashion is the artificial stimulant that incites an unnatural need where no natural need exists: . . . fashion is the most unheard-of, insane tyranny ever to be produced by the perversity of human nature: it demands absolute obedience from nature and requires the most total self-denial on the part of a genuine need in favor of an imaginary one" (ibid., 3.56–57).

The Responsibility of the Jews

It is against this background that we need to see the violent anti-Semitic thrust of "Judaism in Music." There is no mention of Jews in *Art and Revolution* and only three brief references in *The Art-Work of the Future*: "Thus Columbus discovered America only for the mawkish Jew's traffic of our time!" (1849m, *GS* 3.98); at a later point Wagner denounces "modern Jewish utilitarianism" (ibid., 3.144); and at the very end of the essay he asserts that even at the time when they crossed the Red Sea, the Jews "had already turned into dull-witted, dirty beasts of burden" (ibid., 3.175).

In *Opera and Drama* Wagner refers to Meyerbeer's Jewishness only once: "being Jewish, he had no maternal tongue that might have grown together with the nerve of his innermost being: he spoke with the same interest in every modern language, which he set to music accordingly, without any genuine sympathy for its individual features, save for its ability to be subordinated to absolute music whenever it pleased him to do so" (1851a, *GS* 3.293). It was between the writing of these two essays that Wagner vented his spleen in his all-too-notorious article.

"Judaism in Music" was published under the pseudonym of R. Freigedank and appeared in two consecutive issues of the *Neue Zeitschrift für Musik* on 3 and 6 September 1850, shortly after its completion. Almost immediately afterward Wagner turned his attention to *Opera and Drama*.[3] In other words, the composer's anti-Jewish outburst needs to be included in our paradigmatic survey, not least because the line of argumentation that he adopts is closely bound up with his criticism of the state of contemporary art and with his conception of the art-work of the future.

The essential idea that needs to be registered here is that Wagner clearly and explicitly attributes the contemporary decline of music as an art to the Jews as repositories of financial power: "As things stand in the world at present, the Jew is already more than emancipated: *he rules*, and will continue to rule so long as money remains the power before which all deeds and actions must pale into insignificance. . . . That the impossibility of creating anything natural, necessary, and genuinely beautiful at the stage of development that the arts have now reached, without altering the basis of this development entirely—that this impossibility has brought public taste within the active grasp of the Jews is a question that we must now consider in somewhat greater detail" (1850c, *GS* 5.68).

"Judaism in Music" is an essentially racist piece of writing. Wagner attempts to justify the "involuntary feeling of abhorrence" (ibid., 5.67) that the Jew allegedly excites in the *Volk* by expatiating on what he describes as the grotesque appearance of "this unpleasant freak of nature" (ibid., 5.69). In discussing Jewishness in music, Wagner reserves his particular scorn for the Jewish language, insisting that in Europe, the Jew always speaks a foreign language (ibid., 5.70), producing a "gurgling, yodeling, and babbling sound" (ibid., 5.76), and drawing his musical inspiration from the absurd melismas of synagogue singing. In Mendelssohn, Wagner sees an example of a composer "who may possess the greatest wealth of specific talent, the most refined and varied culture, and the most intense and delicate sense of honor, without, however, being able to produce any deep impression on us or move our hearts and souls in the way we expect art to move us" (ibid., 5.79). As for Meyerbeer—who is not even mentioned by name—the reader might be inclined to endorse the scathing aesthetic judgment that Wagner reserves for him, were it not for the fact that the insufferable context in which that judgment appears predisposes us to pity its victim: "Coldness and sheer absurdity are the distinguishing features of that particular manifestation of Judaism in which the famous composer in question reveals himself to us in his music" (ibid., 5.83). Above all, however, Wagner reproaches Meyerbeer for currying the basest type of public favor and for having played a by no means negligible role in the decline of contemporary opera. In this respect the Jewish composers whom he pillories are held largely responsible for the fact that the dance of the three primeval sisters of art has fallen apart:

> The true poet is the prophet who foretells what is yet to come. . . . Divorced from its kindred arts, music has been raised by the greatest geniuses' instinct and effort to a pitch of universal expressiveness at which it could articulate either the most sublime of truths through renewed interaction with the other arts or, if it were to remain separated from them, the utmost indifference and triviality. What the cultured Jew inevitably articulated whenever he sought to express himself as an artist in the situation herein described could of course be only the indifferent and trivial aspect of art, since his entire artistic impulse was grounded in luxury and inessentials. (Ibid., 5.74)

Is there any way out for the Jew? Yes. Wagner is always ready to offer a chance of redemption to anyone who will listen. "For the Jew to become human in common with us is tantamount to his ceasing to be a Jew. . . . But bear in mind that one thing alone can redeem you from the curse that weighs upon you, *the redemption of Ahasuerus—destruction!* (ibid., 5.85).

Signs of Disintegration

All the elements that Greek society and Greek tragedy had held together now began to unravel. Instead of a single genre, several now took its place: dance, music, and poetry went their separate ways. Forms that were naturally human sank into a state of decadence. Words and music were wrenched apart.

There was no longer a unified work of art: "We can no longer recognize genuine drama—that unique, indivisible, supreme creation of the human mind—in our public, theatrical art: our theater offers merely a convenient space for the tempting exhibition of individual artistic or, rather, artificial achievements, achievements that are scarcely connected on even a superficial level" (1849h, *GS* 3.20). The unified work of art has been fragmented into two separate genres, spoken drama and opera. Whereas the former has been "robbed of music's idealizing expression, opera is denied, from the outset, the living heart and ultimate aim of genuine drama" (ibid.). On the one hand, drama fails to take off poetically while, on the other, opera contents itself with superficial attractions such as vocal exercises, lavish scenery, and rousing orchestration: "The only aim that the deployment of such manifold means can justify is the great aim of drama, but such an aim no longer occurs to people" (ibid., 3.21).

The constituent elements of Greek tragedy would henceforth go their own separate ways: "Drama dissolved into its component parts: rhetoric, sculpture, painting, music, and so on abandoned the round dance in which they had moved in perfect unity, each of them going its own autonomous way, developing independently but, at the same time, in a solitary, egoistical way" (ibid., 3.29). It was love, above all, that the three sister arts—dance, music, and poetry—now lacked in their newfound separation. In consequence, each isolated genre becomes confined within an unforgivable egoism, since it is individual rather than oriented to the goals of a whole community: "Here is that true egoism in which each *individual artistic genre* would like to give itself the airs of universal art, whereas by doing so, it merely forfeits its true originality" (1849m, *GS* 3.71).

Wagner now examines the fate of the solitary sisters, underscoring, as he does so, those elements that would allow each one of them to be reunited with her sister arts. Thus he writes of rhythm in dance: "Although dance now ceased to offer the hand of fellowship to Euripides' mawkishly tendentious and pedantic poetry but found that offer rejected in sullen arrogance, . . . it was unable nonetheless to dispense altogether with the help of its closest and most kindred art, the art of music" (ibid., 3.76). Dance was not unconnected with the theater: "Our modern art of dance attempts to realize the aim of drama in pantomime" (ibid., 3.80). Ultimately, it seeks to narrate actions and conflicts without recourse to language: "it wants to produce verse without the comradeship of poetry" (ibid.).

Music has suffered a similar fate:

> When music broke free from the sisters' round dance, she took with her the words of her thoughtful sister Poetry as the most immediate and indispensable condition of her life, in much the same way that her frivolous sister Dance had robbed *her* of her rhythmic tread; it was not, however, the humanly creative, spiritually poeticizing word that she took but only the physically imperative word—the word, in short, that was condensed into sound. Having left departing Dance with a rhythmic beat to use as she now thought fit, she built upon the word alone, the word of the Christian faith, that flexible and spineless word that, unresistingly and happily, soon gave her total power over it. The more this word dissolved into stammering humility and the babbling sounds of unconditional childlike love, so much the more did Music see herself obliged to fashion herself from the inexhaustible depths of her own fluid nature. Her struggle to achieve that form is the basis of all *harmony*. (Ibid., 3.86)

The final stage in the breakdown of the arts was the fragmentation of tragedy, which was broken down into its constituent parts, essentially words and music. *Opera and Drama* lingers over this development.

Opera is divided into two genres, the serious and the frivolous. Among the practitioners of the former are Gluck, Cherubini, Méhul, and Spontini, while the second group includes such names as Mozart, Rossini, Auber, and Meyerbeer, albeit with enormous differences in their relative values.

As a genre, comic opera belongs to the art of distraction, which, in turn, is a product of general decadence. Wagner's essential thesis is that the musicians who fall under this subheading are concerned less with action than with music, which they consider in isolation from the poetry. "Strictly speaking," the opera poet "simply translated the drama into the language of opera, so that, for the most part, he produced operatic adaptations of dramas that, already long familiar, had been presented ad nauseam in the spoken theater" (1851a, *GS* 3.243). As for Mozart, "it never occurred to him to give any thought to the aesthetic problem underlying opera, so that it was with the utmost unconstraint that he began setting the text he had been given, heedless of whether it was a thankful or thankless task for him as a pure musician" (ibid., 3.246). In his own case, of course, Wagner knew that a distinction needed to be made: "This purely musical ability of his he developed to such a pitch that in none of his works of absolute music, and still less in his instrumental pieces, do we see the art of music so broadly and richly deployed as in his operas." Mozart, Wagner believed, had "involuntary possession of the essence of his art." He was "the most abundantly gifted of all musicians" (ibid., 3.246–47).

For Wagner, Rossini represented the ne plus ultra of opera: he had removed every vestige of drama from the work in order to concentrate on absolute melody and the virtuosity of the performers (ibid., 3.257–58). In the case of Auber, *La Muette de Portici* embodied "the dumbstruck muse of drama, who, sad and lonely, wandered brokenhearted among the singing, tumultuous crowds, before finally making away with herself and her hopeless sorrow in the artificial fury of a stage volcano" (ibid., 3.265). Meyerbeer, of course, is the butt of Wagner's most vicious attacks and, if we did not know the anti-Semitic background of "Judaism in Music," we might well be disposed to find them justified and, indeed, as amusing as the drubbing that Meyerbeer received at Schumann's hands:[4] "Meyerbeer wanted a monstrously multicolored, historico-Romantic, diabolico-religious, fanatico-libidinous, . . . roguishly sentimental dramatic hotchpotch, wherein to find the incentive for monstrously curious music—an aim that, given the invincible obduracy of his actual musical temperament, he was never likely to achieve. He felt that something previously unknown could still be produced from the garnered store of musical effects, if only he were to sweep it together from every corner, pile it all up in a heap of motley confusion, add a quantity of stage gunpowder and colophony, and blow it all up with a mighty bang" (ibid., 3.300). Although even Wagner had to acknowledge the success of the love duet from *Les Huguenots* (ibid., 3.306), he could not forgive the composer for "having destroyed the poet from start to finish, so that on the ruins of operatic poetry the *musician* was crowned as the only *authentic poet*!" (ibid., 3.301).

Even with Weber the melody was conceived independently of the poetry; in *Euryanthe*, the music was even written in advance of the words. Under the influence of Christianity, the organs that originally constituted art became separated from each other. Christianity "stifled the organic impulse of the folk's artistic life, suppressing its natural procreative force: it had cut into its flesh and destroyed its artistic organism with its dualistic dissecting knife" (ibid., 3.310). Weber had taken an interest in popular melodies (ibid., 3.259), but he tore them from their natural context:

> He could not resist the loving impulse to bring this healing vision to his unnerved fellowmen, offering them this life-giving perfume to redeem them from their madness, and tearing the flower itself from its divinely creative wilderness in order to present it as a holy of holies to a world that, corrupted by luxury, craved its blessing:—*he plucked it*!—Unhappy man! . . . Behold! Its rigid petals, chastely closed before, unfold as though to languid sensuality; shamelessly it bares its noble generative organs, offering them with appalling indifference to the prying nose of every roguish libertine. . . . One by one the petals fall. . . . "I am dying because you plucked me!" (Ibid., 3.260–61)

Only composers of *serious* operas find a modicum of grace in Wagner's eyes. If, in the case of Gluck, the position of the poet has not really changed vis-à-vis the composer to whom he is subject, the composer himself is seen as the "starting point of a complete sea change" in the interrelationship between the different factors that constitute opera: Gluck, after all, had "*expressed his conscious, fundamental belief* in the proper need for a form of expression in aria and recitative that reflected the underlying text" (ibid., 3.237). Thanks to Gluck and his successors, including Cherubini, Méhul, and Spontini, "what has been achieved, once and for all, is that something natural—in other words, something that, in the best sense of the word, is logical—could evolve on the original basis of opera" (ibid., 3.240). Unfortunately, Spontini stopped some way short of his goal, convinced though he was that he had raised drama to a hitherto unprecedented level: "His drama was always a mere *make-believe* of drama" (ibid., 3.243). Everything still depended too much on the composer alone. The music was expected to portray the drama, a state of affairs that Wagner was unable to accept. Nonetheless, Spontini evinced an "honest, clear avowal of what could be achieved in this genre" (ibid., 3.244). It was he as much as anyone whom Wagner saw as the precursor of modern opera.

Parallel to all this, there had been a change in the very substance of art as Greek myth had been supplanted by its Christian counterpart: "The ability of Christian myth to enthrall our minds derives from the fact that it depicts *transfiguration through death*" (ibid., 4.36). Germanic myth had the merit of linking up with the natural basis of Greek myth. What we see in the Siegfried myth, for example, are "natural phenomena such as those of the day and night, the rising and setting of the sun, transformed by an act of poetic imagination into dramatic characters who are honored or feared because of their actions, so that gods who are thought of as human are turned into heroes who have been fully anthropomorphized, who are reputed to have actually once existed, and from whom real nations and tribes vaunted their descent" (ibid., 4.38). But Christian myth grafted itself onto this framework, denying "this basic insight into the essence of nature and replacing it by a new faith" (ibid., 4.39). The result was a confusion of disparate forms. Once again, we find ourselves confronted by a dislocated form: "No longer capable of regenerating itself, myth was fragmented into its individual, self-contained component parts, its unity dispersed into a thousandfold plurality, the nucleus of its action broken down into a plethora of disparate actions" (ibid.).

In Wagner's day, the major literary forms were the drama and the novel, which pursued conflicting goals: drama was interested in the fate of individuals as representatives of the human race, while the novel sought to capture the mechanisms of history through its interest in individual destinies. By describing reality from too close at hand, the novel had ceased to be a work of art and degenerated into journalism. When would it succeed in regaining its former greatness? "The romance attained its highest pitch as an art form when, on the basis of purely artistic necessity, it appropriated myth's method of creating types" (ibid., 4.48). In a word, the romance or its modern counterpart, the novel, could survive as a work of art only by falsifying history. "The romance descended from its former heights and, abandoning the purity that it had earlier sought to achieve as a work of art, set out to provide a faithful representation of history" (ibid., 4.50). Myth could be reborn only by turning its back on history.

Unity Regained

Better times are coming, however, when it will be possible to rediscover the lost sense of unity. Let us move on, therefore, to the third act of the drama in which Wagner, needless to say, is the principal actor.

The Conditions Necessary to Restore Unity

The title of the first essay in the series that we have been examining—*Art and Revolution*—already hints at the solution: "Only the great *revolution of mankind*, whose earliest stirrings caused the fragmentation of Greek tragedy, can produce this work of art for us; for only revolution can bring forth from its innermost depths a more beautiful, noble, and universal version of what it had once torn from the conservative spirit of an earlier period of beautiful but limited culture and, having torn it, consumed it" (1849h, *GS* 3.29).

Even if, in *Opera and Drama*, the revolutionary enthusiasm of the earlier essay has become somewhat muted, Wagner still believes that the artwork of the future can be brought to fruition only by a change in the social context: "No one can be more conscious than I of the fact that the realization of the drama that I envisage depends upon conditions that do not lie within the will or even within the capability of the individual, though that capability be infinitely greater than my own, but only in a common state and in the mutual cooperation made possible by that state: yet only the direct opposite of these conditions exists at present" (1851a, *GS* 4.210). It is clear—as other writers have often stressed—that revolution did not have an intrinsically social aim for Wagner but that it was the means by which to revolutionize art. In this regard, his standpoint could not be further removed from Marxist thought. "It is the theater that must be liberated first of all, for the theater is the most comprehensive and influential artistic institution" (1849h, *GS* 3.38). Audiences must be admitted free of charge, with state subsidies guaranteeing the independence of the performances that they attend. "Theater performances will thus be the first collective enterprises from which the concept of money and profit will totally disappear" (ibid., 3.40). The result will not only be an aestheticization of politics, but art, in its practical manifestations, will become a model for society to follow: "It is incumbent on art, and on art above all else, to grant this social instinct its noblest significance and to reveal its true direction" (ibid., 3.32). In this way the revolutionary spark acts as a commutator that gives a positive charge to all the negative elements that typify the period of lost unity.

The first priority is to shake off the shackles of money: "Let us break free from the dishonoring yoke of universal artisanship, whose soul has the pallor of silver, and soar aloft to free artistic humanity with its radiant universal soul" (ibid., 3.30). Once the power of money has been destroyed, humanity can reassert the fundamental, original value represented by nature: "Nature, and nature alone, can unravel the tangled thread of this great universal fate. . . . Nature—human nature—will proclaim this law to the two sisters, Culture and Civilization: 'Inasmuch as I am contained within you, you shall live and flourish; inasmuch as I am not in you, you shall perish and decay'" (ibid., 3.31). The same idea returns in *The Art-Work of the Future*: "True art will not flourish until its manifestations need be subject no longer to fashion's despotic whim but to the laws of nature" (1849m, *GS* 3.44). For Wagner, nature and revolution are closely bound up with each other: "This whole accumulation of culture would merely have taught nature to acknowledge her own tremendous force: but the motivation behind this force is *revolution*" (1849h, *GS* 3.31). Revolution is the catalyst that turns Culture back into Nature.

Wagner insists on the difference between art as it existed at the time of the Greeks and art as it will exist tomorrow, yet we must be wary of investing the terms he employs with present-day connotations. It is in an entirely positive sense that he uses the word "conservative," for example, when he describes Greek art as "*conservative* because it existed in the public awareness as a valid and adequate expression of that awareness; with us, true art is *revolutionary* since it exists only in opposition to the ruling spirit of the community" (ibid., 3.35). The human race has not yet returned to the conservative stage because recent art, reacting against what is currently accepted, is the product of isolated individuals. But Wagner places his hopes in the man of the future, a free man who will no longer be forced to earn his living or rely on industry and whose only education will be his art. "Tragedies will be celebrations of humanity: freed from every convention and etiquette, the free, strong, and beautiful human being will celebrate the joys and anguish of his love, performing the great love-sacrifice of his death with dignity and sublimity. Art will once again become *conservative*" (ibid., 3.35). At least Wagner's language has the merit of reminding us that the majority of revolutionaries—when not adopting the concept of permanent revolution—aim to establish a new *order*. This is as true of politics as it is of aesthetics, so that, in this respect, the concept of avant-garde art may be something of an illusion.

According to Wagner, the egoism of the age of lost unity will be replaced by a sense of communism that we must not make the mistake of interpreting in the Marxist sense. Rather it comes close to Rousseau's notion of "primitive communism," as is clear from the following definition, which Wagner proposed some twenty years later: it is "a principle, a sociopolitical ideal according to which I interpreted the 'people' in the sense of the incomparable productivity of the prehistoric primitive community" (1871p, *GS* 3.5). Wagner's communism is inseparable from the notion that egoism will be superseded by the collective will and is ultimately bound up, therefore, with the major Wagnerian concept of redemption. At the time of *Art and Revolution* and *The Art-Work of the Future* Wagner was inclined to argue that, having rediscovered the conservative art of a communist society, the true redemptive poet would emerge in the person of the common people or *Volk*:

> Who will redeem humanity from this deplorable state? *Want*—that want which will teach the world to recognize its own *true need, which, in keeping with its innermost nature, must also find satisfaction*. . . . Together we shall form the bond of hallowed necessity, and the brother's kiss that seals this bond will be the communal *art-work of the future*. In it, our great benefactor and redeemer, necessity's representative incarnate, in other words, the common people, will no longer be separate and distinct; for we shall be as a single person in this work of art—heralds and agents of necessity, knowing the unconscious, willing the involuntary, witnessing nature, *happy human beings*. (1849m, *GS* 3.49–50)

In other words, the new work of art will be the product of a powerful social ground swell: "The work of art of the future is a communal product and can issue only from a communal desire" (ibid., 3.162). The role of the *Volk* is forcibly reaffirmed at the end of *The Art-Work of the Future*: "But who will be the *artist of the future*? The poet? The performer? The musician? The sculptor?—Let us say it in a single word: the *folk* . . . *to whom, alone, we owe art in general*" (ibid., 3.169–70).

At the time he wrote his first two essays, Wagner still believed in universal redemption. On only one point were the Greeks not to be imitated: "We must turn *Hellenic* art into *human* art in general, freeing it from the conditions that made it *Hellenic* rather than *human* and *universal*" (ibid., 3.62). "History shows us two *principal moments* in the evolution of humankind: the *generically national* and the *nonnational, universal*. . . . Let us now look forward to the realization of the second stage of this development" (ibid., 3.61). In *Art and Revolution* Wagner had been in no two minds on the subject: "Whereas the Greek work of art expressed the spirit of a beauteous nation, the art-work of the future will express the spirit of free humanity, divorced from all national boundaries; the national element in it must be no more than an ornament, an added individual charm" (1849h, *GS* 3.30). Little more than twelve months later the language has already shifted in tone: *Opera and Drama* ends with the claim that only the German language is an adequate vehicle for the music drama of the future, even if German singers have undermined its virtues (1851a, *GS* 4.211–17). Nonetheless, "the day will come when this legacy will be revealed to the world for the greater good of our fellow human beings" (ibid., 4.228).

With its universal mission, the work of art has a quintessentially religious role to play, since it is intended to become a work of art for the whole community, beyond egoism, luxury, and money. "The work of art is the living presentation of religion; it is not, however, the artist who invents religions—rather, they issue from the *folk* alone" (1849m, *GS* 3.63).

The subject matter of such works cannot be chosen at random, therefore, but is precisely defined by Wagner: "Only through his death can man evince the ultimate and total abandonment of his personal egoism; only thus can he demonstrate his complete absorption into the universality of men: but, far from being *fortuitous*, that death must be *necessary*, the logical sequel to his actions and the natural outcome of the fullness of his being. *To celebrate such a death is the most worthy act that humanity can perform*" (ibid., 3.164). This act of celebration will take the form of a myth, "*myth that is vindicated by the clearest human consciousness, invented anew to reflect our intuitive perception of an ever-present life and presented in drama in the most intelligible of forms*" (1851a, *GS* 4.88). Whose death was to be celebrated?

There is a close parallel here between Wagner's theoretical discourse and his artistic plans. In *Art and Revolution* it is said that the theater of the future will glorify Christ, the present-day incarnation of the radiant figure of Apollo in the Greek *polis*. A few months earlier, Wagner had sketched out a scenario headed *Jesus of Nazareth*, in which Christ appeared as a social reformer: "This heavenly father will be none other than humanity's social conscience, which avails itself of nature and her riches for the weal of all mankind" (1849h, *GS* 3.33). When he came to writing *Opera and Drama*, Wagner replaced Christ with another paradigmatic figure: Siegfried, the sun god, supplants the Christian hero with his promise of redemption through death (1851a, *GS* 4.38). Wagner had already written the libretto for *Siegfrieds Tod* in October–November 1848. Two years later, in August 1850, he made a desultory attempt to sketch the music but soon abandoned the plan.[5]

Wagner sums up all these ideas in a single striking formula: "The egoist thus becomes a communist; the one becomes all; man becomes god; the individual species of art becomes Art" (1849m, *GS* 3.67).

Reunification of the Constituent Parts

We saw that in the two preceding "acts," the three sister arts had joined together in a single dance, before being wrenched apart. They will resume their dance only when the right conditions have been reinstated, allowing the total work of art to be born anew. By reassembling the forms of expression that correspond to the separate faculties, it will be possible to rediscover the entire being. In turn, that fusion will be feasible because "the *highest* human need is *love*" (1849m, *GS* 3.69).

Dance can be reunited with music thanks to the rhythmic parameter that they share: "This other type of art, into which the art of dance necessarily yearns to pass, therein to recognize and rediscover itself, is *music*, which, in turn, receives the solid framework of its vertebration from the rhythm of that art" (ibid., 3.74).

Poetry and music were finally reunited in Beethoven's *Choral* Symphony:

> The Master set out to explore every last possibility of absolute music . . . , penetrating to the point where the mariner begins to sound the depths with his plumb line. . . . Staunchly he threw out his anchor; and this anchor was the *Word*. . . . This *final symphony* by Beethoven represents the redemption of music from its own most characteristic element into realm of *universal art*. It is the *human* gospel of the art of the future. Beyond it no further *progress* is possible, since only the consummate art-work of the future can follow immediately after it, the *universal drama* of which Beethoven has forged the artistic key for us. *Thus music, of itself, has achieved what none of the other arts could do in isolation*. (Ibid., 3.96)

What we need now, therefore, is a total work of art: Shakespeare and Goethe, Gluck and Mozart were no more than isolated heroes. Above and beyond drama, a more comprehensive art form suggests itself, opera hitherto having provided a focus for egoistical efforts alone. These efforts must be superseded by the new work of art:

> The drama of the future will come into being of its own accord when neither spoken theater nor opera nor pantomime can survive any longer and when the conditions that allowed them to arise and that sustain their unnatural life have been wholly superseded. . . . Only when the ruling religion of egoism,

> which has split the whole of art into stunted and selfish trends and types of art, is pitilessly driven from every corner of human existence and torn up root and branch can the *new religion* enter into existence of its own accord, a religion that contains within itself the preconditions of the art-work of the future. (Ibid., 3.122–23)

There is no doubt that architecture, sculpture, and painting all have a role to play in the art-religion of the future. Certainly, Wagner includes them in the general movement toward reunification, tracing their development from their Hellenic origins. If they have not been mentioned previously, it is because Wagner does not accord them the same status in the original unity as their three remaining sisters. Of course, architecture provides not only the temple but also the theater—said to be derived "from the altar of the gods" (ibid., 3.125)—for the performance of the collective work of art. Sculpture and painting did not come into their own, however, until tragedy was already in decline (ibid., 3.134 and 141). Of the first, Wagner insists that "*the beauty of the human body* was the basis for all Hellenic art" (ibid., 3.134), while he writes of the second that, with it, Greek artists invented a way of depicting nature.

During the period of lost unity these three arts have clearly become corrupted: architecture now sacrifices at the shrine of Pluto, the god of money (ibid., 3.126), while the virile love of the Greeks, embodied in their sculptures, degenerated into "repulsive sensuality" (ibid., 3.137). Only painting, essentially devoted to capturing landscapes, attests to the victory of nature over degrading civilization thanks to a handful of isolated artists of genius (ibid., 3.143).

If Wagner needs these three arts to define the art-work of the future, it is because at this stage in his thinking he has to integrate every form of art into this irresistible movement toward reunion. A special theater will be built, modeled on the Greek amphitheater, to meet the specific needs of the art-work of the future. (Already there is a pointer here to the Bayreuth ideal.) "In designing a building uniquely intended, in each of its parts, to reflect a collective artistic aim, in other words, in designing a *theater*, the architect must proceed as an *artist*, taking account of the *work of art* alone" (ibid., 3.150–51). As for sculpture, the art-work of the future will retain the beauty and plasticity of the actor's body, while painting will provide the scenery: "It will teach us to set up the *stage* for the dramatic art-work of the future in which, imbued with life, it will represent the warm *background of nature* for *living*—as opposed to counterfeited—*humankind*" (ibid., 3.148). "The *artistic human being* will now step forth upon the architect's and painter's stage" (ibid., 3.155). Within this framework everything is now in place for the reunification of dance, poetry, and music: "The illusion of the visual arts is turned into truth in drama: the artist holds out his hand to the *dancer* or *mime* in order to be subsumed by him and thus, in turn, become dancer and mime. . . . But at the point where his ability ends, where the wealth of his willing and feeling yearns to express the inner man through *language*, the Word will reveal his clearly conscious intention: he will then become a *poet* and, in order to become a *poet*, will also become a *musician*. But as dancer, musician, and poet, he is one and the selfsame person, none other than the *performing artist, who communicates with the highest receptive power in accordance with the fullness of his abilities*" (ibid., 3.155–56).

The Union of Words and Music

In passing from *The Art-Work of the Future* to *Opera and Drama*, Wagner abandons his trinitarian sisters in favor of a couple, Poetry and Music. Having recently conceived a work—*Lohengrin*—in which dance, in the form of a *ballet de divertissement*, was conspicuous by its absence, he must have felt how specious it would have been to slip from dancer to mime and thence to actor (1849m, *GS* 3.74–75), even if, in his later essays, he was to return to the subject and advance a new theory of mime.[6]

In reality, however, Wagner is merely abandoning one triunity for another. In *The Art-Work of the Future*, as in his other essays, there is talk of the same "imperative need to achieve one thing alone," a unity that can be attained only through the intermediary of love. But what exactly is the nature of this ménage à trois? It is at this point that Wagner adds a further layer of complexity to the basic symbolic configuration: it is not a question of simply relying on the metaphorical analogies that can be inferred from the male/female dichotomy but, by endowing womankind with her twofold identity as wife (or lover) and mother, of invoking the image of the nuclear family, with its father, mother, and child. In *The Art-Work of the Future* this new trinity allows Wagner to conceive of the relations among music, poetry, and dance in sexual terms and yet relate them to a single entity:

> Just as, in love, man sinks his whole nature into that of the woman in order to be subsumed through her into a third being, the child, rediscovering *himself* in that trinity and, at the same time, discovering in that self an expanded, complemented, and completed being, so each of the individual arts may rediscover itself in the perfect and wholly liberated work of art, indeed, may even look upon itself and its innermost being as having expanded to form this work of art, which it will do as soon as it reverts to itself along the path of true love, sinking within its kindred arts and finding the reward of its love in the perfect work of art to which it knows itself expanded. (Ibid., 3.117)

It is the transmutations of this triadic model, in its theoretical and artistic manifestations, which I intend to trace in detail by examining, in turn, Wagner's poetic outlook and the content of the *Ring*.

Wagner does not forget dance entirely in *Opera and Drama*, where it is absorbed, so to speak, by symphonic music thanks to the rhythm that they have in common (ibid., 3.74). It is the function of the orchestra, therefore, to communicate the "inexpressibility of gesture," a function exemplified by Beethoven's Seventh Symphony, which Wagner subtitles "The Apotheosis of the Dance": "The gesture of dance, like gesture in general, is to orchestral melody what the spoken verse is to the vocal melody that conditions it" (1851a, *GS* 4.176).

The parametrical problem of the art-work of the future, at least on the level of poetry and music, is one that Wagner has no difficulty in envisaging from the sexual angle: "For procreation, the 'I' is as necessary as the 'You,'" Wagner had already announced in *The Art-Work of the Future* (1849m, *GS* 3.51). But before expanding the fundamental metaphor and sexualizing the art-work of the future, Wagner embarks on a painstaking study of those points of contact between poetry and music that are likely to favor their union.

Wagner's description of this fusion relies on two fundamental categories that recur on frequent occasions in *Opera and Drama*: poetry, he argues, is the manifestation of *understanding*, while music is the expression of *feeling*. The spoken language is the "*organ* of understanding" (1851a, *GS* 4.71), while feeling is governed by a different organ: "The *language of sounds* [*Tonsprache*] is the beginning and end of the language of words, just as *feeling* is the beginning and end of understanding" (ibid., 4.91). But music—the language of sounds—is not enough. "The poetic intent[7] is realized only when communicated from the understanding to feeling" (ibid., 4.99). It is on the basis of these two categories that Wagner introduces his decisive metaphor: "Understanding is forced by necessity, therefore, to unite with an element that is able to assimilate the poetic intent as a fructifying seed" (ibid., 4.102). This sentence is taken from the end of the second part of *Opera and Drama*, and it is to these three pages that we must now turn our detailed attention.

"If we take a closer look at the poet's activity, we shall see that the realization of his intent consists solely in depicting the intensified actions of the characters he has invented and that he achieves this by allowing us to feel what their motives are" (ibid., 4.101). Wagner has already introduced the idea of "motive" when he writes of those motives that constitute myth, myth being the poet's field of action: mythic motives must be made intelligible by being "reinforced," in other words, by being "cast in musical form" (ibid., 4.91). It is the orchestra, of course, with its "ability to reveal the inexpressible" (ibid., 3.173), which reinforces the mythic motives. In *The Art-Work of the Future*, Wagner had defined the orchestra as "the basis of infinite, universal feeling, from which the individual feeling of the individual actor can develop to its fullest potential" (1849m, *GS* 3.157).

The poet's aim, Wagner continues, is to set forth his mythic motives

> through a form of *expression* that occupies his activity to the extent that it is *the invention and creation of this expression that in fact enables him to expound those motives and actions*. . . . However, the only expression that is possible here is *altogether different* from that of the poetic understanding's own organ of speech. Understanding is forced by necessity,[8] therefore, to wed an element that can assimilate the poetic intent as a fertilizing seed, nurturing that seed through its own necessary essence and fashioning it in such a way that it can bring it forth as the realizational, redemptive expression of feeling. (1851a, *GS* 4.101–2)

This, it need hardly be added, is the art-work of the future.

A third term makes its appearance here. Issuing from feeling, the product of this union is described as an organ both feminine and maternal:

> This element [i.e., the element with which understanding conjoins] is the same maternal element whose womb—the expressive potential of primal melody—is fructified by the natural, real object that lies outside it, thereby producing the word and the language of words in the same way in which understanding developed out of feeling and thus condensed this female element into a male element capable of communication. Just as understanding must, in turn, fructify feeling, . . . so the intellectual word is impelled to recognize itself in sound, while the language of words finds itself vindicated in the language of music. (Ibid., 4.102)

Behind the rhetoric of this passage is the idea that the feminine element that already exists as part of understanding impels it in the direction of feeling, the quintessential female element.

> The stimulus that rouses this impulse [i.e., the desire of understanding for feeling, hence of the poetical for the musical element] and raises it to the highest pitch of excitement . . . is the influence of the "Eternal Feminine," which draws egoistical male understanding out of itself. This, in turn, is possible only when the feminine element excites that element in it which is already related to it: but the element by which understanding is related to feeling is the *purely human*, in other words, the element that constitutes the essential nature of the human *race* as such. Male and female elements alike are nurtured by this purely human essence and, *linked by love, aspire to humanity*. (Ibid., *GS* 4.102)

Stopping briefly to draw breath, Wagner launches into the final part of his metaphor:

> It is *love*, therefore, which, in the poetic process, provides the impulse necessary to the poetic understanding, to be precise, the love of *man for woman*. Not the frivolous obscene love in which man seeks only his own gratification through sexual pleasure but the deep yearning to know himself redeemed from his egoism as he shares the rapture of the woman who loves him; *this yearning is the poeticizing aspect of the understanding*. The element that must, of necessity, bestow itself on others, the seed that only in the most ardent transports of love can form a concentrate of its noblest forces—a seed that grows only from the impulse to give itself to others, to communicate itself for procreative ends, a seed, in short, that, in itself, is this impulse incarnate—*this procreative seed is the poetic intent, which provides music, that gloriously loving woman, with the subject matter that she must bear*. (Ibid., 4.102–3)

The art-work of the future will issue, therefore, from the fusion of a masculine principle in the form of the poetic intent transmitted by the libretto and a feminine principle in the form of music.

Wagner Androgyne

Our investigation of *Opera and Drama* alone makes it plain that we are already at the heart of the system elaborated by Wagner. The long passage quoted above comes at the end of the second part of the study, which is devoted to the "Nature of Dramatic Poetry" and leads directly into the third and final section, "Poetry and Music in the Drama of the Future." We have external evidence to indicate the importance that Wagner attached to this metaphor. It comes in the form of a letter written by Wagner to Liszt on 25 November 1850, some six weeks before he completed his magnum opus:

> My essay on the nature of opera, the final fruits of my deliberations, has assumed greater dimensions than I had first supposed: but if I wish to demonstrate that music (as a woman) must necessarily be impregnated by a poet (as a man), then I must ensure that this glorious woman is not abandoned to the first passing libertine but that she is made pregnant only by the man who yearns for womankind with true, irresistible love. The necessity of this union between poetry and music in its fullness and entirety (a union desired by the poet himself) was something I could not demonstrate simply by means of abstract and aesthetic definitions—which generally fail to be understood or to make any impression: I had to attempt to show, with the most manifest clarity, that it derives from the state of modern dramatic poetry itself. And I hope to be fully successful in this.[9]

Wagner offers an even more detailed explanation in a letter to Theodor Uhlig, probably written on 12 December 1850. (Wagner was on a more friendly footing with Uhlig at this time, hence, presumably, his greater willingness to confide.) He sets out the overall plan of the essay on which he is currently working:

> I. Account of the nature of opera through to our own day, concluding that "music is a life-bearing organism (Beethoven practiced it, so to speak, with the aim of giving birth to melody)—in other words, a female organism."— II. Account of the nature of drama from Shakespeare through to our own day. Result: the poetic understanding is a procreative organism; the poetic intent is the fertilizing seed, which arises only in the transports of love and constitutes the impulse to impregnate a female organism, which has to give birth to the seed that has been received in love." III. (This is the point I have now reached.) "Account of the birth of the poetic intent by perfected music."[10]

It is clear from this résumé of *Opera and Drama* that the essay as a whole was conceived, at its most fundamental level, as an extended sexual metaphor.

It was necessary to reunite words and music, Wagner believed, because in his search for totality, the artist can no longer be satisfied with the conceptual language of words alone: the poet "can no longer be effective through his use of the merely descriptive, interpretive language of words, *unless that language be made more intense*, . . . which can be achieved only by casting it as *music*" (1851a, *GS* 4.91). But how is this union possible? Just as music and dance share a common grounding in rhythm, so there is a musical element in language in the form of alliteration: "In *alliteration* cognate linguistic roots are fitted together in such a way that just as they sound the same to the sentient ear, so they link together similar objects to form a single collective image" (ibid., 4.94). The phenomenon described by Wagner is one familiar to linguists under the name of *paronomasia*: the similarity between certain words and their neighboring sonorities helps to suggest and even to create semantic links. It will be noted that the process is fundamentally paradigmatic by nature. Wagner turns it into a means by which to establish the union between poetic and melodic line, illustrating it at a later point in the treatise by reference to the line "Die Liebe bringt Lust und Leid" [love brings weal and woe] (ibid., 4.152). It is clear that the repetition of the initial liquid consonant in *Liebe*, *Lust* and *Leid* places love, weal, and woe in the same relationship to one another, thereby producing a semantic confrontation among these three concepts.

Now, the function of consonants and vowels is related sexually to the musical sound. Vowels constitute the melody of words (ibid., 4.92) and it is through them that feeling can be communicated (ibid., 4.93 and

130), while consonants, by contrast, are harmful to the expression of feeling (ibid., 4.130). The vowels in a language represent its musical aspect, so that both spoken and musical language need to be brought together for the two halves of each human being to be merged together as one. These two halves are the intellectual element, understanding, and the emotional element, feeling: "By dissolving the vowel of the accented and alliterating root word into its maternal element, which is the musical sound, the poet emphatically enters the world of music" (ibid., 4.137). It is at this point that the musician must intervene: "It is not the word-poet but, rather, the *tone-poet* who can allow us to feel the relationship between those vocalic sounds that have become musical sounds" (ibid., 4.138).

The contact that is made in this way with the feminine element of music allows the poet to escape from "the wintery cold of language" (ibid., 4.127). The poet of the future will be both poet and musician and, as such, a redemptive figure who, in turn, will be able to save humanity:

> Music resembled the dear Lord of our legends who descended from Heaven to Earth but who, in order to make himself visible, had to assume the form and raiment of common everyday folk: no one recognized the dear Lord in the often ragged beggar. But the true poet shall come who, with the clairvoyant eye of the poet's need and insatiable craving for redemption, will recognize the redeeming god in the grime-encrusted beggar and who, removing his crutches and rags, soars aloft into infinite space on the breath of his yearning desire, entering into that realm where the liberated god exhales the ineffable joys of utmost bliss. (Ibid., 4.139–40)

Melody is thus "love's greeting from woman to man" (ibid., 4.146); and it is love that ordains the alliterative patterns that underlie the poetic diction (ibid., 4.152). One tonality conjoins with another "according to love's inevitable law" (ibid., 4.151). Harmony is the "*child-bearing* element, which assimilates the poetic intent only as a procreative seed, turning it into a finished product in keeping with the most characteristic conditions of its female organism" (ibid., 4.155); and it is the orchestra that is entrusted with the task of expressing harmonic ideas (ibid., 4.165). Confronted by the sounds of the alliterative text, it plays the same role as that played by consonants in their relationship with vowels: "In its determinative influence on the characteristics of the note that it is to play, each musical instrument could be described as the *initial root consonant*, which acts as a *linking alliterative rhyme* for all the notes that can be played on it" (ibid., 4.166). Again: "*In its purely physical manifestation, the orchestra is completely different from the equally purely physical manifestation of the vocal tone-mass*" (ibid.). It is for this reason, Wagner argues, that the chorus no longer has any place in the new musical drama: the orchestra is able on its own to underline the mythic motives and comment on the action (ibid.,

4.162–63). It is the womb of music, the "maternal matrix" from which the bond of expression is born. "*The chorus of Greek tragedy* had an importance in terms of the drama that was felt to be instinctively necessary and that it bequeathed to the *modern orchestra* alone, in order that, free from all constriction, it might express itself here in immeasurably varied ways" (ibid., 4.190–91). Wagner is all for fusion through dissolution: the plasticity of dance has passed into the body of the actor, while its rhythmic dimension has been assimilated into the rhythm of the symphony; finally, the classical chorus's function as a commentator has been taken over by the modern orchestra. All that remains is the parental poet whose poetic intent impregnates music qua wife and mother. Wagner has passed from the trinity of dance, music, and poetry to the poetico-musical couple of *Opera and Drama*, a transition necessitated by his need to ensure the victory of the One and truly Perfect, the need to produce a third reality in the form of the art-work of the future.

Poet and musician merge: "They are as one; each of them knows and feels what the other knows and feels. The poet has become a musician, the musician a poet: *both* are now a consummate artist and human being" (ibid., 4.159). "Assuming that poet and musician do not restrict one another . . . but that they are *mutually consumed* in sacrificing their highest potential, drama will be born in its highest manifestation" (ibid., 4.207). And, in these final pages of his essay, Wagner comes to the crucial question: "Should we think of poet and musician as *two people* or as *one*?" (ibid., 4.208). Having hesitated for a moment, he ends by stating:

> It is impossible at present for *two* people to be struck by the same idea of creating the perfect drama together, since, in discussing this idea, they would be forced to admit, with inevitable candor, that such a drama was impossible to realize in the present climate of public opinion and this avowal would nip their undertaking in the bud. Only the solitary individual, urged on by his instinctual desire, can transform the bitterness of this avowal into a sense of intoxicating joy that drives him on, with drunken courage, to undertake the task of making the impossible possible; for he *alone* is impelled by *two* artistic forces that he cannot resist and by which he willingly allows himself to be driven on to the point of self-sacrificial abandon. (Ibid., 4.209)

It was probably unnecessary for Wagner to explain, in a somewhat embarrassed footnote (ibid., 4.209–10), that he was thinking of himself here. What is clear, however, is that as the poet of the future, Wagner himself is an androgynous being, bearing within him the active male principle, in the form of the poetic seed, and the passive female principle, embodied in music. And the work that results from this inner impregnation is itself an androgynous creation, since Wagner's musical drama bestows its blessing on the union of male poetry and female music.

So far as I have been able to establish, Wagner never uses the word "androgyny" in the context of his own works. It would be a serious methodological error, however, to reduce a system of thought to the terms that it employs. If we judge him by what he wrote about Beethoven—the only historical figure to whom he appeals in evoking the image of a fusion of male and female elements, it is difficult to believe that he was not thinking along these lines. We have seen him reproach an opera composer such as Weber for having uprooted popular melody from its rightful context. The melody for Schiller's ode *To Joy*, by contrast, "does not as yet appear to have been invented for, or through, the poet's verse but merely written with an eye to Schiller's poem and inspired by its general content" (ibid., 3.315). In other words, it was thanks to Beethoven that the music of the final movement of the Ninth Symphony was impregnated by Schiller's poem. With Beethoven,

> We recognize the natural, vital urge on the part of music to produce melody from within its inner organism. In his most important works he presents melody not as something completed in advance but as something that comes into being before our eyes, so to speak, being *born* from music's own organs. . . . The most decisive thing that the master finally revealed to us in his principal work is the *necessity*[11] he felt as a *musician* to throw himself into the poet's arms in order to *beget* the true, infallibly real, and redeeming melody. In order to become a *human being*, Beethoven had to become a whole person, a social being subject to the sexual conditions of both *male and female*. (Ibid., 3.312)

There could be no clearer indication than this that the "purely human" individual who is Wagner's constant preoccupation, especially at the end of the second part of *Opera and Drama*, is a fusion of masculine and feminine elements within a single individual who is certainly male and perhaps also female.

Wagner's fundamental androgyny is thus all-embracing. It explains the birth, development, and future of the arts over a period of two millennia, starting with Greek tragedy. It explains the nature of the musical drama that Wagner bears within him, and, at the heart of the drama, it explains the relationship between verse and melody, the role of alliteration, the raison d'être behind the leitmotifs, and the function of the orchestra.

It must be stressed, moreover, that the idea of androgyny is bound up with the whole thrust of Wagner's thinking and cannot be reduced to an isolated symbol. What our analysis has shown is the concept of an original unity based on love, the dislocation of that unity, and, finally, the eschatological promise of a return to that pristine state through the artwork of the future. This outline is basically similar to that found in those religions in which androgyny figures:

> Certain themes recur throughout the Jewish, Christian, and Muslim traditions in which gnosis, neo-Platonism, cabbala, alchemy, and mysticism converge: an androgynous god, a god of origins, the appearance of a nonbegotten protofather, an initial celestial power that gives birth to a series of eons symmetrically divided into male and female couples; the first androgynous man possessing the attributes of both sexes and thus finding himself created in the image of God; the fall of man as he is cut off from universal life and for whom the division between the sexes marks the advent of evil in the world, that evil being separation; and, finally, a return to the light that will reestablish primordial androgyny at the end of time. Thus androgyny marks the beginning and end of history, to which it gives its meaning. (Molino 1981, 27)

From this perspective, the "history" of tragedy, opera, and musical drama, as seen by Wagner, no longer appears simply as a somewhat eccentric vision of aesthetic evolution comparable to the poetic and Romantic vision of history advanced by Victor Hugo in his preface to *Cromwell*. Wagner reveals himself as an inventor of myths in exactly the same way that the Pygmy or Dan invents a myth to explain the origins of music. This gives an extra dimension to Wagner's preoccupation with the idea of founding a new religion through his work and underscores yet again the essential unity of his approach.

It would be surprising if the total, not to say totalitarian, coherence of this system stopped here and if it did not also affect, at least on one level, the very content of the musical drama that Wagner was gestating at the time he was writing these essays: the *Ring*. In order to show that theory and practice are indeed related, we need to turn our attention to a little-known work of the composer's, an operatic sketch that remained unfinished but that, unlike all his other aborted projects, he held in sufficiently high regard to include in the third volume of his collected writings, where it appears immediately after *The Art-Work of the Future*. The work in question is *Wieland der Schmied*.

Chapter Two

WIELAND THE SMITH

FOUR PAGES before the end of *The Art-Work of the Future* there is a veritable rhetorical upheaval—the theorizing stops and a brief transitional passage introduces a fictional narrative: "Since the poor Israelites once led me into the realm of the most beautiful type of all poetry, that of eternally new and eternally true *folk poetry*, I intend to take my leave by retelling a glorious legend that the rough, uncivilized tribe of ancient Teutons once created for no other reason than inner necessity" (1849m, *GS* 3.175). The pretext ("I want to tell you a story") is feeble in the extreme. It is only when we notice the links between this narrative and the theoretical content of *The Art-Work of the Future* that we understand rather better why Wagner concludes his essay in this way: the legend of Wieland is juxtaposed, virtually without a break, with the theoretical section of the essay, a device that constitutes the most condensed form of metaphor—one thinks, for example, of Hugo's *vautour aquilon* (literally, "the north-wind vulture"). But if *Wieland the Smith* is a metaphorical narrative, in what does that metaphor consist? We may begin by quoting the tale as told by Wagner in *The Art-Work of the Future.*

> In his joy and delight at his handiwork, Wieland the smith created the most elaborate trinkets, glorious weapons both keen and fair to behold. As he was bathing by the seashore, he noticed a swan-maiden, who came flying through the air with her sisters. Laying aside her swan's apparel, she plunged down into the waves. Wieland was fired by the flames of love; he threw himself into the floodwaters and wrestled with and won the wondrous woman. Love, too, broke down her pride; in blissful care for each other, they lived in rapturous union. She gave him a ring, saying that he must never let her win it back from him; for, greatly as she loved him, she still yearned for her ancient freedom, longing to fly through the air to her happy island home; it was the ring that gave her the power of flight. Wieland made a large number of rings, each of which resembled his swan-wife's ring, and he hung them on a hempen cord in his house in the hope that his wife would not recognize her own among them.
>
> One day he returned from a journey. Alas, his house lay in ruins, his wife had flown away.
>
> A king there was by the name of Neiding, who had heard much talk of Wieland's skill; he longed to catch the smith in order that he might work for

him alone. He even found a valid excuse for his violent deed: the gold from which Wieland wrought his trinkets came from Neiding's land, so that Wieland's art amounted to stealing the king's possessions.—It was Neiding who burst into his home, falling upon him, binding him, and dragging him away with him.

Back at Neiding's court Wieland was forced to make all manner of useful, solid, and durable objects for the king: harnesses, tools, and weapons with which the king extended his realm. Since Neiding had to loose the smith's bonds to allow him to work in this way and since he had to let him move about freely, he had to ensure that his captive could not escape; and so he hit on the cunning idea of cutting the tendons in Wieland's feet, for he rightly guessed that the smith needed not his feet but only his hands to perform his work.

And so he sat there in his grief, the inventive Wieland, the carefree, wonder-working smith. Crippled he sat behind the forge at which he had to work, swelling his master's wealth—limping, lame, and ugly, whenever he tried to stand. Who might tell the extent of his misery when he thought of his freedom, his art, and his beautiful wife! Who could say how great was his anger against this king who had caused such terrible shame!

From the forge he gazed up longingly to the blue sky above him, through which the swan-maid had once flown to join him; this air was her blissful realm through which she soared in joyous freedom, while he had to breathe the stench and fumes of the smithy—and all for Neiding's gain. The shame-filled, self-bound man—would he never be able to find his wife again?

Ah, if he was to be wretched forevermore, if he was to find no joy or consolation, one thing at least he might gain—revenge upon Neiding, who had plunged him into such endless grief for the sake of his own base self-interest. If only it were possible to destroy this wretch and the whole of his brood!—

He plotted terrible vengeance; day by day his wretchedness grew, day by day his implacable longing for vengeance increased. But how could he, the limping cripple, prepare for a fight that would cause his tormentor's ruin? A single bold and daring step and he would fall dishonored to the ground, the object of his enemy's scorn.

"You dearest, distant wife! If only I had your wings! If only I had your wings to wreak my revenge and rise above this misery!"

Then *Need itself* beat its mighty wings in the tormented Wieland's breast and fanned the flames of inspiration in his brooding brain. Through Need, through terrible all-powerful Need the enslaved artist learned to invent what no man's mind had yet conceived. *Wieland found a way of forging* WINGS! *Wings* on which to mount aloft and wreak revenge on his cruel oppressor,—*wings* on which to soar away to the blessed island of his wife!—

> He did it, he achieved *what utmost Need had inspired him to do.* Borne upward by the product of his art, he soared aloft and struck at Neiding's heart with his deadly dart, then flew through the air in joyous, daring flight to where he found his youthful love.—
>
> *O unique and glorious folk! This is the poem that you created, and you yourself are this Wieland! Forge your wings and soar aloft!* (Ibid., 3.175–77).

It is clearly this final paragraph that provides a key to understanding precisely why Wagner appended this narrative to the end of a theoretical essay: Wieland, he explains, represents both the *Volk* and the poet. But who, then, is the virgin swan with whom the smith is in love? All the evidence points to the fact that it is music, but since Wagner does not state this explicitly, it is perhaps worthwhile spelling out the reasons for this suggestion and adducing a number of philological arguments in its support.

We may begin with the key concept of need or want (German *Noth*):[1] it is need that gives Wieland the idea and strength to forge a pair of wings in order to rejoin the virgin swan just as, in the opening chapter of *The Art-Work of the Future*, it is need that drives the three sister arts to reunite, the same need that, in *Opera and Drama*, leads the poet to impregnate music and subject it to his poetic intent. Let us remind ourselves of the passage from *Opera and Drama* cited above:

> Music resembled the dear Lord of our legends who descended from Heaven to Earth but who, in order to make himself visible, had to assume the form and raiment of common everyday folk: no one recognized the dear Lord in the often ragged beggar. But the true poet shall come who, with the clairvoyant eye of the poet's *need*[2] and insatiable craving for redemption, will recognize the redeeming god in the grime-encrusted beggar and who, removing his crutches and rags, will soar aloft into infinite space on the breath of his yearning desire, entering into that realm where the liberated god exhales the ineffable joys of utmost bliss. (Ibid., 4.139–40)

Over and above the image of the beggar, there is the same paradigmatic parallel between the virgin swan and music, an analogy that clearly suggests itself inasmuch as it is the swan-maiden whom the poet rejoins in the heavens.

But more than that: the swan-maiden is both bird and marine animal—"she plunges beneath the waves"—that same element in which the poet achieves his conquest and which is clearly associated with music in both *The Art-Work of the Future* and in *Opera and Drama*. "The sea separates and unites lands, just as music separates and unites the two most extreme poles of human art, dance and poetry" (1849m, *GS* 3.81). "Rhythm and melody are the *arms* of music with which the latter locks her sisters in loving embrace: they are the *shores* through which the sea unites two continents" (ibid., 3.82). "But this endless expanse of water is the sea of *harmony*" (ibid., 3.83). Gluck and Mozart are described as "merely isolated lodestars on the desolate, night-enshrouded sea of operatic music" (ibid., 3.122). As evidence of the persistence of this metaphor in Wagner's theoretical writings, here is a characteristic passage from *Opera and Drama*:

> [The poet is] initiated into the deep and infinite secrets of woman's nature through that melody's redemptive kiss of love. . . . The bottomless sea of harmony from which that blissful apparition rose is no longer an object of shyness, fear, or terror, as it previously appeared to his imagination as a strange and unknown element; not only can he now swim on the surface of this sea but, endowed with newfound senses, he can plunge beneath the waves and explore the deepest seabed. (1851a, *GS* 4.146–47)

In writing *Opera and Drama* Wagner did not forget the poet Wieland plunging into the waves to win the swan-maiden who symbolizes music.

Let us extend the parameters of our comparison. Wagner prepared two detailed drafts of *Wieland the Smith*, the first written between 12 and 28 January 1850 and the second completed on 11 March 1850.[3] Briefly intended for the Paris Opéra, the work is of particular relevance in the present context in view of the parallels that it reveals between the legend of Wieland and Wagner's theoretical writings.

In the first place, it is works of art that the poet Wieland produces: "Who made as many wondrous things as you?" Helferich asks him (*GS* 3.180). As in the essays, here is a poet who is *free*: "No king can bid me do those things I gladly do" (3.179). Like Wagner himself, this poet has to be looked after by others: "You would have died of hunger," his brother Eigel tells him, "had I not brought you my spoils from the hunt" (ibid.). The swan-maiden falls to Earth, breathless, while her sisters continue their journey, abandoning her to her fate. The poet-smith takes her up. Schwanhilde's family (for such is the swan-maiden's name) has been attacked by Neiding, who embodies those negative forces that undermine the original unity of art, symbolized in turn by the new couple, Wieland and Schwanhilde. Of course, pure music always wants to be borne aloft on its own wings alone, but it has to sacrifice itself to the poet and do so, moreover, out of love.

Enemy forces enter the fray. Neiding's daughter, Bathilde, wants Wieland as her own. She represents the corruption of grand opera, a type of music that seeks to enslave the poet for the sake of pure entertainment: "What is human art when compared with the power of magic?" (*GS* 3.184). Together with her brother Gram, Bathilde sets out to capture Wieland. His home is reduced to ashes, while Schwanhilde takes refuge in flight. He himself is forced to fashion consumer goods for Neiding—"useful, solid, lasting" objects, according to *The Art-Work of the Future* (1849m, *GS* 3.176), that leave him with no interest in basic aesthetic projects. Wieland discovers a tree trunk washed up on the shore and attempts to use it as a boat in which to pursue Gram and his followers. The curtain falls on Act I.

At Neiding's court, the relationship between Bathilde and Gram has proved a disaster. "Since I was fired by love for you, misfortune has dogged my every step" (*GS* 3.188). But Wieland desires Bathilde, and Neiding, still ignorant as to her true identity, promises her to him. Bathilde uses her magic powers to exercise an irresistible sway over Wieland: "At the very sight of her, Wieland feels bound by magic fetters" (*GS* 3.191). Even if she promises herself to another (Gram), third-rate music succeeds in making the great poet forget that sublime form of music (Schwanhilde) with which he could produce the art-work of the future. This second act embodies that sense of unity that has been lost in the modern world. Wieland is even prepared to take on Gram in Bathilde's name. "He is on the point of recalling the swan-maiden when he catches sight of Bathilde turning away to the right. . . . He thinks he is going mad" (*GS* 3.195). And with that he kills Gram. From now on Wieland is Neiding's plaything, an artist in the service of power. To ensure that Wieland remains attached to him, he severs the tendons in his feet. Wieland is now a slave twice over: as the curtain falls on Act II it is to Bathilde that he turns his love-struck gaze.

At the beginning of Act III, Wagner tells us, Wieland "would like to fashion the most elaborate and unique jewel to see this princess tread it underfoot, if only she might smile at him over the ruins of his handiwork" (*GS* 3.197). And, indeed, Bathilde comes to offer herself to him, but her reasons are mercenary: she wants him to repair her ring. Although lame, Wieland wants her to see in him a thing of beauty; for her own part, she would like him to love her freely. But the dice are loaded and Wieland recognizes Schwanhilde's ring. He utters the swan-maiden's name. Love exists only in authenticity: "How slyly you thought to snare me through love, you who never felt its flame!" (*GS* 3.199). As he raises his hand to kill her, Bathilde reveals that Schwanhilde is still alive and has flown away westward. The poet Wieland suddenly becomes aware of his misery and solitude. While Bathilde grows more and more impressed by his reborn strength ("One of the gods stands before me!" [*GS* 3.201]), Wieland delivers himself of a speech, already familiar from *The Art-Work of the Future*, describing the way in which artistic creativity is motivated by need: "A man! A man in direst need! Need beat its wings, fanning inspiration into my brain! I've found what no man had yet devised!—Schwanhilde! Fairest woman, I'm near you! To you I soar aloft!" (*GS* 3.201). It was this same concept of need that Wagner had introduced at the end of the theoretical discourse leading into the Wieland story in *The Art-Work of the Future*: "Through Need . . . the enslaved artist learned to invent what no man's mind had yet conceived. *Wieland found a way of forging* WINGS" (1849m, *GS* 3.177).

Can one doubt that Wagner is speaking of himself here? "He wants to create his greatest masterpiece," he comments in the draft, as Schwanhilde calls him by name. Music expresses its regret at being so remote from the poet, even in the heights of the absolute. In order to rejoin her, he creates a work of art and Schwanhilde promises eternal union. This brings us back to the idea of original unity, a return effected—according to the essay—by "his youthful lover" (ibid.). And already the poet who is to be united with music raises his voice in song, even if that song cannot find favor with Neiding. Wieland sets fire to his forge, and Neiding and his court perish in the flames. The poet-smith regains his freedom thanks to the wings he has forged for himself and rejoins Schwanhilde—music—in the ethereal vault.

The essential point to emerge from this parallelism is that the opera libretto is clearly an artistic reflex of the line of reasoning advanced in the theoretical essay. *Wieland*, however, assumes an additional resonance when one realizes that this project is nothing less than a prefiguration of the *Ring* and especially of *Siegfried*, a work on which Wagner had yet to embark at this date.

The links with *Lohengrin* are particularly noticeable in the first draft of January 1850, in which the outline of Act I is still extremely rudimentary (one and a half pages in the manuscript versus two and a half for Act II and three and a half for Act III). Here Wieland is introduced as the son of the Erl-King who has been turned into a swan because his wife had demanded to know from where he came. It is in the first act of the second draft, by contrast, that we find the greatest number of themes and images common to the *Ring*.

The setting of this opening act is not so very far removed from that of *Siegfried*, with its forge and forest in the background. Wieland sings what, set to music, could have been Siegfried's Forging Song. There is even the theme of gold—the "glittering trinket of golden trumpery," which, according to Fricka, "would also serve as a fair adornment for women" (*GS* 5.227). Wieland's brothers busy themselves with food while the artist gets on with his work, just as Mime does with Siegfried. And, of course, Wieland forges an avenging sword analogous to that produced by Siegfried. Wachhilde is clearly a water-sprite, while the swan-maidens as a group have certain features in common with the wanton Rhine daughters. Moreover, the opening description of the swan-maidens in the sketch already suggests the Valkyries: "Wherever they have come from, many a hero no doubt lies bleeding" (*GS* 3.180). A few pages later the comparison becomes explicit: "She bade them fly to the northern lands as Valkyries" (*GS* 3.182). Although airborne steeds replace swans' wings as the form of locomotion in *Die Walküre*, the characters concerned remain creatures of the air: "In a cloud bank lit by lightning, moving past from the left, Grimgerde and Roßweiße appear, similarly on horseback, each with a dead warrior in her saddle" (*GS* 6.60). The care that Wieland lavishes on Schwanhilde inevitably recalls that of Sieglinde for Siegmund. Above all, however, there is a parallel between Wieland's removal of Schwanhilde's wings and discovery that she is a woman and Siegfried's removal of Brünnhilde's armor and discovery that she, too, is a woman. And, whereas Schwanhilde is overcome by fear and astonishment, Brünnhilde feels herself "without protection or defense" (*GS* 6.170) when roused from her slumber by Siegfried. Schwanhilde falls into a mortal's power, just as Brünnhilde succumbs to Siegfried. And, like Siegfried, Wieland offers her his love, receiving a ring from her in return. Like the ring in the later work, this one has a twofold function, not only inspiring love and as acting as a pledge of Wieland's love but guaranteeing power—qualities that the Nibelung's ring will have for Siegfried, even though he never regards it as an instrument of power. But Schwanhilde does not ignore the power of the ring, so that when it passes into Bathilde's hands, it is as baleful in its effect as Alberich's ring ever was while in *his* possession or that of Wotan. There is no mistaking the thrust behind Bathilde's words: "It confers on women the charms of love and on men the victor's strength" (*GS* 3.193). Bathilde forces her way into Wieland's lodgings and steals the ring. Gram and his followers are able to capture Wieland in the same way that Wotan and Alberich capture Loge. Although the context is radically different, Wieland—like Alberich—is punished for having stolen the gold. The underlying stratum of ancient Germanic legend is briefly visible here in the form of Iduna, the initial version of Freia, who guarantees the gods' eternal life, while Freia—the early version of Fricka—is abandoned by Odur/Wotan. Had *Wieland* been set to music, we should no doubt have heard Siegfried's horn call and perhaps the whispering waters of the Rhine.

For the second act we leave behind the tetralogy's forest and littoral setting to enter a palace hall worthy of the final act of *Lohengrin*. But Siegfried's selective amnesia (he loses all memory of Brünnhilde and falls in love with Gutrune) is already prefigured here in the use of a magic device, the ring playing an analogous role in *Wieland* to the philter in *Siegfrieds Tod*. In this case, however, Gram too is affected by the power of the ring. Bathilde tells her father about its double function, placing him under the kind of pressure that Fricka exerts on Wotan ("What you decreed in anger, you should now revoke" [*GS* 3.193]) and demanding

Gram as her husband. Bathilde is depicted here as an androgynous being. She had earlier hurled the reproach at her father: "Do you recall the day when you insulted me because my mother bore you a daughter?" (*GS* 3.192). Now she assumes the powers of a man: "Let me be the one who wields the power here" (*GS* 3.193). To which Neiding replies: "Brazen, insolent child! Would you turn yourself into a man?" (*GS* 3.194). Bathilde answers: "What use would your vassals be to you if I were not here now?" (ibid.). At the sound of his name, Wieland begins to recover his memory, and, just as Siegfried remembers Brünnhilde, so Schwanhilde passes through Wieland's thoughts, in an initially bewildering vision. Not until the third and final act does his memory of her return in full.

When the curtain rises on the final act, we are back in Wieland's smithy—but it is a much later work by Wagner that suggests itself here. It is as though Kundry had entered Mime's cave. Bathilde comes, anxious to have him repair her ring as an instrument of power. Wieland takes it in his hands, and immediately calls out Schwanhilde's name. Bathilde is nonplussed, in much the same way that Kundry is taken aback when Parsifal rejects her. Wieland denounces the illusory nature of a love that is not authentic. Bathilde's conversion is instantaneous—even more so in the second sketch than in the first—and she tells him everything: "Deepest anguish takes possession of her soul." A sense of pity overwhelms her and Wieland assumes the aspect of a redeemer in her eyes: "One of the gods stands before me" (*GS* 3.200–201). From now on she wants to serve him: "Can I help you? Tell me how I can save you!" She herself wants to be redeemed: "How can I atone for my guilt?" (*GS* 3.201–2). There is no escaping the theme of redemption through love, a theme common to all Wagner's heroines: "Feel only love! And you will be free from all guilt!" Wieland tells her, assuming the guise of Wagner's Blameless Fool (*GS* 3.202).

The swan-maiden calls out Wieland's name from on high, just as the Wood Bird tells Siegfried of Brünnhilde. Confronting Wieland, Neiding thinks he can still insist that the smith goes on making swords for him, a relationship redolent of that between Siegfried and Mime or Alberich and Mime. But Wieland wafts the flames in the direction of Neiding and his followers, setting fire to the forge, which collapses on top of them. In this way the final scene of *Wieland the Smith* prefigures the end of *Götterdämmerung*.

There is some controversy surrounding the question of why Wagner did not set this draft to music. Can one rely on the much later account of *Mein Leben*, in which he claims that he was not particularly interested in a project that would have had to be performed in Paris? "Not only did I really loathe the idea but I also realized that I was being dishonest with myself in doing it, because it was perfectly clear to me that I would never be truly serious about the enterprise" (*ML*: 431). Not without reason do the authors of the *Wagner Werk-Verzeichnis* believe that Wagner had already seen the material for an opera in the Wieland legend well before he considered adapting it for Paris (*WWV*, 342). The French version was to have been realized by Gustave Vaëz (see Wagner's letter to Theodor Uhlig of 9 August 1849) and at this stage Wagner himself was hoping to set the completed libretto to music (see his letters to Uhlig of 9 August and to Liszt of 5 December 1849). It is possible that the denials contained in *Mein Leben* relate only to the Parisian aspect of the project, since a letter of 13 March 1850 finds him renouncing the Paris Opéra while retaining the draft for his own future use: "I have only to write the verses for my Wiland [*sic*]," he told Uhlig; "otherwise the whole poem is finished."[4] A few months later he abandoned the project[5] for essentially aesthetic reasons: "I shall not complete my Wiland," he told Julie Ritter in a long letter of 26/27 June 1850; "the faults of this poem are all too clear to be hidden from me now by my tired and subjective feelings. Wiland is dead: he will not fly!—I think what I shall do next is compose my thoughts for an essay on genius—the communal and the solitary."[6]

The essay in question was to be *Opera and Drama*. But the *Wieland* project was not in fact abandoned. Just as, at a later date, many of the ideas contained in *Die Sieger* [The victors] passed in part into *Parsifal*, so the themes of *Wieland the Smith* were assimilated into the *Ring*. The motif whereby Wieland forgets Schwanhilde and later remembers her is already found in *Siegfrieds Tod*, the poem of which dates from November 1848. We have already noted that the majority of the analogies between the opening act of *Wieland* and the *Ring* are confined to *Der junge Siegfried*, the work that Wagner resolved to write in May 1851, once he had completed his theoretical essays. There may be some truth in the suggestion, therefore, that as one idea led to another, Wagner's involvement in the *Wieland* sketch played a part in his decision to preface *Siegfrieds Tod* with the earlier parts of the narrative, including *Der junge Siegfried*. Equally influential, perhaps, may have been the fact that in August 1850—or perhaps even earlier—he was inspired to start sketching the music to two of the scenes from *Siegfrieds Tod*[7] containing themes that were to be taken over not only into *Götterdämmerung* but also into the other parts of the cycle.

There remains the central argument of *Wieland*, which, underscored at the end of *The Art-Work of the Future*, revolves around the metaphor of Wieland the poet pursuing Schwanhilde as the embodiment of music, seeking to win, tame, and impregnate her. There is no doubt that for Wagner, *Wieland the Smith* was the mythical and artistic illustration of the theory expounded in *The Art-Work of the Future*. From this point of view, Wagner could abandon the *Wieland* project because the theoretical idea embodied in the artistic metaphor was shortly to be taken over into the *Ring*. If, as we have seen, Wieland prefigures Siegfried, if Schwanhilde adumbrates Brünnhilde, and if, moreover, Wieland embodies the poet and Schwanhilde music, what new depth of meaning must the *Ring* assume if Siegfried were to be seen as the poet incarnate and Brünnhilde as the embodiment of music? By appealing to this primordial myth of the art-work of the future, as traced by Wagner in his four theoretical essays of 1849–51, we may perhaps be permitted to read into the plot of the *Ring* a metaphorical history of music. It is this particular avenue that I intend to explore in the course of the following chapter.

THE *RING* AS A MYTHIC ACCOUNT OF THE HISTORY OF MUSIC

IT MUST BE STATED at the outset that the following exposition of the *Ring*, while reflecting our working hypothesis, does not claim to provide a comprehensive reinterpretation of the cycle as a whole. I am merely suggesting—as the previous chapter set out to show—that there is an organic link between the contents of Wagner's theoretical essays and that of the works of art conceived at the selfsame time. Wagner finished *Opera and Drama* on 10 January 1851 and began work on the first prose sketch of *Der junge Siegfried* between 3 and 10 May of that year, two months before starting *A Communication to My Friends*. As we know, he then went back to *Das Rheingold* and finally drafted *Die Walküre*. Let us reread the cycle from the beginning, following the thread of the "interested" history of music, which, expounded by Wagner in the essays examined in chapter 2, posits three major stages in its development: the original state of unity, the loss of that unity, and its ultimate rediscovery.

THE PRELUDE OF *DAS RHEINGOLD* AND THE BIRTH OF PURE MUSIC

Most commentators agree that the undulating theme that develops over 136 bars from the opening E♭ pedal is an evocation not only of the Rhine but also of nascent nature. It is a theme that returns, moreover, at the end of *Götterdämmerung*, as the Gibichung Hall is engulfed by the Rhine and Valhalla goes up in flames. From a strictly musical point of view—as several musicologists have pointed out (Chailley 1954–55, 162; Cooke 1959, 57)—it is clear that Wagner builds up this section on the basis of natural acoustic resonance. What we hear initially is the tonic sustained over four bars, with a perfect fifth added from bar 5 onward. In bar 17 a canon for eight horns enters: its theme (bars 17–21) is based on the fourth, fifth, and sixth notes in the harmonic series and is repeated, latterly densely overlapping, through to bar 48. In bar 49 Wagner introduces the interval of a second naturally present between the seventh and eighth, the eighth and ninth, and the ninth and tenth notes of the harmonic series, together with the eighth, ninth, and tenth notes themselves. From bar 81 onward the tempo of bars 49 to 52 is doubled. With bar 97, the

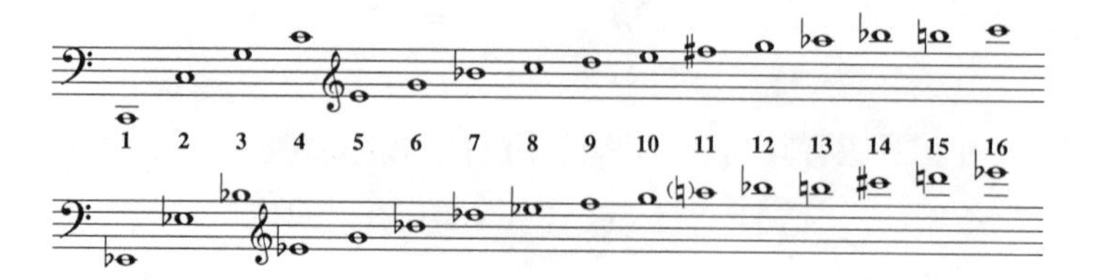

Example 1

Example 2

Example 3

bass line takes up the theme from bars 50 to 52, and this theme is turned into an ascending and descending melodic line in bar 105. For the last eight bars of the prelude (bars 129 to 136), the whole space is saturated with sound, as scales of E♭ major surge simultaneously back and forth.

The music is born from primordial sound. Is there anything in Wagner's writings to support this interpretation? The following passage from *Opera and Drama* might almost have been conceived as a description of the prelude to *Das Rheingold*: "Starting out from the fundamental note of harmony, music grew to fill an immensely varied expanse in which the absolute musician *swam*[1] aimlessly and restlessly to and fro, until he finally grew afraid: ahead of him he saw nothing but an endless billowing mass of possibilities, while being conscious in himself of no single purpose to which to put those possibilities" (1851a, *GS* 4.149). Suffice it to recall at this juncture the maritime associations of music that Wagner develops in *The Art-Work of the Future* and that were discussed in detail in the previous chapter. The persistence of the image in Wagner's thinking is attested by an entry in Cosima Wagner's diary, in which we read, "In the morning we discussed music: 'It is the element into which everything plunges, the fluid element'" (*CT*, 25 May 1871).

This is something that Thomas Mann fully understood: the surging floodwaters of the Rhine represent "*the beginning of music itself.* And it was not just the music of myth that he, the poet-composer, would give us but the very myth of music itself, a mythical philosophy and a musical poem of Creation" (Mann 1937, 189). This is, no doubt, a brilliant insight—but, like the majority of writers whom we shall have occasion to quote, Mann fails to attach any wider metaphorical significance to it. In fact, the opening of *Das Rheingold* evokes the birth not only of music but of pure, absolute, solitary music, a type of music that must be fused with its two Hellenic sister arts to produce the art-work of the future.

The Rhine Daughters and the Three Sisters of *The Art-Work of the Future*

The three sisters in question are not slow in coming forward but appear on cue as the curtain rises. In this case, moreover, my work has been made much simpler by the Berlin musicologist Tibor Kneif, who has provided convincing proof of the analogy between the Rhine daughters and the three sisters of Wagner's essay. I may restrict myself, therefore, to repeating Kneif's main arguments (Kneif 1969, 298–304).

Kneif begins by underscoring the parallelism between the description of the round dance of the sister arts in *The Art-Work of the Future* and the stage directions that litter the opening scene of *Das Rheingold*. Let us remind ourselves of the relevant section of the 1849 essay:

> *Dance*, *Music*, and *Poetry* are the names of the three primeval sisters whom we see entwining their measures the moment that the conditions necessary for the manifestation of art arise. By their very nature they cannot be separated without destroying the graceful round that is art; for in this round, which is the motion of art itself, they are so wondrously entwined, sensually and spiritually, by the fairest affection and love, so firmly and life-enhancingly enlaced that each of the three, unlinked from the chain and thus bereft of life and movement, can lead but an artificial, borrowed life, not giving forth her sacred ordinances, as in their trinity, but merely receiving coercive rules for mechanical movement.
>
> As we gaze upon this entrancing measure of the artist's truest and noblest muses, we now perceive all three of them, each with her arm affectionately entwined about her sister's neck; then, now this one and now that frees herself from the others' embrace in order to show them her beauteous form in full independence, merely brushing the others' hands with the tips of her fingers; now one of them, entranced by the sight of her sisters' tight embrace, bowing down gently before their twin beauty; then two of them, transported by the charm of the third, greeting her with tender homage;

> until at last all three are tightly clasped, breast on breast and limb to limb, melting together with the fervor of love's kiss to create a single, wondrously living human form.—Such is the love and life, the wooing and winning of art, the one true art whose several parts, ever for themselves and ever for one another, diverge to create the richest contrast and reunite in blissful harmony.
>
> This is art that is free. The sweet and forceful impulse in the sisters' dance is the *yearning for freedom*; the kiss of love as their arms entwine is *the joy of newfound freedom.*
>
> *The lonely man is not free*, because, in the absence of love, he is fettered and dependent; *the sociable man is free*, because, unfettered, he is made independent by love. (1849m, *GS* 3.67)

Here, by way of comparison, is the parallel passage in *Das Rheingold*: "With merry squeals Woglinde and Wellgunde separate: Floßhilde tries to catch first one then the other; they slip away from her and finally come together in order to join in pursuit of Floßhilde" (*GS* 5.201). They insist, moreover, on the inevitability of love:

denn was nur lebt, will lieben;	all that lives must love;
meiden will keiner die Minne.	no one wants to shun its delights.
	(*GS* 5.211)

We have already seen to what extent love was an essential element in the union of the three sisters (see Kneif 1969, 301).

At the end of *Götterdämmerung* the Rhine daughters reappear to fulfill the same function as that performed by the sister arts in *The Art-Work of the Future*: they demonstrate their future reunification.

Kneif also observes that the Rhine daughters enter in the sequence Woglinde, Wellgunde, and Floßhilde, reflecting the order *Tanzkunst* (Dance), *Tonkunst* (Music), and *Dichtkunst* (Poetry) of *The Art-Work of the Future*. The parallelism of *W-W-F* with *T-T-D* would thus suggest a similarity between the Rhine daughters and the sister arts. The fact that Wagner changed the names of the Rhine daughters (they are still called Bronnhilde, Floßhilde, and Wellgunde in the prose draft of March 1852) shows clearly that he had a particular aim in mind here.

Without seeking to distinguish between Woglinde and Wellgunde, Kneif argues that "in all likelihood," Floßhilde represents poetry: it is poetry that takes pride of place in Wagner's theoretical essays and it is Floßhilde who, in *Das Rheingold*, appears as the wisest of the sisters and who, in *Götterdämmerung*, holds up the regained ring while her other two sisters drag Hagen down into the depths of the Rhine. To this may be added the fact that, in the stage directions quoted earlier, it is Floßhilde who, in keeping with the active role that Wagner ascribes to the poet, seeks to bring her sisters back together. As I shall show in a moment, there are additional factors that reinforce this interpretation of Floßhilde as the embodiment of the poet.

Kneif has not attempted to place his interpretation within a wider framework and has in fact indicated the difficulty of such an approach. It could be argued, however, that his exegesis is more plausible within the framework of my own more global hypothesis.

What do we hear *musically* just after the end of the prelude, as the curtain rises? Wagner uses a technical device to indicate that we are listening to a primordial form of music, a kind of *Urmusik*, embodied in Woglinde's pentatonic melody. Even in Wagner's day this type of melody was considered typical of *Naturvölker*, those nations deemed closest to nature and hence the most "primitive." In 1854—the very year in which Wagner was writing the music of *Das Rheingold*—we find Eduard Hanslick, for example, commenting in his monograph *On The Beautiful in Music*: "Hand (*Aesthetik der Tonkunst* I, 50) also very justly directs attention to the fact that the musical scales of the Scottish Gaels and the various tribes of India are alike in the peculiarity of having neither fourth nor seventh, the succession of their notes being C, D, E, G, A, C" (1854, 107).

Example 4

This is confirmed by the ethnomusicologist Constantin Brailoiu in a famous article devoted to pentatonicism, "Sur une mélodie russe": "The five-note scale is the *symbol*,[2] therefore, of the beginnings [of music] and the first stage that human music has passed through in every corner of the globe" (1953, 313). Jacques Chailley, in turn, has drawn attention to the way in which Wagner not only exploits natural harmonics in the prelude but passes *instinctively* "from the harmonic structure of the prelude to the vocal melodic structure" (1954–55, 162). Undeniably true though this is, it is only half the story, as we shall see in a moment.

According to *Opera and Drama*, the appearance of this melody *after* the prelude signifies the birth of melody out of harmony, that melody which fecundates the language of words and, specifically, of poetry.

> The melody to whose birth we are now listening is the complete antithesis of that other primeval maternal melody. . . . In tracing its progress from spoken language to the language of music, we reached the horizontal surface of harmony on which the poet's linguistic phrase was reflected back as a musical melody. By taking this surface as our point of departure, we may gain possession of the whole content of *harmony's unfathomable depths—that primordial womb of the whole family of sounds*[3]—and thus achieve an ever more extensive realization of the poetic intent by *plunging*[4] that poetic intent, as the procreative factor, into the utmost depths of that archetypal maternal element. (1851a, *GS* 4.145)

Or consider the following passage: "The musician must rise to the surface from the depths of the sea of harmony, for only on that surface can the rapturous wedding be celebrated between the procreative poetic idea and music's infinite potential for giving birth" (ibid., 4.142). The aquatic metaphors of *Opera and Drama* remind us of the opening of *Das Rheingold*, while the opening of *Das Rheingold* recalls the theoretical tract: by electing to sing a folk melody, Woglinde attests to the union of poetry and music at the very dawn of human history. Moreover, as Jean-Pierre Juliard has shown (1979, 59), the words that she sings celebrate, from the very first line, the *musical* union of vowels and consonants:

	W	*ei*		*a*	
	W	*a*	*g*	*a*	
	W	*o*	*g*	*e*	
du	*W*	*ell*		*e*	
	W	*all*		*e*	
zur	*W*	*ie*	*g*	*e*	
	W	*a*	*g*	*a*	*la*
	W	*ei*		*a*	
	W	*all*		*a*	*la*
	W	*ei*		*a*	*la*
	W	*ei*		*a*	

(*GS* 5.200)

With the constant repetition of the semivowel *w* and the rarer appearance of the palatal *g* and liquid *l*, it is above all the interplay of vowels that strikes the listener here: *ei*, *a*, *o*, *e*, *ie*. Now, as Wagner writes in *Opera and Drama*, "Inner man's primal organ of expression is the *language of music*, being the most spontaneous expression of an inner feeling stimulated from without. . . . If we imagine these vowels stripped of their consonants and see in them only the varied and intensified interplay of inner feelings, whether those feelings express pain or joy, we shall obtain *a picture of man's first language of feeling*,[5] a language in which each excited and intensified feeling could no doubt find expression only in *a combination of expressive musical sounds that was bound, of its own accord, to assume the form of melody*"[6] (1851a, *GS* 4.91–92). Following the birth of harmony, Woglinde allows us to witness the birth of that melody which issues from harmony—a melody, moreover, that is superimposed on a prolongation of the preceding chords over the broken chord of A♭ major and that is clothed in the most elementary form of poetic expression, the varied vowels that constitute the *musical* element of language.

But let us go on with our analysis. The German text reads: "Woge, du Welle, / walle zur Wiege!" (literally, "Welter, you wave! Flow to the cradle!" [*GS* 5.200]). The alliteration on *w* has not been chosen at random, since Wagner is clearly at pains to evoke the emergence of melody from the primordial aqueous element. No less fortuitous is the use of *l*, a sound that phoneticians rightly describe as a "liquid." In those of the following lines that alliterate, it is again the semivowel *w* that predominates:

*W*oglinde, *w*ach'st du allein?	Woglinde, watching alone?
Mit *W*ellgunde *w*är' ich zu zwei.	With Wellgunde there would be two!
Lass' seh'n, *w*ie du *w*ach'st.	Let me see how you watch.
. . . . . .	. . . . . .
Heiala *w*eia!	Heiala weia!
*W*ildes Geschwister!	High-spirited sisters!

(Ibid.)

The fricative *f* then appears, prolonging the name of Floßhilde, whom Wellgunde calls on to join in their game:

*F*loßhilde, schwimm'!	Floßhilde, swim!
Woglinde *f*lieht:	Woglinde's fleeing:
hilf mir, die *f*ließende *f*angen!	Help me catch your sleek sister!

(Ibid.)

And when Floßhilde, the poet, speaks for the first time, it is to introduce a harsher kind of consonantal alliteration and assonance in the form of sibilants and spirants:

Des Goldes *Sch*laf	The sleeping gold
hütet ihr *sch*lecht;	you guard badly;
be*ss*er bewacht	pay better heed
des *Sch*lummernden Bett,	to the slumberer's bed
sonst bü*ß*'t ihr beide das *Sp*iel!	or you'll both atone for your sport!

(*GS* 5.201)

Why this introduction of voiceless consonants? Woglinde's opening words expressed feeling pure and simple, a vocalization of words virtually devoid of meaning ("Weia! Waga! . . . Wagalaweia! Wallala weiala weia!"). In *Opera and Drama* Wagner describes the origins of language as follows:

> When, in the pure language of sound [*Tonsprache*], feeling communicated the impressions that it received, it revealed only itself, which it was able to do because, supported by gesture, the sounds in question rose and fell, were extended or abbreviated, intensified or reduced in the most varied manner: but, in order to describe and distinguish external objects, feeling had to clothe the sound in a distinctive garment in a way that answered to and evoked the impression of each object, and that garment it took from that impression and, through it, from the object itself. *It wove this garment from mute articulations, which it added to the open sound either initially or finally or both*[7] . . . The vowels thus clothed and distinguished by this clothing form *linguistic roots*. (1851a, *GS* 4.93)

It is thus this birth of language that we witness in the first nineteen lines of *Das Rheingold* (bars 137–65); and here, too, it is significant that it is Floßhilde who finally introduces consonants.

When the Rhine daughters begin their games, they are separated from one another ("Woglinde, watching alone?"). Soon, however, they are reunited. The beginning of *Das Rheingold* offers a comprehensive illustration of the birth and original unity of the three sororal arts.

But here comes Alberich.

Alberich and Meyerbeer

Alberich has come to destroy the beautiful, natural, original unity of the three sister arts. He is a Jew, one of the Jews in the *Ring*: "The gold-grabbing, invisible, anonymous, exploitative Alberich, the shoulder-shrugging, loquacious Mime, overflowing with self-praise and spite, the impotent intellectual critic Hanslick-Beckmesser—all the rejects of Wagner's works are caricatures of Jews" (Adorno 1952, 23). The notoriety of the author of *In Search of Wagner* has no doubt helped to consolidate this image, yet it seems to me to be confirmed by Wagner's own writings.

In a letter to Uhlig of 30 October 1851, he reports: "Minna has come up with a splendid joke: she called our doctor an aquatic Jew [*Wasserjude*]. Priceless! Well, he hasn't done me any harm!"[8] A rereading of "Judaism in Music" reveals a striking portrait of Alberich, as three key sentences make abundantly plain: "We must explain the *involuntary feeling of abhorrence* that the Jew excites in us by virtue of his *person*[9] and his *very being*"[10] (1850c, *GS* 5.67). "Incomparably more important, however, indeed of crucial importance here, is the *effect*[11] that the Jew produces upon us by virtue of his *method of speaking*" (ibid., 5.70). The Jew "*rules* and will continue to rule so long as money remains the power before which all deeds and actions must needs pale into insignificance" (ibid., 5.68).

It is not difficult to demonstrate that the character of Alberich in *Das Rheingold* illustrates these three aspects of Wagner's anti-Semitism.

We may begin by considering the physical and linguistic aspect and noting that Wagner speaks of the "effect" produced by the sight of Jews and by the sound of their language. The Rhine daughters have the specific function of giving explicit expression to this feeling of abhorrence. Their reaction must be read in parallel with the corresponding description in "Judaism in Music": "In ordinary life the Jew . . . strikes us first and foremost by his *outward appearance*,[12] which, no matter which European nationality he belong to, has something about it that is foreign to that nationality and that we find insuperably unpleasant: we wish to have nothing to do with such a person. . . . Ignoring the moral aspect of this *unpleasant freak of nature*[13] and confining ourselves to the realm of art, we may mention merely that this exterior can never be used as a subject for one of the visual arts"—unless it be a basis for caricature (ibid., *GS* 5.69).

After Woglinde has fanned the flames of Alberich's lust, Wellgunde paints an unflattering portrait of him:

Bist du verliebt	If you're in love
und lüstern nach Minne?	and lusting for its delights,
Lass' seh'n, du Schöner,	let's see, my beauty,
wie bist du zu schau'n?—	what you're like to look at!
Pfui du haariger,	Ugh! You hairy,
höck'riger Geck!	hunchbacked fool!
Schwarzes, schwieliges	Brimstone-black
Schwefelgezwerg!	and blistered dwarf!
Such' dir ein Friedel,	Look for a lover
dem du gefällst!	who looks like yourself!

(*GS* 5.205)

Floßhilde pretends to like the sound of his voice:

O singe fort	O sing on
so süß und fein;	so sweetly and subtly:
wie hehr verführt es mein Ohr!	how it bewitches my ear!

(*GS* 5.206)

The 1850 essay leaves its reader in no doubt on this point:

What strikes our ear as particularly odd and unpleasant is a hissing, buzzing, humming, and growling sound that is typical of the Jewish way of speaking: a use of inversion that is utterly uncharacteristic of our own national tongue

> and the arbitrary way in which the Jew twists words and constructions give his pronunciation the unmistakable character of an intolerably confused babble of sounds, so that, when we hear it, our attention is involuntarily held by this offensive manner of articulating the *how* rather than by the *what* that his discourse contains. (1850c, *GS* 5.71)

From discourse Wagner passes to singing: "Everything about his outward appearance and language that strikes us as repulsive will have an infinitely off-putting effect upon us when he starts to sing, unless we allow ourselves to be held enthralled by the sheer ridiculousness of it all" (ibid., 5.72). It is this doubly ridiculous aspect of the Jew that Floßhilde mocks:

Deinen stechenden Blick,	Your piercing stare,
deinen struppigen Bart,	your bristly beard
o säh' ich ihn, faßt' ich ihn stets!	might I always see and grasp!
Deines stachligen Haares	May your prickly hair's
strammes Gelock,	unruly locks
umflöss' es Floßhilde ewig!	float round Floßhild' for aye!
Deine Krötengestalt,	Your toadlike shape,
deiner Stimme Gekrächz,	the croak of your voice,
o dürft' ich, staunend und stumm,	could I, amazed and mute,
sie nur hören und seh'n.	hear and see only them!

(*GS* 5.207)

The "croak" of Alberich's voice is clearly heard in the abrasive alliteration of such lines as:

Garstig glatter	Slimily smooth and
glitschriger Glimmer!	slippery slate!
Wie gleit' ich aus!	I can't stop sliding!

(*GS* 5.203)

Or:

Wie fang' ich im Sprung	How can I catch
den spröden Fisch?	this coy fish in flight?

(*GS* 5.204)

Or, finally, in reply to Floßhilde's "O sing on so sweetly and subtly: how it bewitches my ear":

Mir zagt, zuckt	My heart quakes and quivers,
und zehrt sich das Herz,	and burns with desire
lacht mir so zierliches Lob.	when such fulsome praise smiles upon me.

(*GS* 5.206)

Nor should we forget the music. On this point, Wagner writes in his anti-Jewish tract: "Who has not had an opportunity to convince himself that the sound of Jews singing at their divine services is no more than a caricature? Who has not been overcome by feelings of the most utter revulsion, mixed with horror and ridicule, on hearing that gurgling, yodeling, and babbling sound that throws both sense and mind into utter confusion and that no attempt at caricature can ever make more repulsively distorted?" (1850c, *GS* 5.76). The music that accompanies the lines cited above ("Garstig glatter glitschriger Glimmer!") is particularly characteristic, its complicated rhythms and convoluted chromaticisms typifying the style that Wagner was seeking to caricature. There is one particular point that needs to be emphasized here. From his very first entrance, Alberich is characterized by syncopated, limping rhythms, but one searches in vain for a leitmotif that is uniquely his. Neither Lavignac (1897, 343) nor Burghold (1980, 10) nor the anonymous compiler of the *Buch der Motive* (n.d., 2–3) mentions such a motif. The only motif that Deryck Cooke associates with the figure of the dwarf is a tiny descending cello figure (Cooke n.d., no. 165).

Example 5

This is no accident. For Wagner, the Jewish composer "has never had an art of his own" (1850c, *GS* 5.76), his only art being that of the synagogue. "Those curious melismata and rhythms absorb his musical imagination" (ibid., 5.77). In consequence, he cannot be integrated into the artistic creations of non-Semites. He should "be deterred from ever venturing to work alongside us in our artistic activities. His entire position among us, however, discourages the Jew from becoming intimately involved in such a world as ours. . . . He responds only superficially to our artistic world and its life-giving inner organism" (ibid., 5.77–78). From a musical point of view, Alberich cannot be treated like the other characters in the *Ring*. "The most accidental similarities between different phenomena in the sphere of our musical life and art are bound to strike him [the Jew] as their very essence, so that if he then reproduces them in his art and reflects them back to us, they will appear strange, cold, indifferent, odd, unnatural, and distorted" (ibid., 5.78). Alberich is not entitled to have a leitmotif of his own but is characterized by a style that is both ridiculous and grotesque.

That Alberich embodies a third characteristic of the Jew, whose rule is said to be based on the power of money, will become only too clear in the course of the work as a whole: he steals the gold from the Rhine and exerts his sway over the race of Nibelungs, a sway that he hopes to extend to embrace the entire world.

It will be recalled that Wagner's economic critique of the Jews is closely bound up with his denunciation of the mercantilism that plagues modern opera in general. If, in spite of a number of criticisms, Wagner retains a certain sympathy for Mendelssohn, he is relentless in his assault on Meyerbeer: "A universally famous Jewish musician of our own day has addressed himself in his works to that section of the public whose confused taste in music he had less need actually to create than to exploit for his own ends" (ibid., 5.81–82). The parallels between this negative portrait of Meyerbeer (which extends over three whole pages) and the "description" of the physical appearance, language, and music of the Jews are enough to suggest, if not to prove, that Alberich embodies the composer Meyerbeer in this allegorical history of music. A detailed examination of the score may serve to confirm this supposition.

Between bars 375 and 387 the style of the music changes. It is clear that in this section of the scene Wagner is parodying a grand operatic love duet from the 1840s. In *The Composer's Voice* Edward T. Cone has emphasized the fact that if, in an opera, the composer wants to show that a character is singing, this has to be explicitly indicated (Cone 1964, 30):

Holder *Sang*[14]	What sweet singing
singt[15] zu mir her!	wafts this way!

(*GS* 5.206)

Floßhilde confirms this indication: "O *singe*[16] fort / so süß und fein!" (O sing on so sweetly and subtly! [ibid.]), before concluding: "Wie billig am Ende vom *Lied*"[17] (As befits the end of the song [*GS* 5.207]).

The words of these twelve bars of music are typical of a grand operatic "number":

FLOSSHILDE

Wie deine Anmuth	How your charm
mein Aug' erfreut,	cheers my eye,
deines Lächelns Milde	how your gentle smile
den Muth mir labt!	lifts up my spirit.
Seligster Mann!	Dearest of men!

ALBERICH

Süßeste Maid!	Sweetest of maids!

FLOSSHILDE

Wär'st du mir hold!	Did you but love me!

Example 6

ALBERICH

Hielt' ich dich immer!	Might I hold you forever!
	(*GS* 5.206–7)

There is clearly a parody—and a very specific parody it is, too.

VALENTINE

Mais, sans défense, on vous immole,	But defenseless you'll be slain!
Gardez-vous, ah!, gardez-vous de fuir!	Beware, oh! beware of fleeing!
Raoul!	Raoul!

RAOUL

Hélas!	Alas!

VALENTINE

Toi, mon seul bien, toi mon idole!	You are all I have, you, my idol!

RAOUL

Ce sont mes frères qu'on immole!	It is my brothers who'll be slain!

VALENTINE

Et te laisser serait mourir!	To leave you is to die!

RAOUL

Ah! laisse-moi, laisse-moi partir!	Ah, leave me, let me go!

VALENTINE

Oui, je saurai . . .	Yes, I shall . . .

RAOUL

L'honneur le veut.	Honor demands it.

VALENTINE

. . . te retenir . . .	. . . keep you here . . .

RAOUL

Je dois te fuir.	I must flee from you.

VALENTINE

. . . te retenir! Ah! par pitié . . .	. . . keep you here! Ah! For pity's sake . . .

RAOUL

Ah! laisse-moi!	Ah! Let me go!

VALENTINE

. . . entends ma voix!	. . . hear my voice!

RAOUL

L'honneur le veut.	Honor demands it.

[etc.]

This stichomythic exchange, characteristic of the love duet from *Les Huguenots*, is echoed in Wagner's score. But, more than that, the orchestral line doubles Floßhilde's vocal line, revealing a style of writing typical of "modern opera," as the example from *Les Huguenots* reveals. It might be thought that this feature was not relevant here, were it not for the fact that this is demonstrably the only passage in *Das Rheingold* where Wagner uses this device.

Example 7

A further analogy confirms that in this scene, Wagner is pillorying background music and the grand operatic style in vogue in Paris at this time. A comparison between this scene and the love duet (no. 5) in Auber's *Fra Diavolo* reveals analogies not only in terms of rhythm but also in the shape of the melodic line. Is it a chance reminiscence, of a kind that is commonly found? One might be inclined to dismiss it as such, were it not for the fact that Scribe's libretto for *Fra Diavolo* takes on a quite specific meaning here. "We were making music, how I loved music, I liked it a lot, but I see that I was alone in liking it, it was boring Mylord," Paméla says, to which Mylord replies: "I didn't like the music"—that grand operatic music with which Floßhilde the poet does not want to be compromised. Can it be mere chance that Floßhilde engages in dialogue with Alberich to the accompaniment of a melodic line that sets these very words to music?

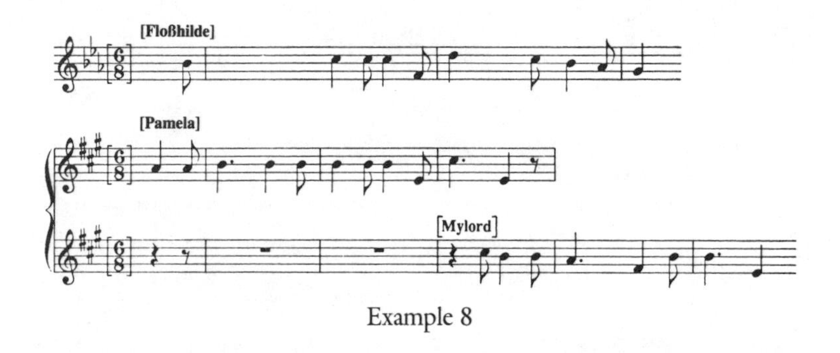

Example 8

Finally, not only does Alberich disturb the unity of the three sisters when he appropriates the gold and seizes power, he renounces the very thing that, according to Wagner's explicit pronouncement, made that union possible—love.

Until the *Ring*'s authentic couples, Siegmund and Sieglinde, and Siegfried and Brünnhilde, experience a love that is deep and natural, the mood remains one of dislocation and disunity. From this point of view, Tibor Kneif, in the article from which I have already quoted, is certainly right to point out that Valhalla is depicted as a work of egotistical pride, an isolated monument (see 1849m, *GS* 3.148–60), which is built only *after* the three sister arts have become separated and which is destroyed immediately before their final reunification in *Götterdämmerung* (Kneif 1969, 304). It is precisely this laborious progress towards the restoration of unity that the *Ring* invites us to follow.

Siegfried and Mime: The Poet of the Future and the "Modern" Creative Artist

Our analysis of *Wieland the Smith* showed clearly that Wieland prefigures Siegfried and that, in the figure of Wieland, Wagner is saluting the poet. The transitive relationship between Wieland and Siegfried would no doubt be sufficient to lend credence to the idea that, in the *Ring*, Siegfried embodies the poet of the future. The identification becomes patently obvious when we come to the love duet for Siegfried and Brünnhilde in the final act of *Siegfried*. For the moment, however, a few textual observations will not come amiss.

The sword Nothung plays the same paradigmatic role as Wieland's wings—that supreme example of the artist's skill, which he succeeds in fashioning when driven on by necessity. Nothung, too, is an altogether exceptional piece of work:

Nur wer das Fürchten	Only he who never
nie erfuhr,	knew fear
schmiedet Nothung neu,	will forge Nothung anew,

Wotan tells Mime (*GS* 6.108). The man of the future will reveal his courage not only by killing the dragon Fafner but also by taking in hand a piece of work that will allow him to produce a synthesis of dislocated fragments.

In this scene Mime's relationship with Siegfried is similar to Alberich's with the Rhine daughters. As Alberich's brother, he is evidently Jewish, too, and Wagner does not scruple to place in Siegfried's mouth words similar to those uttered by the Rhine daughters:

seh' ich dich steh'n,	When I see you standing,
gangeln und geh'n,	waddling and walking,
knicken und nicken,	weak-kneed, nodding,
mit den Augen zwicken:	blinking your eyes:
beim Genick' möcht' ich	I long to seize the scruff
den Nicker packen,	of his nodding neck,
den Garaus geben	and finish off the filthy
dem garst'gen Zwicker!	twitching creature!

(*GS* 6.91)

Later, Siegfried describes Mime as a "garstiger Gauch" (filthy fool) and compares him with a toad. In Act II he ridicules his foster father in virtually identical terms:

Das ek'lige Nicken	The loathsome nodding
und Augenzwicken,	and blinking,

wann endlich soll ich's	when finally shall I
nicht mehr seh'n?	see it no more?
Wann werd' ich den Albernen los?	When shall I be rid of the fool?

(*GS* 6.132)

A little later, Siegfried returns to the subject while musing on his parentage:

Denn wär' wo von Mime ein Sohn,	If Mime were to have a son,
müßt' er nicht ganz	must he not look
Mime gleichen?	just like Mime?
G'rade so garstig,	Just as filthy,
griesig und grau,	fearful and wan,
klein und krumm,	short and misshapen,
höck'rig und hinkend,	hunchbacked and halting,
mit hängenden Ohren,	with drooping ears
triefigen Augen. . .?	and rheumy eyes?

(*GS* 6.133–34)

It is impossible not to be reminded here of the "unpleasant freak of nature" described in "Judaism in Music" (1850c, *GS* 5.69).

Like Alberich, moreover, Mime is another manifestation of the Jewish composer, the creative artist who has sold his art to industry. In this he anticipates the character of Beckmesser in *Die Meistersinger*, a character who, as we know, was inspired by the Jewish critic, Eduard Hanslick. "Hättest du fleißig / die Kunst gepflegt," Mime tells Siegfried in Act I (Had you applied yourself to your art [*GS* 6.114]). Siegfried himself provides a response to this reproach in the final act of *Götterdämmerung*:

doch, was der Künstler	but what the artist
selber nicht konnt',	himself could not do,
des Lehrlings Muthe	the prentice's courage
mußt' es gelingen.	was bound to achieve.

(*GS* 6.242)

It is on his own that Siegfried succeeds in forging the sword. He derides Mime as an "artist"—"Mime der Künstler"—whose only skill lies in the kitchen and in his ability to make egg soup. And yet, like Meyerbeer and his kind, Mime is not without ambition:

Nothung's Trümmer	Nothung's *fragments*[18]
zertrotzt' er mir nicht:	he'd not wrest from me,
könnt' ich die starken	could I but weld
Stücken schweißen,	the massive pieces
die meine Kunst	which my *art*[19]
nicht zu kitten weiß.	can't knit together.

(*GS* 6.86)

But Siegfried denies him this talent: the dwarf

rühmt seine Kunst,
als könnt' er was recht's.

boasts of his art
as though he could do things
aright.

(*GS* 6.89)

Musically, Wagner characterizes Mime through the systematic use of appoggiaturas, aiming to evoke the "yelping" sounds associated in the composer's mind with synagogue chanting. It should come as no surprise, therefore, to read Wagner's letter to Ernst Koch of 10 August 1874, in which the composer states explicitly that Mime, like Alberich and the Rhine daughters, *sings* (Newman 1933, 2.362).

Example 9

It should be clear, when we turn to the text, why the style of this passage has nothing gratuitous about it. Mime abandons himself to a veritable trafficking in emotions, and the vocabulary that Wagner has chosen is certainly not fortuitous:

Das ist nun der Liebe
schlimmer Lohn!
Das der Sorgen
schmählicher Sold!

That's the sad *reward*[20]
for all my love.
That's the paltry *pay*[21]
for so much care!

(*GS* 6.90)

Mime draws up an inventory of all that he has done for Siegfried, concluding:

Und aller Lasten
ist das nun mein Lohn,
daß der hastige Knabe
mich quält und haßt!

And that's my *reward*[22]
for the burdens I've borne,
that the quick-tempered boy
torments and abhors me!

(Ibid.)

Mime embodies and synthesizes all those artists who are incapable of creating a unitary work of art. The image of shards and fragments is one that Wagner uses to describe those artists who are condemned to a certain impotence. Of Weber, for example, we read in *Opera and Drama* that "wherever his long-breathed melody—which was generally written in advance and spread out over the text like a glittering garment—would have done excessive violence to that text, he broke down the melody into fragments, before fitting together the separate sections of this melodic structure to produce an elaborate mosaic that reflected the declamatory requirements of the words" (1851a, *GS* 3.291). The post-Hellenic myth is characterized in comparable terms: "No longer capable of regenerating itself, myth was fragmented into its individual, self-contained component parts, its unity dispersed into a thousandfold plurality, the nucleus of its action broken down into a plethora of disparate actions" (ibid., 4.39). Goethe, by contrast, "took the ready-made subject matter of *Iphigenia* and broke it down into its constituent parts, which he then proceeded to fit together by means of an organically vitalizing act of poetic restructuring in order to enable the organism of the drama to produce the perfect form of dramatic art" (ibid., 4.22). It is this that Mime fails to achieve but that Siegfried succeeds triumphantly in doing. In contrast to Mime, Siegfried embodies the poet of the future.

Confusing fear with a form of aesthetic activity, Siegfried asks: "Ist's eine Kunst, / was kenn' ich sie nicht?" (If it's an art, why don't I know it? [*GS* 6.111]). In a letter to Mathilde Maier of 15 January 1863, Wagner mentions Siegfried's Forging Song and says specifically that Siegfried is "a terrible type of artist" whose singing resembles nothing so much as a "majestic lament."[23] In *A Communication to My Friends* he describes Siegfried explicitly as "the male embodiment of the spirit of eternally and uniquely creative spontaneity, the doer of true deeds" (1851h, *GS* 4.328). It is an analogy that he takes up in his article on Liszt's symphonic poems:

> Because, even without knowing it, the artist always creates forms, whereas those others [art critics[24]] create neither forms nor anything else. [. . .] In fact, this favor has only ever been shown them by those who could never produce anything of their own and who sought the expedient of—forms: and what that means we know very well, do we not? Swords without blades! But when someone comes along who forges blades (*as you can see, I've just been in my young Siegfried's smithy*[25]), the fools cut their fingers by grabbing them in the way in which they used to grab the empty hilts that were proffered to them before; of course, they then grow angry at the fact that the spiteful smith holds the hilt in his hand—as is necessary when wielding a sword—and that they cannot even see what others had already offered them. (1857, *GS* 5.187–88)

The analogy between Siegfried and the poet is also evident in *Opera and Drama*, where Wagner writes: "the language of words was the child that left its father and mother in order to find its way alone in the big wide world" (1851a, *GS* 4.54). While waiting, he demonstrates his ability to reweld the fragments of the shattered sword: "was entzwei ist, zwing' ich mir so" (what lies in twain I force back together like this [*GS* 6.115]). And once Nothung has been reforged, Siegfried can exclaim:

War'st du entzwei, ich zwang dich zu ganz; kein Schlag soll nun dich mehr zerschlagen.	Though you lay in twain, I forced you to be whole; no blow shall shatter you again.

(*GS* 6.122)

Siegfried is now capable of surmounting the obstacles that lie in the way of reunification.

The Poet Siegfried Eliminates the Obstacles That Prevent the Work of Art from Achieving Its Former Unity

Before awakening Brünnhilde as the embodiment of music and attempting to father the art-work of the future on her, Siegfried has to remove two obstacles from his path in the form of Fafner and Mime. How do these two characters constitute an obstacle to the unity of the projected work?

At this stage of the *Ring* Fafner symbolizes the power that accrues through money and its sterile accumulation. He guards the money beneath his belly: "Ich lieg' und besitz'" (What I lie on I own [*GS* 6.128]). Corrupted by the renunciation of love that enabled Alberich to acquire the Rhine gold, Fafner and the ring constitute an obstacle in the way of both womankind and the unity of the work of art: both are accessible only in loving union. Once Fafner has been killed, the meaning of the ring is transformed: Siegfried does not understand its terrible import and offers it to Brünnhilde as a token of his love. At the same time, he now understands the language of birds.

This new understanding constitutes an initial symbol, presaging the coming union between Siegfried the poet and Brünnhilde as the embodiment of music. Unable to understand the Wood Bird's singing, Siegfried hears only a flute—in other words, pure instrumental music. The poet attempts to imitate the music he hears, thus illustrating the total powerlessness of the poet who submits to music, a powerlessness described by Wagner in his theoretical writings. "Ich versuch's, sing' ihm nach" (I'll try to imitate his singing [*GS* 6.135]). A modern artist suggested this idea to him:

Ein zankender Zwerg hat mir erzählt, der Vöglein Stammeln	A querulous dwarf once told me one could

gut zu versteh'n,	come to understand
dazu könnte man kommen.	the babbling of little birds.

(*GS* 6.134)

The premises of this argument are fundamentally flawed:

entrath' ich der Worte,	*If I dispense with the words*
achte der Weise,	*and attend to the tune*,[26]
sing' ich so seine Sprache,	if I sing his language thus,
versteh' ich wohl auch, was er spricht.	I'll no doubt grasp what he's saying.

(*GS* 6.135)

For the Wagner of the early 1850s this is exactly the opposite of what should be involved. Thanks to the loving relationship that has become symbolically possible through Fafner's death, music will be charged with meaning(s) following its contact with poetry: understanding impregnates feeling, the flute becomes song, and music is semanticized. Wagner explains this clearly enough in *Opera and Drama*: "Music cannot think, but it can clothe thoughts in material form. . . . It can do this, however, only if its own manifestation is *conditioned*[27] by the poetic intent and if this intent, in turn, is revealed not as something merely conceptualized but as clearly expressed by the organ of understanding, in other words, the language of words" (1851a, *GS* 4.184–85). "Expression in music will remain completely vague and indeterminate until such time as it assimilates the poetic intent" (ibid., 4.189).

It is not surprising, therefore, that there are not one but three explicit references to the fact that the Wood Bird *sings*.

O holder Sang!	O lovely singing!
Süßester Hauch!,	Sweetest breath!,

Siegfried says when he hears its singing (*GS* 6.150).

Lustig im Leid	Joyful in grief
sing' ich von Liebe.	I sing of love;
Wonnig aus Weh'	delighting, I weave
web' ich mein Lied—	my lay from woe:
nur Sehnende kennen den Sinn!	lovers alone know what it means.

(Ibid.)

Is there any need of further proof to demonstrate the link between the Wood Bird and music? Suffice it to mention Wagner's own commentary on this scene, as reported by Cosima in her diaries: "We pass the evening in conversation; he is still delighted with the picture of Beethoven: 'That is how he looked, this poor man who gave us back the language men spoke before they had ideas; it was to recover this language of the birds that Man created the divine art'" (*CT*, 3 July 1869).

Example 10

The forest bird represents the passage of instrumental music to true unitarian music, vocal music, in its original form. And, like Woglinde, the Wood Bird sings a pentatonic melody. The first incarnation of the poetico-musical synthesis for Siegfried, the Wood Bird plays the part of intermediary and tells him where to find Brünnhilde. That the latter assumes the Wood Bird's musical properties is confirmed by Siegfried himself in the final act of *Götterdämmerung*:

Seit lange acht' ich des Lallens nicht mehr.	It's long since I've heeded their woodnote.
. . . .	. . . .
Seit Frauen ich singen hörte, vergaß ich der Vöglein ganz.	Since I heard women singing, I've quite forgotten birds. (*GS* 6.241–42)

At the same time that it introduces him to Brünnhilde, however, the forest bird also reveals that Siegfried can read Mime's evil thoughts: the "modern" artist plans to kill the artist of the future. In consequence, Siegfried has to remove Mime from the scene. In doing so, he destroys a character who not only embodies the quintessential Jewish artist but who has tried to pass himself off as androgynous. The link between these two aspects is one that needs to be emphasized, since true androgyny—the type of androgyny that is uniquely worthy of the artist of the future—awaits Siegfried on Brünnhilde's rock in the union of her embrace.

The character of Mime is closely bound up with the question of Siegfried's origins. The dwarf tries to pass himself off as Siegfried's father in the first act and, for a time, Siegfried pretends to believe him. In that case, who is his mother? "Ich bin dir Vater / und Mutter zugleich" (I'm both father and mother to you [*GS* 6.94]), Mime replies. Siegfried has seen his own reflection in the forest stream: he does not look like Mime. And he has seen the wild animals mating. Mime divulges Sieglinde's name but not that of Siegmund, even though he knows it. "Mein Vater bist du nicht" (You are not my father [*GS* 6.98]), Siegfried asserts in Act I and, later, in Act II:

Daß der mein Vater nicht ist,	That he is not my father
wie fühl' ich mich drob so froh!	fills me with feelings of joy!

(*GS* 6.133)

Siegfried thus removes a double obstacle, that of an impossible androgynous father and that of a Jewish father. But the problem of his own identity still remains unresolved:

Wie sah mein Vater wohl aus?	What must my father have looked like?
Ha! gewiß, wie ich selbst!	Ha! Of course, like me!

(Ibid.)

At least he does not bear within him the curse of those Judaized composers who are concerned solely with the immediate effect of their works on their audiences and with the profit that they can draw from their performance. Within moments Siegfried will join Brünnhilde-music—on the Valkyries' rock.

Siegfried and Brünnhilde: Poet and Music

As pointed out in the Introduction to Part One, the love duet in the third act of *Siegfried* is dominated by the idea of androgyny.

We may begin by examining the way in which Wagner has explicitly given Brünnhilde male characteristics, while Siegfried is endowed with female ones.

The mannish nature of the breast-plated Valkyries is well known. Although the forest bird tells Siegfried that he will discover a woman asleep on the mountainside, it is a "man in armor" whom he first examines in his astonishment. But before he discovers Brünnhilde's true nature and exclaims, "Das ist kein Mann!" (It's not a man! [*GS* 6.165]), there is a highly poetical passage that includes the first indications of androgyny, indications that appear not to have been previously noticed. Siegfried removes the sleeping Valkyrie's helmet and compares her hair to a bank of clouds, adding:

leuchtender Sonne	the radiant sunlight's
lachendes Bild	smiling image
strahlt durch das Wogengewölk!	shines through a billowing bank of clouds.

(*GS* 6.164)

The sun plays on Brünnhilde's hair. But the sun is Siegfried himself and, in modern German, the word *Sonne* is feminine. When, a few moments later, Brünnhilde starts to speak or, more correctly, to sing, her first words are addressed to the orb of day:

Heil dir, Sonne!	Hail to you, sun!

(*GS* 6.166)

In his 1849 essay *Die Wibelungen* (The Wibelungs) Wagner had already assimilated Siegfried with the solar deity: "In its most remotely distinguishable form the family saga of the Franks shows us the individualized light or sun god conquering and slaying the monster of the primeval night of chaos: —this is the original meaning of *Siegfried's fight with the dragon*" (1849a, *GS* 2.131).[28] It is his own image, therefore, that Siegfried recognizes glinting through Brünnhilde's hair: the first stage in their union is already evident here. He removes her armor and, discovering a woman, calls on his mother to help him, since he finally knows the meaning of fear. Let us not forget that Siegfried has never seen a woman in his life, having lived in an entirely male world. But his fear is not only the result of his discovery of sexuality and the otherness of the female sex, it is also caused by his confrontation with the irremediable breakdown of the original unity, the realization, in short, that *half of himself* exists outside himself. Siegfried is explicit on this point:

Daß ich selbst erwache, muß die Maid ich erwecken.	That I myself may wake, I must awaken the maid.

(*GS* 6.166)

In a letter to August Röckel of 24 August 1851 Wagner expresses himself in exactly the same terms, while at the same time providing a gloss to the whole of the passage under discussion: "Siegfried passes through the fire and awakens Brünnhilde—*womankind*—in the most blissful of love's embraces. —I cannot intimate any further details here: but perhaps I may be allowed to send you the poem itself. —Only one other thing: —in our animated conversations we already touched on the subject: —we shall not become what we can and must be until such time as—*womankind* has been *wakened*."[29] There could be no clearer endorsement than this of Wagner's conception of the androgynous nature of every human being.

The date of this letter is important. It was written on 24 August 1851, barely nine months after Wagner's letter to Uhlig of 12 December 1850, announcing that *Opera and Drama* was based on a sexual metaphor. (The essay itself was completed on 10 January 1851.) *Der junge Siegfried* was conceived between 3 May and 24 June 1851. The textual concordance between Wagner's theoretical androgyny and its poetical counterpart is thus reinforced by chronological considerations.

Another letter to Röckel, this time of 25/26 January 1854, confirms the androgynous gloss that must be placed on this scene: "The highest satisfaction of individual egoism is to be found in its total abandonment, and this is something that human beings can achieve only through love: but *the true human being is both man and woman*,[30] and only in the union of man and woman does the true human being exist."[31] Siegfried intuitively glimpses the need for self-abandonment even before embracing Brünnhilde:

So saug' ich mir Leben	So I suck life
aus süßesten Lippen,	from the sweetest of lips,
sollt' ich auch sterbend vergeh'n!	though I should perish and die!

(*GS* 6.166)

In other words, Siegfried prepares to abandon his individuality and merge with music in the total work of art.

It is this union of male and female that we witness following Brünnhilde's awakening. She herself is conscious of the fact that she is the female half of Siegfried:

Du selbst bin ich,	Your own self am I
wenn du mich Selige liebst.	if you but love me in my bliss.

(*GS* 6.168)

And she recognizes her masculine half in him:

Liebe dich,	Love your own self
und lasse von mir:	and let me be:
vernichte dein Eigen nicht!	do not destroy what is yours!

(*GS* 6.173)

The scene ends with a celebration of the perfect union between them, a union rendered possible by the sexual complementarity of the two partners involved:

SIEGFRIED

Sie ist mir ewig,	She's mine forever,
ist mir immer,	always mine,
Erb' und Eigen,	my heritage and own,
ein' und all'!	my one and all!

BRÜNNHILDE

Er ist mir ewig,	He's mine forever,
ist mir immer,	always mine,

Erb' und Eigen,	my heritage and own,
ein' und all'!	my one and all!

(*GS* 6.176)

This union is also explained by Wagner in his letter to Röckel of 25/26 January 1854: "Not even Siegfried alone (man alone) is the complete 'human being': he is merely the half, only with *Brünnhilde* does he become the redeemer; *one* man alone cannot do everything; many are needed, and a suffering, self-immolating woman finally becomes the true, conscious redeemer: for it is love that is really 'the eternal feminine' itself."[32] This letter may be read alongside the passage from *Opera and Drama* quoted toward the end of Chapter One: "Assuming that poet and musician do not restrict each other but excite each other's abilities through love until those abilities reach their highest potential, and if, in this love, they are all that they can ever be and if they are *mutually consumed* in sacrificing their highest potential, drama will be born in its highest manifestation" (1851a, *GS* 4.207).

Brünnhilde embodies music. The convergence of the two androgynies—androgyny in the theoretical tract and androgyny in the opera—together with the analogy Wieland-Siegfried-poet, on the one hand, and Schwanhilde-Brünnhilde-music, on the other, would at least be sufficient to encourage such a hypothesis. Once again, however, Wagner confirms this supposition by placing the following words in Siegfried's mouth and by insisting so emphatically on them:

Wie Wunder tönt,	How wondrous it sounds,
was wonnig du singst,	what you *sing* so blithely;
. . . .	. . . .
deiner Stimme Singen	the sound of your *singing*
hör' ich süß:	is sweet to hear:
doch was du singend mir sag'st,	but what you say to me, *singing*,[33]
staunend versteh' ich's nicht.	amazed, I cannot grasp it.

(*GS* 6.168–69)

If Brünnhilde were not protected by the fire that she herself had demanded, she would have been abandoned to the mercy of any vainglorious coward. This same image is found, in an even more radical form, in *Opera and Drama*, where Wagner uses it to characterize popular melody: "Shamelessly it bares its noble generative organs, offering them with appalling indifference to the prying nose of every roguish libertine" (1851a, *GS* 3.261). It is a persistent image in Wagner's writings. In an important letter to Liszt of 25 November 1850, in which he discusses the encounter between poet and musician, the composer alludes directly to Brünnhilde's protective circle of flames: "My essay on the nature of opera, the final fruits of my deliberations, has assumed greater dimensions than I had first supposed: but if I wish to demonstrate that music (as a woman) must necessarily be impregnated by a poet (as a man), then *I must ensure that this glorious woman is not abandoned to the first passing libertine*, but that she is made pregnant only by the man who yearns for womankind with true, irresistible love."[34] Also worth citing here is the following passage from *Opera and Drama*, describing the meeting between the "melody of joy" and Schiller's poem in terms of Brünnhilde's awakening:

> This melody is exactly the same as that which rose to the surface from the unfathomable depths of *Beethoven*'s music in order to *greet the sun's bright light*.[35] . . . This melody was woman's loving greeting to man; the all-embracing "Eternal Feminine" showed herself here to be more loving than the egotistical male. . . . Only the poet whose aim we have expounded here feels so irresistibly and powerfully driven to enter into the most intimate marriage with the "Eternal Feminine" of music that he also celebrates his own redemption in this marriage. (1851a, *GS* 4.146)

This is the same act of redemption of the man and poet, on the one hand, and of the woman and music, on the other, as that described by Wagner in his letter to Röckel.

Everything about Brünnhilde as a character corresponds with the features that Wagner ascribes to music, which, as noted above, is described as feeling impregnated by understanding. Now, Brünnhilde is still the *feeling* woman rather than the *knowing* woman:

doch—wissend bin ich	but I am knowing
nur, weil ich dich liebe!	only because I love you!
. . . .	. . . .
Der Gedanke, . . .	The thought . . .
den ich nicht dachte,	that I did not think
sondern nur fühlte;	but only felt;
. . . der Gedanke—	. . . that thought—
. . . .	. . . .
mir war er nur Liebe zu dir!	was only my love for you!

(*GS* 6.168)

But that is not all. Brünnhilde embodies music's precarious position when confronted by the poet: in consequence, she senses from the very first moments of her union with Siegfried how unstable the androgynous union is bound to be. When Siegfried takes her impetuously in his arms, she repulses him:

Trauriges Dunkel	Grieving darkness
trübt meinen Blick;	clouds my gaze.
mein Auge dämmert,	My eye grows dim,
mein Licht verlischt:	its light dies out:
Nacht wird's um mich;	night enfolds me.
aus Nebel und Grau'n	From mist and dread
windet sich wüthend	a confusion of fear
ein Angstgewirr!	writhes in its rage:
Schrecken schreitet	terror stalks
und bäumt sich empor!	and rears its head!

(*GS* 6.171)

On the most obvious level—in other words, the level addressed by any conscientious director—Brünnhilde reveals the fear of a virgin about to give herself to a man for the first time. But Brünnhilde's role also allows us to understand the ambiguous situation of woman and music within the metaphorical language that Wagner uses, artistically and theoretically, to express the idea of androgyny.

Brünnhilde exhibits a certain strength. There is a masculine element in every woman, as she herself tells Siegfried and as Wagner himself recognizes: "in her perfect womanhood, in her love for the man, and in immersing herself in his being, the woman also develops the male element of her womanhood" (1849m, *GS* 3.135). Brünnhilde has inherited Wotan's masculinity on several counts. At the end of *Das Rheingold* Wotan envisaged the figure of Siegfried and, had he not been in thrall to his own laws, as defended by Fricka, he would have gone to Siegmund's defense. In seeking to save Siegmund and in taking charge of Sieglinde, who later gives birth to Siegfried, Brünnhilde is entirely conscious of the fact that she is carrying out her father's wishes:

Zu Wotan's Willen sprichst du,	To Wotan's will you speak
sag'st du mir, was du willst:	when you tell me what you will;
wer—bin ist,	who am I,
wär' ich dein Wille nicht?	were I not your will?

To which Wotan replies:

Was Keinem in Worten ich künde,	What I tell no one in words,
unausgesprochen	shall remain forever
bleib' es denn ewig:	unspoken;
mit mir nur rath' ich,	with myself I commune
red' ich zu dir.	when I speak with you.

(*GS* 6.37)

Siegfried and Brünnhilde are an externalization of Wotan's own nature, which is itself androgynous. Brünnhilde's function in the *Ring* is, therefore, entirely in keeping with the tendency of music to develop in isolation and, like Schwanhilde, to soar aloft supported by its own wings alone. This male component of music is one that Wagner underscores musically in the character of Brünnhilde, when she exclaims:

Wie mein Blick dich verzehrt,	As my gaze consumes you,
erblindest du nicht?	are you not blinded?
Wie mein Arm dich preßt,	As my arm holds you tight,
entbrenn'st du mir nicht?	do you not burn for me?
	(*GS* 6.174)

At this very moment we hear Fafner's motif in the lower strings, establishing a link between the present danger and the risk that is posed by the domination of music—music that, in Wagner's view, was leading modern opera to its ruin. The error nowadays, he argued, was to "*create real drama on the basis of absolute music*" (1851a, *GS* 3.233). It is this that encouraged Metastasio to play a subservient role (ibid., 3.232) and allowed Meyerbeer to indulge in corrupt frivolity (ibid., 3.228–29). In his dealings with Scribe, "the musician ruined the poet utterly" (ibid., 3.301). In the art-work of the future, by contrast, it was the converse that had to be achieved, as Mozart sensed on an intuitive level: "Take his *Don Giovanni*. Where has music ever achieved so infinitely rich an individuality, where has it been able to provide a surer and more definite characterization in the richest and most transcendent abundance, except here, where the musician, in keeping with the nature of his art, was never anything other than an unconditionally loving woman?" (ibid., 3.320).

In the course of the foregoing pages I emphasized woman's double function as lover and mother. At this stage of Wagner's thinking, there is no doubt that the latter must yield to the former. It is the male poet who retains the creative initiative. Wagner's androgyny, here, is plainly dominated by the masculine principle:

> Music is the child-bearer, while the poet is the begetter; music had reached the very pinnacle of madness, therefore, when it sought not only to bear but also to *beget*.
>
> *Music is a woman.*
>
> The nature of woman is *love*; but this is a love that *receives* and, at the moment of conception, *surrenders* itself without condition.
>
> Woman achieves her full individuality only at the moment of self-surrender. . . . The look of innocence in a woman's eye is the pellucid mirror in which the man sees only the general capacity for love until such time as he sees his own likeness in it. Once he has recognized himself in it, the woman's

> all-embracing ability becomes a single pressing need to love him with the all-powerful force of her all-consuming desire for total self-surrender. (Ibid., 3.316)

It is precisely this that Siegfried demands of Brünnhilde:

Sei mein! Sei mein! Sei mein!	Be mine! Be mine! Be mine!
. . . .	. . . .
War'st du's von je,	If you were before,
so sei es jetzt!	then be so now!

(*GS* 6.173)

"What kind of a woman should *true music* be? A woman *who really loves*, a woman who places her virtue in her *pride*, her pride, however, in her *sacrifice*, in the sacrifice with which she surrenders not just one part of her being but her *entire being*, which she surrenders to the fullest extent of her ability at the moment of *conception*" (1851a, 3.319).

Total union is possible only in death, therefore, which explains the apparent contradiction in Wagner's "logic": if—as we shall shortly have occasion to see—the majority of his heroines institute the action, it is also they who sacrifice themselves in order to make the ultimate union possible.[36] At the climax of her union with Siegfried, as both of them celebrate the One and All, Brünnhilde calls down negative forces:

Götter-Dämm'rung,	Dusk of the gods,
dunk'le herauf!	let your darkness arise!
Nacht der Vernichtung,	Night of destruction,
neb'le herein!	let your mists roll in!

(*GS* 6.175–76)

And the act ends with a premonition of the final scene of the whole tetralogy:

Leuchtende Liebe,	Light-bringing love
lachender Tod!	and laughing death!

(*GS* 6.176)

When we rediscover Siegfried and Brünnhilde in the prologue to *Götterdämmerung*, the androgynous nature of their relationship is amply confirmed. In giving the ring to Brünnhilde, Siegfried transfers his masculine characteristics to her: "Nun wahre du seine Kraft," he tells her (Now keep safe its power [*GS* 6.184]), before continuing:

Durch deine Tugend allein	Through your virtue alone
soll so ich Thaten noch wirken?	shall I go on performing deeds?
Meine Kämpfe kiesest du,	My battles you will choose,
meine Siege kehren zu dir?	my victories will be yours:

Auf deines Rosses Rücken,	upon your stallion's back,
in deines Schildes Schirm	within the shelter of your shield,
nicht Siegfried acht' ich mich mehr,	I no longer think of myself as Siegfried,
ich bin nur Brünnhilde's Arm!	I am Brünnhilde's arm alone.

(*GS* 6.185)

Brünnhilde replies: "So wär'st du Siegfried und Brünnhild'?" (So you would be Siegfried and Brünnhild'? [ibid.]).

Now that their androgyny is hallowed by sexual union, the two lovers no longer feel the fragility of the balance they have achieved:

Weidet eu'r Aug'	Feast your eyes
an dem weihvollen Paar!	on the blessed pair!
Getrennt—wer will uns scheiden?	Parted—who would divide us?
Geschieden—trennt es sich nie!	Divided—they'll never part!

(*GS* 6.186)

At the same time, however, we hear a motif in the orchestra described by some commentators as the "Wanderlust" motif. And, sure enough, Siegfried will soon be setting out for new adventures. The androgynous union is a fragile union: each of the two partners may be tempted to resume his or her isolated career. The poet in particular may turn aside, not in favor of the woman who loves him and gives herself to him entirely, but to music the courtesan, music the operatic whore, whose only function is to entertain the masses. It is precisely this fate that befalls Siegfried when he forgets Brünnhilde and turns his attentions to Gutrune.

Gutrune and Prostituted Music

It seems as though there was a link in Wagner's mind between Gutrune and light music. This becomes clear when we turn to Act II, scene 2 of *Götterdämmerung*, which is a conversation, chiefly between Siegfried and Gutrune, involving brief rejoinders and witty sallies, and which resembles nothing so much as a scene from a French *opéra comique*. Gutrune wants to know if Siegfried has slept with Brünnhilde, while Siegfried avoids answering her directly by playing on the ambiguities of the situation:

GUTRUNE

So folgt Brünnhild' meinem Bruder?	So Brünnhilde's following my brother?

SIEGFRIED

Leicht ward die Frau ihm gefreit.	The woman was easily wooed.

GUTRUNE

Sengte das Feuer ihn nicht?	Didn't the fire singe him?

SIEGFRIED

Ihn hätt' es auch nicht versehrt;	It wouldn't have harmed him either,
doch ich durchschritt es für ihn,	but I passed through it for him,
da dich ich wollt' erwerben.	because I wanted to win you.
. . . .	. . . .

GUTRUNE

So zwang'st du das kühne Weib?	So you overcame the undaunted woman?

SIEGFRIED

Sie wich—Gunther's Kraft.	She yielded—to Gunther's strength.

GUTRUNE

Und vermählte sie sich dir?	And yet she wedded you?

SIEGFRIED

Ihrem Mann gehorchte Brünnhild'	Brünnhild' obeyed her husband
eine volle bräutliche Nacht.	for the whole of the bridal night.

GUTRUNE

Als ihr Mann doch galtest du?	But you yourself were deemed her husband.

SIEGFRIED

Bei Gutrune weilte Siegfried.	Siegfried tarried behind with Gutrune.

GUTRUNE

Doch zur Seite war ihm Brünnhild'?	But Brünnhild' was at his side.

[etc.]

(*GS* 6.213–15)

Wagner made explicit reference to this style when superintending the 1876 rehearsals in Bayreuth: this scene, he told Heinrich Porges, should be "performed with the greatest possible ease and facility." It was "a very detailed dialogue," he explained, "a kind of lively conversation on the stage to be kept wholly in the style of comic opera" (Porges 1896, 129). A review that Wagner wrote for the Dresden *Abend-Zeitung* in 1841 proves that it was, indeed, the light operas he heard in Paris at this time that served as a model here: "This opera," he writes of Halévy's *Le Guitarrero*, "has once again confirmed my views on the nature and essence of modern French composers: —they have all passed through the school of comic opera, . . . as a result of which their music is, for the most part, witty conversation" (1840f, *SS* 12.79). Or take Auber's *La Muette de Portici*, which he describes in *Opera and Drama* as "the muse of drama rendered mute" (1851a, *GS* 3.265). In fact, Gutrune says very little in *Götterdämmerung*, and Pierre Boulez is entirely right to note that "everything about Gutrune is light in character, not to say frivolous, both brilliant and empty, thus reflecting the character herself (Wagner said, not without irony, of course, that these passages should recall French opera and, in particular, Auber)" (Boulez 1980, 34).[37]

This parallelism between the character of Gutrune and the music of *opéra comique* is confirmed by Wagner's theoretical writings. Whenever he speaks of comic opera, it is always the image of a woman of easy virtue that recurs:

> *French* opera music is rightly regarded as a *coquette*. The coquette is keen to be admired, even to be loved: but the particular pleasure she feels at being admired and loved is one she can enjoy only if she herself is not overcome by admiration or love for the object whom she inspires with these feelings. The profit she seeks is delight in herself, the desire to gratify her own vanity: to be admired and loved constitutes the whole pleasure of her life, a pleasure that would be marred the moment she herself were to feel admiration or love for another person. (1851a, *GS* 3.318).

This could well be a description of Gutrune. She says little, but one thing she does say is:

wie sollt' ich Siegfried binden?	How should I bind Siegfried to me?
Ist er der herrlichste	If he's the world's
Held der Welt,	most glorious hero,
der Erde holdeste Frauen	the loveliest women on earth
friedeten längst ihn schon.	would have wooed him long ago.
	(*GS* 6.189)

She wants Siegfried not, however, out of love but for the prestige that their marriage would bring her.

The link between Gutrune and Auber is confirmed by the music. When she rejoins Siegfried in this comic-opera exchange in Act II, scene 2, she begins as follows:

Example 11

As in the Alberich-Floßhilde duet, the orchestra doubles the vocal line, a feature entirely characteristic of the genre. There is more to it than this, however. The theme itself is one that Wagner had heard before—in *La Muette de Portici*:

Example 12

The two themes are almost identical. In Auber's opera it accompanies the bridal procession in Act I, as Elvire and Alphonse emerge from the chapel (no. 4; Garland edition 1980, 173ff.) and returns in the orchestra when Fenella, the mute girl of the title, is supposed to evoke their union (Act II, no. 8, p. 330). A comparison between the two texts suggests a conscious reminiscence, an intentional quotation from an opera widely known throughout this period. Whereas Gutrune sings the words "Freia grüße dich / zu aller Frauen Ehre" (May Freia greet you in honor of all women [*GS* 6.213]), the chorus in *La Muette de Portici* raises a prayer to "almighty God": "Daigne exaucer notre prière et bénis, bénis, ces heureux époux" (Deign to hear our prayer and bless, bless, this happy couple). Is it mere chance that at the very time he was writing the music of *Götterdämmerung*, Wagner sang one of Auber's tunes to Cosima (*CT*, 19 March 1873) and that, on another occasion, he played excerpts from Auber's works at the piano (*CT*, 8 August 1874)?[38]

What role does Siegfried play here? He is the victim of Alberich's son, Hagen, who is thus at least a half-Jew (having renounced love, Alberich can satisfy his natural instincts only by violating Grimhilde) and who encompasses all the intrigues and machinations in this final part of the cycle. It is a half-Jew, therefore, who lures Siegfried into the arms of French opera. Hagen proffers Siegfried a potion that induces selective amnesia, making him forget Brünnhilde, the loving woman with whom he was to create the art-work of the future.

Of course, a glance at the genealogical table of the *Ring* shows quite clearly that Siegfried is guilty, in particular, of exogamy. Gutrune, in fact, is a member of a clan manipulated by Hagen, who keeps himself apart for racial reasons:

SIEGFRIED

Was nahm'st du am Eide nicht Theil?	Why did you take no part in the oath?

HAGEN

Mein Blut verdürb' euch den Trank!	My blood would mar your drink;

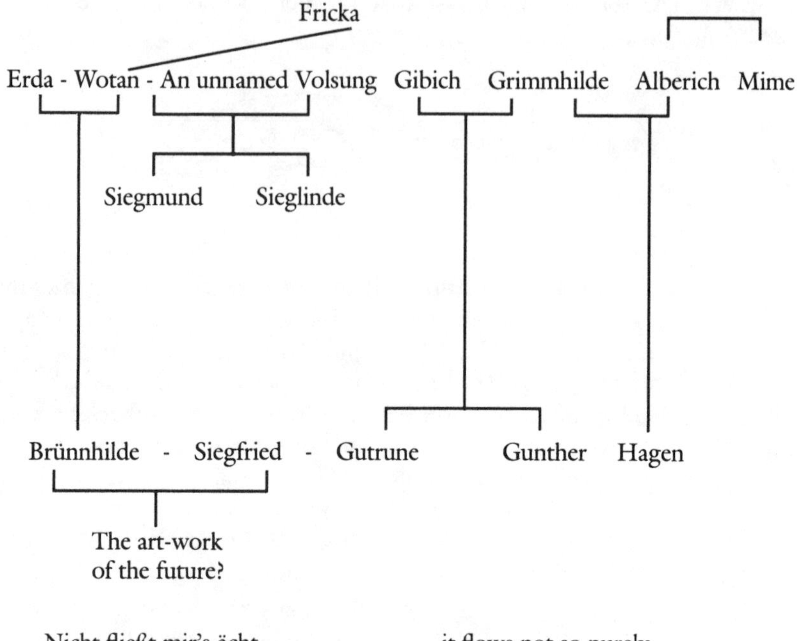

Nicht fließt mir's ächt und edel wie euch.	it flows not so purely and nobly as yours.

(*GS* 6.197)

Once again, Wagner's aesthetic stance is based on a racist attitude. Siegfried dies because he betrays the endogamic imperative, just as he perishes for having succumbed to the blandishments of a frivolous brand of opera. And, like Alberich at the beginning of *Das Rheingold* and like Mime in *Siegfried*, he now becomes an opera singer encouraged to perform his star turn:

Hei! Gunther! Grämlicher Mann! Dank'st du es mir, so sing' ich dir Mären aus meinen jungen Tagen.	Hey, Gunther, woebegone man! If you'll be grateful, I'll *sing*[39] you tales about my younger days.

(*GS* 6.242)

And Hagen sets him off: "So singe, Held" (*Sing*[40] on then, hero [ibid.]). By now Siegfried is completely contaminated. He will be punished for having forgotten the woman with whom the poet could have achieved the perfect union of poetry and music. Moreover, when we know the overriding importance played by the motif of amnesia in the plot, it is not altogether surprising to discover that a lengthy passage in *Opera and Drama* treats this same subject of memory and lapse of memory in the context of the function of motifs, of a musical element that makes sense only in conjunction with the libretto (1851a, *GS* 4.181–85). Essentially, Wagner tells us that thought is possible only in relation to memory: "This nonpresent entity is a real, physically apprehended object, which made a specific impression on us in another place or at another time: this impression lay hold of our power of perception so that, in order to communicate it to others, we were forced to invent an expression that, in keeping with the impression of the object, reflected the power of perception of the human race in general" (ibid., 4.182). It is through music that we can elicit a response by means of association: "Thought, too, is aroused by emotion, . . . for *it is the bond between an emotion that is not present and one that is currently struggling to express itself*" (ibid., *GS* 4.183). Again: "Even where the performer no longer seems conscious of that emotion, its characteristic sounding in the orchestra is able to stir an emotion within us that becomes a *thought* capable of completing an association of ideas or of making a situation perfectly intelligible by interpreting motifs that, albeit contained within that situation, cannot find clear expression within those moments that are presentable on stage" (ibid., 4.184). Now, "music cannot think," since this is something only the poet's verse can do, "but it can give material form to thoughts, in other words, it can reveal their emotional content as something no longer remembered but actualized" (ibid.). Unless there is a link with music, memory—and hence thought—cannot function. And it is the orchestra that has the ability "to waken presentiments and memories" (ibid., 4.191). Without music, Siegfried sinks into oblivion.

Brünnhilde, the pure, loving woman, is contaminated by Hagen: her lapse, though momentary, is fatal. She is contaminated, however, not only on the level of the plot, as might have been expected, but also on a musical plane: in contrast with the rest of the work, the trio that ends the second act resembles a section from a number opera in terms of both style and form.

Nonetheless, it is through Brünnhilde that the final act of redemption comes about. She is the anti-Alberich of the work, since at the most dramatic moment in the destiny of the gods, it is love that she still holds out as an alternative to Waltraute's entreaties:

Von meinem Ringe	Of my ring
raune ihnen zu:	tell them only this:
die Liebe ließe ich nie,	I shall never relinquish love,
mir nähmen nie sie die Liebe—	they'll never take love from me,
stürzt' auch in Trümmern	though Valhalla's glittering pomp
Walhall's strahlende Pracht!	were to molder into dust!

(*GS* 6.205)

It is the motif of renunciation of love that we hear in the orchestra at this point, just as it is through her love of Siegfried that Brünnhilde will immolate herself at the end and return the ring to the Rhine daughters, allowing the three sisters to rediscover their lost sense of unity.

For the other characters in the cycle, too, the return to a primal state of unity is brought about through death. The great lesson to be learned from the *Ring*, through the metaphor of androgyny, is, of course, the precarious nature of the union of male and female. Yet the tetralogy also confirms that only in oblivion can any real union ever take place. Unity is achieved by destroying what is different. Even if Alberich remains at large, his son Hagen obeys the injunction of "Judaism in Music": "But bear in mind that one thing alone can redeem you from the curse that weighs upon you, *the redemption of Ahasuerus—destruction!*" (1850c, *GS* 5.85). The return to the state of primal unity has an apocalyptic smell to it: "Join unreservedly in an act of redemption that involves rebirth through self-destruction, and we shall be united and indistinguishable!" (ibid.).

Wagner was being perfectly consistent when he realized that even the art-work of the future could not escape the coming cataclysm: "When everything has been properly organized, I shall then arrange for three performances of Siegfried[41] to be given in the space of a week: after the third the theater will be torn down and the score burned," he told Theodor Uhlig in a letter of 20 September 1850.[42]

In fact, Wagner was more than keen to trace his name in the sands of history. One thing alone was needed and that was for the work of art of the future to succeed in merging poetry and music, male and female, and for Wagner's labors as an artist to bear aesthetic fruit—an artist for whom the male poetic intent had to be capable of impregnating its other female—musical—half in order to bring forth an androgynous *Ring*.

Chapter Four

ART AS A METAPHOR OF ITSELF

THE READER may be tempted to ask whether it was legitimate to superimpose a reading of Wagner's theoretical writings on the *Ring* while at the same time exploiting the linking role that *Wieland the Smith* appears to play between aesthetic reflection and artistic creation. I am all the more convinced of the rightness of this approach in that the case we have been studying—the *Ring* as the artistic metaphor of a theoretical construct elaborated in tandem with it—is far from being unique in Wagner's overall oeuvre.

There is a remarkable note in *Opera and Drama* discussing the relationship between understanding and feeling, a relationship that, as we have seen, has a crucial role to play both in the theory relating to the art-work of the future and in Wagner's androgynous metaphor. Wagner begins as follows:

> Understanding is forced by necessity, therefore, to wed an element that can assimilate the poetic intent as a fertilizing seed, nurturing that seed through its own necessary essence and fashioning it in such a way that it can bring it forth as the realizational, redemptive expression of feeling.
>
> This element is the same feminine maternal element whose womb—the expressive potential of primal melody—is fructified by the natural, real object that lies outside it, thereby producing the word and the language of words in the same way in which understanding developed out of feeling and thus condensed this female element into a male element capable of communication. Just as understanding must, in turn, fructify feeling—just as, in being impregnated, it is impelled to find itself encompassed by feeling, to be justified by, and reflected in, that feeling and to recognize itself in that reflection, in other words, to find itself generally recognizable—so the intellectual word is impelled to recognize itself in sound, while the language of words finds itself vindicated in the language of music. (1851a, *GS* 4.102)

Fearing—not without good reason—that he may not have been properly understood, Wagner adds a footnote here: "Would it be thought trivial of me if I were to remind the reader—with reference to my account of the relevant myth—of Oedipus, who was born of Jocasta and who fathered the redeeming figure of Antigone on her?" (ibid.).

It is by means of a *myth* that Wagner illustrates a theoretical point, adding, as it were, an equals sign between two patterns of thought, which may be schematized as shown below. The explicative and illustrative function of the Oedipus myth is remarkable in that the idea of androgynous union is assimilated with that of incest with the mother as wife.[1] This is a point to which we shall return.

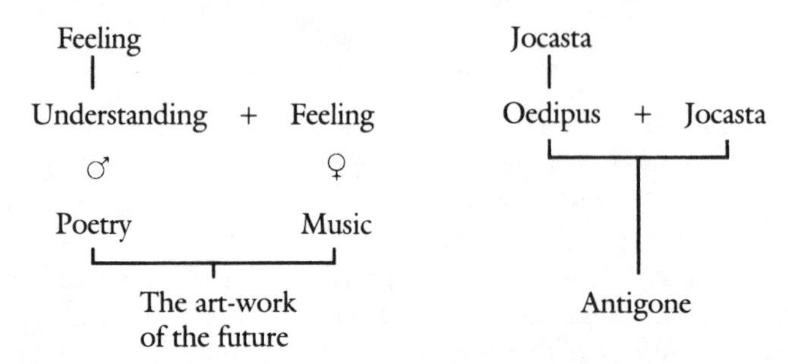

An early link between a theoretical idea, as expounded in Wagner's writings, and the contents of an opera is already discernible in "The Virtuoso and the Artist," one of the novellas that Wagner wrote at the time of his first stay in Paris. In contrast to *The Art-Work of the Future*, Wagner begins by recounting the ancient legend of a jewel that bestows on all who behold it "every spiritual gift and the happiness of a contented mind" (1840e, *GS* 1.167). But the jewel "lies buried deep beneath the earth" (ibid.). Miners attempt to locate it, but in vain. A miner from Salzburg succeeds in finding it but disappears forever. Another, from Bonn, sets out on a similar quest but, finding himself in the presence of the jewel, is blinded by the sight of it: "Seized by a divine frenzy, he plunged into the giddy depths, and the whole mine collapsed on top of him with a mighty crash" (ibid., 1.168). At the end of the tale, Wagner writes explicitly that the legend could be "understood in an *allegorical*[2] sense. Its meaning would easily be grasped if the magic jewel were held to represent the genius of music" (ibid., 1.169). And he goes on to offer the key to a metaphorical interpretation:

> The names of the two miners would not be hard to guess. As for the mass of rubbish and rubble that covers them, it lies all around, cluttering the path whenever we attempt to get through to them. Whoever in his dreams has glimpsed that legendary light, whoever in hours of holy rapture has been fired by the genius of music and then looked round for a means of preserving his vision, stumbles at once over that mass of rubble. He has to get out his shovel and dig; the site is full of gold-diggers churning up the earth and flinging their dross and slag in the way as he attempts to burrow down the old mine. The mass of rubbish grows higher and higher and thicker and thicker; the sweat pours from his brow. Poor fellow! And the people around laugh at him. (Ibid., 1.169)

This analogy—which is drawn by Wagner himself—would in itself be sufficient to reinforce our hypothesis. But there is more to it than this. This short story was published in October 1840. A little over a year later, in February–March 1842, Wagner prepared two prose drafts for a three-act opera based on E.T.A. Hoffmann's novella, *Die Bergwerke zu Falun* (The mines of Falun) (*WWV*, 67).[3] Although it differs in terms of its subject matter from the legend retold in the 1840 novella, the underlying idea remains the same. The tale revolves around a young sailor, Elis, who falls in love with Ulla, the daughter of the local mineowner. Following the advice of old Torbern, he becomes a miner. Torbern tells him of the existence of a marvelous precious stone in the deepest part of the mine, a stone that cannot be reached without first having beheld the face of the Mountain Queen. On the day he is due to marry Ulla, Elis announces that he is first going to look for the stone before sharing his love with her, but Ulla tries to prevent him from descending into the mine. Elis ignores her protestations, plunges into the mine, and makes his way to a dangerous gallery, where he hopes to find the Queen herself, but is buried beneath a rockfall.

Little would be gained by insisting on the profoundly Wagnerian character of this sketch, with its hero torn between an earthbound woman and one who embodies the absolute. It will be noted, however, that the Mountain Queen plays exactly the same role as the buried jewel in the 1840 novella, so much so, indeed, that it would be no exaggeration to read into this operatic project a symbolic quest for the absolute art of music. In both cases, a woman is presented as an obstacle to the artist's search for an artistic absolute. There are also striking analogies between Elis and Tannhäuser, who is caught between Elisabeth and Venus, but the light cast by the 1840 narrative reveals closer parallels between Ulla and Elsa than between Ulla and Elisabeth. Whereas in *Tannhäuser* the moral victory is on the side of Elisabeth and the Christian faith, in *The Mines of Falun* and *Lohengrin* it is on the side of the poet in search of the absolute.

Lohengrin can, in fact, be seen in a similar comparative perspective. In *A Communication to My Friends* Wagner writes, "Anyone who, in Lohengrin, understands nothing more than the category 'Christian Romantic' understands only a random, superficial feature, not its underlying essence. This essence, the essence of a truly new, unknown phenomenon, will be understood only by that faculty which feeds our categorizing understanding, and that faculty is the faculty of pure, physical feeling" (1851h, *GS* 4.298). Thus the character of Lohengrin, understanding incarnate, expects to be loved by Elsa, who is the embodiment of feeling. A few lines later, Wagner indicates clearly that, like Wieland and Elis, Lohengrin embodies the poet: "Here I touch on the principal feature of the true artist's tragic relationship with life in the present day, *that same situation to which I gave artistic form in the subject matter of Lohengrin*:[4] it is this artist's most necessary and most natural longing to be accepted and understood, unreservedly, by feeling" (ibid., 4.298–99). In exactly the same way, Lohengrin demands that Elsa accept him without asking where he comes from. "And the *impossibility*—under the conditions of modern art—of encountering this feeling in the uninhibitedness and undoubting certainty that he needs in order to be understood,—the *compulsion* of having to address himself almost solely to the critical understanding rather than to feeling—it is this that, first and foremost, constitutes the tragedy of his situation" (ibid., 4.299). In other words, it is through the theoretical discourse of understanding that the poet, whom no one understands, attempts to make his intentions known, when feeling, embodied in the figure of Elsa, fails to place any trust in him.

And it is the figure of androgyny that stands out here in the form of a double:

> In Elsa I saw from the outset my desired antithesis to Lohengrin—not, of course, so absolute an opposite as to be far removed from his own nature but, rather, the *other half* of his own being—the antithesis that was contained within his own nature and that is only the complement of his specific masculine essence, a complement which he necessarily longs to embrace. *Elsa* is that unconscious, involuntary element in which Lohengrin's conscious, voluntary nature longs to be redeemed. (Ibid., 4.301)

Lohengrin is a clear illustration of one of Wagner's theoretical preoccupations, the relationship between understanding and feeling, coupled here with the situation of the artist in relation to his audience.[5]

With his project for *Die Sieger* (The victors) Wagner went even further. In his autobiography he states explicitly that he chose this subject because he saw in it a metaphorical analogy with his leitmotivic technique:

> Burnouff's *Introduction à l'histoire du Bouddhisme* was the book that stimulated me most; I even distilled from it the material for a dramatic poem, which has remained with me ever since, if only in a very rough outline, and might one day even be brought to fruition. I gave it the title *Die Sieger*; it was based on a simple legend of a Jandala maiden who is received into the elevated order of mendicants known as the Cakyamounis as a result of her painfully intense and purified love for Ananda, the chief disciple of the Buddha. Apart from the beauty and profound significance of the simple tale, I was influenced to choose it as much by its peculiar aptness for *the musical procedures that I have since developed*.[6] To the mind of the Buddha, the previous lives in former incarnations of every being appearing before him stand revealed as clearly as the present. The simple story owed its significance to

the way that the past life of the suffering principal characters was entwined in the new phase of their lives as being still present time. I perceived at once how the musical remembrance of this dual life, keeping the past constantly present in the hearing, might be represented perfectly to the emotional receptivities, and this prompted me to keep the prospect of working out this task before me as a labor of especial love. (*ML*, 528–29)

There is no longer any distinction in Wagner's mind between the mythic narrative and the artistic procedures used to narrate that myth.

Moreover, there are at least two of Wagner's works in which, this time explicitly, aesthetic problems are presented on stage: in *Tannhäuser und der Sängerkrieg auf Wartburg* (Tannhäuser and the Wartburg tournament of song) the characters enter into a vocal debate on the respective merits of Platonic and sensual singing, while *Die Meistersinger von Nürnberg* revolves around the confrontation of two conceptions of poetry, with Hans Sachs finally speaking out in favor of German art. Much earlier, Wagner had already seen Beethoven as "the master who was called upon to write the *world history of music* in his works" (1849m, *GS* 3.93). Add to this the fact that Beethoven was the hero of whom he saw himself the spiritual, German heir, and it is difficult not to believe that in establishing links between the content of his theoretical writings and that of the *Ring*, Wagner himself was not aware that the latter work contained a history of music, as I have tried to show.

Wagner's thinking was fundamentally metaphorical and there is no doubt that Adorno was not entirely wrong when he wrote that, in Wagner's works, "anything can signify anything." At all events, reasoning by analogy is omnipresent. If, for example, Wagner wants to evoke the solitude of music, caught between dance and poetry, he treats the musician as a swimmer breasting the waves between two different continents. Indeed, this entire chapter in *The Art-Work of the Future* is shot through with this maritime metaphor (1849m, *GS* 3.81–101 and 120–21), a metaphor taken up shortly afterward into *Opera and Drama* (1851a, *GS* 4.146–47), where the theme of love and desire is extended to other aspects of the drama of the future: modulation, for example, is explained in terms of sexual love on the part of the individual "who transcended the barriers of the patriarchal family and forged a link with other families" (ibid., 4.148; see also 4.151–52), while love's necessary law is invoked to explain the function of alliteration (ibid., 4.152).

Wagner was fully conscious of the essentially metaphorical character of his thinking—"I believe I can best make myself clear in metaphorical form" (1860c, *GS* 7.128)—but he disliked overusing the device. Otherwise, he argued, there was nothing that could not be maintained in this way: "No object can ever be entirely like the thing to which it is compared, rather can the similarity be maintained in only one direction, not in all" (1851a, *GS* 4.171). Is this really so certain? Of course, Wagner himself knows why he has recourse to a given image, but are we ourselves certain that we are *interpreting* it in the way he intended? What is the real meaning behind his recourse to male and female imagery when he speaks of the impregnation of music by the poetic intent? Is the male-female distinction in itself so self-evident that it gives us an immediate key to the relationship that it is meant to illustrate?

In fact, Wagnerian androgyny is the scene of some unexpected semantic relationships. Does the composer's recourse to androgyny not become, on a second level, a kind of symbol of the symbolic decoding? It is Cosima herself who suggests such a reading: "I tell him that R.'s article[7] theoretically bears almost the same relationship to the poem as his words on music (the *loving* woman) and on drama (the man) in *Opera and Drama* bear to Brünnhilde and Siegfried" (*CT*, 2 August 1878). In saying this, Cosima confirms not only that in the *Ring* Brünnhilde and Siegfried embody music and poetry but also that the relationship between female and male is analogous to that which exists between a work of art and its theory. She also invites us to regard the link that is forged between the symbol and the object symbolized as an androgynous relationship.

This raises two further questions. Is there a theory capable of explaining the presence of the metaphor of androgyny in Wagner's works and, if so, what is the relationship between this explanation and its object? It is to an elucidation of this problem that the remainder of this study is devoted.

PART TWO

Music and Poetry: The Metamorphoses of Wagnerian Androgyny

La querelle des intrigues

The first part of the present study was an attempt to propose a first level of interpretation of the figure of androgyny in two different orders of discourse. A parallel was drawn between these two different orders on the assumption that the complex symbolic configuration that resulted did not vary in the course of Wagner's life.

This analysis must be extended a stage further, however, since the link between androgyny and Wagner's conception of the relationship between poetry and music turns out to be far more complex when one realizes that the image of androgyny appears only sporadically in Wagner's theoretical discourse and that the relationship between poetry and music is unstable in its conception.

Only a handful of remarks on the subject are to be found in the articles and letters written before 1848. In the post–*Opera and Drama* period, the idea returns in *A Communication to My Friends* (1851h) and *"Zukunftsmusik"* (1860c), to mention only the most important. To anyone familiar with only these essays, the *Beethoven* study of 1870 (1870d) must come as a surprise, inasmuch as the monograph acknowledges the supremacy of music and seems to mark a decisive turning point in Wagner's thinking. However, three articles written in 1879 appear to bring us back to the perspective of the Zurich essays of the period from 1849 to 1851.

The first question that springs to mind is whether we can explain these variations. How can we interpret and explain this evolution? What meaning can we ascribe to each of these stages? Even the best writers on the subject fail to agree, but it seems as though their "plots" (using the term in the sense spelled out in the Introduction to Part One) can be grouped together in three major families. (The present remarks are based largely on Glass 1981, 9–16.)

1. There are those writers who interpret the majority of the contradictions that characterize Wagner's oeuvre as symptomatic of a drastic change of conception in the evolution of his ideas. The most famous of these writers is undoubtedly Nietzsche, who wrote in *On the Genealogy of Morals*:

> Let us here consider straightaway the remarkable and for many kinds of men even fascinating attitude Schopenhauer adopted toward *art*: for it was obviously for the sake of this that Richard Wagner *initially* went over to

> Schopenhauer . . . , and did so to such an extent that there exists a complete theoretical contradiction between his earlier and his later aesthetic creed—the former set down, for example, in *Opera and Drama*, the latter in the writings he published from 1870 onward. Specifically, he ruthlessly altered—and this is perhaps most astonishing—his judgment as to the value and status of *music*: what did he care that he had formerly made of music a means, a medium, a "woman" who required a goal, a man, in order to prosper—namely, drama! He grasped all at once that with the Schopenhauerian theory and innovation *more* could be done *in majorem musicae gloriam*—namely, with the theory of the *sovereignty* of music as Schopenhauer conceived it: music set apart from all the other arts, the independent art as such. (1887, 539)

It is this same thesis—copiously illustrated—that Jack M. Stein advances in an influential study, *Richard Wagner and the Synthesis of the Arts*, first published in 1960. A similar point of view is expressed in the writings of the leading German musicologist, Carl Dahlhaus (see, for example, Dahlhaus 1971, 1–6; Dahlhaus and Deathridge 1984, 115–17).

2. Alongside this view, there is the standpoint of those writers who recognize the existence of changes in Wagner's outlook but who interpret them as passing contradictions that do not impair the unity of his thinking. In order to maintain this position, they have to admit that Wagner himself was mistaken in giving priority to the poem when everything indicates that he was, first and foremost, a musician. This is the point of view adopted by Alfred Einstein in his major study on *Music in the Romantic Era*: "Nothing was really changed in this situation by Wagner's demand that in opera the drama must have supremacy over the music, and that music should be the feminine, drama the masculine principle. The effect of his own work gives the lie to his theory, for this effect rests almost entirely on the music. The only difference is that, in the Wagnerian music drama, it was no longer the singer who bore the brunt of the expression, but the symphonically enlivened orchestra" (1887, 25).

Édouard Sans, an expert on the relations between Wagner and Schopenhauer, says of the Zurich essays:

> It is in vain that Wagner writes page after page, piling up the arguments in an attempt to demonstrate that it is wrong to accord supremacy to any one particular art, since every single line reveals the extent to which he is unconsciously convinced of the superiority of music. Here, too, in spite of a certain number of sensational theoretical remarks, his mind was fully prepared to receive confirmation of his own deepest convictions from the philosopher [Schopenhauer]. Schopenhauer would find himself preaching to the converted. (1887, 263)

From this perspective, the true Wagner is the Wagner of the *Beethoven* essay of 1870. The rest of his writings are merely waffle and, as such, irrelevant to his fundamental belief, as a composer, in the supremacy of music.

3. The third group of writers also adopts a unitarian standpoint but reverses the perspective: the true theory of the Wagnerian drama is to be found in *Opera and Drama*. Such writers either have to ignore the *Beethoven* essay of 1870—as is the case, curiously enough, with Henri Lichtenberger (1898)—or they bend over backward to show that this essay does not represent a fundamental modification of the outlook of the Zurich tracts. To this group belong Shaw (1898, 106–7), Lorenz (1924), Magee (1968, 9–28), Bailey (1969, 10), Cooke (1979, 73), and, especially, Frank Glass, whose book *The Fertilizing Seed: Wagner's Concept of the Poetic Intent* (1981) is one of the most detailed relatively recent studies of Wagner's theoretical concepts. Glass bases his interpretation on the fundamental observation that Wagner's musical drama results less from the union of poetry and music than from the fertilization of music by the poetic intent—Wagner's "dichterische Absicht."

We ourselves have approached the problem of the relationship between poetry and music in Wagner's thinking not from an evolutionary point of view but from the starting point of a different "plot," so that it has not yet been possible to propose a definitive pronouncement on that relationship. Nonetheless, it has been possible—I believe—to uncover an intimate link between Wagner's theories and the content of his operas. It is this particular avenue that I intend to explore in the course of the following pages. In order to provide a more detailed definition of the significance of androgynous symbolism in his oeuvre, we need to reexamine the writings in which it figures and relocate them in terms not only of his artistic activities at the time but also of the philosophical and intellectual context that produced them. The result of this approach will be to reveal a complex network of multiple, shifting meanings bound together in a configuration that confers its specificity on it.

A difficult epistemological problem arises: do we have the means to choose between the three plots summarized above? Does my own view of the situation supersede the three preceding views? In a word, is it possible to adduce a stable truth that, once and for all, will provide a key to the relationship between poetry and music in Wagner's works?

Chapter Five

WAGNERIAN ANDROGYNY AND ITS ROMANTIC COUNTERPART

The Relationship between Poetry and Music in Wagner's Works from 1834 to 1848

I spent some time in Part One identifying the existence of the metaphor of androgyny in Wagner's writings of the years 1848–51 and in the *Ring*. More specifically, I tried to show how love—the cornerstone of Greek homogenized society in *The Art-Work of the Future*—persists in the androgynous union of poetry and music in *Opera and Drama*. It is impossible to proceed to an interpretation of this metaphor without first seeing how it relates to Wagner's other theoretical ideas. Certainly, its very evolution between *The Art-Work of the Future* and *Opera and Drama* invites us to pay due heed to the genetic nature of its emergence. Although the writings of 1848 to 1851 occupy a central position in Wagner's thinking in terms of their chronology and quantity, it is nonetheless imperative that we extend our field of investigation in both directions and examine the writings of the earlier and later periods. How did Wagner conceive of the relationship between poetry and music in the years before 1848? And what became of the metaphor of androgyny afterward?

At the time that Wagner wrote his earliest completed operas, *Die Feen* (*WWV*, 32) and *Das Liebesverbot* (*WWV*, 38)—that is, during the mid-1830s—he was already in the habit of writing articles and essays in tandem with his activities as a creative artist.[1] With his first known text, "Die deutsche Oper" (German opera), we already find him seeking a specifically German type of opera divorced from the French and Italian influences that manifest themselves musically in *Die Feen* and *Das Liebesverbot*, both of which resemble a kind of stylistic patchwork on which Mozart, Boieldieu, Bellini, Weber, and others have all left their mark. Nonetheless, Wagner attributes the weakness of German opera to the inability of his fellow German composers to heed the voice of the people and capture "true, warm life" (1834a, *SS* 12.4). We do not need to linger over the second text, "Pasticcio," the authenticity of which has recently been called into question (Konrad 1987, 218–23). It is, of course, a shame to exclude such a sentence as the following: "a composer will no doubt come one day who will restore this lost unity of poetry and singing on stage" (1834b, *SS* 12.9). But Stein (1960, 13–14) had already expressed surprise at finding so precocious an expression of unity within the context of Wagner's early writings. The misattribution explains the note of discordancy. This text reminds us in any event that the idea was in the air at the time. Certainly, the search for a similar balance recurs in a brief article, "Der dramatische Gesang" (Dramatic singing; 1837a), in which Wagner places Mozart's musical genius on the same footing as Weber's dramatic genius. In one of three other texts devoted to Bellini and written that same year (1837), Wagner compares the quality and force of singing in *Norma* to the effectiveness of Gluck and Spontini: "Singing is the language in which man should express himself musically" (1837d, *SS* 12.20). "Here, where the poetry rises to the tragic heights of the ancient Greeks, this form—which Bellini decisively ennobles—elevates the solemn and grandiose character of the whole" (ibid., 12.21).

With his 1840 novella "Eine Pilgerfahrt zu Beethoven" (A pilgrimage to Beethoven), Wagner inaugurates a long series of texts that, throughout the rest of his life, he was to devote to the composer of the Ninth Symphony. It is an invaluable collection of texts, not least because it allows us to capture Wagner's changing attitude toward the relationship between poetry and music and to do so, moreover, on the basis not only of a single composer but, more often than not, of a single movement, the setting of Schiller's ode *To Joy*.

In the case of the 1840 novella, Wagner puts words into the mouth of a fictional Beethoven, explicitly stating ideas that we might have conjectured when reading his earlier, shorter articles:

> Instruments represent the primal organs of Creation and Nature; their expression can never be clearly defined and formulated since they convey the primal feelings as they first issued forth from the chaos of the Creation, perhaps even before there was any human heart to hear and feel.[2] The genius of the voice is completely different: this represents the human heart, the separate individual sensibility, limited, but clear and definite. Imagine, now, these two elements brought together and united! Imagine the instruments that convey the primal feelings—those raw wild feelings encompassing the infinite—united with the voice that represents the limited, but clear, definite sensibility of the human heart. That second element, the voice, would have a beneficial effect upon the instruments' expression of the struggle of primal feeling in that it would set it within the framework of a definite, unifying course; on the other hand, the human heart itself, represented by the voice, would be infinitely strengthened and expanded by gathering to itself those primal feelings: for now its former vague awareness of the Highest would be transformed into a God-like consciousness. (1840f, *GS* 1.110–11)

Here Wagner insists on more than just the necessary complementarity of musical instrument and human voice: the latter is vindicated by the denotative nature of language and by the more connotative character of music. If Wagner uses Beethoven as his mouthpiece in advancing a semiological conception of these two symbolic forms (a conception that will remain unchanged in the writings of 1848–51), he does not yet state that music is impregnated by the poet. Quite the opposite: "Voices must have words, and where is poetry to be found worthy of such a union? The poem would be overshadowed: words are too feeble an instrument for such a task" (ibid., 1.111). Announcing the appearance of his Ninth Symphony, Beethoven goes on to specify the relationship: "You will soon be hearing a new composition of mine, a symphony with choruses, which will bring home what I've just been saying. Words had to be found, and the task of finding them was a great problem. In the end I decided to use our Schiller's beautiful ode *To Joy*—a very noble uplifting poem, of course, yet a very long way from expressing what in this case no poem in the world could possibly utter" (ibid., 1.111). Music would add a degree of precision to the words through the expression of feeling.

Two months later Wagner returned to this idea of complementarity in discussing the overture as a genre:

> After *Gluck*, it was *Mozart* who gave the overture its true significance. Without attempting in meticulous detail to express what music neither can nor should express—in other words, those individual details and complications of the plot that the prologue had earlier been at pains to set forth—he took in the drama's leading thought with the eye of the true poet, stripped it of all that was random, all that was incidental to the actual event and reproduced it as a musically transfigured structure, as passion personified in sound, presenting it to that leading thought as its musical counterpart, a counterpart in which the idea, and hence the dramatic action itself, found an explanation intelligible to feeling. Alternatively, what emerged was an entirely independent piece of music, irrespective of whether or not it was superficially connected with the opening scene of the opera. (1841a, *GS* 1.196)

Wagner thus defines the status of instrumental music, insisting that it is capable of grasping the *idea* of the drama that is to follow. The idea is sparked off by the drama with an inevitability that recalls the relationship between poem and music in the theoretical writings of 1848–51. Nonetheless, it is still music that is the dominant force: "The composer will do well to weave into the characteristic motifs of his overture certain melismatic or rhythmic features that will later be of importance in the dramatic action itself; . . . of course, these features must in themselves be of a purely musical nature, hence ones that, setting out from the world of sound, extend allusively into human life" (ibid., 1.204). Within weeks of these lines appearing in print, Wagner published his novella "Ein Ende in

Paris" (An end in Paris), with its celebrated closing formula: "I believe in God, Mozart, and Beethoven, likewise in their disciples and apostles; I believe in the Holy Ghost and in the truth of the one and indivisible art" (1841b, *GS* 1.135). Yet this unity continued to be dominated by music even when the composer's task was to translate the dramatic intention.

This is confirmed by the last of the three novellas of the Paris years. Written shortly after the other two, in May 1841, it first appeared under the title "Une soirée heureuse: fantaisie sur la musique pittoresque." In it Wagner endorses the following words, placed in the mouth of a friend of the novella's first-person narrator: "It is an eternal truth that music begins where speech ends. Nothing is so intolerable as those tasteless pictures and stories with which some people try to buttress instrumental works. What poverty of intellect and sensibility is revealed by people who can only manage to maintain their interest in a Beethoven symphony by imagining that the stream of music represents the plot of some novel or other" (1841h, *GS* 1.140–41). Music has its own semiological system and, above all, its own autonomy. We are still some way short of the later idea of music subject to poetry: "The impulses and inspirations behind an instrumental composition must be of a kind that could only originate in the soul of a musician!" (ibid., 1.144). "Thus in the moment of creative inspiration the determining factor is no longer the external event, but the musical feeling that it engendered" (ibid., 1.147), as a result of which Wagner refuses to take seriously the Napoleonic program said to have inspired the *Eroica*:

> Can you point to a single passage that could be taken to describe an event in the young general's career? . . . The feeling may have been occasioned by some external event or it may have sprung from some mysterious inner source. Though it may manifest itself as melancholy, joy, longing, contentment, love, or hate, nevertheless in the mind of the musician the feeling always takes a musical form and expresses itself in tones before it has been cast into notes. (Ibid., 1.146–47)

"What music expresses is eternal, infinite, and ideal. It speaks not of the passion, love, and longing of this or that individual in this or that situation, but of passion, love, and longing in themselves" (ibid., 1.148). Hanslick would later express himself in all but identical terms.

The numerous reports on Paris's musical life that Wagner filed in the course of his years in the city (17 September 1839 to 7 April 1842) insist, above all, on the frivolous nature of French operatic music and underline the mercantile aspect of composers' lives. Indeed, he was almost happy for Auber not to have been familiar with Beethoven's symphonies (1841g, *SS* 12.88). Wagner had already opted in favor of serious music: in spite of certain reservations, which speak volumes for his critical acumen, he drew a resolute, symbolic contrast between Berlioz's *Symphonie fantastique* and Adam's *Le Postillon de Longjumeau*. It was above all Halévy's *La Reine de Chypre* that left its mark on the indigent composer during these years in Paris: no fewer than five of the texts he wrote at this time are devoted, wholly or in part, to the work (1841p, 1841q, 1841s, 1842a, and 1842b). Against the background of a possible *national* opera, Wagner returns to the idea of a text that adequately fires the composer's imagination: "Is it then so infinitely hard to write a decent opera libretto? . . . Try to write a sound *drama*, scene by scene, a drama, moreover, that is full of feeling. In this way you will also make it possible for the musician to write dramatic music, which you now obstinately refuse to let him do" (1841s, *GS* 1.244–46). The libretto must be written with the music in mind so that the composer is not tempted to correct the words in trying to meet the demands of the music (ibid., 1.246–47). However, this is possible only on the basis of a close relationship between librettist and musician: "What is needed for a good opera is not only a good poet and a good composer but also a particularly felicitous sense of harmony between their two abilities. The best opera can come into being only when both are equally enthusiastic about the same idea, but the *very best* opera of all emerges *only when this idea strikes both men simultaneously*"[3] (1842b, *SS* 12.131). Wagner goes on:

> To the *poet* belongs the ability to give clear and definite form to what reveals itself to his imagination; but it is to the *musician* alone that the task belongs of imbuing this idea with the entire charm of the *inexpressible* and of merging reality with the presentiment of the highest ideal. What both men then produce in hours of calm, artistic contemplation may justly be called a perfect opera. Unfortunately this mode of production belongs in an ideal world; or at least we must assume that its results never come to public attention, since the art industry certainly has nothing to do with it. (Ibid., 12.131–32)

Here are the earliest glimmerings of Wagner's ideal, with its insistence on a high-quality libretto, capable of meeting the demands of the music and enhanced by the composer who underscores its emotional content. Wagner does not yet suggest that poet and composer should be one and the same person, although he has already adopted this option himself. The article from which I have been quoting dates from December 1841: *Der fliegende Holländer* had been completed the previous month.

Halévy's *La Reine de Chypre* is not the realization of Wagner's ideal unity, although it came close to that ideal at this point in his development. He praises the quality of Saint-Georges's libretto and contrasts Halévy's talents with Auber's gifts in *opéra comique*. In *La Juive*, he argues, Halévy was able to invest the different scenes with a sense of overall unity, while the emotional force of his melodies transcends Auber's overobvious national character. The concept of "the purely human" ("*rein menschliche* Verhältnisse" [ibid., 12.137]) appears here, apparently for the first time, and is followed up by a reference to "universal human feelings": "When [the melody] paints universal human feelings, the listener should never be reminded, at an initial hearing, of its origins in *French*, *Italian*, or any other type of music" (ibid., 12.138). It is for these reasons that Wagner holds out Halévy as a model for German musicians to imitate, the antithesis of Mendelssohn, with his lack of passion (ibid., 12.145): "The impulse given by Halévy, coming from a talent that, although foreign, has an intimate affinity with the German spirit, will be of far greater and more decisive import" (ibid., 12.145).

Wagner's contact with Halévy's works seems, therefore, to have been of crucial importance for his thinking. "A Happy Evening" was written in May 1841. In December Wagner saw *La Reine de Chypre* and under the impact of the performance returned to the position he had adopted in January 1841 in his article on the overture. Even here we find ourselves faced with a wavering attitude on Wagner's part to the exact definition of the relationship between poetry and music. Nor is it the last time we shall find Wagner hesitating. For all the force of his personality, Wagner was easily influenced. Just as the *Eroica* could persuade him to write in defense of purely instrumental music, so *La Reine de Chypre* could inspire an ideal image of the union of poet and composer.

In none of these texts does Wagner allude directly to his own works. He is slowly seeking his own way. In his "Autobiographical Sketch" of 1843, he denounces the French and Italian influences revealed by *Das Liebesverbot* (1843a, *GS* 1.11) and criticizes Halévy for resorting to a "mercantile" approach to his art following the success of *La Reine de Chypre* (ibid., 1.15). Not until we turn to two letters written in 1844 and 1845 do we find Wagner alluding to the links between poetry and music in his own creative oeuvre. In the first of these letters—written to Karl Gaillard on 30 January 1844—Wagner states clearly that when he writes a libretto, it is as a function of the music:

> In the first place I am attracted only by those subjects that reveal themselves to me as not only poetically but, at the same time, musically significant. And so, even before I set about writing a single line of the text or drafting a scene, I am already thoroughly immersed in the musical aura of my new creation, I have the whole sound & all the characteristic motives in my head so that when the poem is finished & the scenes are arranged in their proper order the opera is already completed, & its detailed musical treatment is more a question of calm & reflective revision, the moment of actual creativity having already passed. But for this to be so, I must choose only subjects that are capable of an exclusively musical treatment: . . . for music offers us the

means to forge links that the poet alone does not have at his command, at least when faced with today's actors.[4]

In other words, the libretto is drafted in the light of the musical treatment to which it is then subjected. A year later, in a letter to Gustav Klemm of 20 June 1845, Wagner draws the consequence of this relationship and places poet and musician on an equal footing:

> I am now fully convinced that if anything of significance & validity for the history of art is to emerge from this particular genre (which I see as diametrically opposed to the "opera industry" of the present day), this can only be so if the poet and musician are one & the same person. By following the old dispensation you will at best produce a decent libretto or decent music, but never a genuine musical drama, indeed, I shall never be able to understand how two artists could ever create a single work of art. The fact that I have grasped a subject that came to me alone, that I elaborate it in such a way that I myself can no longer say which parts show the influence of the poet & which the influence of the musician, and that I finally complete both words and music just as the subject originally appeared to me in vague outline—all this I find adequate justification for my exclusively creative and, more especially, my *musically* creative powers.[5]

Music still appears to dominate, but Wagner hesitates, at least in the second of these two letters. Be that as it may, we are clearly in the presence of the first theoretical expression of a necessary union. A later letter confirms Wagner's growing obsession with unity and complementarity: writing to Hermann Franck on 30 May 1846 he speaks in terms of unity between Lohengrin and Elsa—albeit a unity that proves impossible to sustain—and between the libretto and music of the opera as he himself conceived it.[6] By 1 January 1847—the date of his letter to Eduard Hanslick—Wagner is once again to be found insisting on the primacy of music: "I have no special ambition to see my poetry overshadowed by my music, and I should be guilty of dismembering myself & exposing an untruth if I were to insist upon doing violence to the music for the sake of the poem. I cannot broach a poetic subject if it is not already conditioned by music."[7] It is hardly surprising that the author of *Vom Musikalisch-Schönen* (The beautiful in music) should have been so bemused, seven years later, by the contents of *Opera and Drama*.

Jack Stein argues with some plausibility that Wagner's ambivalence is reflected in *Rienzi*, the music of which occupied the composer's attentions between summer 1838 and November 1840. Certainly, as Stein shows (1960, 15–24), there are passages here in which the poetic line is clearly violated by a music that was conceived in advance, most notably in Rienzi's Prayer (ibid., 23–24). In other passages, by contrast, the dramatic recitative is reinforced and supported by the orchestral accompaniment.[8] However, as Stein himself remarks, the situation changes gradually from *Der fliegende Holländer* onward: here the musical expression exploits and reinforces the emotional intensity of the drama (ibid., 32), even if, in many cases, we are still in the presence of a "number" opera of traditional stamp. In *Der fliegende Holländer* the music in the dialogue sections does not do violence to the rhythm of the poetry but highlights its dramatic contours. Stein's analysis of *Tannhäuser* (July 1843 to October 1845) confirms this development, for here the lack of alignment between verse and music is very much the exception (ibid., 40), while in *Lohengrin* (spring 1846 to April 1848) the music is largely adapted to the rhythm of the words.

Frank Glass's 1981 study of *Tristan und Isolde*, *Die Meistersinger*, and *Parsifal* is intended as an explicit rebuttal of Stein's line of argument. For the earlier period of Wagner's development, however, Stein's observations do not contradict Glass's thesis, for, according to Glass, the music from *Der fliegende Holländer* onward is "fertilized" by the poetic intent, that is, the libretto is written in such a way that the music underlines its logic and dramatic scope—whereas in traditional number opera, the libretto was no more than a foil for brilliant musical pieces that bore no relation to any truly theatrical aim.

In April 1846, shortly before beginning the music of *Lohengrin*, Wagner conducted a performance of Beethoven's Ninth Symphony in Dresden's old opera house and prepared a program note for the occasion that, after his earlier hesitancy on the question of the relevant primacy of music and text, comes out clearly in favor of the dramatic content as mediated by the music. He begins by reaffirming the complementarity of poetry and music: "The essence of higher instrumental music consists in its ability to express in sound what is inexpressible in words" (1846c, *GS* 2.56). And whereas, five years previously, he had condemned those who sought a program in Beethoven's symphonic movements, he now proposes an interpretation of the Ninth Symphony based on passages from Goethe's *Faust*, albeit passages that essentially express states of mind. But joy irrupts at the very moment when music calls on poetry to reveal what music itself cannot say. Wagner quotes Ludwig Tieck at this point: "In these symphonies we hear insatiable yearning rising up from the lowest depths, a yearning that wanders away before returning to itself." He then goes on: "It almost seems as though, in conceiving this symphony, Beethoven was prompted by a similar awareness of the nature of instrumental music" (ibid., 2.61). In introducing the idea of "yearning" (*Sehnen*) on the part of the poet, Wagner broaches the sexual metaphor examined in the earlier part of this study. In the fourth movement of the symphony, he concludes, the music strives toward the text: "In order to proceed, *the musical poem*[9] demands a decision of a kind that can be expressed only in human speech" (ibid., 2.61). The human voice enters in response to a sense of "necessity" (*Nothwendigkeit*), Wagner writes, and, drawing on an image that he reserves not only for music as a female element but for women in general, he goes on to speak of the "*dominated*[10] element of instrumental music" (ibid., 2.62)—the first such reference in his writings to the victory of the word.

The theme of unity finds increasingly frequent expression in Wagner's writings. In May 1848 he completed his *Entwurf zur Organisation eines deutschen Nationaltheaters für das Königreich Sachsen* (Plan for the organization of a German national theater for the Kingdom of Saxony), in which he envisaged a German national theater as a place where composers and men of letters would "in themselves represent the full artistic and scientific vigor of the nation" (1848b, *GS* 2.238). And in his speech to the *Vaterlandsverein* in June 1848 he demanded that his fellow citizens be "brothers of a *single* family" (1848c, *SS* 12.221), encouraging them to break free from the blandishments of gold: "Like some hideous nightmare, this demonic concept of money will vanish, taking with it the whole of its ghastly retinue of open and clandestine usury, financial swindles, interest, and bankers' speculations. This will mean the *complete emancipation of the human race*, the *fulfillment of Christ's pure teaching*" (ibid., 12.223).

It is a purely occasional text, however—the toast delivered on 22 September 1848 to mark the tercentenary of the Dresden Staatskapelle—that deserves our particular attention. Ever since 1834 Wagner had insisted on the complementarity of music and poetry. Initially he had inclined in the direction of the supremacy of music, after which the poetic intent had asserted its rival claims. Here, for the first time, he gives a sexual gloss to the comparison. The instrumental orchestra is likened to a man lacking a vocal ensemble, which latter is compared with a woman. Together they make a whole: "I know of no finer comparison for such a guise as that in which this artistic institution now reveals itself to us except to say that it is a man!" (1848f, *GS* 2.231). And Wagner goes on: "The man requires a *wife*, in other words, the instrumental orchestra requires an equally capable vocal institution entrusted to its keeping as its natural property: I consider this latter to be a woman since, as we know very well, the present orchestra issued from the womb of a chorus of singers" (ibid., 2.232). As we can see from this passage, the masculine is not yet associated with the poetical element, nor the feminine with the musical. Indeed, the opposite appears to be the case. The passage is significant, nonetheless, since it is the first time that Wagner introduces sexual imagery into his discussion of art or, in this case, artistic institutions. Thirteen days later he completed his essay *Die Nibelungensage (Mythus)* (The Nibelung legend [Myth];

1848g) and, on 20 October, finished the first prose draft of *Siegfrieds Tod*. The idea of a sexual metaphor was already occupying his mind at this juncture, therefore. There followed *Art and Revolution*, *The Art-Work of the Future*, and "Judaism in Music"—but we have to wait until August 1850, it seems, before the androgynous metaphor becomes central to Wagner's thinking in *Opera and Drama*. As such, it *precedes* the definitive version of the libretto to the four-part *Ring*.

Thus it was between September 1848 and August 1850 that the idea of sexualizing the relationship between poetry and music took root in Wagner's thoughts. On what basis was that idea formed? Against what literary and philosophical background was it fashioned? And what significance did it have for Wagner at the time he took it into account? These are questions to which we must now turn our attention.

Romantic Androgyny and Wagner

The presence of androgyny in Wagner's works and writings would be less surprising to modern audiences if we had retained the same sort of direct link with the important ideas of early nineteenth-century German Romantic thought as that which binds us, even indirectly, to the writings of Marx and Freud. Nonetheless, it would be wrong to conclude that androgyny was a dominant feature of German Romanticism. Certainly it was an important element but one that needs to be seen in the context of far more decisive features such as the search for totality and the absolute. A glance at the writers and major anthologies of literary history makes it clear that unity is the Romantics' principal preoccupation, of which the myth of a return to androgyny is the natural expression. "For Romanticism, it was a question, come what may, of rediscovering the lost sense of unity. The individual is but a creature of transience, an accident, who will inevitably disappear with a return to the unity of absolute existence" (Sans 1969, 277). Fortunately, those writers who have examined the history of thought, literature, and religion have provided us with a faithful picture of the androgyny of this period,[11] allowing us to define the common early nineteenth-century background against which Wagner's own brand of androgyny emerged.

The first manifestation of this interest appears at the end of the eighteenth century and could be described as a veritable characterology of the sexes, with such writings as Brandes' *Ueber die Weiber* (On women; 1787), Heydenreich's *Mann und Weib: Ein Beitrag zur Psychologie der Geschlechter* (Man and woman: A contribution to the psychology of the sexes; 1798) and—the only work still remembered today—Kant's *Anthropologie* (1798). Admittedly, we are still a long way from an androgynous vision of humanity: Kant's characterization of women, for example, would make even the most lukewarm feminist shudder with disbelief.[12] For Brandes, the woman is first and foremost a body through which she expresses her particularity and her strength. Refinement, devotion, profound sensitivity, and gentleness of temperament are her essential characteristics. The problem at this time is to find ways of understanding the difference between the sexes. This is the question addressed by Fichte in his 1796 essay, *Grundlagen des Naturrechts nach Prinzipien der Wissenschaftslehre* (Rudiments of natural law according to the principles of epistemology): "Why are there two sexes?" Humboldt's vision differs only slightly: if the woman is clearly different from the man, the sexes are nonetheless seen in terms of their complementarity and interaction. Theodor Hippel, in his *Über die bürgerliche Verbesserung der Weiber* (On the civic improvement of women) of 1792, recognizes that men and women are fundamentally similar and that, as a result, they ought to receive the same education, a development that was to lead to the true emancipation of women. Under Goethe's influence, the *Sturm und Drang* movement of the 1770s gave thematic expression to every form of polarity, including the difference between the sexes. In turn, this trend led to the emergence of natural philosophy as a discipline and to the search for a single indivisible whole.

As yet, there was no question, therefore, of androgyny as such, but the discoveries of medicine and research into art history resulted in—or, rather, revived—an interest in hermaphroditism. In 1764 Winckelmann published his *Geschichte der Kunst des Altertums* (History of the art of antiquity). For him, artistic representations of the hermaphrodite were an expression of ideal beauty: "Nature offers us isolated beauties as great as those of art; relatively speaking, however, art has the edge over nature. . . . By intensifying its efforts, art seeks to combine the beauties and characteristics of both sexes in the figures of hermaphrodites, which, as represented by ancient artists, are ideal products" (cited in Molino 1988, 282). Winckelmann lists the most eloquent examples of classical androgynous statuary, including specimens from the Palazzo Pitti in Florence and from the Villa Borghese and Villa Albani in Rome.

To the contribution of art history must be added that of medicine. The cases of hermaphroditism attested by clinical observations posed an enigma: was there not an original hermaphrodite, as the Platonic myth appeared to indicate? And were rare present-day instances of hermaphroditism not related to that first example? Questions such as these were the starting point for a terminological confusion or, rather, of a semantic ambiguity that is still far from resolved today but that requires us to distinguish eunuchs (as transmitted by the Freudian concept of castration) from biological hermaphroditism and symbolic androgyny.[13]

Scientific discoveries of the day were in themselves a model for androgynous thinking. Electricity, the researches of Luigi Galvani into electrical impulses, which led, in turn, to the invention of the battery, together with animal magnetism, the fluids that Anton Mesmer thought could be used to cure every illness—all these provide concrete examples of clear-cut polarities that could nonetheless harmonize in union. The physician Johann Wilhelm Ritter (1776–1810) had discovered the polarization of electrodes in batteries. A friend of Novalis, he was typical of a whole generation of Romantic scholars, seeking to bolster up a semireligious, semiphilosophical theory of androgyny in a study posthumously published in 1810 under the title *Fragmente aus dem Nachlaß eines jungen Physikers* (Fragments from the posthumous papers of a young physician). In addition to numerous references to magnetism as an explanation of the reunion and disjunction of the sexes, he conceives of Eve as a

> female Christ; she has ensured that all creatures are redeemed, she has sinned as a human being. Every birth is a sin, every death a redemption. . . . One day a Christ will come who will be androgynous. Eve was born of man without the help of a woman, Christ of a woman without the help of a man; the androgyne will be born of both at once. Both will dissolve completely into a blaze of glory; it will be a miracle, and the light will assume the form of a sexless and hence immortal body comparable to gold transmuted into flesh. The whole of alchemy consists in grieving for our earthly existence and its particular finality; it is an elixir of life, a rejuvenating philter, the annunciation of the heavenly kingdom, the prophecy of the androgyne. (2.188–89)

The androgyne that is born of Eve and Christ will be a sexless androgyne but as immortal as the gold of the alchemists. Continuing in this philosophico-religious vein is Franz von Baader (1765–1841), a writer largely forgotten today,[14] who is without doubt the most important and influential exponent of the theory of androgyny during the whole of the Romantic period. His writings are scattered throughout a myriad of articles and slender volumes and might be thought of as an extension of the teachings of Jakob Böhme (1575–1624), whose *Mysterium Magnum* is a theosophical reinterpretation of the Old Testament shot through with alchemical and cabbalistic ideas. Androgyny is essential to Baader's thinking: "Without the concept of androgyny, the central concept of religion, that of our image of God, remains unintelligible" (1822–25, 3.303–4). It is "the union of sexual forces within a single body" (ibid., 9.211). For Baader, Adam was created in the image of an androgynous God (see Genesis 1.27–28), and is himself androgynous. Tempted by woman and yielding to his animal nature, he loses his androgyneity. "If woman was created from man, it is simply because at the time of his first temptation or in the very first moment of that temptation, he felt the same kind of desire for *external* assistance in self-multiplication as is felt by animals, so that he lost the desire for *inner* assistance" (Baader 1822–25, 7.229). Adam failed to achieve inner union with the Sophia and so he was condemned to egoism. In consequence man now seeks to regain his lost androgyneity. Christ will restore our "natural humanity," and love will strive to recreate the original androgynous being, struggling to overcome the division between the sexes. For Baader, the function of sexual love is "to help men and women to complement one another inwardly and form the complete human being, in other words, the original image of God" (ibid., 3.309). True love, however, is embodied in the love match, which is synonymous with self-abandon (ibid., 2.179). It is no doubt for this reason that Baader conceives of sexual pleasure as synonymous with sacrifice, a cataleptic, unconscious state akin to death.

It is clear from this to what extent it is possible, in philosophico-religious terms, for the idea of androgyny to convey the Romantic longing for unity and totality. "Every division into two opposing poles represents a form of evil for Baader," according to Eugène Susini (1942a, 2.355).

Even if Baader's writings are occasionally contradictory and even if they do not represent a systematic study of androgyny, they nonetheless constitute the most comprehensive approach to the subject. To that extent, they are entirely typical of their age. It comes as no surprise, therefore, to find other creative writers of the period touching on the topic, albeit in a way that is both more fragmentary and less systematic than that of Baader himself. Among the foremost of these writers are Friedrich Schlegel and Novalis.

In the case of Schlegel (1772–1829), androgyny finds expression not only in his theoretical writings but also in his literary works. His self-styled *Fragmente* are shot through with professions of androgynous faith. His "Idea for a Rational Catechism for Noblewomen" (which modern editors attribute to Schlegel's co-author, Friedrich Schleiermacher) contains the following credo: "I believe in infinite humanity, which existed before it assumed the integument of male and female. . . . I believe in the power of the will and education to approach the infinite once again, to free myself from the fetters of misguided education, and to make myself independent of the limitations of sex" (142–43). The "true nature" of marriage is one in which "several people become only one" (ibid., 108). It is not surprising, therefore, that in his 1795 essay, "Über die Diotima" (On Diotima), Schlegel writes: "The goal to which the human race should aspire is the progressive reintegration of the sexes." A similar sentiment invests the essay "Über die Philosophie (An Dorothea)" (On philosophy: To Dorothea) of 1799: "As normally practiced and understood, masculinity and femininity are the most dangerous obstacles in the way of humanity" (173). But the figure of androgyny becomes particularly interesting from our own point of view when Schlegel applies it to the realm of aesthetics. In his essay "Gespräch über die Poesie" (On poetry), he writes: "Each muse seeks and finds the other, and all the rivers of poetry flow together into the vast universal sea" (1800, 186). True literature, he writes in "Vom kombinatorischen Geist" (On the combinatory mind), is "a vast whole, completely interconnected and interrelated, embracing many modes of art within its unity—in short, a unitary work of art" (1804, 67). Another of the *Athenäum* fragments, finally, prefigures Wagner's own preoccupations: "Perhaps a wholly new era in the sciences and arts might begin when symphilosophy and sympoetry are so universally and so intimately bound up together that it is no longer unusual for several complementary natures to form communal works of art. It is often impossible to avoid the idea that two minds might actually belong together, like two divided halves, and that only when combined could they be everything they had it in their power to be." And Schlegel dreams of "an art by which to unite individuals" (1798, 116).

Androgyny is also central to Schlegel's novel *Lucinde* of 1799, a sensational work in its day, which was seen as dangerously erotic. As before, the same theme of androgynous unity and totality is present here: "You know of no divisions: your nature is one and indivisible. . . . I can no longer say my love or your love; both are identical and a perfect unity, as much the love that I feel for you as the love that you feel for me. It is marriage, eternal unity, and the merging of our minds . . . for our whole eternal being and our lives" (56–57). "Let us exchange roles and vie, in childish delight, to see who can imitate the other more convincingly. . . . I see here a strange and highly meaningful allegory of the perfection of male and female when merged to form a full and total humanity" (ibid., 59–60). Sexual confusion abounds: "The fantastical boy could equally well have been taken for a mischievous girl who had disguised herself on a whim" (ibid., 68). "The third and highest degree is the lasting feeling of harmonious warmth. The youth who feels this loves not just as a man but also as a woman" (ibid., 77). And Schlegel draws a parallel between erotic and aesthetic union: "He lived only in the future and in the hope of one day completing an immortal work as a monument to his virtue and dignity" (ibid., 131). "He longed for a homeland and thought of a wonderful marriage that would not interfere with the demands of art" (ibid., 135). Julius thinks he has achieved the aesthetic perfection for which he has been searching: "He felt he could never lose this unity, that the riddle of his existence was solved, he had found the word" (ibid., 145). In love, it is the kiss that provides that transcendent moment of unity beyond the confines of mortality and immortality. At that moment "we are both one, and only when the individual sees and imagines himself as the center of the whole and the spirit of the world will he become one and be himself" (ibid., 171).

A similar but more somber perspective is found in the writings of Novalis. As Busst has shown in his study of the androgyne in nineteenth-century literature (1967, 59), it is possible to reconstruct a mythical and religious concept of androgyny on the basis of Novalis's various texts, a concept that, moreover, conforms to the pattern unity-fall-reintegration, which, as pointed out in the course of the foregoing pages, recurs in all the texts of this period. Nonetheless, the theme of androgyny seems far more diffuse here, where the conflict between man and nature, spirit and matter is resolved in the figure of the androgyne (Novalis 1800a, 1.167):

Einst ist alles Leib,	One day all will be flesh,
Ein Leib,	*One* flesh,
In himmlischem Blute	In heavenly blood
Schwimmt das selige Paar.	The blessed pair swims.

But it is perhaps the link between androgyny and death that Novalis emphasizes more than his fellow Romantics.

In his major study of androgyny in the writings of the early German Romantics, Fritz Giese attaches an enormous degree of importance to what he terms "the mystique of the embrace" (1919, 335), the concrete figuration of the fusion of two beings that, at the same time, represents the indissoluble link between love and death to the extent that their bodies are held motionless between Heaven and Earth. "The problem of the difference between the sexes," Giese comments, "is now located at the farthest frontier of all earthly existence. . . . In death there is no longer any division between the sexes. . . . Death through love [*Liebestod*] is an extreme demand placed on the individual" (Gliese 1919, 338–39). "Death will not separate us," say the lovers in *Heinrich von Ofterdingen*, "we shall be eternal so long as we love one another" (Novalis 1802, 1.288). And in the first of the *Hymnen an die Nacht* (Hymns to night): "All hail to the queen of the world, to the august proclaimer of hallowed worlds, she who cultivates blessed love—she sends you to me—sweet belovèd—lovely sun of the night,—now I awaken—for I am yours and mine—you have revealed the night to me as a source of life—made me human—consume my body with spiritual glow, that I might merge with you more inwardly, airily, that our bridal night might last forever" (1800b, 1.133). In a letter to Tieck, the artist Philipp Otto Runge (1777–1810) appears to have been influenced by Novalis in his comments on a painting on an androgynous theme, *Die Quelle* (The source): "The I and Thou are joined only in death; it is in this that the human being consists: love comes between longing and will, between man and woman" (quoted in Gliese 1919, 356–57). Mention of the *Liebestod* brings us very close to the familiar world of Wagnerian thought.

All this was in the air at the time, as is clear from the picture painted by a considerable number of historical investigations in the fields of the history of ideas, philosophy, and literature. Moreover, it is now admitted that one or more writers may have influenced a creative artist without it being possible to furnish factual evidence of that influence. The names of Böhme, Humboldt, Ritter, Baader, Schlegel, and Novalis figure neither in the indexes to the volumes of Wagner's correspondence for the period until 1852 nor in his autobiography, *Mein Leben*. None of their writings were represented in Wagner's Dresden library (1842–49), of which Curt von Westernhagen published a complete catalog in 1966. Conversely, we know that Wagner borrowed a copy of *Lucinde* from his uncle Adolf's library in Leipzig (Gregor-Dellin 1980, 64–65) and that he read it during the early part of 1828 (Gregor-Dellin 1972, 14). We may suppose that it was through the intermediary of Adolf Wagner—an eminent writer and translator originally destined for theology (*ML*, 9)—that the young Wagner came into contact with the subject of androgyny, which, as noted, was very much an aspect of the early nineteenth-century zeitgeist. Suffice it to recall the letter to August Röckel of 24 August 1851, quoted above, in which Wagner mentions that androgyny had been the subject of numerous conversations between the two of them. Even if Wagner never mentions the name of Novalis, musicologists have not been slow to point out, from an early date, line-by-line parallels between the *Hymnen an die Nacht* and the love duet from Act II of *Tristan und Isolde* (see, for example, Prüfer 1906 and Seidl 1912). It is clear, however, that there is an equally striking analogy between these mystical poems by Novalis and the love duet between Siegfried and Brünnhilde in the final act of *Siegfried*. Certainly, Wieland Wagner's staging of the moment when Siegfried kisses Brünnhilde, in his first postwar Bayreuth production of the *Ring*, was a superb illustration of Novalis's concept of *Umarmung* in this passage where, according to the stage direction, Siegfried "sinks, as though dying, on the sleeping woman and, his eyes closed, presses his lips to her mouth," and where, at the same time, the union of their two bodies takes place on the cusp of Earth and Heaven, of nature and the absolute. Confronted by this glorious image, it is impossible not to be reminded of Gusdorf's comment that with the Romantics, "masculine and feminine are not characteristics suited to humanity. . . . They are cosmic categories at work in reality in its totality. The opposition between complementary elements and the tension that results between them suggests a particular case of that universal polarity whose law is imposed on the cosmos" (Gusdorf 1984, 225–26).

Siegfried's and Brünnhilde's love duet in Act III of Wieland Wagner's staging of *Siegfried* (1954). Photo by Siegfried Lauterwasser; copyright © Bayreuther Festspiele GmbH, Foto Lauterwasser

Our reconstitution of the spirit of the age has the advantage of showing that when Wagner availed himself of the image of androgyny, it was against a background shared by some of the major thinkers of his time. Yet this, in itself, is not sufficient to demonstrate the specific significance of this borrowing for him. Nor is the probable influence enough to explain why, at some point between 1848 and 1850, it entered Wagner's thinking in so decisive a manner, to the point where it came to constitute the pivotal concept in his most important theoretical essay.

THE SOURCES OF WAGNERIAN ANDROGYNY

It is surprising, perhaps, that in this poststructuralist age, when deconstruction continues to exert so notable an influence, we should insist on identifying, as closely as possible, the sources of Wagner's concept of androgyny. Certain readers may be additionally surprised to discover that I am attempting to do so in the name of semiology, since a growth in semiological studies during the 1960s[15] helped to undermine "university criticism." I have always considered it one of the ironies of the history of ideas that structuralism and semiology at this time conjointly abandoned the concept of "situation," which a linguist such as Bloomfield had identified in 1933 as a decisive constituent of meaning (see Mounin 1969, 255–96). The texts that Wagner read are very much part of a situation that seeks to define the network of meanings invested by an author in a text or work of creative artistry. If it is important for us to know what these texts were, it is not to point out that Wagner simply reproduced their contents but because he based his own thinking on them. My own genetic approach is not concerned to show how the composer mimicked the thoughts of others. Instead—and it was a major error on the part of the New Criticism not to see this—it allows us to define the originality of the thinker or artist in question. It is this originality that, on the basis of the body of influences, constitutes the "poietic space" that I have defined in detail elsewhere (Nattiez 1984, 7).

Baader's ideas represent an early nineteenth-century revival of the classic model of religious androgyny—a model that, already present in Böhme, is typical of the theoretical thrust of Wagner's own line of thought with its basic pattern of an original unity that, lost for a time, is finally rediscovered. Of course, one could "explain" this aspect of Wagner's thinking by adopting a universalist hypothesis and simply stating that he exemplifies a characteristic model of esoteric thought found in the Jewish, Christian, and Muslim traditions.[16] Of course, a religious historian can point out the most striking similarities between one train of thought and another in any number of cultures, but in doing so he neither provides an explanation for them nor reveals their underlying meaning. It is not an explanation, since religious themes are common currency (there is a whole body of influence at the basis of Böhme's thinking, just as there is with Baader or Wagner); and it does not reveal their meaning, since, if there are features common to two systems of thought, it is only by going beyond (or looking behind) these common features that we have any chance of understanding the semantic specificity of any one particular system.

Seen from this perspective, Wagner's view of androgyny seems to be the result of his demonstrable familiarity with several currents of contemporary thought. We have seen that the sexualization of musical ideas makes its first appearance on 22 September 1848 on the occasion of his toast to the Dresden Staatskapelle. It was between 18 June and 2 August 1847, during his annual summer holiday, that Wagner read Plato's *Symposium*. Although his interest in Old and Middle High German literature, which, according to *Mein Leben*, coincided with his reading of Plato, did not develop until the following year, it is not straining the truth to claim that Wagner came into contact with Plato's myth of androgyny at about the same time that he was immersing himself in the mythological material that was to provide him with the subject matter of the *Ring*. At all events, we know from *Mein Leben* and Cosima Wagner's diaries that Plato's dialogue continued to reverberate through Wagner's mind long after his initial encounter with it.

It is interesting to note the way in which Wagner himself reports his reading of *The Symposium*. There is certainly something significant—especially when we bear in mind that *Mein Leben* is a dictated work—about the fact that Wagner passes without transition, within the same paragraph, from his account of the comedies of Aristophanes (whose literary counterpart recounts the myth of androgyny in *The Symposium*) to that of Plato's dialogue itself:

> I used to slink away into the depths of the shrubbery in the part of the garden allocated to me to take refuge from the increasingly obtrusive summer heat; there I would read, to my boundless delight, the plays of Aristophanes, after having been introduced by *The Birds* to the world of this ribald darling of the Graces, as he boldly called himself. Side by side with him, I read the best of Plato's dialogues, and from the *Symposium* in particular gained such an intimate insight into the wonderful beauty of Greek life that I felt myself palpably more at home in ancient Athens than in any circumstances afforded by the modern world. (*ML*, 343)

From the summer of 1847, therefore, Wagner had the image of androgyny within his grasp. Moreover, the tendency to sexualize music by treating the themes of sonata form as masculine and feminine (a treatment found more recently in the writings of Vincent d'Indy[17]) is not much older. As Peter Bloom pointed out in 1974, it seems likely that the sexual characterization of the subject groups in sonata form was first proposed by Adolf Bernhard Marx in the third volume of his *Die Lehre von der musikalischen Komposition*, first published in 1845. In contrast to the first subject group, the second is said to be "more tender and flexible by nature, rather than emphatically structured—in a sense it is feminine in character in contrast to the masculine character of what has preceded it" (Marx 1845, 3.282). Although Marx does not use the word as such, he goes on in the very next phrase to describe the sonata in terms of an androgynous whole: "In this sense, each of the two subject groups is an Other and it is only together that they create a more elevated, more perfect order."

The topos of androgyny is already here, therefore, in the musical theorizing of the time. What is missing is the myth, in other words, a narrative. As noted earlier, Wagner's line of thinking is close to that of those same mystical traditions of which Plato's myth is a part: "In the first place there were three sexes, not, as with us, two, male and female; the third partook of the nature of both the others and has vanished . . . . Man's original body having been thus cut in two, each half yearned for the half from which it had been severed. . . . It is from this distant epoch, then, that we may date the innate love that human beings feel for one another, the love that restores us to our ancient state by attempting to weld two beings into one and to heal the wounds that humanity suffered" (189d and 191d).[18] There is much to be said for the suggestion that this tripartite development was reinforced and reactivated for Wagner by his study of Hegel, not least because the latter's three-stage process of thesis, antithesis, and synthesis is paralleled by the sequence of original unity, lost unity, and rediscovered unity that emerges from our reading of Wagner's Zurich essays. As Gregor-Dellin points out, Wagner spent several months during the winter of 1848–49 reading Hegel's *Vorlesungen über die Philosophie der Geschichte* (Lectures on the philosophy of history), so that he now had at his disposal both the theme and the framework of the myth of androgyny (Gregor-Dellin 1972, 49). In turn, that myth was to provide him with the material for his theory of the art-work of the future, allowing him to flesh out an idea that, even if never expressed in so many words, was far from being new in the history of German ideas. In "The Poet and the Composer," for example, E.T.A. Hoffmann had written: "A true opera seems to me to be the one in which the music springs directly from the poem as a necessary product of the same" (Hoffmann 1819, 1.111). In much the same vein, Friedrich Schlegel had written in his *Athenäums-Fragmente*: "In the works of the greatest poets, it is not unusual for us to feel the breath of another art" (Schlegel 1798, 144). And was it not Schiller—whose complete works graced the shelves of Wagner's Dresden library—who, in his essay *Über naive und sentimentalische Dichtung* (On naïve and sentimental poetry [1795–96]), had contrasted the synthetic art of antiquity with the decadence of humanity? Lessing too—another writer whose complete works were in Wagner's library and whom the composer quotes in *Opera and Drama* in the context of the limits of painting and poetry (1851a, *GS* 4.1–3)—had devoted the second part of *Laokoon* to a discussion of the way in which each art could make up for the deficiencies of the others. Finally, Ludwig Tieck (a twenty-volume edition of whose works was in Wagner's possession in Dresden) had called for a general fusion of the arts. We shall not be guilty of ascribing undue premonitory significance to the fact that in 1813—the year of Wagner's birth—Jean Paul wrote in Bayreuth: "Until now Apollo has always cast the gift of poetry with his right hand and the gift of music with his left to two people so far apart from each other that to this day we still await the man who will write both words and music of a genuine opera." After all, what Jean Paul was expressing here was a recurrent theme of the time, such as he might have found in Schelling's *Philosophie der Kunst* (Philosophy of art), first published in 1809 but containing lectures from 1802–03. Here we find the whole program of Wagner's Zurich essays already mapped out in full:

> The most perfect combination of all the arts, the synthesized union of poetry and music through song, of poetry and painting through dance, is the supreme theatrical manifestation, such as was the drama of antiquity, of which all that remains today is a caricature, *opera*. And yet it is opera that, by dint of a nobler and loftier style in terms not only of poetry but of those other arts that compete with it, is best equipped to lead us back to an enactment of that ancient drama that is bound up with music and singing. (Schelling 1802–03, 3.387)

It was this that Hoffmann had attempted to achieve in his various operas, including *Undine*, and that Herder, too, had hoped to see realized:

> There is no reason to question the exalted effect that could be produced by the intelligent combination of music, poetry, and dance, those arts that belong together so naturally. In the fullness of time a man will come who, despising the current farrago of music deprived of words, will see the need for an intimate union of purely human feelings, of history itself, and music. He must descend from those lofty heights where the common composer ostentatiously declares that poetry must serve his art, and allow music to serve the words of feeling and of action as such. . . . He will overturn the whole disordered and tattered framework of operatic singing and build a coherent lyric structure in its place, a structure in which poetry, music, action, and scenery will be a single entity.

Wagnerian hagiography considers this text prophetic. I myself prefer to see in it one of the possible sources of *The Art-Work of the Future*: after all, a volume of Herder's selected writings formed part of Wagner's private library in Dresden.

Possible contact with the religious philosophies of the time, the influence of the Platonic myth of androgyny, and contemporary theories of a synthesis of the arts would be of little consequence if Wagner had not woven them into the philosophical fabric of a writer—Ludwig Feuerbach—who was to influence him at the very moment when he was working on his Zurich essays and the text of the *Ring*. If the works from which I have quoted define the poietic space that allowed Wagner to construct his own androgynous myth of music history, there is no doubt that it was Feuerbach who played the role of catalyst. In dedicating *The Art-Work of the Future* to Feuerbach, Wagner took the liberty of attaching the philosopher's name "to a work that owes its existence to the impression" left on him by Feuerbach's writings (1849m, *SS* 12.285). It is the result of this deep-seated "contamination" that I should like to analyze in the course of the following pages.

We know from Wagner's letter of 4 August 1849 to his publisher Otto Wigand[19] that, by this date, he had read Feuerbach's *Gedanken über Tod und Unsterblichkeit* (Thoughts on death and immortality), but even without Wagner's own testimony, a cursory reading of the sketches for *Jesus of Nazareth*, which were probably drawn up between 31 March and 16 April 1849 (but see *WWV*, 538–39), would be enough to convince us of this fact. It was this essay that Wagner recommended to Karl Ritter in a letter of 21 November 1849.[20] On 4 June 1850 we find Wagner writing to Theodor Uhlig, asking him to invite Wigand to send him other works by Feuerbach. The request was repeated on 27 July in a letter (now lost) to Feuerbach himself.[21] Around 20 September 1850 he told Uhlig[22] that Feuerbach had written to thank him for sending him a copy of *The Art-Work of the Future*, which—as already noted—had been dedicated to the philosopher.[23] On 8 June 1853, finally, we find Wagner writing to August Röckel and announcing that he is sending the latter a copy of Feuerbach's lectures on *Das Wesen der Religion* (The essence of religion).[24]

We do not know when Wagner read Feuerbach's other works, but Albert Lévy is no doubt right when he claims that even though Wagner may not have owned copies of them, he had evidently read them, as is clear from certain verbal parallels not only between *Grundsätze der Philosophie der Zukunft* (Principles of the philosophy of the future) and *The Art-Work of the Future* but also between *Das Wesen des Christentums* (The essence of Christianity) and *Jesus of Nazareth* (Lévy 1904, 449–64).

In 1830, in his *Thoughts on Death and Immortality*, Feuerbach had not yet advanced the belief, put forward eleven years later in *The Essence of Christianity*, that God is made in man's image, a projection of man's most sublime ideas; nor does he yet state, as he does in his lectures entitled *The Essence of Religion* (1848), that theology is a branch of both anthropology and physiology. Indeed, in *Thoughts on Death and Immortality* Feuerbach still adopts the standpoint of a polytheistic metaphysician: the Christian God is simply the incarnation of egoism.

For now, Feuerbach was content to subsume his conception of unity, love, and death under a single heading. In *The Essence of Christianity* he adds the concept of communism—which must not be confused with the strictly societal associations that the word acquires in Marx's writings: "The Thou belongs to the perfection of the I: only together do human beings form a single human being, only together are human beings what they are, and what they can and must be" (1841, 187). As a card-carrying Young Hegelian of the Romantic School, Feuerbach invests this notion of communism with a metaphysical totality: "Only the one and all, the universal, the whole, existence, and the absolute can be perfect and complete" (1830, 90). Feuerbach's standpoint is metaphysical, moreover, in its interpretation not only of love but also of death as a positive entity:

"Death is the total and complete dissolution of your total and complete being: there is only one death, and that death is total" (ibid., 101). "In love, one is all, all is one, since all other feelings are instinct with multiplicity, dispersion, and division" (ibid., 108). That is why, in Feuerbach's view, love and death are connected: "Love is the unity of personality and essence and, for that reason, presupposes both separation and unity. . . . Love resides only in the unity of the two" (ibid., 109).

It is scarcely surprising, therefore, that Wagner was able to find in Feuerbach a number of statements that are clearly androgynous in character: "When you are in love, . . . you exist only in the being who is the object of your love" (ibid., 118). That is why a life lived to the full is so closely related to death: "You who without love are indivisible from your specific existence will be destroyed, with that existence, in love. But at the same time this passing away is a new and more glorious existence. In consequence you exist and you do not exist in love; love is both existence and nonexistence, life and death as life" (ibid., 119). Love would not be complete if death did not exist. Death is the ultimate sacrifice of reconciliation, the ultimate proof of love.

Moreover, Feuerbach makes a connection between the search for totality, androgyny, and music, and he does so in terms that recall those used in *Opera and Drama*. The work of total art, Wagner had argued here, must spring from the union of poetry and music, of understanding and feeling, a union that he even compared to the incestuous marriage of Oedipus and Jocasta, with its issue in Antigone. For his part, Feuerbach writes: "God the Father is *I*, God the Son *Thou*. The *I* is *understanding*, the *Thou* is *love*; only when *love* is accompanied by *understanding*, and *understanding* by *love* does *spirit* exist, only then is the total human being [*der ganze Mensch*] created" (1841, 82). Music is related to feeling (ibid., 4). "The third person in the Trinity expresses only the mutual love of the two divine persons; it is the unity of Father and Son" (ibid., 82). In order to be able to claim this, however, Feuerbach—like Böhme and Baader before him—has to invest Christ with an androgynous dimension:

> The son of God is a gentle, tender being, who pardons and reconciles, the feminine mind [*Gemüt*] of God. . . . The Son is therefore the feminine feeling of dependency in God; involuntarily, the Son imposes on us the need for a *real* feminine being. In himself and for himself the son—I mean the natural, human son—is an intermediary between the masculine essence of the father and the feminine essence of the mother; *he is, so to speak, half man, half woman,*[25] since he is not yet fully and rigorously conscious of that autonomy that characterizes men and because he feels drawn more toward his mother than toward his father. The son's love of his mother is the first love felt by the male for the female being. (Ibid., 87)

In other words, it is in the form of androgyny, both in love and in society, that the human being finds full realization: "The Thou belongs to the perfection of the I: only together do human beings form a single human being, only together are human beings what they are, and what they can and must be" (ibid., 187). And in the wake of this line of reasoning, *The Essence of Christianity* also provides us with the androgynous "justification" for anti-Semitism, a justification that runs along similar lines to those adopted by Marx in his essay "On the Jewish Question" (1843): "The Jews have retained their individuality until now. Their principle—their God—is the *most practical* principle in the world—egoism or, more specifically, *egoism in the form of religion*" (Feuerbach 1841, 137). "If we remove the barriers of national consciousness, what we obtain in place of the Israelite is the *human being*" (ibid., 144). Elsewhere, in his *Principles of the Philosophy of the Future*, Feuerbach follows up this idea: "the highest and last principle of philosophy, is, therefore, the unity of man with man" (1843, 72). The truth and universality of the human being are achieved both through the loving union of man and woman in death and through the abandonment of all that is specifically Jewish.

As we can see, Feuerbach's androgyny is not an isolated, autonomous trope but an integral, organic part of a symbolic complex involving totality, communism, love, death, and anti-Semitism. And this same nexus of ideas recurs in Wagner's writings. Indeed, the parallels are so close that it is tempting to interpret the significance of Wagner's concept of androgyny as a function of Feuerbach's metaphysics at this particular point in the composer's career.

In an unfinished essay, "Das Künstlertum der Zukunft" (The artists of the future), Wagner envisaged an extension of Feuerbach's concept of communism: "It is in communism that egoism achieves its greatest satisfaction, in other words, through the total denial and supersession of egoism, since a need is satisfied only when it exists no longer" (1849j, *SS* 12.256). This same concept resurfaces in *The Art-Work of the Future* and *A Communication to My Friends*, as well as in *Jesus of Nazareth*, where there is a clear connection between communism, the abolition of egoism, and death: "The ultimate dissolution of the individual life into the life of the community is death; it is the ultimate and most definite abolition of egoism" (*SS* 11.299). "Through his death the individual achieves his creative involvement in life, for we know that, according to the law of nature, death is the result of expending a multiplying force" (*SS* 11.302–3). In this same draft Wagner rediscovers Feuerbach's Christian androgyny: "Jesus is quite right, therefore, to say: 'Man and wife are *one* flesh, God (love) had joined them together, and it is impermissible, just as it is impossible, to put them asunder'" (*SS* 11.305).

It is not possible, therefore, to interpret Siegfried's and Brünnhilde's androgynous union in death simply from the viewpoint of a writer like Novalis. Instead, we have to adopt the sociometaphysical standpoint of Ludwig Feuerbach, for whom death enables the individual to pass beyond his or her own individuality, transcending the difference between being and nonbeing and, by merging with the Thou, rejoining the great timeless All. It is this idea that lies behind Brünnhilde's words to Siegfried: "Du selbst bin ich" (Your own self am I [*GS* 6.178]) and behind Siegfried's words to Brünnhilde: "Nicht hab' ich mehr mich" (I no longer possess myself [*GS* 6.173]). Their union is finally crowned by death:

lachend lass' uns verderben,	Laughing let us perish,
lachend zu Grunde geh'n!	laughing go to our doom!

(*GS* 6.175)

The final lines of the act sum up this whole idea:

Erb' und Eigen,	My heritage and own,
ein' und all'!	my one and all!
Leuchtende Liebe,	Light-bringing love
lachender Tod!	and laughing death!

(*GS* 6.176)

Wagner himself confirmed this interpretation to Cosima after playing Act III of *Siegfried* to her on the piano: "The kiss of love is the first intimation of death, *the cessation of individuality*;[26] that is why a person is so terrified by it" (*CT*, 15 August 1869). As Wagner had told Röckel in his letter of 25/26 January 1854, individuation is an illusion. The fear that Siegfried feels on waking Brünnhilde may be apprehension at his awakening sexuality but it is also, and above all, a metaphysical sense of disquiet.

It would be wrong, therefore, to confuse the *Liebestod* announced and hoped for at the end of *Siegfried* with the Schopenhauerian *Liebestod* that forms the climax of *Tristan und Isolde*: for now, the kiss that presages death enables the couple to break down the egoism of the I in favor of that supreme unity through which one can taste immortality, a prelude to a return to the state of nature, the downfall of the gods, and the advent of a free society prepared for by Siegfried, that modern incarnation of Christ. At this stage in his development, Wagner's androgyny is the response—both social and metaphysical—to the drama of individuation.

It is clear that the thirst for the absolute, for totality, and for love is heavily scented with death, which is why Wagner was able to pass with such apparent facility from the "optimism" of Feuerbach to the "pessimism" of Schopenhauer. On 25/26 January 1854—several months *before* discovering *Die Welt als Wille und Vorstellung* (The world as will and representation)—Wagner was already able to write to Röckel, meditating at length on ideas that, more often than not, are simply a paraphrase of Feuerbach: "The true human being is both man and woman, and only in the union of man and woman does the true human being exist, and only through love, therefore, do man and woman become human."[27] "Egoism, in truth, ceases only when the 'I' is subsumed by the 'thou': this 'I' and 'thou,' however, no longer show themselves as such the moment I align myself with the wholeness of the world: 'I' and 'the world' means nothing less than 'I' alone; the world will not become a complete reality for me until it becomes 'thou,' and this is something it can become only in the shape of the individual whom I love."[28] Is such a union possible? Drawing on his own experiences, Wagner concludes that "love has now become wholly impossible."[29] Yet hope remains: his goal, he goes on, is "to render love possible as the most perfect realization of reality—truth; not a conceptual, abstract, nonsensuous love (the only kind possible *now*) but the love of 'I' and 'thou.'"[30] And this hope is given dramatic form in the mountaintop meeting of Siegfried and Brünnhilde: "Not even Siegfried alone (man alone) is the complete 'human being': he is merely the half, only with *Brünnhilde* does he become the redeemer; *one* man alone cannot do everything; many are needed, and a suffering, self-immolating woman finally becomes the true, conscious redeemer: for it is love that is really 'the eternal feminine' itself."[31]

This comes as no surprise: tomorrow's humanity presupposes the fusion in death of the two halves of the human being. "We must learn to die."[32] "Wotan rises to the tragic heights of *willing* his own destruction. This is all that we need to learn from the history of mankind: *to will what is necessary* and to bring it about ourselves."[33] Wagner was now ripe to respond to Schopenhauer, whose principal work he read in September–October 1854.

Chapter Six

MUSICA TRIUMPHANS (1851–1873)

Problems of Exegesis

Until now I have proceeded on the assumption that Wagner's writings pose no particular problems of interpretation. The reader may be surprised, therefore, on perusing the introduction to this second section, to discover that different writers on the subject have arrived at such widely differing views of the relationship between words and music—so widely differing, in fact, that I was able to divide them into three completely distinct families of "plots."

In fact, each of Wagner's essential concepts can all too easily lend itself to confusion. First, there is the word *dichten*, which essentially means "to compose a poem, to write verse." But, just as the Greek verb *poieîn* has the primary meaning of "to make, execute, prepare" and just as the noun *poiêsis* means "creation" before it means "the art of composition" or "poetry" in general, so Wagner's terms *dichten* and *Dichtung* may be used to refer to artistic creation in general and only secondarily to distinguish poetry from music. It is in this general sense that Wagner uses the term *Dichtkunst* in his open letter to Liszt, "On the 'Goethe Foundation,'" of 8 May 1851: "If we had a genuine art of poetry [*eine wirkliche Dichtkunst*], the other arts would be contained within it and would acquire their effectiveness through it" (1851g, *GS* 5.6). A few pages later he uses the word *Dichter* first in the sense of "poet," then in that of "creative artist" in general: "We can take account of the musician only from the point where he comes into contact with the poet [*Dichter*] and shares the latter's fate in the theater; in this regard he falls entirely into the category of creative artist [*Dichter*]" (ibid., 5.12). There seems to be little doubt that Wagner is intentionally playing on the word here.

As soon as we realize that whenever he uses the word "poet," Wagner may mean not only the creative artist in general but also the poet as opposed to the musician, a potential confusion arises, since it is no longer clear whether the libretto or the music plays the more important role in the art-work of the future.

The word *drama* is equally unclear. Let us take as our starting point one of the central claims of *Opera and Drama*: "The error into which opera as an art form has fallen is that a means of expression (music) has been made the end, while the true end (drama) has become the means" (1851a, *GS* 3.231). Glass is quite right to complain about the ambiguity of this phrase (1981, 23). In order for it to be intelligible, the word "drama" needs to be read in two different ways: the "means" is clearly the libretto, considered on the same level as the music, that is, as a constituent part of the work; the aim or end is the dramatic *content* of the work, mediated *by* the libretto and often described by Wagner as the "poetic intent." Elsewhere in Wagner's writings the word acquires a third meaning when it is used in the sense of drama as a specific art form, distinct from the genre of "opera."

It is tempting, therefore, to paraphrase the formula from *Opera and Drama* and convey its meaning in a less contradictory form: "The error consists in the fact that music has been turned into the aim of opera, when it ought to be a means to the end of drama as a genre, while the libretto has been treated as an operatic means, whereas, in drama as a genre, it is the dramatic content, mediated by the libretto, which should be the aim."

This paraphrase seems to me to be in keeping with Wagner's pronouncements elsewhere in *Opera and Drama* and also to reflect the legitimate distinction that Glass draws between the poetic intent and the poem. Nonetheless, to the extent that we have to explain the train of Wagner's thought, including what appears to be a radical change of position in 1870, it seems important that we should accept Wagner's terminological confusion as a given fact—a fact, moreover, that may explain how the composer-cum-theoretician can openly admit to having changed his standpoint. It may be noted, in fact, that in emphasizing the distinction that needs to be drawn between the poem of the libretto and the dramatic intent—and for this alone he deserves our thanks (1981, 15)—Glass presents us with a classic case of *reculer pour mieux sauter*. In my own view—and this is borne out by the interpretation of the word *dichten* proposed above—the poetic intent can mean *either* the subject matter mediated by the libretto *or* the poetic and musical dramatic design, which imposes an organic structure on the work. And that work in turn is produced by a single creative artist who, in writing the libretto, takes account of the expressive and formal possibilities inherent in music.

To these two levels of semantic ambiguity must be added a third, to which I drew attention in the first part of this study: music, in its embodiment as a woman, can be seen either as lover or as mother. As lover, it receives the fertilizing seed of the poetic intent and is therefore subject to the poet. As mother, it is in a creative situation comparable to that of the poet to the point of providing his poetic intent with its sense of orientation.

Only by bearing in mind these different levels of potential confusion when reading Wagner's post-1848 essays can we hope to understand the evolution in his conception of the relationship between poetry and music and thus come to terms with the transformations in his concept of androgyny.

Problems already arise with *Opera and Drama*. Can one claim, as Glass does, that Wagner conceives of poetry and music on an equal footing? "It is wrong," he writes, "to assume that Wagner, because he assigned poetry the masculine role, intended for poetry to dominate music; or that he meant for music, because he assigned it the feminine role, to be subservient to poetry. . . . I suggest that a more accurate way of viewing it might be in terms of balance or equilibrium rather than dominance and subservience" (Glass 1981, 273). Is this so certain?

After all, there is no mistaking the meaning of certain of Wagner's pronouncements. Take the crucial section of *Opera and Drama* in which he declares that music is a woman, before going on to specify how he conceives of it: "Woman achieves her full individuality only at the moment of self-surrender. . . . The look of innocence in a woman's eye is the pellucid mirror in which the man sees only the general capacity for love until such time as he sees his own likeness in it. Once he has recognized himself in it, the woman's all-consuming ability becomes a single pressing need to love him with the all-powerful force of her all-consuming desire for total self-surrender. The true woman loves unconditionally, since she *must* love" (1851a, 3.316). Wagner goes on to paint a portrait of Italian music as a whore, of French music as a coquette, and German music as a prude, before asking:

> What kind of a woman should *true music* be? A woman *who really loves*, a woman who places her virtue in her *pride*, her pride, however, in her *sacrifice*, in the sacrifice with which she surrenders not just one part of her being but her *entire being*, which she surrenders to the fullest extent of her ability at the moment of *conception*. But to *bear* what she has conceived, joyfully and gladly, is the woman's *deed*—and to perform deeds, woman needs only to be *entirely what she is*, not to *will* anything: for she can will one thing alone, and that is *to be a woman*! (Ibid., 3.319)

The music of the future will be a subjugated woman who will not be her own mistress.

This idea is not entirely new, since it had already appeared in slightly different form in *The Art-Work of the Future*: "Music acquired the power of the greatest, most loving self-sacrifice, namely, the power of self-mastery, the power to deny itself in order to hold out its redeeming hand to its sisters" (1849m, *GS* 3.96–97). Wagner's remarks are even more explicit and radical in the theological commentaries contained in the *Jesus of Nazareth* sketch:

> The essence of woman, like that of children, is egoism: woman does not give, she receives or simply returns what she has received. . . . Woman is imperfect in herself and can become active only in responding to a man's love. Only by merging with the man whose love she receives does she find the means by which to communicate her egoism to the generality of mankind. . . . But woman also complements man; his giving himself to her is the first outward expression of his own egoism, without which it would be impossible for him to merge creatively with the generality. (*SS* 11.304–5)

It is thanks to man, therefore, that woman has the opportunity to redeem herself.

Can one really claim that there is not in all this the idea of the poet's domination of music and that the variations that can be observed between the different texts are only questions of emphasis (Glass 1981, 269)? I do not think so. At the time of the Zurich essays, Wagner's view of androgyny was clearly one in which the feminine component was dependent upon the dominant masculine component.

In *Opera and Drama* the poetic intent that fertilizes music is defined, in no uncertain terms, as "the *subject matter*[1] that music must bring forth" (1851a, *GS* 4.103). The power of creation lies within the poet's fertilizing seed: "*Every musical organism is feminine by nature, it is an organism that can only give birth but is not procreative*" (ibid., 3.314). As the means of expression, music "*cannot, of itself, condition the aim of the drama*" (ibid., 3.308). Can we, on the basis of these strategically positioned pronouncements,[2] claim that, according to *Opera and Drama*, it is the poet who must abide by the conditions laid down by the nature of music (Glass 1981, 55)?[3] Can we—still on the basis of *Opera and Drama*—define the poetic intent as "the fertilizing seed that music took up into her womb to bring forth as drama" (Glass 1981, 3)? This will certainly be the case later when the childbearing wife gains ascendancy over the passive lover of the Zurich essays. It is precisely because the symbol of androgyny is so unstable—it has to be represented either as a man endowed with feminine features, as in the paintings of the pre-Raphaelites or Gustave Moreau, or as a woman with male attributes (one thinks, for example, of the chimera in Paul Chenavard's *Divina Tragedia*)—that it is important to bear in mind the ambiguity that lies at the very heart of Wagner's concepts. Otherwise it will not be possible to understand his conceptualization of the relationship between poetry and music or to explain why, on two occasions, Wagner openly admitted to having changed his mind (*CT*, 11 February 1872 and 4 August 1878). We shall return to this latter point in due course. For the moment, however, the forcefulness of the relationship is expressed in the clearest possible way. Only gradually will it be modified in favor of music.

From the Domination of the Poet to the Domination of Music

Scarcely had he completed *Opera and Drama* when Wagner returned to practical reality and broke a lance in favor of a theater worthy of that name in Zurich, which would be the embodiment of dramatic and musical unity. In Wagner's view the same company should run both the spoken theater and the opera: the singers, therefore, would have to be highly accomplished actors. "In consequence we would not have two companies, divided between plays and operas, but a single group of dramatic artists" (1851f, *GS* 5.41). And Wagner repeats his dream of a fusion between art and life, demanding that we abolish the distinction between actor and public and between the theater and society (ibid., 5.47, 51). In order for this to happen, the "force of some communal will" is required (ibid., 5.52), a will that Wagner aims to mold through his writings.

Five months later Wagner completed an essay that, albeit more obviously autobiographical in character, brings to an end the series of writings that I have been analyzing here: the principal merit of *A Communication to My Friends* is that it underscores Wagner's own admission that a change has taken place in his attitude toward the relationship between poetry and music. In his youthful works, the "imitative urge to write poetry was subordinated to the imitative urge to write music and pressed into service only to the extent that I needed to satisfy the latter" (1851h, *GS* 4.252). The most striking example of this is said to be *Das Liebesverbot*, which betrays a "lively leaning toward wild, sensual impetuosity" (ibid., 4.255). And to the extent that he associates this sensuality with music, the latter "exercised a creative influence on the subject matter and its organization from the very outset" (ibid.), encouraging Wagner to follow the bad example set by frivolous light French operas (ibid., 4.256). Having tended in the direction of "solemn seriousness" in *Die Feen* (ibid., 4.255), he now realized that it was necessary to find a balance between the two. Failing to find that balance, he wrote *Tannhäuser*, with its conflict between what Baudelaire termed "the two principles" of God and Satan (1861, 794).

Wagner goes on to insist, once again, on the need for love in uniting the arts (1851h, *GS* 4.264), while emphasizing the fact that the poem takes precedence over the music. Beginning with *Der fliegende Holländer*, he argues, "I was first and foremost a poet . . . and returned to being a musician only when setting the poem as a whole to music." But he introduces a nuance here that will make him veer increasingly toward the opposite view of the relationship between poetry and music, according to which music will no longer be the servant of the drama but its mother: "But *I was a poet who was conscious in advance of the expressive musical potential of his poems.*"[4] It is still, however, the poetic act that dominates: "I had exercised this faculty to the point where I was perfectly aware of my ability to use it in realizing a poetic intent and could not only reckon on the help of this ability when drafting a poetic sketch but, safe in that knowledge, could formulate such sketches *more freely*, more in keeping with poetic necessity, than if I had formulated them merely with an eye to the music" (ibid., 4.316–17). In writing the poem for *Siegfrieds Tod*, Wagner was fully conscious of the fact that "henceforth it was the subject matter that was important, a subject seen through the eyes of music" (ibid., 4.320). In analyzing the *Ring* as a mythological history of music, I showed that the character of Siegfried was clearly associated with the poet. In *A Communication to My Friends* Wagner states explicitly that Siegfried is "the spirit of eternally and uniquely creative spontaneity, embodied in masculine form" (ibid., 4.328) and that it was because of this that he conceived the idea of using alliterative verse for the poem of *Siegfrieds Tod* (ibid., 4.329). Immediately he picks up the sexual imagery that he had used in his last great essay: "In the final section of my book *Opera and Drama*, I spoke at some length about this verse form and about the way in which it acquires that form from the deeply and inwardly generative force of *language*, pouring that force into the female element of music" (ibid.). The choice of vocabulary is significant: as at the end of the second section of *Opera and Drama*, music "gives birth"; it is not procreative. And it will be noted that it is language, the poetic potential inherent in language, that is said to fertilize music.

With the exception of its shift toward music, *A Communication to My Friends* contains little else that is new—little else, that is, apart from an interesting link between the sexual metaphor associated with poetry and music, on the one hand, and, on the other, the concept of communism, which is here contrasted with egoism. In making this connection, the essay offers a kind of synthesis of the essential arguments of *Opera and Drama* and the social perspective that, typical of *Art and Revolution* and *The Art-Work of the Future*, reflects the philosophical teachings of Ludwig Feuerbach.

In *A Communication to My Friends* Wagner distinguishes between what he calls the force of the receptive faculty (*Empfängnisvermögen*), the poetic force, and the communist force. By the "force of the receptive faculty" he means the artist's capacity for giving himself "without reserve to those impressions that strike a sympathetic chord in his emotional being" (ibid., 4.246–47). If he abandons himself to it totally, the artist will become "an *absolute* artist and develop in the direction that we must describe as feminine, in other words, that which embraces the feminine element of art alone" (ibid., 4.247). Once again the feminine element is passive, but the impressions received by this receptive faculty have to be communicated, and this is the work of the "truly *poetic*" force: "Let us define this as the masculine, *generative*[5] path of art" (ibid., 4.247–48). As before, the choice of words comes as no surprise. It is, however, what Wagner describes as the "communist" force (ibid., 4.248) that allows the poetic force to reveal itself. He locates genius on the side of the receptive faculty—a force both individual and feminine—while the communist force, for its part, conditions the effects of the individual genius and allows his work to share the "purely human" attributes of the collective effort. As with Feuerbach, it is the abandonment of female egoism in favor of the male creative force that enables the heterosexual couple of art to transcend individuation in pursuit of a metaphysical and social whole.

In February 1851 and again in February 1852 we find Wagner twice drawing on the sexual metaphor, albeit in the context of instrumental music. In a program note on Beethoven's *Eroica* Symphony, he has the following to say on the fourth movement:

> Around this theme—which we can regard as embodying resolute male individuality—gentler and more tender feelings wind and cling from the very onset of the movement, developing to the point where they announce that pure feminine element, which, with ever more intense, more varied sympathy, finally reveals itself to the masculine first-subject group as the overwhelming power of *love*, as it strides energetically through the entire piece. . . . From the transport of melancholy the jubilant voice of that power breaks forth in which, wedded to love, *the whole, complete human being* now cries out in jubilation, avowing to his godhead. (1851e, *GS* 5.172)

The following year Wagner wrote a program note for a performance of Beethoven's *Coriolan* Overture:

> If, without erring in the least, we can interpret almost all the composer's symphonic works, in terms of the plasticity of their expression, as representing scenes between man and woman, and if we may find the archetype of all such scenes in that very dance from which the symphony, as a work of musical art, is derived, we may conclude that we have such a scene before us here, a scene of the most sublime and affecting content imaginable. (1852c, *GS* 5.173–74)

Written seven years after Adolf Bernhard Marx's *Lehre von der musikalischen Komposition*, these are the first of Wagner's writings, so far as I am aware, in which sonata form is clearly described in terms of androgyny.

They usher in a period in Wagner's thinking where, sexually speaking, music may be self-sufficient.

Between 1852 and 1860 Wagner wrote no fewer than twenty-seven texts of varying kinds, although none of them approaches *A Communication to My Friends* or "Über musikalische Kritik" (On music criticism) in terms of the density of its theorizing. Throughout these nine years Wagner would be largely absorbed by strictly creative ventures—the libretto of the *Ring*, the music of *Das Rheingold*, *Die Walküre*, and the greater part of *Siegfried*, and the music, finally, of *Tristan und Isolde*. Sexual metaphors disappear, although Wagner continues to evoke the relationship between poetry and music.

The open letter to Franz Brendel, "On Music Criticism," dates from January 1852 and is written in the spirit of the great theoretical essays that we have already studied: "In its noblest development, our music has already set out in the direction in which it must necessarily achieve its most genuine significance, through marriage with the *art of poetry*" (1852a, *GS* 5.60). It is the poet "who must necessarily join with the most genuine composer in order to encourage that total harmony from which the flower of true art shall spring" (ibid., 5.61). Rediscovering the Greek conception of *mousikê*, Wagner enjoins music critics to interpret "music in its widest possible significance, whereby poetry and music are indissolubly linked" (ibid., 5.63). In other words, critics must take account of the dramatic and literary aspect of future works of art, rather than concentrating solely on their musical dimension. If, at the same time, Wagner sings the praises of Wilhelm Baumgartner, a composer whose lieder are largely forgotten today, it is because the Swiss composer "was able, by means of his art [music] to express the emotion that a poem evokes in him" and "to find the verses that will provide the living subject matter needed to discover the necessary melody" (1852b, *SS* 12.287–88). From the point of view of the creative process, it is still the poem that fertilizes the music. A letter to Uhlig of around 13 February 1852 advances the same idea: "What is characteristic about Beethoven's great orchestral works is that they are real poems in which an attempt is made to represent a real object."[6] Writing once again about the *Coriolan* Overture, he insists that Beethoven's aim is the drama, a drama that—as the context of Wagner's remarks makes clear—will be told by the plot or narrative. It is for this reason, he concludes, that "Beethoven has hitherto been understood only by the nonmusician."[7]

That same year—1852—Wagner drew up a series of instructions for performing *Tannhäuser* (1852e) and *Der fliegende Holländer* (1852h). In both cases the drama clearly takes precedence. In the case of *Tannhäuser*, for example, we read that the work's "only chance of being effective lies in the accord between stage and music." The conductor must "pay the closest possible attention to the poem and, ultimately, to the numerous special instructions for its stage presentation" (1852e, *GS* 5.125–26). And the same is true of the performers: "The singer who, in keeping with the *poet's* aim, is incapable of declaiming his part with the requisite expression and of treating it as an acting role will also be incapable of singing it in the way that the *composer* intended, still less will he be able to interpret the character" (ibid., 5.127). A similar remark occurs in a letter to Liszt of 8 September 1852, in which Wagner discusses Berlioz: "He needs a poet to fill him through and through, a poet who is driven by ecstasy to violate him, and who is to him what man is to woman."[8] It is difficult to claim, on this basis, that music, as a woman, is not subject to man.

On 1 November 1853 Wagner began work on the score of *Das Rheingold*. The tone changes. In his letter to Röckel of 25/26 January 1854, for example, he writes: "I have once again realized how much of the work's meaning (given the nature of my poetic intent) is only made clear by the music."[9] A similar idea recurs in a famous letter to Liszt of 6 December 1856: "It is strange, but only in the course of composing the music does the essential meaning of my poem dawn on me."[10] Even more significant, however, is his letter to Liszt of 7 June 1855; whereas he had previously lauded to the skies Beethoven's setting of Schiller's ode *To Joy*, he now claims that the final movement is "without doubt the weakest section" and "important only from the point of view of the history of art"[11]—a critical assessment that seems to the present writer to be altogether faultless. In his open letter on Liszt's symphonic poems, begun in December 1856, when he was already working on some of the earliest musical sketches for *Tristan und Isolde*, Wagner assigns to music a metaphysical status that he had not previously accorded it: "*Into no matter what combination it enters, music can never cease to be the supreme redeeming art*. It is in the nature of music that, through it and in it, what all the other arts merely hint at becomes the most indisputable certainty, the most direct and definite of truths" (1857, *GS* 5.191). And in his open letter to Berlioz of 1860, Wagner returns to the point that "only through the combination of *all* the arts" would "the uniquely true, great work of art" be produced (1860b, *GS* 7.84). Here, too, he discusses the complementarity of the arts. But there is no longer any reference to music's dependency on poetry. Although he goes on to mention *The Art-Work of the Future*, Wagner now regrets having published it, because, he claims, critics had gone out of their way to misunderstand it (ibid., 7.85). But might not the reason also be that Wagner no longer held the views to which he had subscribed a decade earlier?

According to Henri Lichtenberger, whose analysis of Wagner's thinking still bears reading, "there is no essential difference between *The Art-*

Work of the Future and *Opera and Drama*, on the one hand, and '*Zukunftsmusik*' (September 1860), on the other" (1898, 202). In fact, the latter essay finds Wagner continuing to move in the direction of the metaphysical superiority of music, a shift of attitude first noted in 1854.

"*Zukunftsmusik*" (originally published in French as *Quatre Poèmes d'Opéra précédés d'une Lettre sur la musique*) purports to be a résumé of the ideas contained in the theoretical writings of 1848–51 with which French audiences were expected to familiarize themselves before reading the four libretti included in the volume (*Der fliegende Holländer*, *Tannhäuser*, *Lohengrin*, and *Tristan und Isolde*) and before seeing *Tannhäuser* for themselves on the stage of the Paris Opéra. The differences between this essay and the writings of ten years earlier are certainly revealing.

As in the earlier essays, Wagner conceives of music as the complement of poetry. If, in the debate between the Gluckists and the Piccinnists, music had sometimes appeared to be the essential component of opera, it was because libretti were too platitudinous to provide the necessary counterweight (1860c, *GS* 7.102). It was only the perfect marriage of poetry and music that would allow perfection to be achieved in drama (ibid.). Up to this point, then, there is nothing new in Wagner's line of thinking. But he then goes on to insist that "only the musician, not the poet, can alter [musical] forms" (ibid., 7.103). That is, it is the poet who has to modify the nature of his collaboration.

What Wagner goes on to claim comes as no surprise, even though it is not what he had said in 1850: "The symphony must strike us very much as a revelation from another world, . . . impressing itself upon us with the most overwhelming conviction and influencing our feelings with such certainty that our powers of logical reasoning are completely confused and disarmed" (ibid., 7.110). As a result of the autonomous development of music, poetry is confronted with a "power that is bound to seem more powerful than any logic" (ibid.). That power is the power of music, as exemplified by Beethoven's symphonies. To the extent that the ideal remains the *union* of poetry and music, the poet has to plan the libretto as a function of the immense expressive possibilities of music. Of course, even in *A Communication to My Friends*, Wagner had written that "as a poet," he was "conscious in advance," when elaborating his poems, "of the expressive potential of *music*" (1851h, *GS* 4.316). But there is no doubt that in "*Zukunftsmusik*," we are dealing with a complete reversal of the relationship between the two component parts:

> Poetry will easily find the means to achieve this end and recognize that its ultimate resolution and merger with music is its own innermost desire as soon as it becomes aware of a need in music that poetry alone can satisfy; . . . Why? . . . The poet who succeeds in answering this question will be the one

> who is fully alive to music's aim and to its inexhaustible expressive potential and who therefore plans his poem in such a way that it can penetrate the finest fibers of the musical texture, allowing the spoken *thought* to resolve entirely into *feeling*. (1860c, 7.111–12)

It is no longer the poet alone who fertilizes music here: thanks to the development of melodic form, the poet "will pick up a secret from the musician—a secret hidden even from that musician—namely, that melodic form is capable of an infinitely more varied development than the musician might yet have thought possible even in symphonic music; and, presaging this development, he will already plan out the poetic conception with altogether boundless freedom" (ibid., 7.129). Increasingly, therefore, the poet is becoming as much a musician as a poet pure and simple. In a word, he is now a creative artist.

It is no longer poetry that will impregnate music. Wagner now speaks of the "intimate merger of music and poetry in drama" (ibid., 7.112), of "*the equal and reciprocal interpenetration of music and poetry*[12] as a precondition of a work of art that, at the moment of its stage performance, would be bound to leave an irresistibly compelling impression" (ibid., 7.116). And even though Wagner refrains from citing *Tristan*, the music of which he had completed as recently as August 1859 (in other words, shortly before beginning *"Zukunftsmusik"*), it is understandable that this recent creative experience should have led to the change in his theoretical position: "Conversely, there had to remain the possibility of finding a poetic counterpart to the symphonic form in the dramatic poem itself, a counterpart that, while completely filling that ample form, should best reflect the innermost laws of dramatic form" (ibid., 7.127–28). At the same time, music adapts itself to the demands of the libretto in order to transcend it through the expression of feeling: "this melody is already poetically constructed"; "the complete foreshadowing of the musical form can already lend a special value to the poem in accordance with the poet's will" (ibid., 7.123).

> The poet will now call out [to the symphonist]: "Plunge fearlessly into the full flood of the sea of music; hand in hand with me you can never lose contact with what is most comprehensible to every human being: for with me you stand on the solid ground of dramatic action, and this drama, at the moment of its representation on stage, is the most directly understandable of all poems. Spin out your melody boldly so that it may pour out across the whole work like some uninterrupted river: in it say what I myself keep silent since you alone can say it; and in silence I shall say everything, since I lead you by the hand." (Ibid., 7.129)

Wagner allowed himself to be borne along by the flood tide of music: in writing *Tristan*, "I completely forgot all my theorizing, . . . since I acted here in total freedom and in utter disregard for every theoretical consideration, so that only during the process of composition did I myself become aware to what extent I had transcended my own system" (ibid., 7.119). Wagner thus places music on an equal footing with poetry, granting it a status that it had not previously enjoyed.

Wagner's Encounter with Schopenhauer and the Composition of *Tristan und Isolde*

The new position accorded to music is one that Wagner had extrapolated from his own experience. Whereas the various Zurich essays, including *Opera and Drama*, had been written at a time when he was exclusively occupied with libretti as opposed to music,[13] *"Zukunftsmusik"* dates from a period when he had already completed the scores of *Das Rheingold* (November 1853–September 1854), *Die Walküre* (June 1854–March 1856), the first two acts of *Siegfried* (September 1856–August 1857), and *Tristan und Isolde* (December 1856–August 1859). As Jack Stein has noted, these are all works in which music, through the treatment of the motifs, assumes an increasingly important role. A close study of *Das Rheingold* shows in fact that only half the motifs originate in the melodic line, where they are closely bound up with the text; the remainder emerge from the orchestra alone, hence the difficulty in attaching a precise semantic label to them (Stein 1960, 95–97). In *Die Walküre* thirteen new motifs make their first appearance in the orchestra, against five in the vocal line (Stein 1960, 110). With the Ride of the Valkyries the music takes over and dominates the action (Stein 1960, 106). The first two acts of *Siegfried*, written between September 1856 and August 1857, underscore this tendency: in keeping with the theoretical standpoint adopted in *Opera and Drama*, the music is certainly subordinated to the rhythm of the poem, but at the same time there are ten new autonomous themes here, and the orchestra grows in size (Stein 1960, 119–20, 126–27, 130).

In September–October 1854, on the recommendation of Georg Herwegh, Wagner read Schopenhauer's *The World as Will and Representation*. Although this new philosophical encounter certainly did not unleash a revolution in Wagner's thinking, it equally certainly helped him to conceptualize what his newfound experience as a composer had taught him, investing it with a metaphysical dimension. And this is as true of his now-blurred relationship with Feuerbach as it is of his dealings with Schopenhauer.

In the third part of his principal work, "The World as Representation: Second Aspect," Schopenhauer accords music the highest place in the hierarchy of the arts, after architecture, landscape gardening, sculpture, painting, poetry, and tragedy. Music, he argues, is not a representational art but "the copy of an original that can itself never be directly represented" (1819, 1.257). In consequence, it has an essential function in his system, representing not ideas (as is the case with the other arts) but the will itself, which, in Schopenhauer's view, is the essence of all things, both material and spiritual. Music thus represents what is inaccessible, "the inner nature, the in-itself, of every phenomenon" (ibid., 1.261). The other arts "speak only of the shadow, but music of the essence" (ibid., 1.257). Melody "portrays every agitation, every effort, every movement of the will, everything . . . which cannot be further taken up into the abstractions of reason" (ibid., 1.259). Thanks to music, the composer is able to reveal "the innermost nature of the world and expresses the profoundest wisdom in a language that his reasoning faculty does not understand" (ibid., 1.260). Hence, no doubt, the music's independence of the text: "Even other examples, just as arbitrarily chosen, of the universal expressed in a poem could correspond in the same degree to the general significance of the melody assigned to this poem; and so the same composition is suitable to many verses" (ibid., 1.263). Wagner clearly had these ideas in mind not only when writing *"Zukunftsmusik"* but also when he came to write his *Beethoven* essay in 1870.

As always, however, Wagner draws no distinction between theoretical reflection and the content of his music dramas. In 1860 he advances a new interpretation of *Lohengrin*, an interpretation defined by the relationship between poetry and music as he now sees it. Thus Elsa's question to Lohengrin—"Whence have you come?"—is comparable to the theoretical question that the artist addresses to himself (1860c, *GS* 7.122): why does poetry yearn in secret to dissolve into music (ibid., 7.111)? This is a question to which the symphony can provide no answer. Only poetry can do so (ibid., 7.112), just as only Lohengrin can answer Elsa's question. Moreover, the true answer can be provided only by the poet who is "fully aware of music's aim and its inexhaustible power of expression"—the poet, in short, who adopts the only possible form of expression, which is drama (ibid.). The spectator "falls into a state of ecstasy in which he forgets to ask the fatal question 'Why?' and, stimulated to the highest degree, allows himself to be guided by those new laws that make music so wonderfully intelligible and that—in a deeper sense—provide the only fitting answer to the question 'Why?'" (ibid., 7.112). The significance of this is clear: the true answer to Elsa's question is *Lohengrin* as a work, while the error committed by Elsa in her guise as music, at least as interpreted by Wagner in 1860, is that, like Brünnhilde, she renounces the power of intuitive knowledge, which is that of both music and womankind.

By 1860 Wagner had ceased to use the metaphor of androgyny to describe the relationship between poetry and music, not least because that relationship was in the process of changing. This does not mean, however, that all references to androgyny have disappeared, for we shall find them again in *Tristan und Isolde*, albeit in a form compatible with the newly defined relationship between the two.

In discussing the love duet in Act II of *Tristan*, specialist writers have drawn attention, above all, to the reminiscences of Novalis's *Hymnen an die Nacht*, which we examined above, and have insisted rather less on the presence of androgyny in this passage. The most notable exception, perhaps, is one of the leading experts in the field, the self-styled Sâr Péladan,[14] who in his 1911 treatise *La Science de l'Amour* asserted that "Isolde is the man and Tristan the woman," before going on to ask whether Wagner had been aware of the fact that, in this way, he was depicting "the highly secret myth of the androgyne" (113). Péladan's interpretation clearly smacks of the ambiguity that typified approaches to androgyny at the end of the nineteenth century, yet what seems to justify his observation is that it is Isolde who effectively controls the action of the opera, playing the role of leader. But is this enough to claim—as Péladan does—that Isolde has homosexual leanings? The situation is more complex and less stereotyped than Péladan makes out.

With the exception of *Die Meistersinger*, all Wagner's operas are built up on the same underlying schema: the man dies (the Dutchman, Tannhäuser, Siegfried, Tristan) or disappears (Lohengrin), and the woman redeems him through her own self-sacrifice (Senta, Elisabeth, Elsa, Brünnhilde, Isolde). (Kundry pays with her death for her belated submission to her redeemer.) At the same time, however, and rather more frequently, it is the woman who, positively or negatively, motivates the plot: Senta dreams of the Dutchman and breaks with Erik; Elsa invokes Lohengrin and asks the forbidden question; and Brünnhilde, as the embodiment of Wotan's real will, obeys the god, provokes the birth of Siegfried, and prepares for the final act of redemption by setting fire to Valhalla. Nonetheless, it is the Dutchman and Lohengrin who decide to leave, and Wotan who, following his initial error, resolves to renounce the world. And it is Hagen who sets in train the intrigue that enmeshes Brünnhilde and leads to Siegfried's death.

In *Tristan* things are more straightforward. Isolde invites Tristan to die in the very first act. She interferes with the potions—of course, it is Brangäne who substitutes the love philter for the death draught but just as Brünnhilde embodies Wotan's will, so Brangäne embodies Isolde's.[15] And it is Isolde who stage-manages the meeting with Tristan in Act II and who, in Act III, informs King Marke of her love for Tristan, which sets in train the drama's final events, with the arrival of Tristan's companions and the deaths of Melot and Kurwenal.

Above all, however, it is Isolde who, in the course of the love duet, invites Tristan to find redemption in death. It is she who is first to utter the words:

dort dir zu trinken	to drink eternal love
ew'ge Minne,	to you there,
mit mir—dich im Verein	in union with me
wollt' ich dem Tode weih'n.	I wanted to mark you out for death.

(*GS* 7.41)

To which Tristan replies:

In deiner Hand	When, in your hand,
den süßen Tod,	I beheld
als ich ihn erkannt	the sweet death
den sie mir bot;	that love had offered:
als mir die Ahnung	when foreboding,
hehr und gewiß	sublime and certain,
zeigte, was mir	showed what atonement
die Sühne verhieß:	held in store:
da erdämmerte mild	then gently dawned
erhab'ner Macht	within my breast
im Busen mir die Nacht;	the exalted sway of night;
mein Tag war da vollbracht.	my day then sunk from sight.

(*GS* 7.41–42)

Thereafter Tristan merely follows the course prescribed by Isolde:

TRISTAN

In des Tages eitlem Wähnen	Amid day's empty fancies
bleibt ihm ein einzig Sehnen,	one longing alone remains:
das Sehnen hin	the longing
zur heil'gen Nacht,	for hallowed night,
wo ur-ewig,	where everlasting,
einzig wahr	uniquely true,
Liebes-Wonne ihm lacht!	love's rapture smiles on him.

BOTH

O sink' hernieder,	Sink down upon us,
Nacht der Liebe.	night of love!

(*GS* 7.44)

It is only after Brangäne's Watch Song, in the midst of the love duet, that Tristan regains the initiative. To quote Wagner himself: Isolde "does not wish to contemplate the death he has resolved on for them, until he persuades her, and both then find their highest happiness in this decision" (*CT*, 11 December 1878). It is in terms of androgyny that Isolde voices this hesitation:

Doch uns're Liebe,	But our love—
heißt sie nicht Tristan	is its name not

und—Isolde?	Tristan and Isolde?
Dies süße Wörtlein: und,	This sweet little word "and"
was es bindet,—	—if Tristan died,
der Liebe Bund,	would that which it binds
wenn Tristan stürb',—	—the bond of love—
zerstört' es nicht der Tod?	not be destroyed by death?

(*GS* 7.47)

As a hero well read in Schopenhauerian metaphysics, Tristan seizes the initiative and, in a spirit of renunciation, replies to Isolde's question:

Was stürbe dem Tod,	What could die
als was uns stört,	save that which impedes us,
was Tristan wehrt	preventing Tristan
Isolde immer zu lieben,	from always loving Isolde
ewig ihr nur zu leben?	and living forever for her alone?
. . . .	. . . .
So stürben wir,	So we would die
um ungetrennt,	that, undivided,
ewig einig,	one forever,
ohne End',	without end,
ohn' Erwachen,	never waking,
ohn' Erbangen,	never fearing,
namenlos	namelessly
in Lieb' umfangen,	by love enfolded,
ganz uns selbst gegeben	given wholly to each other,
der Liebe nur zu leben!	we might live for love alone!

(*GS* 7.47–48)

Whereas Siegfried and Brünnhilde had recognized themselves in the other's features before seeing their androgynous union transfigured by death, it is death that, in the case of Tristan and Isolde, provides the precondition for their androgynous union:

TRISTAN

Tristan du,	Tristan you,
ich Isolde,	I Isolde,
nicht mehr Tristan!	no longer Tristan!

ISOLDE

Du Isolde,	You Isolde,
Tristan ich,	Tristan I,
nicht mehr Isolde!	no longer Isolde!

BOTH

Ohne Nennen,	Nameless,
ohne Trennen,	nevermore parted,

neu Erkennen,	newly perceiving,
neu Entbrennen;	newly kindled;
endlos ewig	endlessly infinitely
ein-bewußt:	aware of our oneness,
heiß erglühter Brust	love's supreme delight
höchste Liebes-Lust!	ardently glowing in our breast!

(*GS* 7.50–51)

Although Joseph Kerman (1956, 162) is doubtless right to remark that as the work progresses from act to act, Tristan's role increases in scope, it is no less true that, dramatically speaking, events remain in Isolde's control, that Tristan merely accepts the death that she has been preparing for him from the opening act, and that she rejoins him in the Love-Death first heard in the prelude to Act I. It is she who, from first to last, actuates the lovers' androgynous union. Jean Matter is right, therefore, to claim that "at every stage in this tragedy, it is Isolde who controls the action: she is bound, as it were, to the fate that has decreed that it shall be so. Here is a definitive instance of that mystery of the woman who guides the man in love" (1977, 269). There is androgyny, certainly, in *Tristan*, but it is an androgyny in which the woman now plays an active role as intermediary. And to the extent that Wagner still associates music with the female sex, we may legitimately look for examples of this more active role within the music itself.

No one can doubt that in *Tristan und Isolde* it is music that predominates. Wagner himself declared as much to Cosima: "In *Tristan* he gave himself up entirely to music" (*CT*, 4 October 1881). "In my other works the motifs serve the action; in this, one might say that the action arises out of the motifs" (*CT*, 15 September 1873). In tracing the "rise" of music in Wagner's theoretical writings, Jack Stein (1960, 141–42) finds an echo of this in Acts II and III of the work: vowels are lengthened and syllables extended to such a degree that "the conceptual meaning is submerged, and little remains but pure tone." This is particularly true of the climax of the love duet ("höchste Liebeslust"). Stein goes on to show that the structure of the musical phrase takes precedence over the logic of the words (1960, 143–44), much as in Wagner's early operas, in which the music was Wagner's foremost concern. (That there is no comparison on the level of style scarcely needs to be added.)

It is the assimilation of music with the female element that is our principal concern here. Against the background of my own interpretation, Édouard Lindenberg's fine analysis stands out in particular and deserves to be quoted at length:

> Wagner wanted to use the orchestra to comment on the action as seen through Isolde's eyes and soul. Musically speaking, the characters—and above all that of Tristan—are presented from Isolde's point of view. So long

> as their feelings remain a secret to her, they engender no response in the orchestra, which is otherwise so quick to underscore the slightest beating of the heroine's heart.
>
> Thus, in the opening act, when Kurwenal intones the words "Message from Isolde," Tristan replies with a shudder: "What's that? Isolde?" only to pull himself together and refer to her with the respect that is her due: "From my mistress?" There is no trace of this agitation in the orchestra, which merely announces Tristan's objective theme to indicate that Isolde has her eyes fixed firmly on him.
>
> By contrast, Isolde's anger reverberates in the orchestra in Act I, scene 5, following Tristan's reply, "Ask custom!" Yet she herself remains calm when replying: "Since you, Sir Tristan, are so mindful of custom." But as soon as her partner's thoughts are revealed to her, the orchestra seizes hold of them. An example of this occurs somewhat later in the same scene, where the words "oblivion's kindly draught" make it clear to Isolde that Tristan has known from the beginning of the scene that she is offering him the death potion. Having believed that she could trick Tristan, Isolde now realizes her mistake, allowing the orchestra to accompany her words with the motif associated with death. When, earlier in the same scene, Tristan asks, "Where are we?" and Isolde replies, "Near our goal!" the same motif allows us to grasp the double meaning with which she wants to invest the word *goal*: for her it means death, whereas for Tristan, whom she believes to be ignorant of her deadly intentions, it means only their journey's end, Marke's Cornish kingdom.
>
> And finally, when Brangäne, unaware of the love that consumes Isolde's soul, attempts to force her secret from her mistress, the orchestra reveals what Isolde conceals: one by one, we hear the Glance motif, fragments of the Tristan motif and—following the phrase "Confide in Brangäne!"—the Desire motif. Isolde replies with the words "Air! Air! I'm suffocating!"
>
> Moreover, not only does the action begin and end with Isolde but she is on stage throughout the entire opera, with the single exception of the beginning of Act III, by which point her absence—however much it may involve Tristan in an impassioned wait—can no longer affect the thematic nature of the work or prevent the spectator from being intimately involved with the character of Isolde.
>
> It is impossible, in the space available, to do more than sketch out my point of view, but if called upon to justify it, I would mention only that, strictly speaking, Isolde does not have her own motif. Why? Because all the leitmotifs (I use the term advisedly in order to distinguish them from themes and melodies) are in fact related to Isolde, images seen through her eyes or reflections of her dream-world. (Lindenberg 1974)

Juliard is not wrong, therefore, to argue that "the androgyne that Wagner was seeking was essentially feminine" (1979, 66), so long as we remember that this is merely a new and temporary phase in the evolution of Wagner's concept of androgyny.[16]

Can we interpret the characters of *Tristan und Isolde* as allegories of Wagner's new theoretical position, as was the case with the *Ring*? In order to answer this question, we need first to have examined the *Beethoven* essay of 1870. Suffice it to observe at this juncture that the principle of analogy continued to preoccupy Wagner's thoughts. In May 1868, for example, at a time when he was still contemplating plans for a stage work on the subject of *The Victors*, he made the following entry in *The Brown Book*:

Truth = nirvana = night
Music = brahman = twilight
Poetry = samsara = day

And he comments on the equation thus: "Brahman becomes desire, as music; the music that is turned toward samsara, poetry; which is the other, the side that is turned away from samsara? Nirvana—untroubled, pure harmony?" (1865g, 148). It is impossible not to be struck by the analogy not only with *Tristan* and its progression from day to dusk and finally to night but also with the dominant, intermediary role played here by music: truth is ultimately associated with night, nirvana, and the union of poetry and music.

Poetry and Music in the *Beethoven* Essay of 1870

After the *"Zukunftsmusik"* essay of 1860, a further ten years were to elapse before Wagner returned to the problem of the relationship between poetry and music. Other preoccupations provided a distraction. The nationalist element to his thinking, which had been temporarily forgotten at the time of the 1848 revolution, now returned with a vengeance not only in *Über Staat und Religion* (On state and religion [1864c]) but also in his proposals for a German school of music (1865b), in his musings on the question "What is German?" (1865h), and, finally, in his definition of German art (1867) and its insufferable corollary, the reprinting, in expanded form, of the 1850 essay "Judaism in Music" (1869a).[17] Still concerned with model performances, he also wrote his magisterial essay *Über das Dirigiren* (On conducting [1869h]), which deserves to be reread even today.[18]

Here and there we find the occasional allusion to "music and poetry holding out their hands to one another" (1865b, *GS* 8.161), and to that "deep and tender passion, the expression of which alone allows music to be raised to the same heights as poetry" (ibid., 8.168). On 25 July 1869

Wagner explained to Cosima "how differently one must work in the symphony and in music drama, where all is [musically] permissible except stupidities, since the action explains everything." And on 16 August 1869 he told her: "In me the accent lies on the conjunction of poet and musician, as a pure musician I would not be of much significance." In all these cases one might perhaps think that Wagner was reverting to his earlier belief in the supremacy of poetry as propounded in the Zurich essays, a standpoint that might well surprise the reader, coming, as it does, only a year before the *Beethoven* study of 1870. (This is certainly the case with Abbate 1989b, 103–4.) There is, however, no contradiction if we assume—as we have assumed since the time of *A Communication to My Friends*—that the poet creates his verses with music's expressive potential in mind and if, in the most general sense of the term, it is he who conceives the work's dramatic development. It is not until some nineteen years after *A Communication to My Friends* that the *Beethoven* monograph, written to mark the centenary of Beethoven's birth, celebrates the triumph of music, bringing to an end this particular period in the evolution of Wagner's thinking.

The entire essay is based upon the Schopenhauerian concept of music: the Sage of Frankfurt, Wagner insists, "believes that he must see in music itself an idea of the world" (1870d, *GS* 9.66). Poetry is suddenly relegated to a lower level, a level at which there is a radical shift in position away from the standpoint adopted in *Opera and Drama*:

> For it is not, in fact, the meaning of the Word that holds our attention on the entry of the human voice [in the Ninth Symphony] but the human character of that voice. Similarly, it is not the ideas expressed in Schiller's verses that continue to lay hold of our minds but the familiar sound of the choral singing, which we feel encouraged to join in, thus participating in some ideal divine service, just as the congregation would join in at the entry of the chorales in Sebastian Bach's great Passions. It is patently clear, especially in the case of the principal melody itself, that Schiller's words have been laid under the vocal line with little skill and as a makeshift measure. (Ibid., 9.101)

If this is so, one is tempted to ask whether the words serve any useful purpose? In the case of the *Missa solemnis*, "we do not understand the conceptual significance of the text, which serves simply as material for the vocal line" (ibid., 9.103). Wagner goes on to generalize and define his own position:

> The relationship between music and *poetry* is altogether illusory, since it can be shown that in vocal music it is not the poetic thought that one hears—in choral singing, in particular, that thought is not even intelligibly articu-

> lated—but at most the mood which that thought aroused in the musician, inspiring him, as music, to create music. The union of music and poetry is bound to end, therefore, in the latter's subordination, so that we can only marvel at the fact that our great German poets have kept on returning to the problem of how to combine both these arts, constantly reassessing that problem and even attempting new solutions. (Ibid., 9.103–4)

There could be no more blatant expression of Wagner's change of attitude toward the Ninth Symphony than the foregoing passage, with its reversal of the views advanced in *Opera and Drama*. Yet Glass refuses to see in *Beethoven* a radical break with the earlier essay (1981, 77). A glance at Wagner's text shows that he is wrong. For the later Wagner, the final movement of the *Choral* Symphony is reduced to the dimensions of a "cantata with words, to which the music bears no closer relation than to any other sung text. We know that it is not the verses of a librettist—be he a Goethe or a Schiller—that *determine*[19] the music; this is something that drama alone can do, by which I do not mean the dramatic poem but the drama that actually unfolds before our eyes, the visible counterpart of the music, where word and speech no longer belong to the poetic thought but solely to the action" (1870d, 9.111–12). According to Glass, Wagner finally draws an explicit distinction here between the drama as a poem and drama as dramatic action, so that, from this point of view, the theoretical position of 1870 could be seen as an extension of the concept of poetic intent advanced in *Opera and Drama*: "Only the poet who has first become a musician is in a position to know what sort of poetry to write for the composer to set" (Glass 1981, 77).

Admittedly, the poetic intent was defined in *Opera and Drama* as one that "provides music, that gloriously loving woman, with the subject matter that she must bring forth" (1851a, *GS* 4.103), yet it is equally clear from the imagery that Wagner uses that the music has to submit to that intent. No doubt Wagner finally managed to clarify the distinction between libretto and the subject matter of that libretto, but to claim that he draws that distinction in *Opera and Drama* is to fall into the trap of a retrospective interpretation. Moreover, the poetic intent in *Opera and Drama* is clearly that of the poet in contradistinction to the musician, whereas what Wagner says in *Beethoven* is that words and discourse are no longer dependent on the poetic thought ("der dichterische Gedanke": 1870d, 9.112) but on the action ("die Handlung": ibid.), as the "visible counterpart of the music" ("als sichtbar gewordenes Gegenbild der Musik": ibid.). In other words, it is now music that plays the leading role, poetry being no more than its reflection; as such, it governs the course of the drama. It is significant in this context that Wagner uses the same word, "Handlung" or "action," to describe *Tristan und Isolde*, thereby acknowledging the supremacy of music. That there has been a complete volte-face on Wagner's part is confirmed by the rest of the essay.

In turning his attention to *Fidelio*, Wagner argues that "this subject matter contained so much that was alien to music, so much that could not be assimilated into it that it is really only the great *Leonore* Overture that reveals the way in which Beethoven wanted the drama to be understood. Who can hear this thrilling piece of music without being consumed by the conviction that music contains within itself the most consummate *drama*?" (ibid., 9.105). And by drama he means something more metaphysical, namely, the direct expression of the thing-in-itself—the Schopenhauerian will—which music alone can reveal:

> Music does not represent the ideas contained in the world's phenomena but is itself an idea of the world, and a comprehensive one at that. *In consequence it includes drama as a matter of course, since the drama, in turn, expresses the only idea of the world that is commensurate with music.*[20] Drama towers over the bounds of poetry in exactly the same way that music towers over those of every other art, especially the visual arts, since its *effect*[21] lies solely in the sublime. Just as a drama does not depict human characters but allows them to reveal themselves directly, so a piece of music gives us, through its motifs, the character of all the world's phenomena according to their innermost essence. Not only are the movement, form, and evolution of these motifs related, by analogy, to the drama alone, the drama that represents the idea of the world can be fully understood only through music's moving, formative, and evolving motifs. We would not go far wrong, therefore, if we were to see in music man's a priori capacity for fashioning drama in general. (Ibid., 9.105–6)

The 1870 definition of drama is no longer that of 1851. Whereas Wagner had earlier argued that music "cannot, of itself, determine the aim of the drama" (1851a, *GS* 3.308), he now sees the drama less as the subject matter that results when the poet's fertilizing seed impregnates music than as the global, transcendent dramatic outline, the essence of which is expressed by music. It will not be long before he describes music as the "mother" of the drama.

On 11 February 1872 Cosima noted in her diary: "Of *Opera and Drama*, which he is correcting, he says, 'I know what Nietzsche didn't like in it—it is the same thing that Kossak took up and that set Schopenhauer against me: what I said about words. At the time I didn't dare to say that it was music that produced drama, although inside myself I knew it.'" One can, of course, cite this passage in support of the argument that it is legitimate to interpret *Opera and Drama* in the light of what followed, and Glass, at least, does not hesitate to avail himself of this possibility (1981, 270). But the fact remains that in admitting this, Wagner recognizes that by 1870 his ideas had changed and were no longer compatible with what he had claimed in 1851. If—shortly afterward—he speaks of the "perfect agreement" between *Opera and Drama* and his latest theoretical writings—which he nonetheless concedes contain certain "new aspects" (1871a, *GS* 9.127), it is partly because he is unable to admit publicly that he was wrong and partly because he believes he has finally succeeded in giving clear expression to the relationship between music and dramatic content.

One would expect every sexual metaphor to have disappeared from Wagner's writings by now. That this is not the case, however, will become clear in the course of the following discussion, in which we need to examine a series of somewhat unexpected texts—much as I examined the draft of *Wieland the Smith* and the poem of the *Ring* in the context of Wagner's Zurich writings.

"The Ancient Tune . . ."

In the third part of his autobiography, Wagner recalls his stay in Venice following his flight from Zurich in 1858:

> On a sleepless night that drove me out on the balcony of my apartment at about three o'clock in the morning, I heard for the first time the famous old folk song of the gondolieri. I thought the first call, piercing the stillness of the night like a harsh lament, emanated from the Rialto, barely a quarter hour's distance away, or thereabouts; from a similar distance this would be answered from another quarter in the same way. This strange melancholy dialogue, which was repeated frequently at longish intervals, moved me too much for me to be able to fix its musical components in my mind. . . . Such were the impressions that seemed most characteristic of Venice to me during my stay, and they remained with me until the completion of the second act of *Tristan*, and perhaps even helped to inspire the long-drawn-out lament for the shepherd's horn at the beginning of the third act. (*ML* 578)

Thus the song of the Venetian gondoliers was one of the possible sources for the Shepherd's *alte Weise* or "ancient tune" in *Tristan und Isolde*.[22] But we need to relate this allegedly autobiographical account to a passage from another text of the same period, namely, *Beethoven*:

> One sleepless night I stepped out on to the balcony of my room overlooking the Grand Canal in Venice; the fairytale city, built upon the Lagoon, lay before me, stretched out in shadow like a deep dream. From out of the breathless silence came the powerful, strident, and desolate cry of a gondolier who had just woken up in his barque; again and again he repeated the cry, calling into the night, until, from the farthest distance, the same call

> came answering back along the midnight-black canal: I recognized the ancient, melancholic melodic phrase to which, in their day, Tasso's well-known lines had once been set but which, in itself, must be just as old as the city's canals and population. After a series of solemn pauses, the distant dialogue grew more lively, seeming to merge into a single unison call until the sounds, both near and far, died away at last in newfound slumber. (1870d, *GS* 9.74)

Although Wagner does not allude to *Tristan* here, the connection that he makes in *Mein Leben* between the singing of the gondoliers and the cor anglais solo in Act III of *Tristan* entitles us to reinterpret his remarks in *Beethoven* about the dialogue of the gondoliers and to read into them a reference to the music of *Tristan*. One is more than ever inclined to do so on reading Wagner's reference, a few lines later, to the "ranz des vaches" sung by the herdsmen in an Alpine valley in the Swiss canton of Uri: there is no doubt, after all, that Swiss folk music has left its mark on the yodeling passage for solo cor anglais in bars 78 to 86 of the Act III prelude.

The passage just quoted comes at the end of a lengthy résumé of Schopenhauer's conception of music and of the links that Wagner establishes with the philosopher's theory of dreams. For Schopenhauer, music is the incarnation par excellence of the idea, through which we gain access to the innermost essence of things, including the actual ego and the will. The section as a whole rests on dichotomous reasoning. Our consciousness may have an intuitive awareness of the external world, but it can also be turned inward toward the self and the inner world, and thereby achieve a state of true clairvoyance. The external world corresponds with light, the visible universe, and the waking state, while the inner world is reflected in night, the sound world, and dreams. Now, according to Wagner's paraphrase of Schopenhauer, a dream is made up of two parts, the deep dream and the language of a second allegorical dream that leads consciousness to a waking state. In much the same way, Wagner explains, there is movement between the will and the immediate image of its intuition, which leads in turn to an awareness of either the inner or the outer world. What is of interest in the context of our present discussion, however, is that Wagner goes on to show that this process is equally characteristic of composition: "For just as in that phenomenon [i.e., the dream] the introverted consciousness achieves true clairvoyance; in other words, it achieves the power of seeing where our waking consciousness, turned toward the day, has only a vague impression of the nocturnal[23] ground of our will's emotions, so it is from this night that sound bursts upon the world of waking perception, as a direct expression of the will" (ibid., 9.68). Or, to put it another way: at the moment of waking, our consciousness gains access to the will—in other words, to the innermost essence of things—by turning back toward the world of dreams that it has just left. The immediate expression of the content of that essence is the sound world. It is the composer's task, therefore, to reveal the very content of the will and bring it to the listener's consciousness: "His music is itself an idea of the world" (ibid., 9.72). Consciousness then launches an appeal aimed at understanding nature in all her infinity, and it is music that provides the response: "The object of the perceived note coincides precisely with the subject of the emitted note: we understand, without the intermediary of reason, the call for help, the cry of lamentation, or the shout of joy, and we reply straightway in a corresponding vein" (ibid., 9.71). A few pages later Wagner asserts that "the will cries out; and it recognizes itself in the countercry: thus cry and countercry become a consoling and, ultimately, delightful game with each other" (ibid., 9.74). It is at this juncture—within the framework of his explanation of this vast metaphysical conception—that Wagner alludes to the calls of the gondoliers and the Alpine herdsmen of Uri.

There is no doubt that we are intended to interpret the Shepherd's *alte Weise* within the context of this metaphysical approach to dreams and music. Immediately after evoking the Venetian gondoliers and Swiss herdsmen and their calls, Wagner goes on to claim that whether we hear calls or whether we listen to music, we immediately recognize "that dreamlike state . . . in which that other world is revealed to us, *a world from which the musician speaks directly to us*"[24] (ibid., 9.75).

The oneiric context of this passage and, in particular, this final phrase will no doubt have reminded the reader of an identical context in Act III of *Tristan*, where the hero is wakened by the Shepherd's call: "Die alte Weise;— / was weckt sie mich? / Wo bin ich? . . . Wer ruft mich? . . . Was erklang mir?" (The ancient tune—why does it wake me? Where am I? . . . Who calls me? . . . What sound was that? [*GS* 7.58–59]). It is the same melody as that which "once told the child of his father's death" and revealed "his mother's destiny" to him (*GS* 7.65–66). In waking, Tristan returns from the kingdom of the dead, of which the dream is a mere metaphor:

Ich war—	I was—
wo ich von je gewesen,	where I have ever been,
wohin auf je ich geh':	where I shall ever go:
im weiten Reich	in the vast realm
der Welten Nacht.	of universal night.
Nur ein Wissen	One lore alone
dort uns eigen:	is ours there:

göttlich ew'ges	divinely eternal
Ur-Vergessen.	age-old oblivion.

(*GS* 7.61)

For Tristan death is the kingdom where he could finally forget and no longer be plagued by desire, but the "ancient tune" reminds him that the death of his parents, doubly linked to his conception and birth, dooms him likewise to death. And this is something he can forget only in death itself.

What, then, is the significance of the solo cor anglais in this context? Tristan himself provides the answer when the Shepherd's tune returns in the middle of the act:

Die alte Weise,	The ancient tune
. . . .	. . . .
die nie erstirbt,	that never dies
sehnend nun ruft	now calls yearningly
um Sterbens Ruh'	to the distant healer,
sie der fernen Ärztin zu.	longing for the peace of death.

(*GS* 7.66)

The "distant healer" is Isolde, the embodiment of love and death. Tristan awakes from a dream, returning to the waking world from a land akin to Hades. If Tristan is seen as a latter-day Orpheus, the cor anglais solo would be the symbolic incarnation of music itself, of that infinite melody that Tristan heard in the oneiric world of death, a melody with which he seeks to defy the march of time itself: "Although music draws those elements of the phenomenal world that are most closely related to it into what we have termed her dream-world, it is only to turn our intuitive faculties inward, so to speak, through a wondrous transformation that enables them to grasp the essence of things in their most immediate manifestation and thus interpret the vision that the musician himself had beheld in deepest sleep" (1870d, *GS* 9.77).

Who, then, is Tristan from the standpoint of the allegorical interpretation of the characters that guided us in our exegesis of the *Ring*? Tristan is the composer of *Tristan*: in his dream he has had access to the essence of those things that are represented by the music and, on awakening, listens to the music as the idea of the world. *Tristan ist der Dichter*: from the perspective of *Beethoven*, he is musician and poet, the creator of that dramatic action that, in turn, is the "visible counterpart of the music" (ibid., 9.112). This begs the question as to the identity of Isolde.

Once again, the answer comes from the *Beethoven* essay under review and, more specifically, from the musical interpretation of Goethe's *Faust* that Wagner offers here:[25] what we understand by the lines "Das ewig Weibliche / zieht uns hinan" (The eternal feminine / draws us on) is "the spirit of music that soared aloft from the poet's deepest consciousness and which now hovers over his head, showing him the way to redemption" (ibid., 9.125). But who is it who guides Tristan—the poet and creator of the musical drama—to redemption if not Isolde, the spirit of music? And is it mere chance that, in her final transfiguration, Isolde asks:

Höre ich nur	Do I alone
diese Weise,	hear this tune
die so wunder-	which, so wondrous
voll und leise,	and gentle,
Wonne klagend,	joy bemoaning,
Alles sagend,	all-revealing,
mild versöhnend	gently consoling,
aus ihm tönend,	sounding from in him,
in mich dringet,	pierces me through
auf sich schwinget,	and soars aloft
hold erhallend,	as, sweetly dying,
um mich klinget?	it echoes around me?

(*GS* 7.80)

The melody that Isolde alone can hear is already familiar to us from the end of the love duet in Act II, where it accompanies Tristan's words to Isolde, "Tristan you, I Isolde, no longer Tristan!" and Isolde's words to Tristan, "You Isolde, Tristan I, no longer Isolde!" Known as the Redemption motif, this theme might legitimately be renamed the Androgyny motif; such is the semantic malleability of Wagner's leitmotifs.

Example 13

In both *Tristan* and the *Beethoven* essay we are no longer dealing with male-dominated androgyny in which the poet, as author of the libretto, joins with the composer of the music, but with a female-dominated variant in which the female spirit of music (*der Geist der Musik*) dictates to the poet-composer (*der Dichter*), telling him what plot he has to construct and what music he has to write.

1575
[Isolde]
Du — I - sol - de,
Tri - - -
[Tristan]
zart dolce
Träu - men: Tri - - - stan. — du, —
dolce
1580
- - stan — ich, —
nicht —
ich — I - sol - de,
p dolce
1585
— mehr I - sol - de!
nicht — mehr — Tri - stan!
più p
pp
morendo

Example 14

Wagner and Nietzsche

Although there is no mistaking Schopenhauer's influence on the *Beethoven* essay of 1870, it is nonetheless worth reexamining the relationship between poetry and music as it affected the relations between Nietzsche and Wagner.

The young Nietzsche published *Die Geburt der Tragödie* (The birth of tragedy) at the end of 1871, a little over a year after Wagner's *Beethoven* essay, which dates from 20 July to 7 September 1870. Most writers have tended, therefore, to emphasize Wagner's influence on Nietzsche (Halévy 1944, 153, 160; Westernhagen 1978, 411–12; Borchmeyer 1986, 117).

There is no question of challenging the generally accepted view that Wagner, now recognized as the master, exercised a certain ascendancy over the much younger man. Nietzsche's correspondence, after all, confirms that this was the case: "What I learn and see, hear and understand there [at Tribschen] is indescribable," he confessed to Rohde on 3 September 1869. "Schopenhauer and Goethe, Aeschylus and Pindar are still alive, believe me." At any rate, it is worth taking a closer look at two of Nietzsche's texts that, although not published until after his death, predate *Beethoven*. Both were familiar to Wagner and Cosima. *Das griechische Musikdrama* (Greek music drama) was the title of a lecture that Nietzsche delivered in Basle on 18 January 1870 but that he had been planning since 28 September 1869, while *Socrates und die Tragödie* (Socrates and tragedy) was delivered on 1 February 1870. Although the text of the first of these lectures was not read at Tribschen until somewhat later (11 June 1870), the second provided the basis for a "lengthy conversation" on 12 February 1870, shortly after its receipt by the Wagner household.

Wagner's influence on Nietzsche is patently obvious. Reporting on the philosopher's first meeting with her husband at Tribschen, Cosima records that Nietzsche "knows R.'s works thoroughly and even quotes from *Opera and Drama* in his lectures" (*CT*, 17 May 1869). Without going so far as to claim that Nietzsche exerted a fundamental influence on Wagner, we may nevertheless ask whether the exchange of ideas that took place between the two men does not explain, in part, the theoretical shift that is discernible in the *Beethoven* essay of 1870. If the Schopenhauerian thrust of this monograph is as evident as it is explicit, why is it only now that music suddenly becomes an "idea of the world," rather than, say, in *"Zukunftsmusik,"* written ten years earlier, at a time when Wagner had not only read Schopenhauer but also composed *Tristan*?

Nietzsche paid his first visit to Tribschen on 17 May 1869. We know that he returned there between 5 and 7 June, 31 July and 1 August, 21 and 23 August, and for the whole of the Christmas vacation, from 24 December 1869 to 2 January 1870.[26] Cosima's diaries contain an echo of the conversations that took place between the two men on the subject of the philosophy of music. The arrival of the text of the lecture *Socrates and Tragedy* at Tribschen elicited enthusiastic congratulations on the part of Richard and Cosima in their letters of 4, 5, and 6 February 1870.

The aim of the first lecture was to remind Nietzsche's audience that all we know nowadays about ancient drama is the text and that in attempting to understand it, we have failed to take account of its musical dimension. Although he picks up an idea from *Opera and Drama*—that "the word impinges first of all on the conceptual world and only subsequently on feeling"—he goes on in the same breath to insist that "music affects the heart directly, as the true universal language that is everywhere understood" (Nietzsche 1870a, 1.528–29). In doing so, he accords music an importance that it did not have in 1851 and that, even in 1860, was not expressed in such unequivocal terms: "We are not qualified to discuss Greek tragedy, since its principal effect rested, in no small measure, on an element that has been lost, namely, music" (ibid., 1.528). "Even in terms of its language, the dominating influence of music had become all-powerful" (ibid., 1.531). In the second of the two lectures, *Socrates and Tragedy*, Nietzsche insists that "tragedy foundered on an optimistic dialectic and ethic, which is as much to say that music drama foundered on a lack of music" (1870b, 1.548). "The effectiveness of antique tragedy rested . . . on those grandiose, broadly structured scenes of great emotion in which the basic musical character of the Dionysian dithyramb was once again to be heard" (ibid., 1.538). The audience of Nietzsche's day would know there was someone in Germany who was able to respond to the philosopher's final appeal and put forward an alternative to grand opera as a form of pure entertainment (ibid., 1.549).

I am not suggesting that Nietzsche had the same degree of influence on Wagner that Schopenhauer did but simply that he could have played the part of a catalyst, more especially on this one particular point.

It is noteworthy that in both these lectures Nietzsche insists on the *effect* of music. Admittedly, Wagner describes Beethoven as a creative artist who, in the act of *composing*, treats Schiller's poem as a mere pretext. But he also underscores the impact of the music on the listener. In their search for a synthesis of the arts, the great German poets "were clearly guided by the effect of music in opera" (1870d, *GS* 9.170), he writes in *Beethoven*. This insistence on the *effect* of music rather than on the *production* of the work of art is a novel development in Wagner, as Dahlhaus has rightly emphasized (1984, 116–17). Wagner—who finally heard his *Tristan und Isolde* on 10 June 1865 and *Die Meistersinger* on 21 June 1868, had every reason to be receptive to Nietzsche's observations. The latter read *Greek Music Drama* to the Wagners on 11 June 1870; on 20 July Wagner began his *Beethoven* essay.

Music as the Mother of Drama

The post-*Beethoven* articles of 1871 and 1872 confirm the shift in Wagner's point of view: music now gives birth to the drama, and the role of the poet, as author of the libretto, definitely appears to be secondary.

In his public lecture of April 1871, *On the Destiny of Opera*, Wagner insists—as he had in the *Beethoven* monograph—that the drama is reinforced by the music. *Don Giovanni* is described here as a "drama that is musically conceived" (1871a, *GS* 9.136). In *Don Giovanni* and *Iphigénie*, Mozart and Gluck "found the drama transported by its music to the sphere of the ideal" (ibid., 9.138). But a new idea appears here—the importance of acting as an extension of the music: it is this, Wagner argues, that can still ensure the drama's impact in spite of the weakness of its libretto and the poverty of its music. As an illustration of what he means, he cites the example of Wilhelmine Schröder-Devrient in Bellini's *I Capuleti e i Montecchi*: "This effect certainly did not lie in any vocal virtuosity, as is the case with the ordinary successes enjoyed by our true operatic sopranos, since her own virtuosity was slight and altogether unsupported by voluptuousness of vocal means: the effect was due simply to her dramatic rendition. Yet not even Schröder-Devrient herself could have succeeded in this regard in the finest of all spoken plays, since her achievement lay only in the element of music, which has an idealistically transfiguring influence even in this most wretched of forms" (ibid., 9.140). What Wagner refers to here as mime or mimic improvisation (ibid., 9.143) is simply acting, which he adduces to explain the effect of the drama as *inspired by the music*, the model for which has been bequeathed to us by Elizabethan actors (ibid., 9.143–46). In consequence, modern opera will not be effective as a genre until such time as the poet conceives his work by latching on to the original affinity that exists not between the poem and the mime but between music and the mime: "What both of them [the musician and the "poetic mime"] directly create and form is the true work of art *of which the poet merely drafts the outline*[27]—a task in which he will be successful only if he borrows that plan from their own nature" (ibid., 9.148), in other words, from the musical and mimic force. "If we abide by this definition of 'mimico-musical improvisation of consummate poetic value fixed by supreme, artistic, conscious recollection' and if we apply it to the work of art as we ourselves envisage it, a surprising light will be thrown on the practical aspect of its performance, when seen from the standpoint of empirical perception" (ibid., 9.149–50). As Stein points out (1960, 173), the work that Wagner was thinking of here was *Die Meistersinger von Nürnberg*, which was written—with interruptions—between November 1861 and October 1867. First performed on 21 June 1868, it was the last work Wagner completed before embarking on the essay currently under discussion and one in which gesture plays a notable role: consider, for example, the Dance of the Apprentices, the Midsummer Eve riot, the scene between Beckmesser and Sachs, and so on. "What, from a practical point of view, was impossible for Shakespeare—that is, to act every one of his roles—the composer achieves with the greatest ease by speaking to us directly through each of his performing musicians" (ibid., 9.150). The gesture of the singing actor is a direct extension of the musical "gesture," and it is in this sense that we should interpret the famous formula found in the essay "On the Term *Music Drama*" of October 1872: "I should have been happy to describe my dramas as *deeds of music made visible*" (1872t, *GS* 9.306). It is the genius of music that, combined with "mimic improvisation," can regenerate German opera.

In the essay *On Actors and Singers* of September 1872 Wagner picks up the idea that the work of art can be amplified by the acting. Drawing on the same maternal imagery, he cites the example of the ancient theater, albeit in a very different sense from the one conveyed by the essays of 1849–50: "The *orchestra* of the antique theater is the magic retort, the fruitful matrix of the ideal drama whose heroes, as has rightly been pointed out, reveal themselves to us on stage only as two-dimensional beings, whereas the magic that emanates from, and is guided by, the *orchestra* is uniquely able to fill each possible dimension in which the individuality that appears there can be revealed" (1872r, *GS* 9.196). As in the earlier essay, where Wagner speaks of Apollonian and Dionysian elements without mentioning Nietzsche by name (1871a, *GS* 9.138), so Nietzsche's influence is evident here, too. In *Greek Music Drama* Nietzsche writes: "During its golden age the chief and overall effect of Greek tragedy still lay in the chorus. . . . It is the chorus that prescribes the limits of the poet's imagination as revealed in tragedy. . . . Action was added only when dialogue came into being" (Nietzsche 1870a, 1.525–27). In Wagner's essay this becomes "It was the whole element of music that pervaded the entire drama, however exiguous its forms, and thus transferred it to that ideal sphere for which even the most meaningful poetic diction had proved inadequate" (1872r, *GS* 9.198). "*The womb that bore [the drama] must be sought in the element of music from which tragedy as a work of art was born*"[28] (ibid., 9.198).

On Actors and Singers was written in September 1872. It seems clear that Wagner is indebted to Nietzsche for the image of music as the mother of the drama. A copy of Nietzsche's first major essay—the very title of which (*The Birth of Tragedy from the Spirit of Music*) is highly significant in this context—was sent to Tribschen on 2 January 1872. Wagner's response was as immediate as it was enthusiastic: "Never have I read anything more beautiful than your book! How splendid it is! I am writing to you quickly now because reading it has left me so inordinately excited that I must first await the return of reason before reading it *properly*."[29] Wagner's enthusiasm is understandable. After all, Nietzsche had begun his essay by recalling that for Schiller, the "act of creation" was preceded by a "*musical mood*" (Nietzsche 1872, 49) and that in folk songs, "melody gives birth to the poem from within itself, ever again" (ibid., 53). And he had gone on to apostrophize Wagner as the artist who had successfully reconciled the two fundamental principles of Greek art, namely, the Apollonian and the Dionysian (ibid., 99–104), even suggesting that through him audiences might soon be able to witness "the yet-impending rebirth of Hellenic antiquity" (ibid., 123). "Having reached its highest manifestation in tragedy, [the Heracleian power of music] can invest myths with a new and most profound significance. This we have already characterized as the most powerful function of music" (ibid., 75). How could Wagner have failed to recognize himself in such descriptions as the following: "Lyric poetry is dependent on the spirit of music just as music itself in its absolute sovereignty does not *need* the image and the concept but merely *endures* them as accompaniments" (ibid., 55)? Nietzsche draws the conclusion that music has the ability "to give birth to *myth* (the most significant example), and particularly the *tragic* myth: the myth that expresses Dionysian knowledge in symbols" (ibid., 103). With the image of music as the mother of myth and tragedy, Nietzsche helped Wagner to overturn what he had written in *Opera and Drama*: "What will become of the eternal truths of the Dionysian and Apollonian when the styles are mixed in this fashion . . . ? A style in which music is regarded as the servant, the text as the master, where music is compared with the body, the text with the soul? . . . Out of the Dionysian root of the German spirit a power has arisen . . . —*German music* as we must understand it, particularly in its vast solar orbit from Bach to Beethoven, from Beethoven to Wagner" (ibid., 119).

It is difficult to know whether Wagner was alive to the existence of an androgynous dimension to Nietzsche's thinking. After all, *The Birth of Tragedy* opens with the words "We shall have gained much for the science of aesthetics, once we perceive not merely by logical inference but with the immediate certainty of vision, that the continuous development of art is bound up with the *Apollonian* and *Dionysian* duality—just as procreation depends on the duality of the sexes, involving perpetual strife with only periodically intervening reconciliations" (ibid., 33). And, a little later, "These two different tendencies run parallel to each other, . . . until eventually, by a metaphysical miracle of the Hellenic 'will,' they appear coupled with each other and, through this coupling, ultimately generate an equally Dionysian and Apollonian form of art—Attic tragedy" (ibid.).

Cosima Wagner's diary for 3 January 1872 (the day after the receipt of Nietzsche's monograph) contains the following striking entry: "[R.] calls me his priestess of Apollo—he says I am the Apollonian element, he the Dionysian, but we made an alliance, a pact, and from it came Fidi [the Wagners' son, Siegfried]." If Wagner is quick to apply the sexual metaphors of *The Birth of Tragedy* to his own domestic situation, he is less ready to reintroduce into his theoretical writings the latent theory of androgyny to which Nietzsche himself had given more explicit expression in one of the posthumously published fragments relating to his essay:

> The fact that nature has linked the birth of tragedy with those two basic urges of the Apollonian and Dionysian may strike us just as much as an abyss of reason as a precaution of that same nature that linked the propagation of the species with the duality of the sexes—which never ceased to astonish the great Kant. The secret that is common to both is that something new can arise from two mutually inimical principles, something, moreover, in which those divisive instincts appear as a unity: in this sense propagation may be regarded just as much as the tragic work of art as a guarantee of the rebirth of Dionysus, as a glimmer of hope on Demeter's eternally grieving countenance. (Nietzsche 1988, 7.179; fragment of late 1870—April 1871)

For Nietzsche, it seems that the Wagnerian drama issued from the androgynous union of the Dionysian and the Apollonian.[30]

Under Nietzsche's influence the image of music as the mother of the drama became a metaphorical constant during this period. Wagner returns to it in October 1872 in an article in which he comments on, and criticizes, the term *music drama*: "What is understood by the name of music is an *art* that was originally the epitome of all art" (1872t, *GS* 9.304). Music, Wagner goes on, quoting Goethe, is "that part which once was all" (ibid., 9.305): clearly he is thinking of the Greek *mousikê* as the union of poetry and what we nowadays call music. Music "now feels called upon to reassume its ancient dignity as the mother's womb of drama. Yet in this higher calling it must stand neither before nor behind the drama: it is not drama's rival but its mother" (ibid., 9.305). In her diary entry of 4 November 1872 Cosima records the following musings on Wagner's part: "In the morning R. says that he has again been thinking about the birth of drama from music: 'As the baby is nourished in the womb by the mother's blood, so does drama emerge from music; it is a mystery; once it emerges into the world, the outward circumstances of life begin to exert their influence.'" Is this the mystery of some latter-day immaculate conception? Wagner's introduction to a public reading of the poem of *Götterdämmerung* in January 1873 seems to offer an explanation:

> By always allowing us to feel the innermost motives of the action in their widest ramifications, music also enables us to present this drama with drastic clarity. . . . While antique tragedy had to limit the dramatic dialogue by dividing it up among separate sections strewn between the choruses, the

archetypally creative element of music, investing the drama with a higher significance in the form of those choruses performed in the *orchestra*, is no longer separated from the dialogue in that greatest of modern artistic achievements, the modern orchestra, but always accompanies the action and, in a deeper sense, may be said to embrace all the action's motives in its mother's womb. (1873b, *GS* 9.309)

Why is music the mother of the drama? Because the dramatic poem—in this case that of *Götterdämmerung*—"owes its existence solely to the possibility of a complete musical realization" (ibid., 9.309). Music is the *fons et origo* of the dramatic action and hence of the poem since it was as a function of the music that the drama was conceived.

Here, too, Stein finds proof of the dominance of music not only in the abundance of motifs that invade the third act of *Siegfried* but also in the presence of symphonic interludes, including Siegfried's Funeral March, in *Götterdämmerung*, where it is often impossible to ascribe a precise semantic function to the musical motifs (Stein 1960, 189–202).

It is only if one neglects the importance of the male-dominated figure of androgyny in *Opera and Drama* that one can see merely shifts of emphasis in Wagner's symbolic approach. In *Opera and Drama* it is the drama that gives birth to the music, whereas it is clear from all the later essays that it is now music that gives birth to drama, both as a genre and in the form of the dramatic action. Of course, Wagner's changing conception of womankind was predictable, since woman can be both lover and mother, but, having previously been passive and submissive, she now becomes active and creative. She no longer engenders but conceives. In the essays of 1871 and 1872—that is, the writings that postdate *Beethoven*—the image of the woman as mother allows Wagner to continue using sexual metaphor to describe the artistic process, even if androgyny as such has disappeared. Needless to say, the author of the libretto is still very much in evidence, but he is no longer a part of the symbolic construction: by this stage in his theoretical development, Wagner no longer conceptualizes his theory in terms of a male-female contrast or relationship. To find such explicitness we must wait for the articles of 1879.

Chapter Seven

THE RETURN OF ANDROGYNY (1878–1883)

The Essays of 1879

There are no significant texts for five years, but there is a good reason for this silence: Wagner was absorbed in preparations for the first Bayreuth Festival in 1876, so that when, in 1879, he was consumed by a new desire for theorizing, he had behind him the experience of staging the *Ring* according to his own instructions, even if the production fell far below his expectations. Not only was he reminded of the intellectual atmosphere of 1848–52, the work itself now *existed*: the score had been performed and the drama realized on stage. Moreover, Wagner had finished the first complete musical draft of *Parsifal* on 16 April 1879.

After the direction adopted in the *Beethoven* essay of 1870, it is clear from Cosima Wagner's diary entry of 4 August 1878 that by the late 1870s, a further shift of emphasis had taken place in Wagner's outlook: "R. says . . . these three books, *Opera and Drama*, *Art and Revolution*, and *The Art-Work of the Future*, are his most significant works." A few weeks later, on 22 September, Wagner repeated the same idea: "He tells Herr L[ipiner] that attention must now be drawn to his theoretical writings." There is a change here, certainly, but the evidence is too incomplete for one to infer that the Wagner of 1878 was still clinging tenaciously to all he had written in the course of his Zurich essays. After all, we have seen him presenting *"Zukunftsmusik"* as a summary of ideas that he had held in Switzerland, whereas the assertions made there were often radically different in kind. In 1871, he even claimed that *On the Destiny of Opera* agreed in every detail with the tenets of *Opera and Drama* (1871a, *GS* 9.127). Cosima Wagner's diaries attest to the fact that in August 1878 Wagner was deeply preoccupied with the problems of staging *Parsifal*, which he was then in the process of setting to music. Although this in itself may well explain Wagner's attitude, it is worthwhile, nonetheless, looking in greater detail at the three 1879 texts, which it seems legitimate to regard as the theoretical counterpart to his final music drama. The essay "On Poetry and Composition" of June 1879 not only returns us to the unitarian concept of a common origin, it also reinstates the poet in his former role, turning him into the person who masters poetry and music and who gives the word "music" the sense that it had in ancient Greece, in other words, the union of poetry and what we today call music: "The writer of lyric tragedies was not a poet, for only by mastering and deploying the highest art [i.e., music] was he able *to create the world desired by the poet*[1] and place the folk in the position of the clairvoyant poet. In this way the art of 'music' came to embody every inspiration by some divine vision, together with the order needed to clarify that vision" (1879c, *GS* 10.145–46).

A month later, in July 1879, Wagner returned, with the additional zest of the Buddhism that he had inherited, in part, from Schopenhauer, to the androgynous metaphor of *Opera and Drama*. In his article "On Opera Libretti and Composition in Particular," we find him writing as follows: "If, as I have explained in figurative terms elsewhere, the poet's task can be described as the male principle, while the music, by contrast, is the female principle in a union that aims to create the greatest synthesis of the arts [*Gesamtkunstwerk*], then I may perhaps be permitted to compare the result of the penetration of the words of *Euryanthe* by Weber's genius as the fruit of the marriage of a Chandala man with a Brahman woman" (1879e, *GS* 10.167).

How are we to interpret this passage? A Chandala man is of a lower caste than a Brahman woman, so that Wagner goes on immediately to say that the union of a Brahman man and a Chandala woman can produce a legitimate offspring, whereas the son of a Chandala man and a Brahman woman is regarded as an outcast. The context in which the comparison appears makes its meaning plain: the problem with German opera—including Weber—is that the musical genius (here compared with a Brahman woman) has been paired with the type of inferior poetry (compared with a Chandala man) that is fabricated by mediocre rhymsters and poetasters. "In the first part of my great treatise *Opera and Drama*," Wagner goes on, "I tried as best I could to explain my ideas concerning the lamentably, not to say heartbreakingly, instructive, state of affairs relating to the work by Weber already mentioned, taking pains more especially to demonstrate that even the richest musical melodist is not capable of making a true work of art out of a compilation of verseless German verses intended for a poetically pretentious opera text" (ibid., 10.168). In true German opera—which, of course, is Wagner's own—the poem will be on a par with the music. Having recently affirmed that music is the mother of the drama, Wagner now returns to the idea that even the best music depends for its success on the choice of a good dramatic libretto, but he does not say—and it makes a significant difference—that the music must *submit* to the poet. Quite the opposite. Whereas in 1851, the poet had been the dominant partner, it is now music that plays the fundamental role, just as it does in *Tristan* and *Parsifal*. This is the lesson of the essay "On Poetry and Composition": "It was no longer the poet who was left to structure the tragedy but the lyric musician" (1879c, *GS* 10.145).

In returning to the original metaphor, Wagner does not make any fundamental change to the dominant place accorded to music in the writings of the immediately preceding period. From a strictly logical point of view, of course, it was no longer possible to imagine the maternal figure of music without a father. But let us look at the texts in detail. In *Opera and Drama*, the poetic intent fertilizes the music; in the 1879 essay "On Opera Libretti and Composition in Particular," it is Weber's genius that fertilizes the words of *Euryanthe* and the music is equated with the caste of Brahman women—the superior caste—while the libretto is equated with the inferior caste of Chandala men. It is impossible to avoid noticing that this final reversion to the 1851 metaphor has been added in the margin of the manuscript,[2] as though in passing. The allusion does not imply the male superiority present throughout *Opera and Drama* but, instead, insists on the triumph of music as attested by *Tristan* and the *Beethoven* essay of 1870.

Wagner simply wishes to indicate that the poem must match up to the musical genius and have been conceived as a function of the musical style that will ensure its effectiveness. It is impossible, therefore, to infer from the remarks of 1878 and the reference, the following year, to *Opera and Drama* that Wagner still believes in a world of ideas propounded in a text of almost thirty years earlier.

The emphasis on music is confirmed in the third of the three essays under discussion. Completed in October 1879, "On the Application of Music to Drama" sets out explicitly to complement the earlier piece. It is here, moreover, that Wagner points out that the term *leitmotif* is Hans von Wolzogen's, not his own, and that he himself prefers to speak of *Grundthemen*, or "basic themes":

> In order to become a work of art as music, the new form of dramatic music must nonetheless demonstrate the unity of symphonic writing—a unity that it will achieve if, intimately linked with the same, it extends over the entire drama rather than merely over individual, lesser, and arbitrarily selected parts of it. This unity results from a web of basic themes that permeate the entire work of art and that, as in symphonic writing, contrast with and complement each other, allowing themselves to be re-formed, divided, and reunited, except that in this case the dramatic action that is elaborated and executed governs the laws of separation and association that were borrowed originally from dance movements. (1879f, 10.185)

Although the poem represents the male principle to the extent that the work of art derives its origins from the dramatic action as conveyed by the libretto (Wagner uses the same word *Handlung* as in the *Beethoven* essay of 1870), the so-called leitmotifs must nonetheless be examined less "from the point of view of their dramatic significance and effectiveness" than "from that of their value for the musical structure" (ibid.). It is musical logic that ultimately decides the issue.

The role that the *Grundthema* plays in ensuring the aesthetic unity of the work (ibid., 10.184) is altogether crucial. It will be recalled that in two program notes dating from 1851–52 and dealing with Beethoven's *Eroica* (1851e) and Overture to *Coriolan* (1852c) Wagner had placed a sexual gloss on the relationship between the first and second subject groups. In "On the Application of Music to Drama" he tries to explain why Beethoven did not attempt another opera after *Fidelio*: it was, he claims, because "what was new and unfamiliar to us had already occurred to him as a writer of symphonies" (1879f, *GS* 10.177). That newness, he goes on, consisted in the thematic complementarity of "male and female elements of an identical underlying character" (ibid., 10.178). In this way Wagner succeeds in killing two birds with one stone: if Beethoven did not attempt another opera, it was because, thanks to the fundamental androgynous unity of his symphonies, he had already raised instrumental music to an unsurpassable pitch of unitarian perfection. It was now up to Wagner himself to apply this principle to the field of opera and to rediscover there the perfection of the Beethovenian symphony.

The relationship between music and drama (as a genre) is dialectical, therefore. In his symphonies Mozart is true to the spirit of drama: "The few symphonic works whose unique value has kept them alive until the present day are the product of that period in his creative life in which he had already revealed his true genius as an operatic composer" (ibid., 10.179). At a time when Wagner was preoccupied with plans for symphonies—between the autumn of 1877 and his death (see *WWV*, 107)—the drama, with its profound underlying unity, remained the model for the instrumental music of the future (1879f, *GS* 10.182). At the same time, "the new form of dramatic music must . . . demonstrate the unity of symphonic writing" if it is to "become a work of art" (ibid., 10.185), and this is the function of the "basic themes," since it is through them that the fundamental unity of music and drama can be realized. But it can no longer be argued, as it had been in 1851, that music is the servant of the drama. On the contrary, it is music that allows the drama to become all that it must be and thus to achieve redemption.

On a musical plane, *Parsifal* confirms this analysis. Stein has shown that this work has a shorter libretto and a longer performance time than any of Wagner's other operas: melodic melismatas on a single vowel are particularly frequent here, and all the motifs, save one, originate in the orchestra rather than in the vocal line (Stein 1961, 203–13). Is there an analogy here between Parsifal and Kundry on the one hand and poetry and music on the other? Wagner will have recourse one last time to the topos of androgyny, albeit to other ends . . .

"On the Feminine in the Human"

At the same time that he was working on the full score of *Parsifal* (23 August 1879–13 January 1882), Wagner was engaged in writing a series of aesthetico-religious essays whose content is sufficiently close to that of the Stage Consecration Festival Drama to explain its significance retrospectively.

Completed in July 1880, "Religion and Art" (1880a) was followed by two appendixes, a new anti-Semitic diatribe entitled "Know Yourself" (1881a) and "Heroism and Christianity" (1881c), from which we learn that the splendor of Christian civilization has been ruined by "a Judaeo-barbarous mixture" (1881a, *GS* 10.268) and that the degeneration of the modern world is the result of the corruption of the blood (1881c, *GS* 10.275). Having completed *Parsifal*, Wagner turned his attention to a third addendum to "Religion and Art." Headed "On the Masculine and Feminine in Culture and Art," it was written at some point between 21 March and 9 April and remained unpublished within the composer's lifetime. Only a heart attack on 13 February 1883 prevented him from completing more than the first four pages of a further essay on the same topic, the androgynous orientation of which is clear from its very title, "On the Feminine in the Human" (1883b).

These last two fragmentary essays attest to Wagner's continuing interest in his sexual metaphor, although a close examination of the context in which it evolves is bound to lead to the conclusion that it has acquired new connotations here.

Starting with "Religion and Art" in 1880, Wagner had begun to develop a racist theory of regeneration. In "Heroism and Christianity" he writes: "Let us not underestimate the enormity of the assumption that the human race is destined to achieve complete uniformity and let us admit that we can imagine this uniformity only in an appalling image of the kind that Gobineau, for example, feels obliged to hold out to us at the end of his book" (1881c, *GS* 10.283). Wagner is convinced that the blood of the German race risks being corrupted by foreign blood, the worst type of all evidently being Jewish blood, since "miscegenation does not harm it: let Jew or Jewess intermarry with even the most foreign of races; a Jew will always be the result" (1881a, *GS* 10.271). And not only Jews but Orientals and barbarians are gnawing away at the heart of Aryan civilization.

These texts confirm—if confirmation be needed—that *Parsifal*, Wagner's "farewell to the world," is indeed an anti-Semitic work, as his contemporaries realized from the outset (see Lindau 1882). This is something we need to bear in mind in order to understand the loathing that Kundry inspires in Parsifal. The "Judaeo-barbarous mixture" is clearly the

Flower-maidens' enchanted garden and Klingsor's castle—"a palace of richly ornamental Arabian style," according to the libretto (*GS* 10.350). Only by refusing the Semite's kiss can Parsifal serve the pure blood of Christ. According to both Wagner and Gobineau,[3] the racial unity of mankind would entail a dilution of specifically Germanic features in favor of Semitic ones.

In the character of Kundry, Wagner succeeds in combining anti-Semitism with misogyny with peculiar force, as Hans Jürgen Syberberg, the director of the 1982 film of *Parsifal*, rightly observed: "Wagner assimilates the problem of woman as a figure of guilt and hostility with that of the Wandering Jew, treating them as stages in a process of seductive temptation and eternal malediction" (Syberberg 1982, 11 and 56; see also 161).

That Wagner is guilty of a fundamental misogyny throughout his works, from *Der fliegende Holländer* to *Parsifal*, and that it is left to womankind to sacrifice herself in order for men to be redeemed, is all too evident. His private remarks too, collected by Cosima during the years preceding the composition of *Parsifal*, leave one in no doubt as to his feelings on the subject. When she asked him whether she ought to read Schopenhauer, he advised her against it: "A woman should approach philosophy through a man, a poet" (*CT*, 2 January 1869). He is unhesitating in his condemnation of women's emancipation (ibid., 8 August 1869, 26 April 1870). Certain expressions verge on caricature: "It is a great shame," Wagner remarked on the eve of his marriage to Cosima, "that the Germans no longer beat their women; if that custom were to return, we should experience a revolution in the literature of today" (ibid., 24 August 1870). Nor did he have any faith in their creative abilities: discussing their literary activities, he opined that "the occupation seems to be connected with a certain morbid condition peculiar to them, a sort of unsatisfied desire to please; they then put on blue stockings in order to dominate through the intellect" (ibid., 23 November 1878). "A man must demand obedience from a woman and allow her to influence him only within limits" (ibid., 9 November 1882). Womankind is irrevocably condemned: "The eternal feminine drags one downward" (ibid., 1 December 1880)—clearly a reversal of Goethe's glorification of women. One can merely note the sycophantic obsequiousness with which Cosima encouraged her husband's beliefs: for her, woman's essential duties were "to raise upright men and good women" (ibid., 19 December 1873). "'I should like to die in you,' I say to R.—a poor expression for my feelings, my longing to be nothing apart from him" (ibid., 12 January 1872). "To me the whole world is recognizable only in him and through him" (ibid., 4 January 1869). "Every utterance from him is a doctrine to me" (ibid., 16 January 1871). "It seems strange to me, too, that women who are loved by great men do not feel that they are what they are because of these men and this love, and imagine they are something else besides in themselves" (ibid., 7 April 1869). Wagner had certainly found "the woman of the future" in Cosima.

It is against this anti-Semitic and misogynistic background that we must read the 1882 fragment (1882f):

On the Masculine and Feminine in
Culture and Art

> The inadequacy of the causal form of cognition of the nature of things may become fully apparent to us on examination of the spatial and, more especially, the temporal priority of male and female considered together.—Does man or woman come "first?" It is an idle question, conception without procreation, like procreation without conception, being unimaginable; accordingly, what we have before us is merely a division of that genus that, once again, is conceivable only as a unity and that achieves not only its actuality but also its ideal dignity only when this division is superseded.
>
> So long as we can see only the division of the sexes in its various manifestations when we judge natural and human things, the genus is bound to remain far short of the ideal. Culture and art, too, could be perfect only if a product of the act of suspending the divided unity of male and female.
>
> Act:—the perfectly matching marriage.—Plato:—his state defective & impossible.—However, the unfortunate experience of a historically propagated humanity serves as a constant warning of racial decline through mis-marriage: physical decline combined with moral. Plato's error must not deter us from examining the problem that he saw so clearly; accordingly it is our task to recognize, as a matter of infallible certainty, that marriage without mutual affection has been more pernicious for the human race than anything else.
>
> Gobineau: definition of the reasons for the superiority of the white race: aim at what is useful by recognizing what is harmful about the unbridled will. To be precise: cautious exploitation of the power of violence in the enjoyment of possessions. (Male.) Apparently: correction to—again only apparently—aimlessly creative nature; at the same time, however, incomprehension of nature's true purpose, which aims at deliverance from within itself. (Feminine.) (1882f, 204)

By juxtaposing this fragment with the opening pages of "On the Feminine in the Human" and also with the "lesson" of *Parsifal*, one can attempt the following hypothetical reconstruction. Marriage plays an essential role in the destiny of the different races to the extent that polygamy favors the commingling of blood. Equally, it is marriage that allows us to rediscover the original androgynous unity. Hence the impossibility of knowing whether man or woman came first. Why are marriage and conjugal fidelity a factor in racial purity? When we observe the behavior of animals, we see that nature is concerned solely with ensuring that the species remains pure (1883b, *SS* 12.345).[4] In the case of human beings, men are driven by the instinct to possess and by the exercise of violence, both of which lead to polygamy or interracial marriage. Women, by contrast, have a natural feeling for fidelity, an instinct due to their status as mothers, even if they do not properly understand nature's aims. (Here is a further example of the opposition between the rational and the intuitive that typifies many of Wagner's other writings.) "It is certain," Wagner goes on, "that the most noble white race is already monogamatic on its first appearance in legend and history" (ibid.), something that Kundry—being neither white nor monogamous—plainly is not.

It remains to explain how this theory is bound up in Wagner's mind with the "artistic perfection" that becomes possible when there is no longer any sense of separateness between the male and female, that is, in marriage. Neither of these incomplete fragments suggests that, in 1882 and 1883, Wagner was preparing to give a sexual interpretation to the constituent parts of the work of art, as he had done in 1851 and, briefly, in 1879. A note entered in *The Brown Book* on 23 October 1881 would tend to suggest that he was thinking of the masculine and feminine as directly represented by the subject matter of an opera: "In the mingling of races, the blood of the nobler male is corrupted by that of the less noble female: the male suffers, character is destroyed, whereas women gain so much as to take over from men. (Renaissance). That is why womankind still owes us redemption: here *in art as in religion*;[5] the immaculate virgin gives birth to the Saviour" (1865g, 202).

This could be a commentary on *Parsifal*, in which Wagner does not hesitate to assimilate "less noble women" with womankind in general ("the feminine"). The Knights of the Grail are sullied by their contact with the Flower-maidens, who are a "Judaeo-barbarous mixture." Parsifal alone resists them. It is for him, therefore, that Kundry—whose blood is tainted and who embodies womankind *tout court*—has to sacrifice herself in order to ensure redemption.

As spectators, we find ourselves once again confronted by a woman who sacrifices herself for the sake of a man. But, without seeking to exonerate the composer, we need to show that for Wagner, Kundry's death has an additional meaning.

If *Parsifal* is the only work, with the obvious exception of *Die Meistersinger*, in which the principal male character does not die, it is not only in order to indicate man's essential predominance but because, by the very end of the work, Parsifal has become the symbolic embodiment of an angelic androgyny, proclaiming a new civilization and culture.[6]

Kundry sinks lifelessly to the ground at the precise moment that Parsifal achieves redemption, as the chorus intones the final words of the text:

Höchsten Heiles Wunder!	Wonder of supreme salvation!
Erlösung dem Erlöser!	Redemption to the Redeemer!

(*GS* 10.375)

This final chorus is the only mixed chorus in the entire work and Kundry dies on a sustained A♭ sung by the sopranos. Through Cosima, Wagner explained the androgynous significance of this ending: he "plays the first theme of *Parsifal* to himself and, returning, says that he gave the words to a chorus so that the effect would be neither masculine nor feminine, Christ must be entirely sexless, *neither man nor woman*;[7] Leonardo, too, in the *Cena*, attempted that, depicting an almost feminine face adorned with a beard. He must appear neither young nor old, he says, the god within the human being" (*CT*, 27 June 1880). In dying, Kundry symbolically destroys the element of femininity and the absence of racial purity that she embodies and that threaten to corrupt the purity and sanctity of the new Christ. There is a palpable difference between *Tristan* and *Parsifal*: "In the introduction to the third act of *Tristan* there is the melancholy of longing, it is 'like a fish out of water'; but in the introduction to the third act of *P[arsifal]* the depression is complete, no longing at all" (ibid., 31 August 1882).

Just as, in 1849, Wagner had declared that the art-work of the future should depict the death of the hero, the aim of *Parsifal* is now to depict the triumph of a certain type of androgyny. But the androgyny of *Parsifal* is no longer the same as that of the *Ring* or of *Tristan*: it is an *asexual* androgyny that transcends all racial differences.

In his Zurich essays Wagner had set out from the belief in an original Hellenic unity but had later put forward the idea of a male-dominated aesthetic androgyny. In *Tristan* and the *Beethoven* centenary essay, it is womankind who has, so to speak, adopted the superior position. Parsifal takes the androgynous myth to its logical conclusion: the *Bühnenweihfestspiel* not only brings to an end Wagner's own life's work in the spirit of its creator, it also rounds off the history of Western music at the same time as opening up a new religious age. "But who is going to make humans out of humans?" Cosima asked her husband on 27 June 1880. "Ah!" he replied. "The founder of a new religion." And he went on to explain that "he feels his new work will not be unwelcome to a limited number of well-wishers" (ibid., 27 June 1880). A few lines later Cosima noted down the androgynous conception of the Saviour quoted above. A new work of ritual, *Parsifal* freezes time and is intended to allow its audience to celebrate the religion of the future. "Zum Raum wird hier die

Zeit" (Here time is one with space), Gurnemanz tells Parsifal as they prepare to enter the Temple of the Grail (*GS* 10.339). The redemptive score will have no successor, just as the Redeemer himself—"neither man nor woman"—can have no offspring.[8] At the end of his life, Wagner abolished all existing hierarchies in a state of sexual neutrality.

The allusion to Leonardo da Vinci might suggest that we were in the presence of that ambiguous androgyny typical of the end of the nineteenth century and much prized by the pre-Raphaelites.[9] But there is almost certainly no truth in this interpretation. Ambiguity is not sexual neutrality. For Wagner, the androgynous Parsifal proclaims the advent of a raceless, sexless society.

Already in "Religion and Art" Wagner had denied that Jesus was Jewish (1880a, *GS* 10.231–2), and an entry in Cosima Wagner's diaries confirms the depth of Wagner's belief: "Then he gets heated about the assumption that Jesus was a Jew; it has not been proved, he says, and Jesus spoke Syriac-Chaldaean. 'Not until all churches have vanished will we find the Redeemer, from whom we are separated by Judaism'" (*CT*, 27 November 1878). What, at the time of *Tristan und Isolde*, had remained within the confines of metaphysical exegesis is now extended to the racial sphere. Regrettable though it may be for him to have said of the third act of *Siegfried*, "That is Gobineau music, . . . that is race," he is merely confirming what we already knew about Mime and Alberich (ibid., 17 October 1882). But one would prefer not to have read this retrospective interpretation recorded by Cosima: "*Tristan* is the music that removes all barriers, and that means all racial ones as well" (ibid., 19 June 1881).

And also all sexual barriers, of course. Only the androgynous Parsifalian angel will survive in the religion heralded by Wagner's final music drama, an angel that at the same time will resolve that fundamental division within each human heart that condemns to failure every attempt to achieve love's union. Wagner wanted to go beyond Schopenhauer: "R. criticizes Schopenhauer for not having paid sufficient attention to the male and female elements, into which everything in this world is divided" (ibid., 8 March 1872). "Love—tragedy" are the final words that he wrote on the day of his death (1883b, *SS* 12.345). Announcing a future religion, an asexual Parsifal preaches the gospel of the renunciation of desire through the intermediary of a work of art in which, at the very end, every form of sexual and racial distinction is abolished.

Conclusion to Part Two

La querelle des intrigues (*continued*)

In the Introduction to Part Two I pointed out that the writers who have discussed the relationship between words and music in Wagner's works fall into three groups: those for whom Wagner always accorded primacy to music, even when he said the opposite; those for whom the true Wagner is the author of *Opera and Drama*; and those, finally, who admit the existence of changing points of view throughout the composer's career. It will be clear by now that my own position is close to that of the third group even if, in singling out the theme of androgyny in Wagner's thinking, I believe I have put forward a new plot that takes account of this highly controversial problem.

Having reached the end of my own exposition, I cannot avoid asking whether one of these plots is more acceptable than the others.

Given the evidence assembled in Chapter Five, there seems little doubt that the plot according to which music reigns supreme even when Wagner claims the opposite is inadmissible inasmuch as everything points to the fact that the problem resides in the nature of the *relationship* between the poetry and the music. Even if, as Paul Veyne argues, there is no one plot capable of taking account of all the events that can be observed in this world of ours, there are nonetheless plots that, compared with other more compelling ones, simply fail to take account of certain decisive elements. One cannot deny that Wagner himself demanded that music should submit to the poet.

The true debate, therefore, is between those writers like Stein who admit to a total shift in Wagner's thinking in the *Beethoven* essay of 1870 and those writers like Glass for whom Wagner's thinking is all of a piece: the poetic intent is elaborated in terms of the demands of the music and every variation in the conception of the relationship between poetry and music is the result of a mere change of emphasis that has no real consequences to speak of.

There are, I believe, three reasons why one may be led to question a plot:

1. because a given fact proves to be wrong from a factual point of view;
2. because a different arrangement of the facts leads one to suggest a different interpretation; and
3. because new facts are introduced into the construction of the plot.

In each of these cases the new observation may mean that the proposed plot is partially or wholly called into question. It is in this spirit that we need to examine the plots propounded by Stein and Glass.

Having systematically constructed his study around the principle of a parallelism between Wagner's theoretical writings and his music dramas, Stein concludes by arguing that the 1872 essay *On the Destiny of Opera* represents the composer's final explicit discussion of the synthesis of the arts (Glass 1960, 171). It is difficult to understand why he has ignored the three essays of 1879, since this leads him to overlook the fact that Wagner returns here to certain of the ideas contained in *Opera and Drama*. It also persuades him that the idea of improvisation on the part of the poet-mime is as integral to *Parsifal* as it is to *Die Meistersinger*. If Wagner's use of gesture in all its forms (the Dance of the Apprentices, the St. John's Eve riot, and so on) sanctions a comparison between the theoretical postulate of the 1872 essay and its practical realization in *Die Meistersinger*, it is by no means certain that the character of Kundry legitimates such an approach: here, after all, is a work whose subject matter demands a solemn and hieratic staging, a work for which Wagner himself—still suffering from the shortcomings of the first production of the *Ring*—said that he would like to have invented "the invisible theater" (*CT*, 23 September 1878).

It remains to consider Stein's general thesis. It seems to me necessary to evaluate its significance by comparing it with the plot proposed by Glass, who presents his own interpretation as an explicit critique and overhaul of his predecessor's work.

Glass's essential contribution to the discussion—and in this sense it represents a real discovery—is the distinction that he draws between the poem and the poetic intent. It is a distinction that rests on a verifiable observation in the text of *Opera and Drama* even if—as he himself admits—Wagner's editorial confusion offers ample excuse for earlier misreadings.

Here, then, is a fact that persuades him to construe things differently. In itself, however, this fact is of no significance unless part of a larger plot. But which? The poetic intent proposes a dramatic action that demands the abandonment of number opera as a form and insists on a new type of poem commensurate with the musical expression of that dramatic content. Starting out from this thesis, Glass considers that the different weights given to the poem, the drama, and the music are merely concomitant variations of emphasis and that, from this point of view, Wagner's thinking is fundamentally unified. This position leads Glass to deny that there is a problem of hierarchical superiority of poetry over music or vice versa.

Stein's plot is different from Glass's, therefore, in two essential respects:

1. ignoring the distinction between poetry and dramatic content, his whole construction rests on a comparison of the relationship between the libretto and the music at various stages in Wagner's career but chiefly in his dramatic works; and
2. Wagner's thinking and practice vary, and the Wagner of 1870 is no longer the Wagner of 1851.

What are we to make of these two contradictory concepts? It is clear that having failed to see the difference between the libretto and the dramatic intent, Stein cannot handle the very real complexity of the evolution in Wagner's thinking but that at the same time, and contrary to Glass's claim, it is not because there is a dialectical relationship between the poetic intent and the music that there is no literal confirmation in Wagner's writings that poetry or music is superior, a superiority subject to later modifications.

The foregoing considerations might appear to be an attempt at reconciliation, but this is not the case. What I am trying to show is that both writers are conducting their respective analyses on two different levels of Wagnerian discourse, that Stein's analysis is less complete than Glass's, however well it treats one reality of this discourse, and that Glass's analysis introduces a vital distinction while reducing the effectiveness of that distinction by glossing over the conceptual differences in the relationship between libretto, drama, and music in order to bolster up his belief that the poetic intent is of permanent importance.

If I appear to insist unduly on this point, it is because it seems to me necessary to explain why, with both these writers, their analysis of Wagner's stage works seems to prove the truth of their theses. The reason is simply that they are not looking for the same sort of evidence in the works themselves. Stein examines the way in which Wagner sets his poem to music, studying the way in which the leitmotifs appear either in conjunction with the sung text or, independently, in the orchestra, and determining the place occupied by a more symphonic style within the opera's general structure. Glass, by contrast, studies the way in which the music adopts a form that fits the contours of the dramatic action as transmitted by the libretto. Stein and Glass are describing two different things, so that it is impossible to adduce the evidence of one in order to refute the theory of the other.

My own plot is based on two principles not found in my predecessors' writings:

1. because I believe in the profound unity of Wagner's thinking at every moment in its evolution, I have tried to show that there is a close connection or parallelism between the content of the theoretical essays and that of the *Ring* and *Tristan*, and that this link is provided by the idea of androgyny. It is noteworthy, moreover, that Stein never once mentions the way in which

the relationship between poetry and music is translated into sexual terms and that even though Glass regards the "fertilizing seed" as so central to his thesis that he names his book after it, the *androgynous* nature of the relationship between the poet and music is never treated as an independent theme. Glass has taken his title from the final chapter of part 2 of *Opera and Drama*; I propose my title on the basis of Wagner's own statement in the final chapter of part 3.

2. Although Stein clearly considers that Wagner's sexual terminology is merely an inessential trimming, we have seen, in fact, that androgyny is a central symbolic figure suited not only to establishing a hitherto unsuspected link between Wagner's theory and artistic practice but also to providing a metaphor whose content deserves to be properly studied in order to understand the composer's various conceptions of the relationship between poetry and music.

Bearing all this in mind, the reader may finally ask which plot lay behind my own analysis in the second part of this study. It must be said at the outset—and this has been said a thousand times already—that, in spite of the thousands of pages that he filled with his prose, Wagner was not comfortable in matters of philosophical discourse. He was an intuitive artist but one who wanted his creative work to have a theoretical counterpart, a desire due, in part, to his need to explain its novelty but also because he considered it worthy of being raised to the level of philosophical speculation.

In short, Wagner does not express himself clearly, and although there is evidently a distinction between the poem and the drama, between the words of the libretto and the poetic intent, Wagner establishes an androgynous relationship between the music and something that is both the poem and the "poetic intent." At least in *Opera and Drama*, where one cannot simply brush aside all that he says on the submissive role of female music, it is impossible to deny that in Wagner's view, the poet is superior to music, a position that he gradually reversed when he began to recognize that the poem was written according to the demands of the music. If I refuse to follow Glass in reducing the two components in the hierarchy to a single level, it is because Wagner's position in 1851 and that of 1870 seem to reveal two different points of view.

It seems to me dangerous to follow the Wagner of 1872 when he declares that, unconsciously, he already knew at the time of *Opera and Drama* that it was music that was the mother of the drama. When, in 1851, he declared that the poet fertilizes the music, he was saying something that he would not have said twenty years later: as a composer of lyric operas he wanted to turn from the world of history in *Rienzi* and from the world of legend in *Der fliegende Holländer*, *Tannhäuser*, and

Lohengrin to the world of myth. The poet does indeed fertilize the music, preceding it in true genetic fashion, in the sense that if Wagner is persuaded to change the musical form, it is because he has something different and new to recount on stage. It will be clear that I have no hesitation in supporting the idea that the musical form adopted by Wagner was provoked not by an autonomous evolution in his musical style but by the fact that at the time of the *Ring*, he had to find a new form of music commensurate with the type of dramatic action that he wanted to set to music. This position seems to square with a fact that otherwise remains inexplicable: why does Wagner insist on taking a particular stance and devoting the equivalent of ten volumes of three hundred pages each to the operas of his day, to the German nation, Judaism, and Germanic and Scandinavian myths, if not because, as an opera composer, he has something to say to us?

As we have seen, Wagner wrote *Opera and Drama* at a time when he was involved in a multiplicity of operatic projects. Here it is the poet who, with his words and the story that he wants to tell us, is to determine the new form of opera. But Wagner soon realized that in order for this to be possible, the poem would have to be drafted according to the possibilities inherent in its musical realization. As soon as he went back to setting his libretti to music, he noticed just how much the music added to the dramatic content: the poetry was a vehicle for the understanding, the music a vehicle for feeling—a position that Schopenhauer would soon confirm with his insistence on the metaphysical superiority of music. In writing *Tristan und Isolde*, Wagner chose a subject that was the quintessential expression of feeling, with its tragic myth of love. Having seen for himself what an effect *Tristan* and *Die Meistersinger* had not only on himself but also on audiences in general, he concluded that music was the mother of the drama since it embodies the very essence of that drama. From now on the poet remains present, but a close reading of the texts in question suggests that this presence is much more discreet than Glass would have us believe. And if, as I would argue, it is important to take seriously this difference of emphasis, it is both because an examination of Wagner's dramatic works shows the dominant role that music has assumed in their structure and also because the relationship between Tristan and Isolde seems to correspond with a change in the hierarchical relationship between poetry and music, and hence between the masculine and feminine elements, as they obtained in *Opera and Drama*. The writings of 1879 constitute the final formulation of the relationship between poetry and music and reintroduce not only the poet (who was absent from the *Beethoven* essay of 1870) but also the sexual imagery of *Opera and Drama*, while retaining the dominant position of music. This supremacy survives into the final period, when Wagner was working on

Parsifal, even though he did not have time to explain the full implications of the abolition of racial and sexual differences in the realm of art. Only the religious significance of Parsifalian androgyny is explicit.

In order to assess the implications of my own androgynal analysis of the relationship between poetry and music, I need to compare it with other types of possible interpretations. Throughout the preceding sections I have followed Stein and Glass, and adopted a method that is philological, historical, and genetic. It is philological to the extent that at each step, I have relied on a reconstruction of the sense of the words; it is historical because I have sought to establish the factors that could explain the emergence of the androgynous metaphor and its metamorphoses; and it is genetic because I have examined its changing morphology from a chronological point of view. As indicated in the Introduction to Part Two of this study, this approach was chosen for basically semiological reasons: the significance of the three successive forms of androgyny in Wagner's works cannot be reconstructed unless it is interpreted in the light of the philosophies that influenced it at every stage of its evolution.

The Feuerbachian androgyny of the *Ring* heralds a new society in which, through the joyous transports of death, man and woman unite in self-sacrifice in order to ward off the drama of individuation. The Schopenhauerian androgyny of *Tristan und Isolde*, embodied in Isolde, signifies the triumph of music and of woman who, renouncing the will to live, shows man the way to redemption. With *Parsifal*, Wagner aimed to institute a new religion centered around an asexual redeemer who symbolizes the suppression of every kind of division, be it sexual, racial, cultural, or aesthetic.

But is this historico-genetic approach sufficient to define these successive networks of meanings? How is it that I can speak of androgyny without appealing to Freud? I have relied only on factual evidence and explicit statements. How could I have the temerity to neglect the work of the unconscious and ignore the unspoken? We shall see.

PART THREE

Wagner and Androgynous Hermeneutics

Chapter Eight

PSYCHOANALYZING WAGNER

WHEN AN IDEA so important and so closely bound up with sexuality as androgyny passes through the mind of a creative artist, psychoanalysis suggests itself as an unavoidable explanational paradigm. Of course, Wagner is no longer here to lie down on the psychoanalyst's couch, so that one of the basic requirements of analytical interpretation—the technique of association—is missing. But psychoanalysis has accumulated sufficient results for it to be possible, on the basis of a given text and of biographical information transmitted by history, to make a connection between what Charles Mauron has called "obsessive metaphors" and "personal myth." Moreover, Freud himself set the tone for the first investigation of this nature with his "Leonardo da Vinci and a Memory of His Childhood" (1910a), in which he combines an analysis of texts left by the painter with contemporary eyewitness accounts, various paintings, and what analytical experience has learned, in a general way, of the etiology of homosexuality.

THE FAMILY ROMANCE

In speaking of the psychoanalytic approach to bisexuality, we need to be clear that what is involved here is an attempt to explain a mental image: why is it that a man (in this case, Wagner) conceives of himself, creatively, as both man and woman?

We have more biographical documentation concerning Wagner than virtually any other composer, and even if a large part of that material emanates from Wagner himself (a fact that renders it suspect in the eyes of the historian who has to use it with all the necessary critical caution), it is all the more valuable to the psychoanalyst to the extent that through it Wagner tells us how he views his own relations with others. It seems, therefore, that one can reconstruct the following "family romance."

The young Richard's neurotic excitability developed against a background of violence. In May 1813 war was raging in Saxony between Napoleon and the allied troops under Friedrich Wilhelm III of Prussia and Tsar Alexander I of Russia. The Battle of Bautzen was fought on 20 and 21 May, and Wilhelm Richard Wagner was born in Leipzig on the 22nd. Early in June the family left the city for Stötteritz, around which the war continued to be waged. Ludwig Geyer, the family friend and future husband of Wagner's mother, Johanna, was performing in Teplitz. At some date between 21 July and 10 August 1813 Johanna crossed the enemy lines in order to join him there, presumably taking the infant with her. The child's unconscious is bound to have been affected by all these upheavals.

And death lay in wait. His brother Carl Gustav had died in infancy on 29 March 1802 and Richard must have heard talk of the family tragedy. His official father, Friedrich Wagner, died of typhus six months after Richard's birth, while his sister Maria Theresia died at the age of four on 19 January 1814, when he himself was only eight months old. At the end of January his paternal grandmother died. His child's mind filled with phantoms, as is clear from his recollection of his uncle's house in Leipzig: "To sleep alone in such a large and remote room, near one of these fearsome pictures, in a sumptuous old bed, was horrible for me: I tried, it is true, to conceal my fear from my aunt when she lighted the way for me to bed in the evening; but never a night passed without my being bathed in sweat at the fear caused by these frightful ghostly apparitions" (*ML*, 9). As a child, Wagner was subject to hallucinatory fears that, as an adult, he associated retrospectively with the world of the theater:

> In particular *Freischütz*, though mainly because of its spooky plot, affected my imagination with characteristic intensity. The excitement of horror and fear of ghosts constitute a singular factor in the development of my emotional life. From earliest childhood certain mysterious and uncanny phenomena produced undue effects on me; I remember, whenever I was alone in a room for any length of time and looked fixedly at such inanimate objects as pieces of furniture, suddenly bursting into a loud shriek, because they seemed to me to come alive. Until late in my boyhood no night passed without my awakening with a frightful scream from some dream about ghosts, which would end only when a human voice bade me be quiet. Severe scoldings or even corporal punishment would then seem to me redeeming kindnesses. None of my brothers and sisters wanted to sleep near me; they tried to bed me down as far from the others as possible, not stopping to think that by so doing my nocturnal calls to be saved from the ghosts would become even louder and more enduring, until they finally accustomed themselves to this nightly calamity. (*ML*, 13)

Music, too, was associated with this imaginative world:

> Even the orchestra's tuning up excited me fantastically: I remember particularly that the striking of fifths on the violin struck me as a greeting from another world—which incidentally had a very literal meaning for me. When I was still scarcely beyond infancy the sound of these fifths had been associated with the ghosts and spirits that had always excited me. . . . Now at last grown to boyhood, I luxuriated nearly every afternoon in the Großer Garten

around Zillmann's band, and one can imagine the voluptuous shudder with which I drank in all the various chaotic sounds to be heard when an orchestra is tuning up: the sustained A of the oboe, awakening the other instruments like a call from the dead, never failed to strain my nerves to fever pitch; and when the swelling C of the *Freischütz* overture announced to me that I had stepped with both feet into the magic realm of awe, anyone observing me at the time could hardly fail to see what the nature of my case was, despite my dismal piano playing. Another work also attracted me just as strongly: it was the overture in E major to *Fidelio*, in which the introduction gripped me especially. (*ML*, 29–30)

Note the Hoffmannesque terms with which Wagner describes the masochistic association that music had for him even at an early age. Even more interesting, however, is the reference to *Fidelio* at the end of our extract. For it was in the role of Leonore that Wagner claims to have seen Wilhelmine Schröder-Devrient in Leipzig in 1828 or 1829, when he was only fifteen:

> Yet another miracle . . . suddenly gave a new direction to my artistic sensibility and proved decisive for a lifetime. This was a brief appearance as guest star by Wilhelmine Schröder-Devrient, who then stood at the pinnacle of her career, young, beautiful, and ardent as no woman I have since seen on the stage. . . . When I look back across my entire life I find no event to place beside this in the impression it produced on me. Whoever can remember this wonderful woman at that period of her life will certainly confirm in some fashion the almost demonic fire irresistibly kindled in them by the profoundly human and ecstatic performance of this incomparable artist. After the opera was over I dashed to the home of one of my friends to write a short letter in which I told her succinctly that my life had henceforth found its meaning, and that if ever she heard my name favorably mentioned in the world of art, she should remember that she had on this evening made of me that which I now vowed to become. (*ML*, 37)

It is difficult to think of a more eloquent account, and what is perhaps the most fascinating aspect of it is that in Schröder-Devrient Wagner was admiring an androgyne: the role of Fidelio, after all, is that of a man played by a soprano. In fact, as John Deathridge has pointed out (1984, 7), the role in which Schröder-Devrient so impressed Wagner appears to have been that of Romeo in Bellini's *I Capuleti e i Montecchi*, which he heard in Leipzig in March 1834. But in telling the truth, Wagner would not have been able to posit a heroic link with German music. Yet this does not affect anything from the androgynous point of view: the singer's silhouette was sufficiently slender to allow her to play men's roles. Much later Wagner confided to Cosima: "How did I ever achieve the rapture of the second act [of *Tristan und Isolde*]? I know, it was through seeing Schröder-D. as Romeo" (*CT*, 23 March 1878). It is a remark that throws even more light on the androgyny of *Tristan und Isolde*. Androgyny and the world of the theater were now associated in Wagner's mind.

But this link was established against a background of anxiety that produced the hallucinatory neurosis described in *Mein Leben*. As we have seen, *Der Freischütz* is clearly bound up with his infantile fears. If he found in the theater a sublimated form of the hallucinatory world of his infancy, it is because that world was associated in his mind with a feeling of pleasure: after all, he speaks of corporal punishments as "redeeming kindnesses." Here he is, ready for masochism: throughout his life he was to show an evident indulgence toward suffering. The later evocation of these scenes, renewed and reinforced by the theater, is maintained by him "in an act of pleasurable autoerotic satisfaction," to quote from Freud's essay, "A Child Is Being Beaten" (1919, 164), thereby predisposing him to perceive the ego as an androgynous being.

There was a second factor, however, that steered him in the direction of the theater, and that was his almost exclusive early involvement with the world of women—an involvement, be it added, that was not necessarily untroubled. Following Geyer's death, he later recalled in *Mein Leben*, he was "received for the first time with a tenderness unusual in our family" (*ML*, 7), while his mother inspired the following remarks:

> I have no remembrance of her as a young and pretty mother. The anxious and trying relations with a large family (of which I was the seventh surviving member), the difficulties in providing the necessities of life, and the fulfillment of a certain desire to keep up appearances even with very limited means, were not conducive to a comforting tone of motherly solicitude in her; I hardly remember ever being caressed by her, just as outpourings of affection did not take place in our family at all; on the contrary, quite naturally a certain impetuous, even loud and boisterous manner characterized our behavior. (*ML*, 11).

To Cosima he later confided: "Also, I lacked a maternal home to which I would have been glad to return; my marriage was a sort of emancipation" (*CT*, 1 April 1874). This portrait is confirmed by a somewhat harshly worded letter of 11 September 1842 to his half-sister, Cäcilie, and her husband, Eduard Avenarius, in which he speaks of his mother's "infinite lack of principle & utterly wayward capriciousness," of her "remarkable penchant for misrepresenting & distorting everything, & for indulging in endless gossip," and, finally, of her "really offensive avarice & egoism."[1] As the final straw, he recalled his mother once having wished him dead and having told him so:

> After one of the common ailments of infancy, which made me so sick that my mother, as she later told me, almost wished me dead owing to my seemingly hopeless condition, I seem to have surprised my parents by thriving. On this occasion, as well, I was told, my admirable stepfather played a splendid part, never despairing despite the cares and complaints of such a large family, remaining patient, and never giving up the hope that I could be pulled through. (*ML*, 5)

The young Richard's natural Oedipal libido toward his mother was quickly repressed, therefore, and must have been directed, instead, at his stepfather. Three essential elements are brought together in this single piece of evidence: the mother's hatred of her son, the link between that hatred and his small stature (from which Wagner would suffer all his life and which he would sublimate by relentless megalomania), and the feeling of gratitude toward his protective stepfather.

But the feminine world of Wagner's upbringing was not only notable for the absence of any affection on his mother's part, it was also represented by his elder sisters.

In 1813, Rosalie was ten, Luise eight, Klara six, and Ottilie two. Recalling his reunion with the twenty-year-old Luise, he writes in *Mein Leben*: "For the first time one of my sisters showed some affection for me" (*ML*, 21). At the same time, however, he speaks of "the gentler imaginative impulses produced by association with my sisters" (*ML*, 16). His sisters, moreover, embodied not only femininity but also the theater: Rosalie was engaged as an actress at the Dresden Court Theater, Luise worked in the theater, while Klara, with her fine soprano voice, would later appear on the operatic stage. Wagner himself gives the clearest possible account of this identification of the world of womankind with that of the theater:

> Despite the fact that, as I have mentioned, there was little tenderness in our family, particularly as expressed in caresses, the predominantly feminine element in my surroundings must have had a strong impact on my emotional development. Perhaps it was precisely because members of my immediate family were restless and impetuous that the other attributes of femininity, particularly insofar as they were connected with the imaginary world of the theater, filled me with an almost passionate delight. (*ML*, 14)

This deviant search for a sexual object has a very precise name—fetishism: "While I tried with playmates to imitate performances of *Freischütz* and devoted myself with great zeal to the production of costumes and masks through grotesque painting, it was the more delicate costumes of my sisters, on which I often observed my family working, that exerted a more subtly exciting effect on my fantasy; touching these objects could cause my heart to beat wildly" (*ML*, 13–14). As Freud points out in his *Three Essays on the Theory of Sexuality*, "What is substituted for the sexual object is some part of the body (such as the foot or hair) which is in general very inappropriate for sexual purposes, or some inanimate object which bears an assignable relation to the person whom it replaces and preferably to that person's sexuality (e.g., a piece of clothing or underlinen. . . . The choice of a fetish is an after-effect of some sexual impression, received as a rule in early childhood" (1905a, 65–67). Throughout his life Wagner would show a pronounced predilection for expensive fabrics and dressing gowns, to Cosima's great displeasure.[2] From our present point of view, this is no doubt an anecdotal consequence. Less easy to dismiss is the fact that Wagner's fascination with women's clothes, which he must surely have put on in the course of these amateur dramatics, came at a time when, between the age of eight and the end of his adolescence, he was being brought up exclusively by women: his substitute father, Ludwig Geyer, had died in 1821.

Wagner was thirteen when he experienced the first stirrings of love. The object of his passion was Amalie Hoffmann:

> I recollect a very beautiful, well-bred young lady . . . coming in immaculate dress to pay one of her rare Sunday visits, whose entrance struck me with such amazement that for a long time I was bereft of speech. On other occasions, I remember pretending to be in a state of stupefied sleepiness in order to induce the girls to carry me to bed, as I had noticed to my excited surprise that their attention in similar circumstances brought me into delightfully intimate contact with the female being. (*ML*, 16)

Although the world of women was forbidden to him by virtue of his age and because of the incest taboo, it is clear that he nonetheless created a replacement form of erotic satisfaction, either by deliberately provoking physical contact or by means of the symbolic substitution of fetishism associated with the theater. Imagine Wagner's dismay, therefore, when the world of the theater was barred to him by his castratory mother: "My mother took pains to let me know that I was not to develop any inclination for the theater . . . . What particularly struck me about her was the strange zeal with which she spoke, in almost histrionic terms, of the great and beautiful in art. She would never let me suppose that she included dramatic art in this category but rather solely poetry, music, and painting" (*ML*, 10–12). Later—and somewhat self-contradictorily (but the very self-contradiction reveals the extent of the grudge he bore his mother)—he tries to explain why she did not allow him to have piano lessons: "I was the sole member of the family who had received no piano lessons, a fact no doubt attributable to my mother's anxious desire to keep me away from any exercises that could stimulate a love for the theater" (*ML*, 29).

The absence of a loving, understanding mother in Wagner's life finds expression in his stage works in his characters' maternal quests: "Hinab! Zur Mutter! Hinab!" (Descend! To our mother! Descend!), the Norns exclaim (*GS* 6.182). When Siegfried dreams beneath the linden tree, it is of his mother that he thinks in a passage of great emotional force:

Aber—wie sah	But—what must
meine Mutter wohl aus?—	my mother have looked like?—
Das—kann ich	That I cannot
nun gar nicht mir denken!—	conceive of at all!—
Der Rehhindin gleich	Like those of the roe-deer,
glänzten gewiß	her bright-shining eyes
ihr' hell schimmernde Augen,—	must surely have glistened.
nur noch viel schöner!—	Only far fairer!—
Da bang sie mich geboren,	When she anxiously bore me,
warum aber starb sie da?	why did she die then?—
Sterben die Menschenmütter	Do all mortal mothers
an ihren Söhnen	perish
alle dahin?	because of their sons?
Traurig wäre das, traun!—	Sad that would be, in truth!
Ach! möcht' ich Sohn	Ah, might I, her son,
meine Mutter sehen!—	yet see my mother!—
Meine—Mutter!	My mother—
Ein Menschenweib!—	a mortal woman!—

(*GS* 6.134)

In the theater Wagner kills the mother who, in real life, wished him dead. When Siegfried awakens Brünnhilde on her rock and discovers that she is not a man but a woman, it is his mother to whom he turns for help:

Wen ruf' ich zum Heil,	To whom can I turn
daß er mir helfe?—	and call on for help?
Mutter! Mutter!	Mother, mother!
Gedenke mein'!	Remember me!—

(*GS* 6.165)

And in Brünnhilde, Siegfried immediately sees a substitute for his absent mother. Parsifal, in turn, reproaches himself for having forgotten his mother, but he clearly chose to do so since her kiss was that of a vampire, as Kundry herself explains:

Wann dann ihr Arm dich wüthend umschlang,	When her arm embraced you in her rage,
ward dir es wohl gar beim Küssen bang?	were you afraid of her kisses?

(*GS*, 10.356)

Repressed affection has left a traumatizing trace.

The conclusions of this first part of our family romance are clear: a hallucinatory neurosis against a background of anxiety left its mark on Wagner's earliest childhood and led him, in a spirit of autoerotic masochism, to embrace the world of the theater. He was all the more inclined to turn to the theater in that as a result of a fetishistic fixation, the latter was identified with the world of women, a world from which he was debarred by his sisters (as a result of the incest taboo) and by his castrating mother. At the same time that she refused the Oedipal affection demanded by a particularly precocious libido, his mother discouraged him from entering the theater, a way of life associated not only with the delightful terrors of childhood but also with the world of womankind. The only alternative left to him was narcissistic introspection. According to McDougall (1973, 264–65), "The hermaphroditic ideal finds its roots in the fusional ideal that unites the child with its mother's breast. . . . The breast is the image of the Other that allows us to become conscious of an Otherness. If this separation goes badly, the element that has been lost must be sought in ourselves." It is impossible to imagine a better description of what happened to the young Wagner, an experience that produced the fantasy of androgyny, the "Aristophanes complex" that lies at the root of the theoretical formulations that I examined in the first part of the present study and in which one should not hesitate to see a sublimation of narcissistic and autoerotic tendencies: "In an erotic game, the masturbatory act realizes a relationship between two people, the hand playing the role, in reality, of the sex of the Other" (ibid., 268).

But the family portrait is not complete. We need to examine the role played by Wagner's male entourage. The negative influence of the women in his life and the barrier they erected against his libido, both actual and sublimated, is counterbalanced in fact by three positive figures in the world of men, all of whom gave him encouragement. First there is his brother Albert, fourteen years his senior and a singer, actor, and director. We know how much Wagner admired Weber and the role played by *Der Freischütz* in his relations with the spectral world of his early infancy. For Wagner, Albert was the model of success, a success encouraged, moreover, by his musical hero, Weber: "My eldest brother (Albert), originally destined to study medicine, had, on the advice of Weber, who admired his tenor voice, begun a theatrical career in Breslau" (*ML*, 10). With such prestigious patronage, Albert was not discouraged. "Why not me?" Wagner must have wondered.

Then there was his uncle Adolf, a distinguished translator and man of letters, for whom Wagner felt the liveliest admiration and with whom he remained on affectionate terms. "The fact that my bizarre inclinations were not merely caused by a desire for superficial amusement was shown by the zeal with which I attached myself to this learned relative" (*ML*, 22). His earliest memory of his uncle was of a man "amid a chaotic mass of books" (*ML*, 9), and it was to Adolf Wagner that he owed his love of literature and speculation: "Originally destined for theology, he soon gave this up to devote himself solely to philosophical and philological studies" (ibid.). "His manifold knowledge, which embraced not only philology but also philosophy and belles lettres with equal warmth, made his conversation extremely appealing, as many people freely conceded" (*ML*, 22). As a young man, Wagner profited a great deal from this in the course of long walks in and around Leipzig (*ML*, 22–23).

Such was Adolf Wagner's influence on his nephew that the portrait that the composer paints of him contains features that would later be numbered among Wagner's own negative characteristics. Dilettantism: "His huge library had excited me to feverish reading in all directions, so that I jumped avidly from one area of literature to another, without achieving a basic grounding in any of them" (*ML*, 23). A rambling prose style: "The fact that he was denied the gift of writing as winningly, or even with adequate clarity, was one of the curious imperfections of this man, which markedly weakened his impact on the literary world, and at times even subjected him to ridicule on account of the incomprehensible and pompous sentences that were to be found in his occasional polemical writings. This weakness did not, however, frighten me away" (ibid.). The narcissism maintained by the admiration of others: "He too appeared to enjoy the company of the ardently attentive boy. . . . My uncle was delighted to find in me a very willing listener" (ibid.).

But Adolf Wagner also embodied the boy's future independence of outlook and wish to succeed outside existing institutions: "Profoundly disinclined to function as a professor or in any formal teaching capacity, he tried from early on to make a meager living from literary work" (*ML*, 9). "What attracted me most strongly in my uncle was his blunt yet still humorously expressed contempt for the modern pedantry of state, church, and school. While his other views on life were quite moderate, he nonetheless impressed me as a truly free spirit" (*ML*, 24). Moreover, Adolf Wagner had positive links with that world of the theater that his nephew so desired: "Gifted with social abilities and particularly with a fine tenor voice, imbued as well with interest for the theater, he seems in his youth to have been welcome as a literary figure among a fairly wide circle of acquaintances in Leipzig" (*ML*, 9).

The third person in this male trinity is Wagner's stepfather, Ludwig Geyer. Wagner himself was born on 22 May 1813; his father, Friedrich Wagner, died six months later, on 23(?) November. On 28 August 1814 his mother, Johanna, married the *actor* Ludwig Geyer and bore him a daughter, Cäcilie, on 26 February 1815. Ludwig replaced Wagner's absent father and, as the boy later discovered, "wanted to make something" of him (*ML*, 6; see also *CT*, 1 April 1872). A police official by profession, Friedrich Wagner "was in general very much interested in poetry and literature, and particularly accorded an almost passionate devotion to the theater, at that time much patronized by the educated classes" (*ML*, 3). But the portrait that Wagner gives us of Geyer is even more positive: his own father's fondness for the theater

> was also evidenced by his selection of the actor Ludwig Geyer as an intimate friend of the family. Although his choice of such a friend was surely attributable mainly to this love of the theater, he thereby bestowed upon his family a most noble benefactor, inasmuch as this modest artist, through heartfelt concern with the destiny of the numerous offspring of his unexpectedly deceased friend Wagner, was moved to devote the rest of his life most strenuously to the support and upbringing of this family. Even while the police official was spending his evenings in the theater, this admirable actor generally filled his place in the bosom of his family, and it appears that he was often obliged to soothe my mother when she complained, rightly or wrongly, about the flightiness of her husband. How deep was the need of this homeless, hard-pressed, and buffetted artist to be at home within a sympathetic family environment was proved a year after his friend's death, when he married the widow and henceforth became a most solicitous father to the seven surviving children. (*ML*, 3–4)

Moreover, Johanna's second husband wrote plays. Wagner later recalled *Der bethlehemitische Kindermord* (The massacre of the innocents), which was "praised by Goethe in a most friendly fashion" (*ML*, 4). Geyer would have liked the boy to become a painter, but it was he who introduced Wagner to the world of the theater:

> My imagination was now dominated by acquaintance with the theater, with which I was brought into contact not only as a juvenile spectator from the concealed loge with its entrance from the stage, and by visits to the wardrobe with its fantastic costumes and all the paraphernalia of illusion, but also by taking part in performances myself. . . . I was obliged to appear in some comedies. . . . I remember playing the part of a child and speaking a few words in Kotzebue's *Misanthropy and Misery*, which furnished me with an

> excuse at school for not having done my homework, as I declared myself to have been overburdened by the obligation to learn by heart a vast role in *Mr. and Mrs. Antropy*. (*ML*, 5)

This predestination was further reinforced by Geyer. On the eve of his death, hearing the young Richard strumming away at the piano, he wondered: "Could it be that he has a talent for music?" (*ML*, 6).

The portrait is clear, therefore. Whereas the women in Wagner's early entourage were viewed as essentially negative, the affection and understanding lavished on him by men encouraged him to turn his libidinal drives toward the male sex. It is for this reason that the image of androgyny is accompanied by signs of repressed homosexuality that biographers and commentators have pointed out in his life as in his works: "It is noteworthy," André Michel comments, "that Wagner suppressed all feelings of hostility toward his father and that he blamed only his mother. There may well be a sort of homosexual understanding here that, although latent, would later reappear" (1951, 68).

It is an orientation that is particularly clearly revealed in his choice of friends and male patrons—Karl Ritter, King Ludwig II, and, above all, Peter Cornelius, to whom he wrote on 9 January 1862, at a time when he despaired of finding a female companion, suggesting, in the clearest possible terms, that Cornelius might like to come and live with him: "*My friend, you must come and live with me, once and for all!* . . . You will belong to me, as my wife does, and we shall share everything equally together, be it good fortune or failure, everything as a matter of course. . . . You'll do what you can, as I shall; but always like two people who really belong to each other like a married couple."[3] Two years later he was still hoping to induce Cornelius to move in with him, as is clear from a letter to his confidante, Eliza Wille, of 26 May 1864: "Perhaps I shall get Cornelius to come. Shall I be able to renounce the 'eternal feminine' completely? Sighing deeply, I tell myself that I ought to wish that I could!—A glance at his [i.e., Ludwig's] dear portrait helps me again! Ah, the dear young boy! I suppose he must now be everything to me; world, wife, and child!"[4] Wagner's passionate declarations of his feelings for Ludwig II have often been dismissed as overblown romantic rhetoric, yet it remains a fact that the very nature of these remarks left Cosima deeply unsettled: "Before lunch he writes his letter to the King and reads it to me. I am overcome by a very curious, indescribable feeling when at the end I read R.'s words that his soul belongs for all eternity to him (the King); it pierces my heart like a serpent's tooth . . . . I suffer, and I disappear, in order to hide my suffering" (*CT*, 15 October 1878).

Thanks to Cosima, we have access to a transcription of 421 of Wagner's dreams out of a possible total of twenty thousand (the calculation is based on the assumption of four or five dreams every night) (Muller 1981, 20). One of them, in particular, commands attention: "R. dreamed that he was thrashing a boy, using a tallow candle, which proved to be unsuitable—too soft—for the task, whereupon he woke up!" (*CT*, 1 January 1882). The blatant symbolism of this account makes any comment superfluous. This homosexual fantasy appears at the very time that Wagner was completing *Parsifal*, the pronounced homosexual component of which cannot be overlooked: after all, Klingsor renounces heterosexual love through explicit self-castration, while Kundry's maternal kiss induces so great a phobia in Parsifal that he rejects her embrace in favor of the strictly male community of the Grail (Fuchs 1903). It is difficult not to recall the testimony of Friedrich Nietzsche, for whom "Wagner was in his old days by all means *femini generis*" (1888, 647).

The Oedipal attraction that Wagner felt toward his "father" was, by definition, homosexual in nature. But Geyer died when Richard was eight. Wagner's works reflect this concern for the absent father. It was a double absence, of course, since Wagner had lost his official father at the age of only six months.

Leubald, begun when Wagner was only thirteen, starts with the death of the hero's father. In *Die Feen*, Arindal laments his father's death; and in *Die Meistersinger von Nürnberg*, Walther von Stolzing is both fatherless and motherless. Siegmund has never seen his father, whose true identity remains unknown to him. And Siegfried, in turn, wonders: "What was my father like?" (*GS* 6.133). Tristan's father dies on his mother's breast at the moment of the child's conception. Parsifal's father died in battle . . .

But, above all, the question of paternal origin is one that must not be asked, one, moreover, on which a whole opera rests: in *Lohengrin*, the hero enjoins his bride-to-be,

nie sollst du mich befragen,	You must never ask me,
noch Wissens Sorge tragen,	nor bear the care of knowing
woher ich kam der Fahrt,	by what journey I have come
noch wie mein Nam' und Art!	nor my name and nature!
	(*GS* 2.75)

Why is this question so traumatizing? Because, for Wagner, the answer may well have been, "My real father was a Jew."

Wagner had grave reasons for doubting who his real father was. In 1870 his half-sister Cäcilie sent him the letters that Geyer had written to Johanna Wagner. Wagner replied on 14 January: "So rarely in domestic life do we find such a clear example of the most total self-sacrifice in pursuance of a nobly conceived end. . . . I believe I now see it all quite clearly, although I am bound to find it extremely hard to say in what way

I see this relationship. It is as though by sacrificing himself to the whole family, our father Geyer believed he was *atoning for some sin* or other."[5]

Throughout his life Wagner had wondered whether Geyer was his father. Two days after the letter to Cäcilie, Wagner wrote to Nietzsche—currently engaged in correcting the proofs of *Mein Leben*—to discuss the crest that was to adorn the edition:

> The crest has turned out very well, and we have every reason to be grateful to you for the care you have lavished on it. But it reminded me of my old misgivings about the *vulture*, which everyone is bound to take for an eagle at first glance, at least until some natural historian explains that there is a "cinereous vulture" that is very similar in appearance to the eagle. But since—because of the allusion—*it is important that the "vulture" be instantly recognizable as such*,[6] we would ask you to prevail upon the engraver to avail himself of the first available picture of such a beast and to hang the vulture's characteristic ruff around the neck of our bird.[7]

What is the nature of this symbol? The German for "eagle" is *Adler*, while the word for "vulture" is *Geier*. What was Wagner wanting to suggest with his choice of an imagery over which he took such infinite pains?

There has been much speculation on the physical resemblance between Wagner and the descendants of his official father, Friedrich, of whom we do not possess a portrait. But, if read correctly, a conversation recorded in Cosima's diaries gives the game away: "R. says that Fidi [Siegfried Wagner], to whom he had each time thrown his cap for safekeeping, had looked magnificent, resembling his father Geyer. I: 'Father Geyer must surely have been your father.' R.: 'I don't believe that.' 'Then why the resemblance?' R.: 'My mother loved him at the time—elective affinities.'" What is important here is not Wagner's reply but what he had said immediately beforehand, when looking at Siegfried: his son resembled Ludwig Geyer.[8]

And it was Nietzsche, now at odds with the man he had once so admired, who blabbed the family secret in a footnote in *The Case of Wagner*:

> Was Wagner a German at all? There are some reasons for this question. It is difficult to find any German trait in him. Being a great learner, he learned to imitate much that was German—that's all. His own nature *contradicts* that which has hitherto been felt to be German—not to speak of a German musician.—His father was an actor by the name of Geyer. A Geyer [vulture] is practically an Adler [eagle].—What has hithero circulated as "Wagner's Life" is *fable convenue*, if not worse. I confess my mistrust of every point attested to only by Wagner himself. He did not have pride enough for any truth about himself; nobody was less proud. Entirely like Victor Hugo, he

> remained faithful to himself in biographical questions, too—he remained an actor. (1888, 638)

If Nietzsche plays on these two names, it is because, as Giorgio Colli and Mazzino Montinari indicate in a note to their edition of the text, the name Adler was widespread in Jewish families (Nietzsche 1988, 14.408). As a result, Wagner's letter concerning the crest takes on a very specific meaning: in his homage to his stepfather, Geyer [vulture], it was important not to confuse him with an Adler [eagle or Jew]. Wagner's psychological dilemma is clear: could it be that he felt admiration and gratitude for a man whose Jewish blood was now coursing through his veins? But why feel repulsion toward a Jew who had saved the family from destitution? Psychoanalysts are in no doubt on this point. The young Richard was endowed with a precocious libido, and anti-Semitism is strongly conditioned by the fear of castration (Freud 1905a, 113–14)—a further theme that occurs in Wagner's works, as is clear from the figures of Klingsor and, in symbolic form, Alberich, both of whom renounce love. Now, if Wagner felt homosexually attracted to his father, that attraction was doubly forbidden. A mother who rejected him, unobtainable sisters, an affectionate—but equally forbidden—father, and perhaps a Jew into the bargain . . . The only way left open to Wagner was the orgasm of the ego, androgyny mixed with anti-Semitism.[9] It is now apparent why Wagner's life and works confirm the ambivalent nature of his relations with Jews.

In Part One we saw that Alberich is the Jew in the *Ring*, which means that his brother Mime must also be a Jew. Now, Martin Gregor-Dellin tells us something that Wagner's own autobiography conceals: Geyer was not only an actor, he was also a *mime* artist (1980, 38). And a Jewish mime artist at that. Androgyny and anti-Semitism come together here. When Siegfried asks Mime who his parents are, the latter replies: "I am your father and mother in one" (*GS* 6.94). Mime refuses initially to tell him their names, although he knows them perfectly well, as is clear from the Riddle scene with the Wanderer. In Act II, as he sinks into a wistful reverie, Siegfried muses: "That he is not my father fills me with feelings of joy!" (*GS* 6.133). Having set this phrase to music, Wagner broke off composition of *Siegfried* on 27 June 1857. Was he relieved? The musings continue:

Wie sah mein Vater wohl aus?	What must my father have looked like?
Ha!—gewiß wie ich selbst:	Ha! Of course, like me!
denn wär' wo von Mime ein Sohn,	If Mime had had a son,
müßt' er nicht ganz	must he not look
Mime gleichen?	just like Mime?

(Ibid.)

But he is still not certain, as he admits to Fafner: "I do not know who I am" (*GS* 6.138); and so, to be on the safe side, he kills Mime, his false true father. Geyer saved the Wagner family, including Wagner himself who, born in Brühl, the center of Leipzig's Jewish quarter, bore his father's name—Richard Geyer—until his fourteenth year. The same ambivalence typifies Siegfied: twice he asks Mime,

in den Wald lauf' ich,	into the forest I run
dich zu verlassen,—	to escape you,
wie kommt das, kehr' ich zurück?	how comes it that I return?

(*GS* 6.91; cf. 6.94)

Wagner's life provides many examples of this same ambivalence in his relationships with Jews. There is, of course, the anti-Semitic pamphlet, from which we know of his hatred of Mendelssohn and Meyerbeer, but there were also close ties of friendship with Leah David, a "Jew named Levy but known as Lippert" (*ML*, 47), and, toward the end of his life, Joseph Rubinstein, Hermann Levi, and Angelo Neumann (Gutman 1968, 5–6). And even the character of Alberich was not seen in a totally negative light by its creator: "R. tells me that he once felt every sympathy for Alberich, who represents the ugly person's longing for beauty," Wagner told Cosima on 2 March 1878, a remark that can be interpreted only as an autobiographical confession. Thus Alberich—who, let us not forget, is one of the few survivors at the end of the *Ring*—is comparable in certain ways to Wagner's dark shadow, just as he is Wotan's dark shadow (Light-Alberich and Black-Alberich they call each other in Act II of *Siegfried*). Since, as we know, wordplay vouchsafes profound insights into the unconscious, Alberich could also be Alb = er = ich, in other words, the dwarf (or Jew) that he is, is I.

The suggestion that Geyer was Wagner's father has one final consequence. We know from Wagner's much later account of his early years that Cäcilie, two years his junior, was his true childhood companion and that there was a particularly deep sense of affection between them. The possibility that the attraction was incestuous cannot be ruled out: if Geyer was Wagner's biological father, Cäcilie was no longer Wagner's half-sister but his natural sister. One should not be surprised, therefore, at the veritable paean to incest in the opening act of *Die Walküre*, in which Wotan's twinborn offspring, Siegmund and Sieglinde, ignorant of their origins, meet and mate, an act of incestuous affection that Wotan himself defends in no uncertain terms:

FRICKA

Wann—ward es erlebt,	When were siblings ever seen
daß leiblich Geschwister sich liebten?	to love each other carnally?

WOTAN

Heut'—hast du's erlebt:	Today you have seen it happen:
erfahre so,	Learn thus
was von selbst sich fügt,	that a thing may come to pass,
sei zuvor auch noch nie es gescheh'n.	though it never happened before.
Daß jene sich lieben,	That they love each other
leuchtet dir hell:	is plain as the day;
drum höre redlichen Rath!	so hear my honest advice:
Soll süße Lust	if sweet delight shall
deinen Segen dir lohnen,	reward your blessing,
so seg'ne, lachend der Liebe,	then smile on their love and
Siegmund und Sieglinde's Bund!	give that blessing to Siegmund's and Sieglinde's bond.

(*GS* 6.27–28)

As we have seen, it is a particularly complex but richly textured family romance. Thanks to the resources of psychoanalysis, however, we are in a better position to understand why three apparently heterogeneous features appear juxtaposed in Wagner's works and thoughts: the apologia for incest, anti-Semitism, and androgyny. Nor is it surprising that Georg Groddeck, the Freudian precursor of psychosomatic medicine, should have described the *Ring* as a "manual of psychoanalysis" (1927, 218).

Bisexuality in Freudian Theory

This overall portrait is so consistent that one might almost think that the "case of Wagner" had been invented with the sole aim of verifying Freud's system of explanation. But can we really believe that the arsenal of psychoanalysis is capable of explaining Wagner's androgynous fantasy? This is a question to which we must now turn our attention.

Although bisexuality is at the basis of psychoanalytic theory, this does not mean that it is clearly defined or that the links between its diverse manifestations have been adequately explained. The evidence of that irreproachable Freudian, Ernest Jones, confirms this point of view: "Psychology cannot yet explain on what the flair or intuition depends that guides the observer to follow up something his feelings tell him is important, not as a thing in itself, but as an example of some wide law of nature" (Jones 1953–57, 1.107).

The idea of bisexuality was not invented by Freud but was borrowed from his one-time friend and colleague, Wilhelm Fließ, who, in a study completed in spring 1896, *Relations between the Nose and the Female Genital Organs from the Biological Point of View*, had posited the idea that, in addition to the woman's menstrual cycle, both sexes operated on periodic cycles of twenty-three days. In his preface Fließ writes: "An examination of these two groups of periodic processes leads to the conclusion that they have intimate and stable relationships with male and female sexual characteristics and the fact that they exist, albeit in different forms for men and women, is entirely in keeping with our bisexual constitution." Fließ's bisexuality, therefore, is biological. Didier Anzieu quite rightly points out that "Fließ's theory of periods involves the idea of suppressing the difference between the sexes," a "fantasy" that finds expression in "assigning to man marks equivalent to those of supposed female castration" (Anzieu 1959, 1.229). Fließ's androgyne is a woman.

For a time, Freud adopted and quoted his friend's theory, as is clear from his letter of 6 December 1896: "In order to account for why the outcome [of premature sexual experience] is sometimes perversion and sometimes neurosis, I avail myself of the bisexuality of all human beings" (Freud 1985, 212). It is possible to gain an idea of the nature of the link that Fließ established verbally between bisexuality and repression from the summary of it that Freud gives in his 1919 essay "A Child Is Being Beaten":

> The first of these theories is anonymous. It was brought to my notice many years ago by a colleague with whom I was at that time on friendly terms. The theory is so attractive on account of its bold simplicity that the only wonder is that it should not have found its way into the literature of the subject except in a few scattered allusions. It is based on the fact of the bisexual constitution of human beings, and asserts that the motive force of repression in each individual is a struggle between the two sexual characters. The dominant sex of the person, that which is the more strongly developed, has represssed the mental representation of the subordinated sex into the unconscious. Therefore the nucleus of the unconscious (that is to say, the repressed) is in each human being that side of him which belongs to the opposite sex. Such a theory as this can only have an intelligible meaning if we assume that a person's sex is to be determined by the formation of his genitals; for otherwise it would not be certain which is a person's stronger sex and we should run the risk of reaching from the results of our enquiry the very fact which has to serve as its point of departure. To put the theory briefly: with men, what is unconscious and repressed can be brought down to feminine instinctual impulses; and conversely with women. (Freud 1919, 188–89)

It was not long, however, before Freud not only abandoned Fließ's theory of different periods but gave bisexuality an alternative meaning. In the crucial manuscript M, of May 1897, he writes: "It is to be supposed that the element essentially responsible for repression is always what is feminine. This is confirmed by the fact that women as well as men admit more readily to experiences with women than with men. What men essentially repress is the pederastic element" (1985, 246).

There are three essential new ideas here. In the first place Freud rejects Fließ's symmetrical vision and does so, moreover, according to a schema whose "masculine prejudice" (i.e., the belief that men's castration anxiety is women's penis envy) has been denounced by contemporary feminist critics. Freud's androgyny is male, and in a letter to Fließ of 15 October 1897, he contrasts his own hypothesis, according to which "repression always comes from femininity and is directed against virility," with that of Fließ, "who says the opposite" (ibid., 273). Second, Freud's bisexuality becomes psychological, not biological—a subject that, according to a later letter of 26 July 1904, was discussed by both men when they met in December 1897 (Anzieu 1959, 2.771): "I was all the more puzzled by your resistance in Breslau to the assumption of bisexuality in the psyche" (Freud 1985, 465). And, finally, bisexuality signified "latent homosexuality" for Freud.

Now, in his letter to Fließ of 15 October 1897, from which I quoted a moment ago, Freud informs his correspondent of a discovery that was to alter our entire picture of man in the twentieth century: the Oedipus complex.

> I have found, in my own case too, [the phenomenon of] being in love with my mother and jealous of my father, and I now consider it a universal event in early childhood, even if not so early as in children who have been made hysterical. (Similar to the invention of parentage [family romance] in paranoia—heroes, founders of religion.) If this is so, we can understand the gripping power of *Oedipus Rex*, in spite of all the objections that reason raises against the presupposition of fate. (1985, 198)

Freud's universalization of his own experience is somewhat suspect. As Anzieu (1959, 2.736–37) reminds us in his account of the epistemological background to this discovery, Freud found the material for his hypothesis in only *two* patients. It was confirmed for him by what he claimed was the universal character of a culturally remote myth. And he sought its validation, in himself, by means of self-analysis.

It is particularly important to emphasize that neither in this historic letter of 15 October 1897 nor in the relevant passage in *The Interpretation of Dreams*, where Freud first brought his theory of the Oedipus complex to public attention (1900, 261–63), does he speak of bisexuality—and, at risk of criticizing Anzieu (to whom this section is much indebted), we may well ask whether there are not good grounds for trying to explain this silence.

As we shall shortly have occasion to see, Freud was obsessed by the wish to be famous and did everything he could to avoid basing his theory of psychology on the idea of bisexuality, since he knew very well that, as a theory, he could not claim it as his own. Instead, the Oedipus complex allowed him to claim a personal triumph, at least in the short term. The role played by plagiarism and by the desire for fame in the formation and development of Freud's theories is nothing new in writings on the history of science and especially of psychoanalysis. In his excellent study *Freud, Biologist of the Mind*, Frank J. Sulloway shows very clearly that Freud borrowed not only the theory of bisexuality from Fließ but also the concept of the Fließian id and the homosexual etiology of paranoia (171–237). But Sulloway does not retrace the steps that Freud himself followed in reintegrating bisexuality into his theory of the Oedipus complex, even though he indicates that Freud did indeed owe the idea of bisexuality to Fließ. This is the reason, however, why Freud subsequently took such great pains to distance himself, little by little, from his former friend's conception. Finally, Freud succeeded in combining the Oedipus complex with bisexuality in his so-called complete version of the complex in 1923. It is this course that I should now like to follow, step by step.

Anzieu (1959) and Sulloway (1979) have both shown perfectly clearly that from the very outset there was a temptation on Freud's part to steal Fließ's idea of bisexuality from him. It is not even necessary to undertake a Freudian analysis of Freud's dreams to prove this point: those writings of Freud and Fließ that have been made public show this all too plainly.

The whole of Freud's correspondence with his friend bears witness to a constant desire to be the first to bring untold joy to humankind with new and important discoveries: "The expectation of eternal fame was so beautiful," he writes on 21 September 1897 (1985, 266). Turning to screen memories, "I'm not rich enough to keep my finest and probably my only lasting discovery to myself" (letter of 28 May 1899; ibid., 353). "Do you suppose that someday one will read on a marble tablet on this house: Here, on July 24, 1895, the secret of the dream revealed itself to Dr. Sigm. Freud?" (letter of 12 June 1900; ibid., 417). On several occasions Freud was on the point of making important neurological discoveries: a method of coloring nervous fibers, the anesthetizing power of cocaine, and the theory of the neuron, for example. On each occasion he either failed to carry his observations through to the end or realized that the discovery had been formulated before him (Anzieu 1959, 1.56, 64, 73). And the letters to Fließ abound in endless fears that others have already expressed what he thought he had discovered himself: "I found the substance of my insights stated quite clearly in Lipps, perhaps rather more so than I would like. . . . The correspondence [of our ideas] is close in details as well" (31 August 1898; 1985, 325).[10] Having abandoned neurology in favor of psychopathology—but still hoping to arrive at his "initial goal of philosophy" (letter of 1 January 1896; ibid., 159), he had to succeed, come what may, in elaborating a new vision of Man—a vision, if possible, without a precursor. In his essay "On the History of the Psycho-Analytic Movement" he states emphatically: "I have denied myself the very great pleasure of reading the works of Nietzsche, with the deliberate object of not being hampered in working out the impressions received in psycho-analysis by any sort of anticipatory ideas" (1914, 15–16). But in a letter of 1 February 1900, initally suppressed from his published correspondence with Fließ, Freud had written that he was starting to read Nietzsche, "in whom I hope to find words for much that remains mute in me" (Freud 1985, 398). A glance at Assoun's study (1980) will suffice to disabuse anyone still inclined to give credence to Freud's public pronouncements that he had not read a word of Nietzsche.[11]

Freud was intellectually indebted to other writers, and this is as true of his theory of bisexuality as of other areas. On 4 January 1898 he wrote to Fließ: "I literally embraced your stress on bisexuality and consider this idea of yours to be the most significant one for my subject since that of 'defense'" (1985, 292). Anzieu is quite right to describe the phrase "for my subject" as "a Freudian slip that reveals Freud's desire to appropriate Fließ's conception of bisexuality" (1959, 1.343). And this is exactly what was to happen.[12]

On 15 March 1898 Freud wrote to Fließ: "I do not in the least underestimate bisexuality either; I expect it to provide all further enlightenment. . . . It is only that at the moment I feel remote from it because, buried in a dark shaft, I see nothing else" (1985, 303). If Freud has the feeling of floundering about, it is because he never really succeeds in dissociating himself from the biological principles of Fließ's bisexuality. On 22 September 1898, for example, we find him writing to Fließ: "I am not at all in disagreement with you, not at all inclined to leave the psychology hanging in the air without an organic basis. But apart from this conviction I do not know how to go on, neither theoretically nor therapeutically, and therefore must behave as if only the psychological were under consideration. Why I cannot fit it together [the organic and the psychological] I have not even begun to fathom" (ibid., 326). This was catastrophically depressing from the point of view of his fantasy of fame and immortality. "How can I ever hope to gain an insight into the whole of mental activity, which was once my proud expectation?" he asked Fließ on 23 October 1898 (ibid., 332).

It is not surprising, therefore, that the first edition of *The Interpretation of Dreams* contains none of the references to bisexuality that are found in later editions (Anzieu 1959, 2.480–81), with the exception of the following quasi-parenthetical remark: "The theory of the psychoneuroses is an indisputable and invariable fact that only sexual wishful impulses from infancy, which have undergone repression . . . during the developmental period of childhood, are capable of being revived during *later* developmental periods (whether as a result of the subject's sexual constitution, which is derived from an initial *bisexuality*,[13] or as a result of unfavourable influences acting upon the course of his sexual life)" (1900, 605–6). Freud still alludes here to Fließ's conception of repression on the basis of biological bisexuality. But, except for a note on the following page in which he announces the need to get more deeply involved "in the still unsolved problems of perversion and bisexuality" (ibid., 607n), we must wait for the *Three Essays on the Theory of Sexuality* of 1905 before Freud returns to the subject in detail. At the time of his completion of *The Interpretation of Dreams* he was still emphasizing his inability to explore the question in any greater depth: as he wrote to tell Fließ on 1 August 1899, "The farther the work of the past year recedes, the more satisfied I become. But bisexuality! You are certainly right about it" (Freud 1985, 364).

It was the question of bisexuality, however, that led to the break between Fließ and Freud. In his 1906 book on the subject, *In eigener Sache*, Fließ recalls the envy that Freud felt toward him. Freud had in fact spoken to Swoboda in the course of treatment in 1900, informing him of the "fact of permanent bisexuality." In turn, Swoboda talked to Otto Weininger, who published his highly influential study, *Sex and Character*, in 1903 (quoted in Freud 1985, 464). From 1900 Fließ had the feeling that he had been robbed of his discovery, as Freud was quick to appreciate in his *Psychopathology of Everyday Life*:

> One day in the summer of 1901 I remarked to a friend with whom I used at that time to have a lively exchange of scientific ideas: "These problems of the neuroses are only to be solved if we base ourselves wholly and completely on the assumption of the original bisexuality of the individual." To which he replied: "That's what I told you two and a half years ago at Br. [Breslau] when we went for that evening walk. But you wouldn't hear of it then." It is painful to be requested in this way to surrender one's originality. I could not recall any such conversation or this pronouncement of my friend's. One of us must have been mistaken and on the "*cui prodest?*" principle it must have been myself. Indeed, in the course of the next week I remembered the whole incident, which was just as my friend had tried to recall it to me; I even recollected the answer I had given him at the time: "I've not accepted that yet; I'm not inclined to go into the question." (1901, 143–44)

It is a fact that, in his later correspondence, Freud admitted his debt to Fließ, while still limiting bisexuality to its biological dimension. In

Dreams and Hysteria,[14] he wrote in a letter of 30 January 1901, "There are only glimpses of the organic [elements], that is, the erotogenic zones and bisexuality. But bisexuality is mentioned and specifically recognized once and for all, and the ground is prepared for detailed treatment of it on another occasion. . . . The principal issue in the conflicting thought processes is the contrast between an inclination toward men and an inclination toward women" (Freud 1985, 434). Seven months later, in a letter of 7 August 1901, he proposes that the two of them should work together, albeit under his own supervision: "As far as I can see, my next work will be called 'Human Bisexuality.' For the time being I have only one thing for it: the chief insight which for a long time now has built itself upon the idea that repression, my core problem, is possible only through reaction between two sexual currents." Here, again, Freud attempts to insist on the originality of his own psychological concept. He then goes on: "I must have a long and serious discussion with you. The idea itself is yours. . . . Perhaps I must borrow even more from you; perhaps my sense of honesty will force me to ask you to coauthor the work with me." (Freud's use of the verb *force* speaks volumes.) "Thereby the anatomical-biological part would gain in scope, the part which, if I did it alone, would be meager, I would concentrate on the psychic aspect of bisexuality and the explanation of the neurotic" (ibid., 448).

But Fließ's reply—which has not survived—must have been chilly, not only because Fließ felt robbed but also, no doubt, because he found it difficult to accept that Freud had long since abandoned his own theory of periods and bilaterality, which he had associated with the idea of bisexuality. Freud made his own position clear in a letter of 19 September 1901:

> I do not comprehend your answer concerning bisexuality. It is obviously very difficult to understand each other. I certainly had no intention of doing anything but working on my contribution to the theory of bisexuality, elaborating the thesis that repression and the neuroses, and thus the independence of the unconscious, presuppose bisexuality. You will by now have seen from the relevant reference to your priority in "Everyday Life" that I have no intention of expanding my role in this insight. But the establishment of some link to the general biological and anatomical aspects of bisexuality would be, after all, indispensable in any such work. Since almost everything I know about it comes from you, all I can do is cite you or get this introduction entirely from you. (Ibid., 450)

The project remained in the realm of fantasy, of course.[15] But is it possible to give Freud a full discharge in matters of intellectual ethics? Discussing the argument over precedence, Anzieu writes: "The idea of a fundamental biological bisexuality belongs to Fließ. It is more difficult to say whether its application to the psychology of nervous disorders and to general psychology is Freud's own contribution, or whether it, too, was suggested to him by Fließ" (1959, 2.681). And, a little later: "Freud subsequently maintained his interest in bisexuality and periodicity, and on each occasion cited Fließ" (ibid., 2.715). Anzieu refers at this point to the *Three Essays on the Theory of Sexuality*, "The Disposition to Obsessional Neurosis" (1913), and *Beyond the Pleasure Principle* (1920). The order of the texts seems to prove, as Sulloway (1979) also believes, that Freud's psychological interpretation of bisexuality owed something to Fließ. If I insist on this point here, it is because what is at stake is not only the problem of the relationship between bisexuality and the Oedipus complex but also, and above all, the status of Freudian interpretation.

The first of the texts quoted by Anzieu takes up and expands ideas contained in the letter of 6 December 1896 in which Freud refers to Fließ's biological theory, before continuing: "In order to account for why the outcome [of premature sexual experience] is sometimes perversion and sometimes neurosis, I avail myself of the bisexuality of all human beings" (Freud 1985, 212). The same idea recurs in the *Three Essays*: "Neuroses are, so to say, the negative of perversions." Freud then goes on to appeal to the idea of psychological bisexuality: "The unconscious mental life of all neurotics (without exception) shows inverted impulses, fixations of their libido upon persons of their own sex. . . . I can only insist that an unconscious tendency to inversion is never absent and is of particular value in throwing light upon hysteria in men" (1905, 80). In a note to this passage, however, he admits: "It is only fair to say that my attention was first drawn to the necessary universality of the tendency to inversion in psychoneurotics by Wilhelm Fließ of Berlin, after I had discussed its presence in individual cases" (ibid.).

Freud alludes here to Fließ's belief, cited above and summarized in the essay on child beating, that repression is the result of an inherently bisexual constitution.[16] Freud's letter of 4 January 1898 seems to indicate that the psychological consequences of bisexuality were not his own invention alone: "If I had a disinclination on personal grounds, because I am in part neurotic myself, this disinclination would certainly have been directed toward bisexuality, which, after all, *we*[17] hold responsible for the inclination to repression" (Freud 1985, 292). The published texts have a different ring to them. In the 1913 essay "The Disposition to Obsessional Neurosis," the reference to Fließ is relatively neutral: alluding, in a note, to Fließ's theory of periods, Freud announces that it is the task of the biologist to determine the causes of those developmental inhibitions that he discusses here (1913, 135). The final explicit references to Fließ are altogether negative. In the 1919 article "A Child Is Being Beaten," for instance, Freud recalls Fließ's theory of periods but only to dismiss it as "incorrect and misleading" (1919, 188). And a year later, in *Beyond the*

Pleasure Principle, he recognizes Fließ's greatness but states that external factors "are of a kind to invalidate the rigour of his formulations and enable us, at least, to call into question the universality of the laws he has formulated" (1920, 57). Freud is now home and dry and can establish a link between bisexuality and the Oedipus complex, thus conjuring up the new theory with which he had earlier hoped to gratify humanity. With this in mind, we may look once again at one of the most frequently cited texts in Freudian literature, "A Child Is Being Beaten":

> The affections of the little girl are fixed on her father, who has probably done all he could to win her love, and in this way has sown the seeds of an attitude of hatred and rivalry towards her mother. This attitude exists side by side with a current of affectionate dependence on her, and as years go on it may be destined to come into consciousness more and more clearly and forcibly, or else to give an impetus to an excessive reaction of devotion to her. (1919, 172)

The aim of the article is to show how children's fantasies of being beaten derive from the Oedipus complex. Freud's line of argument can be summarized as follows. In the case of small girls, the fantasy passes through three phases. In the first, a child of indeterminate sex, who is not the one producing the fantasy, is beaten by an indeterminate adult. In the second, unconscious phase, the beaten child is the one producing the fantasy, and the adult who is doing the beating is the father. In the third, conscious phase, the male adult is undetermined as before, and the girl being beaten is replaced by a boy. Turning his attention to small boys, Freud fails to find any equivalent of the first phase outlined above. Conversely, the fantasy corresponding to the second phase finds unconscious expression with boys in the form "I am being beaten by my father." In the equivalent of the third phase, it is said consciously: "A woman is beating children of the male sex."

The dissymmetry on the basis of which Freud criticizes Fließ's theory is as follows: where girls fantasize about being boys in the third phase, boys maintain their sexual identity but replace the "beating" father by the mother. In the case of girls, the second phase reflects the normal Oedipal position: from a masochistic point of view, "I am being beaten by my father" means "my father loves me." With boys, "I am being beaten by my father" (which also means "my father loves me") reflects an *inverted* Oedipal position. On the conscious level, the girl turns masochism into sadism by changing into a boy in the third phase, while the boy, being the one who is beaten, maintains the masochistic stance in the form of a passive fantasy derived from a feminine attitude toward his father, whom he fantasizes as his mother, which allows him to evade his latent homosexuality. "In both cases," Freud concludes, "the beating-phantasy has its origin in an incestuous attachment to the father" (1919, 186).

It is on the basis of this analysis that Freud refutes Fließ's concept of the "sexualization of the process of repression" (ibid., 190). To the extent that in beating fantasies the girl adopts a feminine attitude toward her father, that attitude corresponds with her dominant sex, which represses the mental representation of the subordinated sex into the unconscious. Her fantasy "becomes unconscious, and is replaced by a conscious fantasy which disavows the girl's manifest sexual character. The theory is therefore useless as an explanation of beating-fantasies, and is contradicted by the facts" (ibid.). "In the last resort," Freud concludes, "we can only see that both in male and female individuals masculine as well as feminine instinctual impulses are found, and that each can equally well undergo repression and so become unconscious" (ibid., 190–91).

In this way Freud has succeeded in linking the Oedipus complex with a bisexual interpretation of fantasies while unharnessing that bisexual dimension from the determinism that Fließ had established between the individual's manifest sexual constitution and repression. From now on the way was open for Freud to combine his discovery of the Oedipus complex with the *idea* of bisexuality that Fließ had offered him at an earlier date. And this, indeed, is what Freud was to do in 1923, in *The Ego and the Id*, with its so-called complete formulation of the Oedipus complex. It is not impossible to see in this study the development of an idea of which he had had a vague intuition as long ago as 1 August 1899: "I am accustoming myself to regarding every sexual act as a process in which four individuals are involved" (Freud 1985, 364).

In the third chapter of *The Ego and the Id*, Freud begins by recalling the structure of the Oedipus complex in its simple form, in which the boy's libido is directed toward his mother, with feelings of rivalry and hostility toward his father. When the Oedipus complex is demolished, the boy's masculinity is consolidated (1923, 32). As in the 1919 article, Freud concedes that there is a certain dissymmetry between the sexes, since girls will "bring their masculinity into prominence" (ibid.). "It would appear, therefore, that in both sexes the relative strength of the masculine and feminine sexual dispositions is what determines whether the outcome of the Oedipus situation shall be an identification with the father or with the mother. This is one of the ways in which bisexuality takes a hand in the subsequent vicissitudes of the Oedipus complex" (ibid., 33).

But, Freud goes on, the complete complex is "twofold, positive and negative, and is due to the bisexuality originally present in children: that is to say, a boy has not merely an ambivalent attitude towards his father and an affectionate object-choice towards his mother, but at the same time he also behaves like a girl and displays an affectionate feminine attitude to his father and a corresponding jealousy towards his mother" (ibid.). And the same is true, mutatis mutandis, in the case of the little girl: "The relative intensity of the two identifications in any individual will reflect the preponderance in him of one or other of the two sexual dispositions" (ibid., 34).

Freud suggests that an appeal to bisexuality may invalidate his explanation of the Oedipus complex in terms of identification resulting from an attitude of rivalry. Above all, however, he admits that it can cause *hermeneutical* confusion: "It is this complicating element introduced by bisexuality that makes it so difficult to obtain a clear view of the facts in connection with the earliest object-choices and identifications, and still more difficult to describe them intelligibly" (ibid., 33). Accordingly, he addresses himself to the very function of psychoanalytic interpretation and demonstrates the mechanics of his line of reasoning. To this end we may conveniently return to the 1919 study "A Child Is Being Beaten," where it will be seen that in order to reach his conclusion—in other words, to show that the Oedipus complex is based on the theory of bisexuality that he had succeeded in making his own—he tolerates repeated shifts in meaning and successive approximations. Something that Freudian theory posits as a universal truth is based on a banal problem of intellectual priority, and the absence of any control that it places at the heart of the hermeneutical approach rests, at bottom, on the question of sexual ambivalence.

The first problem is a statistical one. At the beginning of his article Freud notes that the fantasy occurs with "surprising" frequency (1919, 163) but, only a few pages later, admits that his findings are based on four female cases and two male ones (ibid., 167). Of these, he intends to concentrate exclusively on the female ones, although the male ones make a brief reappearance at a later stage of the argument (ibid., 185). Freud is no doubt aware of the difficulty here, since he writes: "If then on further observation a greater complexity of circumstances should come to light, I shall nevertheless be sure of having before us a typical occurrence, and one, moreover, that is not of an uncommon kind" (ibid., 169). "The six cases I have mentioned so often do not exhaust my material. Like other analysts, I have at my disposal a far larger number of cases which have been investigated less thoroughly" (ibid., 177–78).

From an epistemological point of view, there is no reason why a relatively small number of given facts should be a major obstacle in validating a hypothesis. After all, the theory of relativity was put forward without any empirical evidence and validated only much later. But it is precisely this validation that is missing in the case before us. Freud passes with undue haste from assumption to affirmation. Thus he writes, entirely legitimately, "It would naturally be important to know whether the origin of infantile perversions from the Oedipus complex can be asserted as a general principle. While this cannot be decided without further investigation, it does not seem impossible" (ibid., 179). A few sentences later, however, assumption becomes certitude without any additional proof:

> If, however, the derivation of perversions from the Oedipus complex can be generally established, our estimate of its importance will have gained added strength. For in our opinion the Oedipus complex is the actual nucleus of neuroses, and the infantile sexuality which culminates in this complex is the true determinant of neuroses. What remains of the complex in the unconscious represents the disposition to the later development of neuroses in the adult. In this way the beating-fantasy and other analogous perverse fixations would also only be precipitates of the Oedipus complex. (Ibid.)

And the article ends on an unequivocal note: "Infantile sexuality, which is held under repression, acts as the chief motive force in the formation of symptoms; and the essential part of its content, the Oedipus complex, is the nuclear complex of neuroses" (ibid., 192). Q.E.D.

But what is Freud's evidence for according the Oedipus complex so central a position? The whole of his exegesis is based on a series of subtle shifts in interpretation. In the case of small girls, the narrative that can be summarized as "a child of indifferent sex is beaten by an indeterminate adult" becomes "I am being beaten by my father" in the second phase. But, as Freud himself admits, the second phase "has never had a real existence. It is never remembered, it has never succeeded in becoming conscious. It is *a construction of analysis*,[18] but it is no less a necessity on that account" (ibid., 170–71). Exactly the same is true of small boys: "This second phase—the child's fantasy of being itself beaten by its father—remains unconscious . . . and can only be reconstructed in the course of the analysis" (ibid., 175–76). It is clearly the experience of the psychoanalyst that leads him to interpolate this second phase between the first and third. Yet the theory of the Oedipus complex tells us that in any fantasy, other people are father-substitutes and that even when being beaten by her father, the little girl expresses her unconscious love for him in this way. In other words, the Oedipus complex influences the interpretation and, in its turn, the interpretation justifies the Oedipus complex. The argument is totally circular.

This circularity culminates in the so-called complete theory of the Oedipus complex as set forth in *The Ego and the Id*, where the hostility of the boy, jealous of his father, may be transformed into homosexual affection for him. The same is said to be true, mutatis mutandis, of the girl. This constellation opens up the way to a total flexibility of interpretation, as is clear from the following diagram:

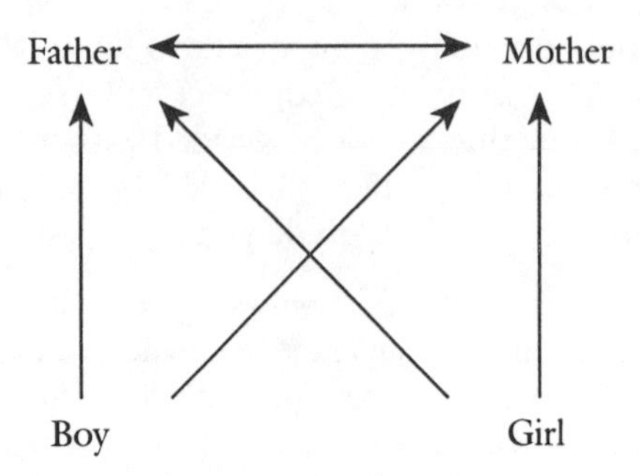

In its complete form—that is, the form that draws on the theory of bisexuality—the Oedipus complex loses in specificity what it had hoped to gain in universality: the theory will always operate while at the same time forfeiting its ability to discriminate between alternative explanations. As Anzieu comments, entirely symptomatically, "In searching hard enough, would one not find an Oedipal problem in every dream?" (1959, 1.194).

It is not surprising, therefore, that Freud thought that the Oedipus myth, as recounted by Sophocles, provided confirmation and validation of his thesis, whereas the reading of it that he proposes is merely the result of his own projection.

There is an important point here. The attempt to explain the human psyche in terms of the Oedipus complex claims to be universalist, in other words, ahistorical and acultural—as a recurrent image in Freud's writings confirms: he is clearly fascinated by archaeology as a symbol of a buried and undifferentiated historical age and a metaphor of depth psychology. In one of his earlier essays, *Totem and Taboo*, he even tries—unsuccessfully and without adducing any evidence—to claim that the Oedipus complex is an intercultural phenomenon. As Gilbert Durand has emphasized (1964, 50), Malinowski's observations of the natives of Trobriand Island have shown that this is not the case. Indeed, Malinowski even goes so far as to conclude that *Totem and Taboo* is pure fiction from beginning to end.

It is doubtful, moreover, whether the Greek myth can be said to offer confirmation of Freud's hypothesis. In an unjustifiably neglected article, "Oedipus without the Complex," the erudite Hellenist Jean-Pierre Vernant has shown that the alleged sensation of terror that we feel when attending a performance of the Sophoclean tragedy is the result not of our reliving the Oedipus complex of our childhood but simply of the mechanisms inherent in Greek tragedy:

> In order for there to be a tragic awareness, the human and divine planes need to be sufficiently distinct to oppose one other without ceasing, however, to appear inseparable. The tragic sense of responsibility arises when the human

> action is already the object of reflection, of inner debate, but has not yet acquired enough autonomous status to be entirely self-sufficient. The true domain of tragedy is situated in this border area where human acts intermesh with divine powers, thereby revealing their true meaning, a meaning ignored by those very people who have taken the initiative and who bear the responsibility for them, inasmuch as they are incorporated into an order that transcends the human individual and escapes his understanding. Every tragedy necessarily takes place, therefore, on two different levels. (1967, 82)

But worse is still to come. In order for there to be a phobia concerning incest (or a desire for it), Oedipus has to suspect who his parents are. Yet "Oedipus states not just once but several times,[19] without any doubt whatever, that he is the son of Merope and Polybus" (ibid., 91). Nor can it be argued that this is evidence of repression. It is simply an essential element in the tragedy.

What Freud found in the Greek myth was not what a patient sociohistorical reading would have allowed him to discover there but a meaning that he needed to find there in order to escape from the impasse in which he found himself as a result of his intellectual rivalry with Fließ. In the short term—and instead of taking bisexuality as the starting point for the science that would ensure his immortality—Freud supported his theory by "discovering" or, rather, inventing the Oedipus complex. Twenty years later he was finally able to combine the Oedipus complex with bisexuality, thereby opening up the way to boundless speculation on a topic that, time and again, has recurred in the course of the twentieth century—androgynous hermeneutics.

Reexamination of the Wagnerian Family Romance

In the light of what has just been said, it is worth returning to the interpretation of the family romance advanced at the beginning of the present chapter. My aim is now to show that the *plasticity* of Freud's exegesis is such that, for reasons that can be described as aesthetic (i.e., for reasons of coherency), it is always possible to arrive at an explanation that carries a degree of conviction.

I explained the constitution of the fantasy of androgyny (or the Aristophanes complex) in terms of two factors: masochism bound up with the violence to which Wagner was subjected when his family tried to stop his screaming because of nocturnal hallucinations, and forbidden access to the female and theatrical world, the latter being fantasized as a fetishistic substitute for the female world.

My use of the term "masochism"—in other words, pleasure in being beaten—is based on Wagner's own phrase: "Severe scoldings or even corporal punishment would then seem to me redeeming kindnesses" (*ML*, 13). It is only because the theater, and especially *Der Freischütz*, was something that he desired and admired that we infer the punishments associated with his hallucinations might also be perceived as something positive. Here, too, as with Freud, the reasoning is circular, resting, as it does, on the following syllogism: I know that the masochist takes pleasure in the violence he receives; Wagner says that the punishment he received helped him to forget his hallucinations, and so he takes pleasure in being beaten. It is this interpretation that, turned into a general rule by Freud on the basis of cases of actual masochism, is projected onto Wagner's autobiography in order to give it a masochistic meaning. A second layer of interpretation is then grafted onto the first: the punishment—accepted as something positive—is a substitute for masturbatory pleasure, predisposing Wagner to fantasize his ego in autoerotic terms.

In moving on to the role of the mother in our earlier interpretation, we find the ground is even more treacherous. The texts from which I quoted—the passages from *Mein Leben* and the letter to Wagner's half-sister—seem to be unambiguous. Yet, if we turn to Martin Gregor-Dellin's 1980 life of the composer, the early chapters of which constitute a clearly Freudian interpretation of Wagner's childhood, we find the author arguing that Wagner felt a very strong filial bond with his mother—and this in spite of the passages from *Mein Leben* quoted above. "One letter . . . assumes special significance," Gregor-Dellin insists. Written in Karlsbad on 25 July 1835, it contains the following lines: "Only to you, dearest Mother, does my mind return with the sincerest love and deepest emotion. . . . See, Mother, now that we are apart, I am so overwhelmed with feelings of gratitude for your glorious love for your child, which you lately showed again with such warmth and affection, that I should dearly like to write and talk of it to you in the fondest tones of a lover to his beloved. Ah, but far more than that, for is not the love of one's mother far more—far more unsullied than any other?" Gregor-Dellin concludes: "This conveys a remarkable, textbook mother fixation that was bound to affect his relations with the opposite sex" (1980, 43). Without examining the matter any further, he accepts that this letter expresses the true relationship between Wagner and his mother. But how do we know when Wagner is telling the truth? We know how many passages in *Mein Leben* need to be treated with caution, but if we believe him here and assume that the relationship was, in fact, a difficult one, it is because the context in which the present letter was written seems to account for its exceptional character: when Wagner wrote to his mother on 25 July 1835 he had just spent two months with her in Leipzig after a year-long stay in Magdeburg, to which he was shortly to return. He was twenty-two years old and finally independent of the family circle: he could now afford to be affectionate toward his mother, even if he expressed that affection with the pomposity authorized by the age.

But ultimately it matters little whether this explanation is correct. If Gregor-Dellin chooses to rely on this particular letter rather than on all the other evidence that indicates a lack of affection, it is because he is obliged to do so. From the standpoint of Freudian theory, only a libidinal attachment to his mother can explain his predilection, in life as in art, for the role of the "injured third party," in other words, his tendency to fall in love with "attached" women and to seek the image of his mother in those other women, whether as lovers or wives. "If the psychologists are to be believed," Gregor-Dellin concludes,

> he suffered from the traumatic notion that he was depriving someone else of a wife (mother). He was even tactless enough to make this clear to Cosima. He had never had an untouched woman in his life, he told her; none of them had ever been "new." Within the basic framework of Wagner's love for the "attached" woman—his mother—Ludwig Geyer undoubtedly represented the "rival." Chained to his mother, Wagner suffered from what psychologists would term an "injured-third-party" requirement—a complex that impels its victims to seek the strangest forms of escape and release. (Ibid.)

This attitude of the "injured third party" is certainly a given fact in Wagner's life and works: he systematically sought to steal other men's wives (Jessie Laussot, Mathilde Wesendonck, Cosima von Bülow, and Judith Gautier) and many of his operatic characters find themselves in the same position: think of the Dutchman with regard to Senta and Erik; Tannhäuser vis-à-vis Wolfram and Elisabeth; and Lohengrin with regard to Elsa and Telramund; Tristan takes Isolde first from Morold and then from King Marke; Siegmund breaks up the marriage of Sieglinde and Hunding; Walther seduces Eva and thereby comes between her and old Sachs; and Parsifal, finally, diverts Kundry from Klingsor's ensnarements.

The explanation of the injured third party is not limited to Gregor-Dellin but is common to most psychoanalytic approaches to Wagner,[20] which, in turn, are based on Freud's 1910 essay "A Special Type of Choice of Object Made by Men." For Freud, the injured-third-party complex results from the "infantile fixation of tender feelings on the mother" (1910c, 235), in other words, from the Oedipus complex. However—and it is here that the malleability of the psychoanalytic interpretation is difficult to accept—there needs to be an attachment to the mother, with the father cast in the role of hated rival, if this Wagnerian attitude is to be explained by means of Freud's hypothesis. We have seen how things stood with Johanna. As for Ludwig Geyer, there is ***nothing*** in Wagner's writings that offers even the tiniest vestige of proof that Wagner felt hostility toward him: quite the opposite, all the evidence indicates how grateful he felt. Of course, this ignores the unconscious element: I can tell my mother that I love her while telling others that I do not love her—which means that unconsciously I have a choice between loving her and not loving her. And the same is true of my father: I can say that my family and I owe him a great deal while at the same time hating him in secret.

When, in the opening section of this chapter, I suggested a psychoanalytic explanation of Wagner's androgyny, I was sufficiently perverse as to borrow the same examples from Wagner's operas as those used by Gregor-Dellin to demonstrate Wagner's attachment to his mother, even though, in my own case, I had opted for the theory that Wagner hated his mother (1980, 44–45). If the same examples can be made to work in both cases, it is because, in keeping with the character of Freudian hermeneutics, they are ambiguous in meaning: I can claim that Siegfried's longing for the mother he never knew could equally well express Wagner's love for Johanna as regret for the affection he was denied as a child. Moreover, the contradiction is part and parcel of the operas themselves. It is by no means certain, after all, that Siegfried's relations with Brünnhilde (in whom he sees, first and foremost, a mother substitute) are the same as those between Parsifal and Kundry (who appears to the hero with his mother's rejuvenated features). Brünnhilde inspires a feeling of fear, although Siegfried does not turn and flee, while Kundry instills a sense of repulsion, causing Parsifal to reject her. By considering the works globally, without taking account of Wagner's own development, and by associating them with the earliest stages of infancy, one simplifies the problem, leaving Freudian hermeneutics to do the rest: one can always propose a coherent interpretation.

It is entirely typical of the situation under review that in seeking to explain the same phenomenon of the injured third party, another writer, André Michel (1951), has succeeded in reconciling the lack of tenderness shown by Wagner's mother with the letter of July 1835 and, in particular, with the sentence "I should dearly like to write and talk of it to you in the fondest tones of a lover to his beloved." Wagner's description of the reproach he bore his mother is now interpreted as proof of his profound feelings for her (ibid., 67), feelings that he turns into a "guilty mother fixation" that conflicts with the "sublimation due to her marriage with his father" (ibid., 71). Michel concludes: "While choosing partners who were younger than he was, he never ceased projecting onto their real image a maternal *imago* that lost nothing of its Oedipal character" (ibid., 77). Nor can Michel resist a play on words, which takes the place of any real analysis: "The Flying Dutchman is literally *fixated on the sea* [la mer]" (ibid., 75), the assimilation of *la mer* (the sea) and *la mère* (the mother) being justified subsequently by a reference to the amniotic fluid of the womb (ibid., 79), even if this play on words is impossible in German.

Michel was no doubt more than delighted to have his analysis confirmed by Wagner himself, who, writing in *Opera and Drama*, had insisted: "Even today we need interpret the *Oedipus myth* only according to its innermost essence in order to obtain a clear picture of the whole history of mankind from the beginning of society to the necessary downfall of the State" (1851a, *GS* 4.65). The only problem is that Michel (1951, 72) cites Wagner out of context and at second hand.[21] If he had referred to the section of *Opera and Drama* that surrounds this sentence, he would have discovered that, for Wagner, the Oedipus myth has a completely different meaning from the one that Freud was to give to it. Wagner invokes the story of Oedipus to show that states are based on a primitive form of property, which in turn provides the basis not only for social order but also for all the crimes that are committed in justifying that order (1851a, *GS* 4.65).

Gregor-Dellin denies that Wagner harbored negative feelings toward his mother; for André Michel those feelings were transformed into an object of reproach. Thanks to the plasticity of Freudian exegesis I can love the mother who hates me (a love that may also involve masochism) or I may be seeking the mother I never knew. Any explanation that draws on the Oedipus complex will work in every case, since my attachment to my mother and the resultant Oedipus complex are universal.

The same is true when we turn to the interpretation of dreams. Can I really claim that Wagner's dream of 1 January 1882, cited in the first section of this chapter, betrays a repressed homosexual desire?[22] If I am convinced that the analytical approach is correct, the answer must be yes, but a non-Freudian commentator on Wagner's dreams proposes a different, yet equally coherent, interpretation: "One can ask whether this dream does not convey his gnawing concern that his son Siegfried might not be capable of taking over and continuing his work, coupled with a critical attack on that work itself ('candle too soft, throws insufficient flame')" (Muller 1981, 188). It is worth noting that of all the dreams reported by Cosima, this is the only one with potentially homosexual connotations, whereas among the corpus as a whole it is feelings of anxiety that dominate Wagner's dreams, particularly the fear of losing Cosima. This certainly seems to justify Muller's explanation. Freud, of course, cites dreams expressive of anxiety in *The Interpretation of Dreams* but, as we know, all dreams are really the expression of a desire and, if a dream signifies the opposite of what it says, it follows that Wagner was actually hoping that Cosima would leave him . . .

It is clear, therefore, that a psychoanalytic interpretation is not decidable. Freud himself had already encountered the problem of the ambiguity of exegesis: "We have already become acquainted with the interpretative rule according to which every element in a dream can, for the purposes of interpretation, stand for its opposite just as easily as for itself" (1900, 471). This admission comes from Freud's first published book, *The Interpretation of Dreams*, written at the beginning of his analytical career. All too soon it was not the context that played a decisive role but rather conformity to a theory believed, a priori, to be true. There is a good example of this toward the end of Freud's life: at the end of *The Future of an Illusion* (1927) he interprets the case of a colleague not by analyzing him but by projecting onto him a fixed interpretation founded on the Oedipus complex and considered as an infrangible truth. Freudian interpretation is no doubt the most perfect kind of noncontrollable plot since it is the theory that, a priori, determines which data are retained for analysis. That this is no exaggeration is clear from Freud's own letter to Jung on the subject of *Totem and Taboo*: "My interest [in this study] is diminished by the conviction that I am already in possession of the truths I am trying to prove" (Freud 1974, 472).

There is an outstanding example of such circularity in a study devoted to the *Ring* and written by Georg Groddeck, a Freudian who, for all his originality, enjoyed the master's esteem. His 1927 article "The *Ring*" is all the more interesting in that it is based, essentially, on my own "primitive scene," namely, the androgynous love duet between Siegfried and Brünnhilde in Act III of *Siegfried*. But although Groddeck is rightly regarded as a writer who has reflected on the question of human bisexuality from a psychoanalytic point of view,[23] the androgynous nature of the relationship between Siegfried and Brünnhilde seems—surprisingly—to have passed him by. He locates the underlying meaning of this scene elsewhere: "It is not his beloved whom Siegfried discovers but his mother. . . . The love between Siegfried and Brünnhilde is the passion between mother and son" (1927, 220). Groddeck expands on this interpretation: "The mother of the man dies of the child" (ibid., 221), which is why both of them will later die.[24] The author never appeals to Wagner's own life since for him the *Ring*—that "manual of psychoanalysis"—contains all the truths of that innate science (ibid., 222), a science that we need only to learn in order to decode all the secrets of our psyche and human relations in general. "Where can one read in psychoanalytic literature that a woman feels love only when the man dies . . . , when her lovesick frenzy has passed, when he is a child once again and she feels she is his mother once again?" (ibid., 229). For Groddeck, the *Ring* expresses an intangible and eternal truth.[25]

But having disposed of the biographical data, psychocriticism ought to go one stage further and overturn the model initially proposed by Freud in "Leonardo da Vinci and a Memory of His Childhood." In this essay Freud examines the painter's life, adopting the model of clinical practice, in an attempt to find an explanation for the homosexual fantasies revealed in the painter's works. With Charles Mauron, by contrast, biography is envisaged only as a means of checking the analytical interpretation of "obsessive metaphors" (1962, 29, 32, 165–88). Epistemologically speaking, Mauron's approach has the great merit of relying first and foremost on thematic recurrences, which is also the approach adopted by the majority of those analyses of Wagner that linger over the figure of the injured third party. But it is an approach that allows one to abandon the historical explanation, and its attitude to biographical data was bound to lead to the position that was soon to be claimed by the New Criticism with its structuralist orientation: I can propose an interpretation of Racine without taking account of the details of his life but basing myself entirely on the text. "The events of adult life are more or less well known, while those of infancy are very rare," writes Mauron. "*It is the works, therefore, that must explain the life*[26] and not vice versa. The evolution of the myth reveals, at least in part, that of the unconscious personality" (1963, 230). In other words, Wagner's works ought to reveal the secret of his birth: since the only references are to questions that must not be asked about origins and to fathers who are unknown or dead, it follows that Wagner's real father was Geyer and that he perceived the latter to be a Jew.

In presenting my own argument I chose a controversial historical interpretation for the purpose in hand, pretending to accept the thesis according to which Geyer was not only Wagner's real father but also a Jew. It may be said straightaway that this double thesis is accepted by another of Wagner's biographers, Robert Gutman, who even goes so far as to suggest that Geyer could be the father of other children beside Richard and Cäcilie (1968, 7). Conversely, the thesis is rejected out of hand by Curt von Westernhagen (1978, 7–8), who points out, quite rightly, that the whole of Geyer's family was Protestant. But it is symptomatic that when citing the entry in Cosima's diaries that I quoted above, he forgets to mention the explicit reference to a resemblance between Geyer and Siegfried. Westernhagen's links with Nazism are now well known,[27] so that it is impossible to avoid the conclusion that he had no interest in admitting to Jewish ascendancy in the case of the composer.

Historically speaking, there are in fact two problems—Wagner's paternity and Geyer's Jewishness—that need to be treated separately. Wagner's possible Jewishness did not become a subject for public discussion until after 1869, when Nietzsche appears to have spoken somewhat too freely on the subject. That conscientious biographer, Ernest Newman (1933, 2.608–13), was able to show that Nietzsche was party to a private confidence in December 1869,[28] and that it is only after that date that cartoons and caricatures began to appear showing Wagner as a Jew.[29] Only now was he accorded the scornful sobriquet "Geyerbeer." Newman considered Nietzsche the source of this titillating information. What is more, no one

Wagner caricatured as a Jew in the Viennese satirical journal *Der Floh*, 1879

is entirely certain as to the Jewishness of the name Geyer. As we have seen, Nietzsche based his insinuations on the name of Adler alone; Newman (1933, 2.610) describes both names as those of German Jews. In his study of Wagner's anti-Semitism, *The Darker Side of Genius*, the Jewish historian Jacob Katz insists: "Unlike Adler, the name Geyer is never found among Jews"[30] (Katz 1985, 121). It will be noted, however, that Nietzsche does not deny this: "A *Geyer* [vulture] is practically an *Adler* [eagle]" (Nietzsche 1888, 638). He equates the two names but does not say that Geyer is a Jewish name.

Gregor-Dellin is right, therefore, to set aside the question of Jewish antecedents and to note simply that Wagner was in two minds about his own paternity. It would be interesting, from the point of view of biographical technique, to retrace Gregor-Dellin's line of argument against the Geyer hypothesis but, whatever the psychoanalytic interpretation that he draws from it, he is right to draw attention to the leitmotivic recurrence of the enigmatic theme of paternity in Wagner's libretti: "Almost all his heroes have a surrogate or foster father, such as Siegfried's weird Mime ('mime' being Geyer's professional designation)" (Gregor-Dellin 1980, 38). But if one adopts the thesis that Wagner projects the frustrations of his private life onto his works, there is no reason not to go one stage further. I believe I have furnished philological proof that Mime is a Jew, in which case this character may be thought of as embodying the ultimate admission of Wagner's family secret that he was at such pains to conceal. But we then find ourselves caught up once again in the vicious circle of psychoanalytic hermeneutics without being able to achieve any certainty, while still being able to use the method as a means of explaining the coincidence of Wagner's androgynous fantasy and anti-Semitism.

In fact there is not a single surviving text that would allow us to maintain that Wagner felt a secret hatred of Geyer and justify both the thesis of the injured third party and his anti-Jewish sentiment. Moreover, if Cosima Wagner's diaries are to be believed, it was only relatively late in life, not during his childhood, that Wagner came to harbor anti-Jewish thoughts: "After lunch he tells me how handsome he was and how at the age of thirty he became so anti-Jewish. Taking off from an article about Vienna and its Israelites, he enlarges upon the subject of how terrible it is to have this foreign Jewish element in our midst and how we have lost everything" (*CT*, 19 February 1881). It is more than likely that the Jewishness of Alberich and Mime can be explained in personal and ideological terms rather than with reference to the enigma of the composer's paternity. As Katz (1985) reminds us, Wagner's anti-Semitism did not find public expression before the appearance of "Judaism in Music" in 1850, a publication that, written at a time when Germany was not yet anti-Semitic, predates the libretto of *Das Rheingold* by only a year. All the evidence, including the chronology of Wagner's life and writings, indicates that the anti-Semitism of "Judaism in Music" originates in the jealousy that Wagner felt toward Meyerbeer, who, he believed, had not given him the help he had hoped for. It will be clear by now that psychoanalysis is not necessarily the key to understanding the reasons why Wagner's androgyny and anti-Semitism were able to coexist.

The theory of latent homosexuality, combined with the idea of a bisexual constitution, turns all of us into creatures whose androgyny is revealed in our relations with our parents through the ambivalence of the libido. There is femininity in masculinity, and masculinity in femininity. When I say "white," I mean "black." In consequence, the sexual ambivalence in the so-called complete form of the Oedipus complex explains the total freedom of psychoanalytic interpretation and also the openness of its conclusions. Ricoeur was quite right when he compared Freud's theory with those of Marx and Nietzsche and described them all as "philosophies of suspicion." At the same time, androgyny and freedom of interpretation involve the suppression of every sociohistorical and chronological framework, since the truths revealed by psychoanalysis are timeless. What remains is the individual's archaeological "history," a history that communes with the universal depths of the human psyche and that analysis decodes by means of an interplay of associations and accumulated experience. It is a circular argument, however, since psychoanalysis merely rediscovers in the patient's words the very thing that the theory had already established once and for all.

With its ideological grounding in androgyny, freedom of interpretation, and a denial of time and history, Freudian exegesis provided the paradigm for later hermeneutics, all of which maintain that they can "establish" that what is said is what is not said, and that I say the opposite of what I say. When I love my mother, I hate my father, but at the same time as hating him, I love him because, being a man, I am also a woman. Psychoanalysis fails to explain androgyny since it is itself an androgynous theory. Its beauty and its powerlessness derive from the fact that it can say anything, including the truth. Unfortunately, we never know when.

Chapter Nine

ANIMUS-ANIMA

EVEN IF JUNG practically never used the word "androgyny," there is no doubt that the concept is central to the school of analytical psychology that he founded. "Of all the schools of contemporary psychoanalysis," writes Gaston Bachelard, "it is the school of C. G. Jung that has shown most clearly that the human psyche was originally androgynous" (1960, 50). In order to demonstrate how this concept operates, there is no need on this occasion to invent a specious interpretation, since the works of both Jung and his disciples contain more than one analysis not only of the relationship between male and female but, more especially, of Wagner's music dramas. This is hardly surprising, of course, when we consider that one of the key ideas of Jungian thought is the belief that beyond the individual unconscious there is a collective unconscious, the "sphere of inherited psychic mass," made up of basic psychological archetypes. The deepest of all these archetypes is the binomial animus-anima. And this archaic psychological layer has been revealed, since the beginning of time, in myths, where it is far easier to observe it directly than in the dreams of individuals.

Unlike Freud, who scarcely ever mentions Wagner and who claimed to have little affinity for music,[1] Jung quotes Wagner on frequent occasions. In *Psychological Types* he suggests a number of analytical approaches to *Parsifal* that need not detain us here (Jung 1913, 76, 192, 219). More interesting from our own point of view is the long and detailed analysis of the *Ring* that he presents in *Symbols of Transformation* (Jung 1912, 358–64, 385–89). More recently, the English musicologist Robert Donington has proposed a strictly Jungian interpretation of the *Ring* in a study that is widely known and read in the Anglo-Saxon musical world. It is Jung's and Donington's analysis of those aspects of the *Ring* that involve the archetypes of animus and anima to which we must now turn our attention.

THE ANDROGYNY OF THE *RING* ACCORDING TO JUNG AND HIS DISCIPLES

In the beacon of light that dominates the opening scene of *Das Rheingold* Donington sees the archetypal symbol of the eternal feminine as manifest in Mother Nature, since the image of the mother, as viewed by man, is radiant in its beauty, the first impression of his mother that man tries to rediscover in his adult life by seeking it in all the women he meets (1963, 49).

If Wotan is an image of both the Self (in the Jungian sense) and paternal authority, two women embody his anima: Fricka and Brünnhilde. In Fricka, Wotan sees an aspect of the eternal feminine, albeit a negative aspect—the anima that has borrowed male logic and inflexibility from the animus (ibid., 72–73). According to Donington, however, there are other representatives of the eternal feminine in the *Ring* in the shape of the Rhine daughters, Freia, Erda (the Earth Mother and anima of the world), the Valkyries, and the Norns (ibid., 75–76), all of whom are colored, to a greater or lesser extent, by our experience of our physical mother and by the quality of the love that she—or a substitute—gave us. Fafner and Fasolt, although male, are interpreted as the blackest incarnation of femininity, the dark aspect of the animus contained in the female sex (ibid., 77–78). In turning to Loge, Donington reminds us that he is a hermaphroditic god according to the Eddas and Germanic legend generally (ibid., 82).[2]

Brother and sister represent perhaps the finest symbol of animus and anima (ibid., 121–23), especially when united by an incestuous bond, as in the case of Siegmund and Sieglinde: just as undifferentiated nature finds expression in the hermaphrodite, in which the two sexes merge, so the incestuous relationship is the image that comes closest to such a figure. Donington is clearly appealing here to the Freudian Oedipus complex, which he describes as "one of his most valuable and irrefutable contributions to our knowledge of depth psychology" (ibid., 122). The twins in the *Ring*, he argues, are a clear demonstration of the fact that animus and anima are archetypes: the two characters have the feeling that they recognize one another and that they have always known each other. But Siegmund exists only as a product of Wotan's will, which is thwarted by the negative animus embodied by Fricka. His death signifies a return to feminine submissiveness (ibid., 151). Sieglinde, too, is a part of Wotan, Donington tells us, drawing on the concept of transformation: just as what is lost in Siegmund passes to Siegfried and what is lost in Hunding passes to Hagen, so Brünnhilde salvages what comes from Sieglinde (ibid., 162).

It is at this point in the narrative that Jung launches into his own analysis. Donington insists on the fact that the Valkyries are the positive aspect of the Great Mother or, rather, the Good Mother. (The Terrible Mother will be the dragon.) For his part, Jung makes Brünnhilde Wotan's anima, the incarnation of the real will. She asks him: "Who am I if not your will?" To which Wotan replies: "I commune with myself when I talk to you" (*GS* 6.37).

This is an aspect on which Donington does not insist, no doubt because it has already been treated by Jung. The latter, in fact, begins by expressing his surprise that Wagner has placed the powers of so martial a god in the hands of a feminine agent. But this, he argues, is because Wagner's Brünnhilde

> is one of the numerous anima-figures who are attributed to masculine deities, and who without exception represent a dissociation in the masculine psyche—a "split-off" with a tendency to lead an obsessive existence of its own. This tendency to autonomy causes the anima to anticipate the thoughts and decisions of the masculine consciousness, with the result that the latter is constantly confronted with unlooked-for situations which it has apparently done nothing to provoke. (Jung 1912, 361)

The birth of Siegfried is that of the sun god. His substitute mother, Mime, is "a chthonic god, a crippled dwarf who belongs to a race that has abjured love" (ibid., 361–62). Mime wants Siegfried to kill Fafner: "he is a masculine representative of the Terrible Mother who lays the poisonous worm in her son's path. Siegfried's longing for the mother-imago drives him away from Mime" (ibid., 362–63). In a footnote to this passage, Jung elaborates this point: "The dragon in the cave is the Terrible Mother. In German legend the maiden in distress often appears as a snake or dragon that has to be kissed; then it changes into a beautiful woman" (ibid., 362). Even if he does not say so explicitly, Jung clearly insinuates that Fafner is an early incarnation of the sleeping Valkyrie. Indeed, he might even have recalled, as Donington does (Donington 1963, 213), that we hear the Dragon motif in Wagner's orchestra at the very moment when the Valkyrie threatens Siegfried with her embrace:

Wie mein Blick dich verzehrt,	As my gaze consumes you,
erblindest du nicht?	are you not blinded?
Wie mein Arm dich preßt,	As my arm holds you tight,
entbrenn'st du mir nicht?	do you not burn for me?
	(*GS* 6.174)

Having turned Fafner into an *imago* of the Terrible Mother "invented" by the substitute mother, Jung goes on:

> Siegfried's longing for the mother-imago has unwittingly exposed him to the danger of looking back to his childhood and to the human mother, who immediately changes into the death-dealing dragon. He has conjured up the evil aspect of the unconscious, its devouring nature, personified by the cave-dwelling terror of the woods. Fafner is the guardian of the treasure; in his cave lies the hoard, the source of life and power. The mother apparently possesses the libido of the son (the treasure she guards so jealously), and this

> is in fact true so long as the son remains unconscious of himself. In psychological terms this means that the "treasure hard to attain" lies hidden in the mother-imago, i.e., in the unconscious. (Jung 1912, 363)

It must be stressed that this interpretation is possible only if the dragon is turned into a negative substitute for the mother.

Siegfried will abandon the terrifying image of his former mother, embodied in the figure of Mime, in order to approach another mother. And it is his tender musings on his true, but unknown, mother that accompany the Forest Murmurs. Donington makes it clear, in particular, that the Wood Bird that guides Siegfried to Brünnhilde plays its traditional role of an associate of the Great Mother (Donington 1963, 195). At this point his own interpretation complements that of Jung: by drinking the dragon's blood, Siegfried ingests Fafner, who now assumes the aspect of the Good Mother and puts him in touch with nature. Donington even sees Fafner's murder as "phallic penetration of his mother-image," an act that "amounts to a psychic incest" (ibid., 195).

Armed with his sword—to which Jung ascribes a solar dimension, comparing it to the sword that "goes out from the mouth of Christ in the Apocalypse" (Jung 1912, 359)—Siegfried breaks the will of his "father," Wotan, as a result of the turn of events that Brünnhilde herself has given to the action: "And the instrument of fate is always the woman, who knows and reveals his secret thoughts; hence the impotent rage of Wotan, who cannot bring himself to recognize his own contradictory nature" (ibid., 361). There follows an episode in which Wotan is confronted by the Great Mother herself: Erda has robbed him of all joy in existence and now tells him that he is not what he claims to be, so that the god abandons the field to Siegfried who, as the embodiment of life, succeeds in passing through the wall of fire, itself a symbol of "the fiery longing of the hero for the forbidden goal" (ibid., 362). Wotan is powerless, writes Donington, because he has cut himself off from his two animas, Erda and Brünnhilde (Donington 1963, 220).

Here is Jung's account of Siegfried's meeting with Brünnhilde: "Brünhilde [*sic*], standing to Wotan in a daughter-anima relationship, is clearly revealed here as the symbolical or spiritual mother of Siegfried, thus confirming the psychological rule that the first carrier of the anima-image is the mother" (Jung 1912, 388). And, just as Brünnhilde was Wotan's daughter-anima, so she now becomes Siegfried's anima—mother, sister, and wife in one:

Du selbst bin ich,	Your own self am I,
wenn du mich Selige liebst.—	if you but love me, blessed that I am.

(*GS* 6.168)

Later in the same scene, Siegfried conjures up the following image:

Ein herrlich Gewässer	glorious billows
wogt vor mir;	surge before me:
. . . .	. . . .
ich selbst, wie ich bin,	just as I am,
spring' in den Bach:—	I plunge into the brook:
o daß seine Wogen	oh, that its waves
mich selig verschlängen.	might enfold me in bliss.

(*GS* 6.173)

The water, of course, represents the maternal depths where Siegfried will rediscover himself with Brünnhilde.

For a psychological account of *Götterdämmerung*, we must return to Donington. When Siegfried and Brünnhilde bid each other farewell, they exchange their respective anima and animus in the form of ring and horse (Donington 1963, 221). When Siegfried arrives at the Gibichung Court, his anima is split in two, half of it now being embodied in Gutrune, who will make him forget Brünnhilde (ibid., 224) and whom he confuses with his own anima (ibid., 241). He rediscovers the archetype of Mother Nature with the Rhine daughters, but he is under the negative influence of the anima embodied in Gutrune (ibid., 248–49), so that he does not listen to what they have to tell him. When he dies at Hagen's hands, his thoughts return to Brünnhilde once again and he rediscovers his true anima (ibid., 254). For her own part, Brünnhilde had lost her animus when she fell in with Hagen's machinations (ibid., 262), but her ultimate sacrifice allows her to reconcile the eternal feminine with the eternal masculine in the final stage of what Donington terms "transformation" (ibid., 263). The "sacred marriage" in the flames of the funeral pyre reunites the psyche's two complementary principles, male and female (ibid., 269), thereby bringing about a return to the original hermaphrodite described in Plato's *Symposium* (ibid., 270).

Only four years before Donington's study, the animus-anima relationship had inspired a similar interpretation by Anne-Marie Matter (1959, 141–50), and there is no doubt that she was the first French writer to start out from the perspective of bisexuality and draw attention to the sexualization of poetry and music that I analyzed in the first section above, even if she did not establish any links with Wagner's artistic oeuvre. She, too, considers the relationship between Wotan and Brünnhilde from the binomial standpoint of animus and anima, equating it with the relationship between Tristan and Isolde, Siegmund and Sieglinde, Lohengrin and Elsa, and, by extension, Wotan and Alberich, whom Wagner himself describes as "Licht-Alberich" (Light Alberich) and "Nacht-Alberich" (Night Alberich, the archetype of the shadow).

If Jung's analyses emphasize the presence of a maternal element in the psyche of male characters, Matter has the merit of underscoring the fact that in those of Wagner's music dramas that center upon the animus-anima dichotomy, it is the feminine component that is dominant:

> It is Isolde who takes the initiative in the search for love, whereas Tristan is defensive and afraid. It is also Isolde who prepares the double suicide, whereas Tristan resigns himself to his fate. It is Sieglinde who serves her detested husband the drink that sends him to sleep, she who decides on their double destiny, who draws the Volsung's attention to the sword buried deep in the ash tree, and who reveals its powers to him; and it is she, finally, who forces her lover to flee with her. (Matter 1959, 147; Donington makes a similar point, albeit belatedly: 1963, 271)

Depending on the situation, the character of Brünnhilde is more ambivalent in her relations with Wotan and Siegfried (Matter 1959, 148).

Finally, if I may be allowed to indulge my penchant for pastiche, one could propose a Jungian interpretation of the sexual characteristics that Wagner lends poetry and music in *Opera and Drama* by claiming that Wagner adopts the *persona*[3] or official image of poet even though he must be aware on some level that he is first and foremost a musician; for the time being, however, he continues to treat music as feminine, assigning to it the role of the masculine poet's unconscious anima.

Psychocritical Analysis According to Jung

The psychocritical analysis of a work of art and, by extension, the explanation of androgyny proposed by Jung are not the same as those advanced by Freud. Jung devoted at least two studies (1922 and 1930) to the analytical interpretation of works of literature and art and harbored very deep reservations about a deterministic explanation of their content on the basis of a knowledge of depth psychology (1930, 86–87), even going so far as to denounce its reductive character. Turning to Wagner, he writes: "There is nothing in *The Ring of the Nibelungs* [*sic*] that would lead us to discern or infer the fact that Wagner had a tendency towards transvestism, even though a secret connection does exist between the heroics of the Nibelungs and a certain pathological effeminacy in the man Wagner. The personal psychology of the artist may explain many aspects of his work, but not the work itself" (1930, 86). Of course, his criticism of Freudian reductivism serves as a springboard for a conception that is based, in essence, on the collective unconscious. What the analytical psychologist can do is scour works of art for any trace of the immutable archaic nucleus that, depending on the personality of the writer and specificity of the age, produces a work that is original in outline. The poet "has plunged into the healing and redeeming depths of the collective psyche, where man is not lost in the isolation of consciousness and its errors and sufferings, but where all men are caught in a common rhythm which allows the individual to communicate his feelings and strivings to mankind as a whole. This re-immersion in the state of *participation mystique* is the secret of artistic creation and of the effect which great art has upon us" (ibid., 105). For Jung, the success of a work is comparable, both creatively and receptively, to successful psychoanalytic treatment: just as one succeeds in curing a sick person when, beyond the personal unconscious, the analyst manages to gain access to that element of the collective unconscious to which the fantasy or neurosis is attached, so the work of art genuinely touches us when the archetypes that it contains rise to the surface. Even more than with Freud, the explanation of the work is resolutely universalist and ahistorical:

> The sum of these images constitutes the collective unconscious, a heritage which is potentially present in every individual. It is the psychic correlate of the differentiation of the human brain. This is the reason why mythological ages are able to arise spontaneously over and over again, and to agree with one another not only in all the corners of the wide earth, but at all times. As they are present always and everywhere, it is an entirely natural proceeding to relate mythologems, which may be very far apart both temporally and ethnically, to an individual fantasy system. The creative substratum is everywhere this same human psyche and this same human brain, which, with relatively minor variations, functions everywhere in the same way. (Jung 1912, xxix)

There is something highly reductive, therefore, about Jung's approach, although the reductionism is, in a sense, the opposite of that proposed by Freud. Freud reduced the work to an infantile sexual fantasy, in other words, to a particular point in the individual's history, albeit one that the Oedipus complex was always able to take into account. Jung no longer needed to trouble himself with the artist's life, as Freud had done in his study of Leonardo da Vinci. Analytical psychology represents a psychoanalysis of dreams that transcend the subject who dreams them. Works of art and myths are all reduced, "from above," to a network of universal, transcultural, and interhistorical archetypes. As Gaston Bachelard writes, "One reads with a different, deeper involvement those scholarly works on the subject of the androgyne if one has taken cognizance of the potentialities of the animus and anima that dwell in the depths of every human soul. As a correlative of this cognizance of the animus and anima, *one could divest myths of the surplus weight of explicit historicity*"[4] (1960, 72). In this way, Bachelard figures as a precursor of the New Criticism of the 1960s. He refuses to "pass from the psychology of the work of art to the psychology of its creator. I shall never be anything other than a psychologist of books" (ibid., 81). "What use is a biography that tells us about the past, the poet's weighty past?" he exclaims elsewhere (ibid., 8). Is this not a similar attitude to that of Roland Barthes, albeit expressed in different stylistic terms? "I dream about words, about written words. I think I am reading. A word stops me short. I leave the page. The syllables of the word begin to stir. Tonic accents start to invert. The word is no longer so weighted down with meaning that it stops me from dreaming. Words then take on other meanings, as though they had the right to be young again. And in the undergrowth of the vocabulary words set out in search of new friends and bad company" (ibid., 15).

In the case of Freud, the freedom of interpretation that we discovered there was the result of the fact that the concept of latent homosexuality allowed him to find the opposite of what he was looking for in everything he analyzed. With Jung, we find a scheme similar to Freud's complete version of the Oedipus complex. In his summary of Jung's "Psychology of the Transference" (1946), Bachelard writes:

> A detailed psychological study that forgets nothing, be it reality or idealization, should analyze the psychology of the communion between two souls along the lines of the following diagram:

> It is over this range of four beings in two persons that one should study the good and the bad in all close human relationships. (1960, 64)

In the case of Jung, however, freedom of interpretation is not only the result of all the possible relationships that are opened up by this generalized schema. (The reader will recognize its kinship with the one drawn earlier of the second version of the Oedipus complex.) The flexibility of Jungian hermeneutics stems from its excessive generality: there is animus and anima everywhere, but instead of asking what they signify in each individual myth and each specific culture, Jung reduces each manifestation of the symbol to its archetypal significance.

Critique of Jungian Interpretations of the *Ring*

Jung's interpretative system is quintessentially allegorical. In other words, phrase after phrase of the text is made to mean something other than what it says: it is no longer Siegfried and Brünnhilde who speak and act but animus and anima, not the Wood Bird but the Good Mother, not the dragon but the Terrible Mother. It may be objected to my own objection that I spent the first part of this study showing that it was possible to read into the libretto of the *Ring* ideas that are not explicitly stated, namely, an allegorical history of music. There is an essential difference, however, between my own approach and that of Jung. I constructed this allegorical edifice simply by relying on philological data and the world of meanings that surrounds the libretto in the form of theoretical writings, letters, and musical allusions. By contrast, Jung turns Wagner's text into a tapestry woven from the store of universal archetypes. In doing so, he condemns himself to misunderstanding the semantic specificity of the *Ring* and, in particular, the meaning of androgyny in this context.

Let us examine the Jungians' interpretation of the Wood Bird, Brünnhilde, and the dragon in order to see whether their approach is acceptable. The principle that will guide us will be as follows: we shall accept the analytical view that there is such a thing as a collective unconscious peopled by archetypes and then see whether the Jungian interpretation is contradicted by an examination of Wagner's own text.

For Donington, the Wood Bird is associated with the Great Mother (Donington 1963, 195), an interpretation that is not contradicted by Wagner himself. According to Curt von Westernhagen (who unfortunately does not give his source), "Wolzogen tells us that Wagner once interpreted the Wood Bird in *Siegfried* as 'Sieglinde's maternal soul'" (Westernhagen 1962, 95). This interpretation is scarcely allegorical, however, since Siegfried's first words to the bird, when he hears it calling his name, are:

Du holdes Vög'lein!	You lovely little bird!
Dich hört' ich noch nie:	I've never heard you before:
bist du im Wald hier daheim?—	do you live here in the wood?
Verstünd' ich sein süßes Stammeln!	If only I understood his sweet babble!
Gewiß sagt' er mir 'was,—	He'd tell me something no doubt—
vielleicht—von der lieben Mutter?	perhaps about my dear mother.
	(*GS* 6.134)

Even more striking in this context is the earlier version of *Der junge Siegfried*, in which Siegfried says, immediately after the Wood Bird's first words (Strobel 1930, 156):

Mich dünkt, meine mutter	Methinks my mother
singt zu mir.—	is singing to me.—

It is the Wood Bird that leads Siegfried to Brünnhilde, so it is scarcely surprising that when confronted by a woman for the first time in his life, Siegfried's initial reaction is to think she is his mother.

But, the reader may ask, how can I fail to see the archetype of the mother-wife in Brünnhilde, as Freud, Groddeck, and Jung have all done? How can I dispute such evidence? Simply because, before seeing Brünnhilde in terms of a supposed constant in the human psyche, it is more important to recall the role she plays in the action, where she literally "invents" Siegfried *not* as Brünnhilde but as Wotan's female double, carrying out her father's innermost wishes and thereby acquiring a psychological depth that is missing from the reductionist archetype. After all, Brünnhilde herself asks her father:

Zu Wotan's Willen sprichst du,	To Wotan's will you speak
sag'st du mir, was du willst:	when you tell me what you will:
wer—bin ich,	who am I,
wär' ich dein Wille nicht?	were I not your will?

(*GS* 6.37)

Can one—as Jung does—see in the dragon an embodiment of the Great Mother, placed there by that negative mother-substitute represented by Mime and, as such, the guardian of the "hoard, the source of life and power" (Jung 1912, 363)?

The first objection is of a logical nature: if Fafner represents the negative mother, why does Wagner never suggest as much, since in the case of Brünnhilde, the comparison with the mother figure is perfectly explicit?

My second objection relates to a gap in the interpretation: Jung fails to consider the implications of the dragon's blood, which Siegfried raises to his lips and which enables him to understand the language of the Wood Bird (ibid., 364). Why should the blood of the Terrible Mother allow him to understand Sieglinde's messenger?

But there is a third objection: why should the psychoanalytic interpretation not be based on a simple philological fact? It is impossible to avoid noticing that only in his essay on the Wibelungs does Wagner use the word *Drache* (dragon) (1849a, *GS* 2.131); in his prose drafts and libretto to the *Ring* he consistently prefers the word *Wurm* (worm) and its compound *Lindwurm*. In 1878 he complained to Cosima that in the Munich production of *Siegfried* Fafner was represented as a dragon rather than as a serpent,[5] and in his essay "A Retrospect of the 1876 Festival," written at the end of 1878, he uses the word *Lindwurm* (1878g, *GS* 10.111). From the psychoanalytic point of view, it is entirely possible, therefore, to see the serpent as a bisexual symbol, a possibility already suggested by Nunberg (1973, 213). Why not argue, for example, that Siegfried, having never met a woman, first has to free himself from every autoerotic and (dare we say it?) masturbatory temptation by killing the hermaphroditic serpent before being able to make any attempt to know true androgynous union with the feminine Other? This interpretation is at least as well-substantiated as that of the Terrible Mother and arguably more so since it rests on an explicit choice of words and fits much more readily into the description that we have of the hero's sexual apprenticeship. But in order to make it work, we should have to abandon an archetypal constant.

Throughout all this, we seem to have forgotten Wagner's own thoughts on the subject, although he expresses himself clearly enough: "In its most remotely distinguishable form the family saga of the Franks shows us the individualized light or sun god conquering and slaying the monster of the primeval night of chaos: this is the original meaning of *Siegfried's fight with the dragon*" (1849a, *GS* 2.131). It matters little whether the legend had this meaning for the Franks; what is important is what Wagner himself has made of it. He goes on: "The age-old battle is now taken up by us in turn, and its changeable outcome is exactly the same as that constant recurrence of day and night, summer and winter—and, ultimately, of the human race itself, which continues to move from life to death, from victory to defeat, from joy to sorrow, actively reminding us, through constant rejuvenation, of the eternal nature of Man and Nature both in and through itself" (ibid., 2.132). In the light of this essay, Siegfried's fight with the dragon Fafner may be seen as a stage in what our late-lamented colleague Jacques Gomila described so aptly as "hominization": Siegfried becomes human not only because he assumes an independent sexual identity when confronted by a woman but also because, having issued from the chthonic world of the forces of literal and metaphorical darkness (i.e., having been brought up by the Nibelung Mime), he will shortly embody a radiant humanity and assume the features of a solar hero. It is as such a hero that Brünnhilde explicitly acclaims him when she wakes:

Heil dir, Sonne!	Hail to you, sun!
Heil dir, Licht!	Hail to you, light!

(*GS* 6.166)

From this point of view, the enigmatic quotation of the Fafner motif as Brünnhilde prepares to embrace Siegfried is clear, and there is no need, therefore, to draw on the archetype of the Terrible Mother to explain it: Siegfried had thought he would encounter fear when confronting Fafner, but true fear is something he discovers only when meeting a woman.[6]

Although some readers may find this interpretation too banal inasmuch as it claims to express Wagner's thoughts on the basis of what he actually says, it seems to me to be confirmed by an examination of one of the sources that Wagner himself is known to have used in drafting the libretto. According to Gustav Kietz's recollection of a conversation he had with Wagner in 1849, the composer had insisted: "I'm not going to write any more grand operas; I want to write fairy tales, like the one of the lad who doesn't know fear" (Breig and Fladt 1976, 31). On 10 May 1852, after he had already decided to compose *Der junge Siegfried*, Wagner wrote to Theodor Uhlig to announce that Siegfried and the "lad who wants to learn fear" were one and the same person.[7] If we turn to the story in question in the Grimms' collection of *Kinder- und Hausmärchen* (1819–22, no. 4), we discover that after surviving various adventures, the hero learns the meaning of fear only when, on their wedding night, his young wife "empties on him a bucket of cold water and gudgeon, so that the tiny fish wriggled to and fro all around him." In other words, it is in the Grimms' text that sexual excitement is described in metaphorical terms. Wagner has simply made the suggestion explicit: in *Siegfried*, the meaning is no longer hidden but transparent.

It will be clear by now that—to borrow Schelling's famous distinction—a tautegorical interpretation rooted in the immediate semantic world of the symbol under consideration is preferable to an allegorical interpretation, which is both uncontrollable and all too often incoherent. It may perhaps be objected to this that in neglecting the "work" of the unconscious (be it individual or collective), I am ignoring the deep significance that symbols may have and thus impoverishing them. But Wagner's symbols certainly do not lack depth and complexity, as is clear from the endless arguments over the labeling of his leitmotifs. And the attention given to philological documents, far from disregarding the rich Wagnerian metaphors, allows us, rather, to give them the exegetical role they deserve. If Wagner himself placed a different gloss on the symbols from the one that the libretto sometimes seems to indicate, it is important, surely, to examine this secondary meaning *first*, before going in search of a third or fourth meaning.

There is an additional reason for proceeding in this way. Appearances notwithstanding, a Jungian interpretation explains nothing since, for Jung, "all the figures [of myth] are interchangeable" (Jung 1912, 390), so that the semantic significance of characters and actions is always reduced to a small number of well-known archetypes. Sieglinde is the anima, Brünnhilde is the anima, Mime is the anima, and even the dragon is the anima. Of course, they have different shades of meaning (the biological mother, the sister-wife-mother, the nourishing mother, and the Terrible Mother), but have we really gained anything in the process?

The essential problem, from a semiological point of view, is that in reducing the multiplicity of symbolic manifestations to a single set of archetypes, we are depriving ourselves of the chance to interpret each individual symbol once it is incorporated into the syntax of a narrative. There is, in fact, a problem of the corpus that Jung has chosen to analyze: as he himself admits, he did not wish to analyze an entire corpus of myths (1912, xxix), since his aim was simply to study how mythologems recur from one dream or myth to another. But this is the whole heart of the problem, for how can one be certain that two mythologems are identical to each other if one has not first studied their meaning in the context in which they appear? Jung's symbol is asyntactical. What interests him is not what the myth recounts but what he rediscovers in it. But it is precisely at the moment when we reinterpret the different symbols within the linearity of the texts from which they have been taken that the difficulties of the symbolic approach (in the sense understood by Jung, Bachelard, and Durand) arise. Admittedly, the idea of conceiving symbols in terms of the way they are inserted into a "constellation," as Durand does in his *Structures anthropologiques de l'imaginaire* (a procedure that entitles him to describe himself as a structuralist; Durand 1960, 6.66 and 437) is in itself remarkable, since the meaning of each symbol is limited and determined by the symbolic environment as a whole. In this, however, archetypology resembles that period in astronomy when stars were grouped according to constellations, without knowledge of whether the stars that were thus laid flat on the two-dimensional heavenly vault were in fact separated from one another by millions of light-years or whether, physically, they did not even belong to the same galaxy. It is impossible, therefore, to agree with Durand when he writes: "What matters in myth is not simply the thread of the narrative but also the symbolic sense of the terms" (ibid., 412). The symbolic sense of the terms depends to no little extent on the thread of the narrative.

According to Durand, symbolology operates by pinpointing vast constellations of images that are "more or less constant and that seem structured by a certain isomorphism of the convergent symbols. . . . Convergence discovers constellations of images that, term by term, are similar to each other in different areas of thought" (ibid., 40). This is not the place to discuss Durand's attempt to distinguish between convergence and analogy. The problem, rather, is that the criterion of convergence between concrete symbolic manifestations (i.e., isotopism) is applied *before* the manifestation in question has been interpreted in its initial context. It is not surprising, therefore, that Durand specifically claims his approach to be "ahistorical" (ibid., 52 and 452). "Archetypes are bound to images that are highly differentiated from a cultural point of view," he notes (ibid., 63). But what happens if a cultural and historical analysis suggests that before becoming the manifestation of hypothetical archetypes, these images had highly specific meanings within each culture, meanings that they acquired at a given moment in history and in each particular text and that, varying from one region of the world to another, might turn out to be contradictory? Jungian and post-Jungian symbology assumes that it is legitimate to state that "the serpent of Genesis is the hermaphroditic intermediary between Adam and Eve, just as the androgynous shaman mediates between Earth and Heaven" (Molino 1981, 6), without first examining in what ways the serpent and the shaman, Adam and the Earth, and Eve and Heaven are comparable. A tautegorical interpretation of symbols begins by reestablishing the semantic constellation to which they belong in order to determine the network of meanings (including metaphorical meanings) that is unique to them in this particular context. A linguistic comparison may make this point clear: in his excellent little study *La Structure des langues* (1982), Claude Hagège compares the phonological structures of different languages, but he is able to do so only because he has first established the phonological system of each of the languages under review. Symbology has failed to pass through the preliminary phase of particular "phonologies" and has tried to jump directly to general phonology. It may be objected to this that such a move was not possible in the realm of symbols, but in that case it must be asked whether, in spite of the brilliance of general constructions, these latter have not in fact prevented us from traveling so far as we might otherwise have done down the road to a better understanding of the symbolic facts. In a word, it is not "the analysis of symbolic and archetypal isotopisms that alone can provide the semantic key to myth" (Durand 1960, 417) but a patient study of the networks of meanings that myth acquires in each specific context.

Jean Libis's Jung-inspired study, *Le Mythe de l'androgyne* (Libis 1980) leads one to the same conclusion. Libis, moreover, is guilty of an apparent contradiction. Setting out from the observation—which no one would deny—that the myth of the androgyne is a universal one (ibid., 15), he associates it with a feeling of nostalgia for a lost original unity and with the persistence of Jungian archetypes (ibid., 49) while at the same time noting "the astonishing plasticity of the androgynous model" (ibid., 19). This forces him to "descend" from the general outline to more specific families of manifestations of the myth, depending on whether that myth deals with power, knowledge, health, or immortality. But Libis fails to take any epistemological advantage of these successive distinctions—"the distinguishing feature of the archetype is its timelessness" (ibid., 66)—in spite of having been on the point of recognizing the specificity of the various manifestations of androgyny. How could he fail to see that each of the authors he quotes constitutes a specific constellation?

Anxious to harness his whole corpus of myths to a single unique meaning, Libis finally comes to the conclusion that "the androgyne seems, above all, to be the fantasmal expression of some impossibility." It implies "a fundamental desire to deny the difference between the sexes . . . and at the same time to abolish the ontological drama that unfolds there." It is "the negation of sexuality" (ibid., 217) and the meeting ground between Eros and Thanatos.

None of this is wrong, of course, and there is certainly a denial of time in Wagner's particular brand of androgyny to which we shall later return. But the fact that androgyny is combined with other philosophical systems, such as those of Feuerbach and Schopenhauer, should have shown that before being yoked, on a more universal level, to sexuality or to the expression of absolute impossibilities, it signified at one moment a solution to the drama of individuation and, at another, the abolition of differences in the context of renunciation—configurations that are as complex, in their different ways, as the system of archetypes into which certain writers have claimed to resolve it. It is important not to adopt the easy Jungian solution of linking up semantically complex and diversified images to isotopisms that happen momentarily to be mythical, so that the animus-anima opposition is robbed, definitively, of all significance.

The Androgyny of the Symbol

The symbol is at the heart of all hermeneutical activity. In the case of Jungian psychoanalysis, it is vouchsafed with a thematic function as the semiological authority that allows an interpretation to be constructed. But here, too, we are confronted by a very real laxity of interpretation. If the binomial animus-anima can include such diverse realities, it is because this symbolic configuration triggers off a series of binary connotations at the heart of which each couple is considered transitively as being the equivalent of the whole of the others:

animus	masculine	exterior	intellectual	conceptual	rational
anima	feminine	interior	sentimental	emotional	arbitrary
logos	power	father	conscious	knowledge	land
eros	love	mother	unconscious	life	water
quarrel	serpent	sun	short hair		
abandon	horse	moon	long hair	etc.	

The proliferation of interpretants at the heart of Jungian hermeneutics is entirely in keeping with the nature of the symbol as conceived by Jung—constantly alive, open to the unknown, and expressive of the inexpressible. Let loose in the world of symbols, the interpreter has to search for the Secret,[8] his work—according to Durand's felicitous formulation (1964, chap. 3)—being an institutional hermeneutics (*herméneutique instaurative*). This is why the chain of connotations can be extended and the mystery deepened. Thus Bachelard adds to the foregoing series:

activity	growth	dream	concept
rest	deepening	reverie	image

It was not surprising, therefore, that the binomial animus-anima could itself become a symbol of the task of exegesis, as Bachelard explicitly points out in his *Poétique de la rêverie* when discussing the twofold orientation of his oeuvre.

On the one hand, there is the epistemology of knowledge, which seeks, in the name of understanding, to pursue the claim that images generate concepts ("the formation of the scientific spirit"; "applied rationalism") and, on the other, the psychoanalysis of perceptible categories ("the Earth and the illusions of the will"; "water and dreams"; "air and dreams"). "If I had to sum up an irregular and laborious career that has been interspersed by various books," he writes, "it would be best to place it under the contradictory signs of masculine *concept* and feminine *image*. . . . Anyone who gives himself up with all his mind to the concept and with all his soul to the image knows that concepts and images develop along two divergent lines in our spiritual lives" (1960, 45).

In his epistemological writings, "the virility of knowledge" pursues the "weakness" or "femininity" of images. In his poetic oeuvre, he refuses to tackle images with the aid of concepts. But in the twilight years of his career Bachelard finally recognizes the unity of his life and work and admits to his own androgynous nature:

> Images and concepts form around these two opposing poles of psychic activity that constitute the imagination and reason. . . . It is necessary to love the psychic powers of two different types of love if one loves concepts and images, and these are the masculine and feminine poles of the psyche. I realized this too late. Too late I recognized a clear conscience in the alternate work of images and concepts, two clear consciences, which are those of broad daylight and of an acceptance of the dark side of the soul. In order for me to enjoy *the clear conscience of my double nature*,[9] which I have finally recognized, and to enjoy it, moreover, with a clear conscience, I need to be able to write two more books, one on applied reason and the other on active imagination. (1960, 46–47)

Bachelard published these lines in 1960 and died in 1962, denied the opportunity to combine the two aspects of his activity and personality in two final works, but at least he was able to dream of his own androgyny in ending his final book with the words "Written in anima, I should like this simple book to be read in anima. Nonetheless, I do not wish it to be said that the anima is the being of the whole of my life and so I would like to write another book that would be the work of an animus" (ibid., 183).

We have found the same constellation of ideas in Jung and Bachelard as we did in Freud—androgyny, a refusal to countenance a historical dimension, and total freedom of interpretation. In the case of Bachelard, however, we find an additional feature: as with Wagner and the world of the artist, androgyny has become a symbol of scientific activity itself. In discussing Bachelard, Gilbert Durand enlarges on this observation: "What the phenomenology of the symbol rediscovers at the basis of the anthropology that it inaugurates is a form of androgyny" (Durand 1964, 80). It is in this sense that Durand interprets Jung, even though he does not refer explicitly to the Swiss psychologist's writings:

> In man, the symbolic function is the place of "passage," the reconciliation of opposites: in its essence and almost in its etymology (*Sinnbild* in German), the symbol "unites pairs of opposites." In Aristotelian terms, it would be the ability to "hold together" the conscious meaning (*Sinn* = meaning) that perceives and divides up objects in a precise manner and the raw material (*Bild* = image) that issues from the substratum of the unconscious. For Jung, the symbolic function is *conjunctio*, marriage, in which the two elements are merged synthetically, within the symbolizing thought, in a veritable "hermaphrodite," a "divine son" of thought. (Ibid., 68)

Libis goes even further: "Every great symbol conceals contrary meanings, oppositional pairings, notably that of the feminine and masculine . . . . The Androgyne and the Symbol (in general) are ultimately interchangeable as terms" (Libis 1980, 272). There could be no clearer expression of the fact that androgyny has come to symbolize that freedom of interpretation whose post-Freudian line of development we have been following in the present section, a freedom that, according to Libis, sanctions "the plurality that emerges from a dynamic unconscious authority" and whose "archetypal productions are timeless, at least on their deepest level" (ibid., 273). From now on hermeneutic activity is explicitly acknowledged to be androgynous (ibid.).

It should come as no surprise that by turning back on itself, the task of psychoanalytic interpretation is conceived in terms of sexual symbolism. More surprising, perhaps, is to discover it in the structuralism of Lévi-Strauss.

Chapter Ten

ANDROGYNOUS STRUCTURALISM

IN THE LIGHT of Lévi-Strauss's claim that Wagner is "the undeniable originator of the structural analysis of myth" (Lévi-Strauss 1964, 15), it is perfectly legitimate to pursue our examination of the possible ways of explaining Wagner's androgyny by appealing to Lévi-Strauss's structuralist method, not least because this approach provides an unexpected opportunity to test the way that dominant paradigms function in twentieth-century human sciences. Among these human sciences the anthropological structuralism of Lévi-Strauss certainly figures prominently.

TWO EXAMPLES OF A STRUCTURAL ANALYSIS OF WAGNER

Does the data collected in our opening section enable us to propose a structural explanation of the relationship that Wagner establishes between poetry and music? For even if the structural approach is, by definition, immanent rather than causal, it claims nonetheless to offer an explanation, as Lévi-Strauss has repeatedly emphasized: there are universal structures because the human mind is universal. It is worth recalling here Lévi-Strauss's provocative and oft-quoted declaration in his "Overture" to *The Raw and the Cooked*:

> For if the final aim of anthropology is to contribute to a better knowledge of objectified thought and its mechanisms, it is in the last resort immaterial whether in this book the thought processes of the South American Indians take shape through the medium of my thought, or whether mine take shape through the medium of theirs. What matters is that the human mind, regardless of the identity of those who happen to be giving it expression, should display an increasingly intelligible structure as a result of the doubly reflexive forward movement of two thought processes acting one upon the other, either of which can in turn provide the spark or tinder whose conjunction will shed light on both. (1964, 13)

The mind explains the structure, and the structure the mind.

Before examining the kind of structural explanation that could be proposed for my own interpretation, it may not be entirely futile to consider an example of Lévi-Strauss's particular brand of analysis. I am grateful to Professor Pedro Penedo da Rocha Calhão of the University of Asa Branca for transcribing key passages from a lecture that Lévi-Strauss gave in Brazil and that, apparently unpublished in French, appeared in the *Revista de Antropologia e de Folclore* under the title "Linguistic Transformations: Mythological Transformations."[1] The text is particularly important in that it takes Wagner as its starting point:

> My studies revealed the extensive connections between all genuine myths and opened my eyes to the marvelous variations that can be found within this rediscovered corpus. It was with a delightful sense of unmistakability that I encountered one such variant in the relationship between Tristan and Isolde as compared with that of Siegfried and Brünnhilde. Just as in languages, a sound shift often produces two apparently different words from one and the same original, so two apparently differing relationships had evolved from this single mythic relationship as a result of a similar shift or transmutation. Their total similarity consists, however, in the fact that Tristan, like Siegfried, acts under the constraint of a delusion that makes this deed of his not free, so that it is on another's behalf that he woos the woman destined for him by primeval law, meeting his death as a result of the ensuing *mésalliance*. But whereas the *Siegfried* poet, while maintaining the cohesion of the overall Nibelung myth, could concentrate only on the hero's downfall, interpreting it as the result of an act of vengeance on the part of the woman who sacrifices herself for him, the *Tristan* poet finds his principal theme in a depiction of the torments of love to which the two lovers are exposed from the time they become aware of their mutual feelings to the moment of their deaths. . . . The theme of *Tristan* has a great attraction for me inasmuch as it complements, as it were, the great Nibelung myth that, for its own part, embraces an entire world of relationships.

It is hard to imagine a finer summary of the whole approach and spirit of the structural method. At the same time, it is impossible to resist the temptation to compare these lines with an interview that Lévi-Strauss gave to Raymond Bellour in 1979:

> How can one doubt that the third act of *Parsifal* is a variant of the equivalent act in *Die Meistersinger*? In both cases an elderly and experienced man (Gurnemanz and Sachs) retires in favor of another, younger man, who is exceptionally gifted and whom he enthrones. In both cases their long conversation precedes a procession to the sacred rite with an intermediate moment of calm and rediscovered unanimity between these two phases (the Good Friday Music and the Quintet). It is impossible to undertake a satisfactory analysis of the one without knowing and appealing to the other. (Bellour and Clément 1979, 169)

In the Brazilian lecture, Lévi-Strauss begins by reaffirming the sense of cohesion that binds human myths together and that, he argues, can be established by pointing out the transformational links that bind them to each other. The myths of Tristan and Siegfried could scarcely fail to attract the attention of Lévi-Strauss, whose "passion for incest" is well known: Tristan is the nephew of King Marke, whose future wife he desires, while Siegfried is Brünnhilde's grandnephew. For the anthropologist, incest is the locus classicus of the conflict between nature and culture, since society's laws proscribe that inclination that results from "the law of nature" and help in founding society (Lévi-Strauss 1949, 561). But this common basis is not sufficient to explain "the complete analogy" between the two. Quite the opposite, since the myths are inversely related. Siegfried gives his wife to Gunther and dies as a result of an act of vengeance on the part of Brünnhilde who, in turn, takes her own life; Tristan abducts Isolde from King Marke, who precipitates his death. Unable to survive him, Isolde dies. Whereas the ending of the *Ring* is negative (Siegfried is prevented from enjoying the love of the woman who loves him in return), that of *Tristan* is positive, since hero and heroine are conscious of their love from the outset. From this point of view, *Tristan und Isolde* reveals the underlying *truth* of the *Ring* and constitutes its conclusion.

This method can be applied without difficulty to the texts that were analyzed in the first part of our study.

There are even stronger links between the libretto drawn from the Nibelung myth and the theory of the total work of art, not least because they were conceived by one and the same person. The structural analogy revealed by superimposing the two texts underscores the essential unity of Wagner's thinking inasmuch as he was able to subsume the fictional and theoretical narratives within a single referential world, yet it obscures the fact that the second is the inverse of the first. What the myth tells us is that the union between Siegfried and Brünnhilde, being founded on their characteristic androgyny, is bound to end in disaster since they wished to transgress the essential fact of nature that insists that procreation should spring from difference. Androgynous union is the utopian aim of procreation based on the concept of the One. Wagner's aesthetic theory states the opposite of this: the work of total art derives from the union of the male poetic principle and the female musical principle. Proof of the viability of this theory is furnished by the *Ring* itself, which succeeds as an androgynous work. The order of culture triumphs, whereas the order of nature ends in failure. The theory is thus the reverse image of the fiction, an opposition between positive and negative poles that is readily explicable in terms of the fact that, for humans at least, procreation involves the production of one from two; cultural procreation is the production of a multiplicity from one. It will be clear, therefore, that for Wagner the work of total art is not simply a form of opera invented to provide a new framework for a modern enactment of Germanic myths. It becomes a myth itself. "The purpose of myth is to provide a logical model capable of overcoming a contradiction" (Lévi-Strauss 1955a, 229). But there is no more fundamental contradiction than the impossibility of a human being fathering a child without a partner. Conversely, as the union of masculine poetry and feminine music, the androgynous work of art results from the gestation of a unique being, an androgynous Wagner who is both poet and musician.

Structuralism and Androgyny

Is this structural explanation not too good to be true? And is it really an explanation? It may be useful to take another look at Lévi-Strauss's 1955 essay "The Structural Study of Myth," in which the anthropologist established his method of structural analysis of myth, and to ask why he chose to analyze the Oedipus myth when he repeatedly refuses to interpret the myth "in literal terms" (ibid., 213), in other words, in a manner acceptable to the specialist (ibid., 213 and 215). Was his aim simply to "illustrate . . . a certain technique" (ibid., 213)?

On rereading the essay, one has the feeling that there is more to it than this. This is not the place to reexamine the intellectual operations that allow Lévi-Strauss to reach his proposed interpretation. (I am thinking, for example, of his setting up of four "bundles of relations" that acquire meaning on the basis of the formula: four is to three as seven is to two [ibid., 216].) Suffice it to quote from the text itself:

> The myth has to do with the inability, for a culture which holds the belief that mankind is autochthonous . . ., to find a satisfactory transition between this theory and the knowledge that human beings are actually born from the union of man and woman. Although the problem obviously cannot be solved, the Oedipus myth provides a kind of logical tool which relates the original problem—born from one or born from two?—to the derivative problem: born from different or born from same? (Ibid.)

In other words, the Oedipus myth is a way of imagining the impossibility of an androgynous origin for human beings. Lévi-Strauss is even more explicit a few lines later, when he introduces the Freudian interpretation of the myth: "Although the Freudian problem has ceased to be that of autochthony *versus* bisexual reproduction, it is still the problem of understanding how *one* can be born from *two*: How is it that we do not have only one procreator, but a mother plus a father?" (ibid., 217). The androgynous utopia figures as a paradigmatic example of the structural method.

One is tempted to ask whether androgyny is not behind one of the fundamental characteristics of this method, namely, its binary structure. A glance at the text that Lévi-Strauss wrote in 1967 as a tribute to Roman Jakobson on the latter's seventieth birthday, "The Sex of the Sun and

Moon," reveals that the birth of the binary method is bound up, for them, with the opposition between masculine and feminine:

> One of the first conversations with Roman Jakobson that I can remember was about the manner in which languages and myths proceed to mark the opposition of the moon and the sun. We were trying to pick out contrasts in the gender of the words designating the sun and the moon here and there, or in the verbal forms denoting their relative size and luminosity. We were very soon to recognize that the problem was not a simple one, and that what seemed so obviously a binary opposition to the Western observer could be expressed in singularly roundabout ways in distant cultures. (1967, 211)

In his analysis, Lévi-Strauss shows that in several North American Indian languages the same word is used to designate the sun and the moon, even though mythology distinguishes them not only on the basis of the parts of the body that correspond with the functions fulfilled by each of them but also according to "the sex of the personage from whom they originate" (ibid., 213). He goes on to suggest that "the sexes assigned to them also seem commutative according to the functions incumbent to each, in the context of a particular myth or ritual" (ibid., 216). Having set out from the opposition of masculine and feminine, Lévi-Strauss discovers more basic antinomies such as light/darkness, bright light/dim light, heat/cold, and so on. But he does not conclude from this that the distinctive criteria between these pairs of opposites are sexual in nature: "Myths do not make an isolated problem out of the sex of the heavenly bodies" (ibid., 221). His approach consists simply in listing what paradigmatic substitutions are possible in each culture on the basis of the opposition between masculine and feminine. This opposition is the starting point, therefore, not for the organization of the object but for the development of the method.

This is confirmed by Lévi-Strauss's English disciple, Edmund Leach, who writes as follows:

> But if a student of primitive art, who could free himself from our assumptions about the notations of arithmetic, were to encounter paired symbols 0/1 he would immediately conclude that the opposition represented "vagina"/"penis" and was metonymic of female/male. A structuralist might argue that this fits very well with his assumptions about the deep structure algebra of human thought. . . . In practice, the bias of choice in symbolic forms is very marked, sexual symbolism which relies on male/female opposition (e.g. penis/vagina representations) being far more common than any other. (1972, 334–35)

There is a question mark, therefore, over the fundamental binary structure of the human species at the very heart of structuralism and of the structural analysis of myths, so that it is not surprising to find it again in the "Finale" of *Mythologies*, a superb piece of writing that deserves to be the subject of as many commentaries as the celebrated "Overture" to *The Raw and the Cooked*.

From mythologue, Lévi-Strauss turns to the invention of myths, as George Steiner has shown in an enthralling series of lectures first published in 1974 (1974, 25, 29, and 30). But whereas Steiner's aim is to show in what way Lévi-Strauss's approach places him, alongside Marx and Freud, in the Jewish messianic tradition, our own concern is with the aspect of his theory that, under the aegis of a comparative semiology of language, music, and myth, becomes a veritable myth of the origins of music—a myth, moreover, that is androgynous in nature.

> If music and mythology are each to be defined as language from which something has been subtracted, both will appear as derivative in relation to language. . . . Music no doubt also speaks; but this can only be because of its negative relationship to language, and because, *in separating off from language*,[2] music has retained the negative imprint of its formal structure and semiotic function: there would be no music if language had not preceded it and if music did not continue to depend on it, as it were, through a private connection. Music is language without meaning; this being so, it is understandable that the listener, who is first and foremost a subject with the gift of speech, should feel himself irresistibly compelled to make up for the absent sense. (Lévi-Strauss 1971, 647)

Conversely, the unities that make up the myth—mythemes—are reduced, according to an idea first advanced in 1955, to "a pure semantic reality," since the linguistic modalities of mythic narrative become immaterial as soon as the *content* of the myth is conveyed. It is conveyed, however, by means of images, which have to be reassembled at a later date: "The myth . . . can, as a vehicle of meaning, become detached from its linguistic base, with which the story it tells is less intimately connected than ordinary messages would be" (1971, 647–48).

In order to clarify his meaning, Lévi-Strauss avails himself of the sort of mirror image that will come as no surprise to anyone familiar with the structuralist method: "In the case of music, the structure which is, so to speak, detached from the sense, adheres to the sound; in the case of mythology, the structure is detached from the sound and adheres to the sense" (ibid., 647). If this is so, it is because in the modern age, music replaced myth at the very moment when the latter became literature:

> It would seem that the point at which music and mythology began to appear as reversed images of each other coincided with the invention of the fugue, that is, a form of composition which, as I have shown on several

occasions . . . , exists in a fully developed form in the myths, from which music might at any time have borrowed it. . . . With the invention of the fugue and other subsequent forms of composition, music took over the structures of mythic thought at a time when the literary narrative, in changing from myth to the novel, was ridding itself of these structures. It was necessary, then, for myth as such to die for its form to escape from it, like the soul leaving the body, and to seek a means of reincarnation in music. In short, it is as if music and literature had shared the heritage of myth between them. (Ibid., 652–53)

Just as man, longing for his original androgynous unity, seeks womankind, so music seeks the meaning that it has lost:

> The listener, as such, is not the creator of the music, either through a lack of natural ability or through the incidental fact that he is listening to someone else's music, but a place exists inside him for the music: he is, then, like the reverse, hollowed-out, image of a creator, whose empty spaces are filled by the music. . . . Thus, the union of the sound proposed by the composer, and of the meaning present in a latent state in the listener, is reconstituted in a pseudo-language. When they encounter the music, meanings drifting half-submerged come to the surface and fit together according to lines of force analogous with those determining the patterning of the sounds. Hence a sort of intellectual and emotional coupling of the composer with the listener. They are both equally important, since *each represents one of the two "sexes" of the music, whose carnal union is realized and solemnized in the performance.*[3] Only then do sound and sense meet up with each other *to create a unique entity comparable to language*,[4] since in this case too there is a coming together of two halves, one consisting of a superabundance of sound (in relation to what the listener could have produced on his own) and the other of a superabundance of meaning (since the composer had no need of it to compose his own work). . . . When they meet, each sort communicates to the other sort the complementary charge which it lacked. Union which had previously been potential is achieved as if through an effect of copulation. (Ibid., 654–55)

Lévi-Strauss's comparative semiology is strictly analogous to the androgynous myth of traditional religion. In the beginning was language, which was divided into music (sound minus sense) and myth (sense over sound). Only the recombination of sound and sense, in other words, of the composer and the listener who lends him that meaning, allows us to rediscover the original lost unity.

In this same study Lévi-Strauss suggests, albeit with less precision perhaps, an identical analysis of myth, a schema codified according to images rather than sounds, to which the listener brings "one of more of the meanings inherent in the schema," just as he would when listening to music. Even if there is not perfect symmetry between music and myth, since mythic discourse already implies a meaning, it is nonetheless true that myth does not really acquire a meaning until taken in charge by the metalanguage that invests it with one. Myths are not gratuitous games: the mythologer exists to discover their logic.

It will be clear now why Lévi-Strauss's androgynous vision of musical and mythological meaning is followed, in this "Finale," by an analysis of Ravel's *Boléro* that borrows its method and categories from structural mythography:

> Music, in its own way, has a function comparable to that of mythology. The musical work, which is a myth coded in sounds instead of words, offers an interpretative grid, a matrix of relationships which filters and organizes lived experience, acts as a substitute for it and provides the comforting illusion that contradictions can be overcome and difficulties resolved. . . . If what has just been said is correct, it is inconceivable that there should be any musical work that does not start from a problem and tend towards its resolution. (Ibid., 659–60)

Suffice it to quote Lévi-Strauss's summary of his analysis of the *Boléro* to show how Ravel's work has been approached as though it were a myth:

> The work as a whole is an attempt to overcome a complex set of oppositions, interlocking, as it were, with one another. The main opposition, which is stated at the outset, is between the melody, announced in the smoothest and most even tone, . . . and two interwoven rhythms, one of which seems to be always trying to move on ahead, while the other insists on lagging behind. The melody, by its tonal oscillations, and the rhythm, by its internal duality, vary between symmetry and asymmetry, expressed respectively by the hesitation between binary and ternary, and between serene and anxious tonalities. (Ibid., 665)

For Lévi-Strauss, these oppositions are reconciled thanks to the composer's treatment of the instrumental timbres, their amplification leading to the modulation in the final fifteen bars, a modulation that he claims has been prepared for by a "rhythmic modulation," so that, binary and ternary rhythms being superimposed on one another, the key of E major finally resolves the tonal hesitation between the two themes. "Thus, like a myth, even a work the construction of which at first sight seems so transparent as to need no comment, is telling simultaneously on several different levels a very complex story, for which it has to find a conclusion" (ibid., 666).

The musicological "truth" of this analysis need not detain us here.[5] What is important is the meaning that it assumes in Lévi-Strauss's mental universe. In applying to *Boléro* the approach he had reserved for myths, he develops a double metaphor—a metaphor for the myth that he claims has transmitted the structures of the fugue to music (ibid., 652)[6] and, at the same time, a metaphor of what he conceives all myths to be: expressions of the fundamental structures of the human mind, each individual myth being simply a manifestation of the One. There could be no better expression of this than Ravel's orchestral piece, since it repeats the same phrase endlessly, albeit with changing colors, before transcending the contradictions in a final modulation, just as the mythologer can combine apparently heterogeneous myths by demonstrating an underlying and immutable logical structure.

In treating music as though it were a myth and in giving the work of art the meaning that it lacks (just as myths are invested with their missing meaning), Lévi-Strauss gives the impression of someone whose task in life is the reunification of the two separate halves of the language. He is the arch-listener who restores to music and myth the sex that they have lost.

At the same time he reunites myth and music, in which he sees a symmetrical relationship between the sixteenth century and the music of the present day, which he feels is growing increasingly remote from myth (ibid., 652–53). Lévi-Strauss the androgyne is arrogating to himself exactly the same role as the one that Wagner had sought to play, aiming at the ultimate reunification of symbolic forms by merging male and female *in propria persona*. Lévi-Strauss's androgyny is fundamentally masculine, therefore. As with Wagner, it even seems to imply the disappearance of womankind,[7] a disappearance that becomes explicit in the final lines of the celebrated analysis of Baudelaire's poem *Les Chats*, which he wrote in collaboration with Roman Jakobson:

> All the characters in the sonnet are male, but the cats and their alter egos, the great sphinxes, are *androgynous by nature*.[8] The same ambiguity is emphasized throughout the sonnet by the paradoxical choice of feminine nouns for so-called masculine rhymes. Of the poem's initial constellation, made up of lovers and scholars, the cats, through their contemplative nature, make it possible to *eliminate womankind*,[9] leaving "the poet of *Les Chats*" face to face, or even merged, with the universe, the former freed from his "highly restricting" love, the latter liberated from the austerity of the scholar. (Jakobson and Lévi-Strauss 1962, 21)

In this classic text of structural analysis, Lévi-Strauss liberates humanity from the difference between the sexes, while at the same time suggesting the sterility of scientific work. All that remains is solitude and the world's ineluctable destiny, he implies in a final tragic and Wagnerian comparison: "I myself," he wrote in *The Naked Man*, "in considering my work from within as I have lived it, or from without, which is my present relationship to it as it drifts away into my past, see more clearly that this tetralogy of mine, now that it has been composed, must, like Wagner's, end with a twilight of the gods" (1971, 693). There follows one of the finest passages in twentieth-century French literature, as Lévi-Strauss abandons the fundamental binary opposition between being and nonbeing, resolving it in a final apocalypse in which humanity and sense are both superseded. All that is left then is the "already canceled evidence that they once were, and were as nothing" (ibid., 695).

The *Ring* Analyzed by Lévi-Strauss

It is not impossible that by destroying all the oppositions on which his work had been based Lévi-Strauss was wanting to indicate, indirectly, the gratuitousness of his game of structuralist mechanics: when a relationship is not symmetrical, it is dissymmetrical; when it is not direct, it is inverted. Lévi-Strauss's structural analysis is founded, perhaps, on nothing more than an immense shrewdness, which allows him always to fall on his feet. In myth, he himself has written:

> we are dealing in all cases with images which are inverted from positive to negative or are reversed from right to left or from top to bottom; all of which transformations are similar to *the mechanism of the pun* which, *when properly used*,[10] causes a word of a sentence to display, as if in the manner of a negative, *the other meaning* that the same word or sentence might take on, if transposed into a different logical context. Transformations of this kind constitute the basis of all semiology. (Ibid., 650)

One can disagree with this, and disagree violently. After all, if $A = B$, if "+" = "−," if masculine is feminine, and feminine masculine, anything can be said about everything. Like Freud and Jung, Lévi-Strauss admits to the total freedom of interpretation.

Let me cite an example that will not take us too far from the subject of our initial inquiry. In his "Note on the Tetralogy," published in *The View from Afar* (1983, 235–40), Lévi-Strauss attempts to explain why the Renunciation of Love motif returns in a number of contexts where, normally, it would not be expected: one thinks, for example, of the passage in which Wotan pretends to abandon Freia (*Das Rheingold*, scene 2), the scene in which Siegmund wins Sieglinde's love (*Die Walküre*, Act I), and the moment, later in the second act of this same work, when Wotan, in his despair, declares himself "the saddest of all living creatures."

As early as 1964, in *The Raw and the Cooked* (1964, 15), Lévi-Strauss had emphasized that with Wagner the structural analysis of myth is carried out by the music: by establishing a link between apparently heterogeneous sequences of text, the return of the leitmotif obliges one to ask what semantic relationship exists between these passages.

It can be shown that Lévi-Strauss's explanation of each of these recurrences rests on hermeneutical approximations that allow him to introduce extraneous elements into the framework of his structural "explanation."

If the Renunciation motif accompanies the dialogue between Fricka and Wotan in the second scene of *Das Rheingold*, it is to show that Wotan is inversely related to Alberich:

> Alberich renounces complete love, which he cannot obtain "by force," but from which he separates physical pleasure, which he can obtain "by trickery." . . . If complete love forms a whole, Alberich will thus give up only a part of it. . . . In contrast, Wotan renounces not the realities of love (he boasts about his adventures to Fricka) but its metaphorical figure as represented by Freia, who, according to Nordic myth, is the patron of carnal appetite and sensuality—the very aspect of complete love that Alberich does not renounce. (1983, 236)

There is undeniably a parallel here, albeit a parallel between a concrete fact and its metaphor, but in order to establish it, Lévi-Strauss has to draw on an interpretation of the character of Freia that derives from a different body of texts (the Old Norse myths), whereas within the context of the *Ring* Freia is presented first and foremost as the guardian of the golden apples that guarantee the gods' immortality.

Lévi-Strauss's second structural explanation similarly fails to convince, although for different reasons. "Likewise, in *Die Walküre*, Act II, scene 2, the return of the musical motif emphasizes that there is both correlation and opposition between the failure of Wotan, who has relied on love to produce a free person, and the success of Alberich, who, by a loveless union, has produced a being subjected to his will. Siegmund and Hagen are thus symmetrical, each the exact reverse of the other" (ibid.). This leads the author to posit the following relationship:

$$\frac{\text{Wotan}}{\text{Alberich}} : \frac{\text{Siegmund}}{\text{Hagen}} : \frac{\text{Siegfried}}{\text{Gunther}}$$

Certainly, Wagner links Wotan and Alberich, describing the former as Light-Alberich and the latter as Black-Alberich. But in what respect is Wotan's action a failure? "Siegmund prefigures Siegfried as a failed attempt" (ibid., 237). One does not have to agree with this. What Wotan's (adulterous) act produces is a pair of incestuous twins. And do not Wotan's words to Fricka in Act II, to say nothing of the love duet between Siegmund and Sieglinde in Act I, with its unsurpassably lyrical strains, tell us that this couple is the most positive, the most successful not only in the entire *Ring* but, with the possible exception of *Die Meistersinger*, in the whole of Wagner's oeuvre? If one wanted to place a Lévi-Straussian interpretation on this scene, it would perhaps be legitimate to say that it has Wagner's sympathy because nature triumphs over culture here. If the interplay of inverse symmetries is really so important, the obvious parallel here is between Siegfried—who is, indeed, a failure, but, as we shall see in a moment, for different reasons from those given by Lévi-Strauss—and Hagen. At all events, it needs to be explained why it is Hagen who murders Siegfried.

Believing that he has demonstrated links between four of the six terms in the relationship, Lévi-Strauss finds himself in a position to state with apodictic certainty (and the phrase he uses speaks volumes): "The two remaining elements, represented by Siegfried and Gunther, *must*[11] [since the structure comes first and explains everything] correspond to one another as well—a relationship that will be realized in *Die Götterdämmerung*" (ibid.). The remainder of his analysis is perhaps less clear, but Lévi-Strauss appears to suggest that Gunther represents the exogamic solution, whereas Siegfried and Brünnhilde are condemned to incest and endogamy.

If my own interpretation of Lévi-Strauss's analysis is correct, it can certainly be countered by an alternative approach, since endogamy has a positive value for Wagner, and Siegfried dies because he forgets Brünnhilde (with whom he could have had a successful endogamous—*and androgynous*—relationship), preferring, instead, his exogamous and negative relationship with Gutrune.

One is tempted to propose an alternative set of relationships:

$$\frac{\text{Wotan}}{\text{Alberich}} : \frac{\text{Siegmund (Sieglinde)}}{\text{Gunther (Gutrune)}} : \frac{\text{Siegfried}}{\text{Hagen}}$$

To these may be added Brünnhilde, Siegfried's one true love, and the "character" of the ring, the object of Hagen's desire. In structural terms, the result could be tabulated as follows:

	Light/Darkness	Brother and Sister		Life/Death	Love/Power
		Endogamy and Incest (+)	Exogamy (−)		
+	Wotan	Siegmund (and Sieglinde)		Siegfried (+) Brünnhilde	
−	Alberich	Gunther (and Gutrune)		Hagen	Ring

Moreover, this diagram underscores the fact that all the positive relationships, be they of kinship or influence, belong to the upper line, whereas the negative relationships belong to the lower line. The "positive heroes" suffer misfortune only when they envisage relationships with characters from the lower line, as is the case with the allegiance between Hagen and Brünnhilde and the seizure first by Siegfried, then by Hagen, of the ring.

It scarcely needs adding that I do not believe any more than is necessary in the "explanatory" value of the new "structure" that has been extrapolated in this way. The relationships between the characters are too complex and subtle to be reducible to such a structure. All I want to show is that it is possible to arrive at a different but, I believe, equally convincing result by selecting aspects of the "lived experience" of the action and characters that differ from those singled out by Lévi-Strauss in constructing his own analysis. The plasticity of the structural categories is such that it is possible, depending upon the way in which they are manipulated, to press the selected categories into the service of whatever one wishes to demonstrate. It is not the structure that organizes the text and that it is left to the analyst to discover. It is the structure that is produced by the analyst,[12] just as with Freud the interpretation was predetermined by the theory.

Lévi-Strauss, Freud, and the Denial of Time

It is not surprising, therefore, to note a close affinity between Freud's approach and that of Lévi-Strauss. The reader will recall the diagram that I proposed earlier in summarizing the Oedipus myth in its complete form:

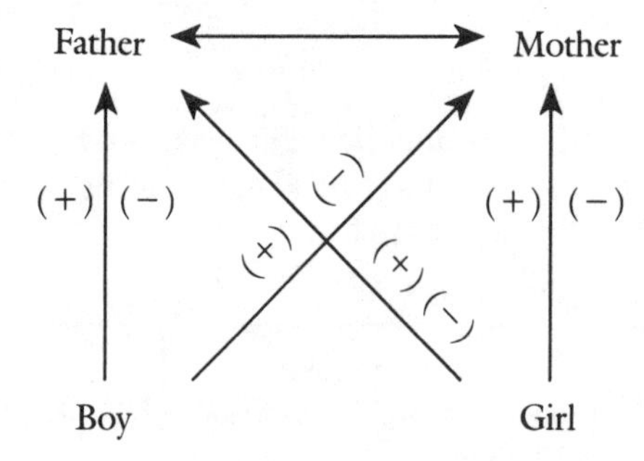

What is this diagram if not a network of structural relationships in which, as we have seen, every negative relationship can be interpreted positively, and vice versa?

Lévi-Strauss has explained his debt to Freud in *Tristes tropiques* (1955b, 67–69): "Beyond the rational there exists a more important and valid category. . . . The order which is thus introduced into a seemingly incoherent mass is neither contingent nor arbitrary." Beyond the variations observable in time, there exist "certain basic characteristics of the physical or mental universe."

The first feature characterizes the hermeneutic dimension not only of the approaches of Lévi-Strauss and Freud but of all "philosophies of suspicion," to quote Ricoeur's memorable phrase. Since every dream is the fulfillment of a desire, it necessarily says the opposite of what it appears to say. Notwithstanding the great diversity of myths, it is the universal structures of the human mind speaking to us here: there is a meaning to the myth beyond the one that it seems to be telling us.

In both cases it is possible to go beyond the incoherence of the surface structure and discover an underlying logic. Thus Freud writes: "If we adopt the method of interpreting dreams which I have indicated here, we shall find that dreams really have a meaning and are far from being the expression of a fragmentary activity of the brain" (1900, 121). In much the same way, Lévi-Strauss notes that while mythology gives the impression of "idle play, . . . the purpose of myth is to provide a logical model capable of overcoming a contradiction" (Lévi-Strauss 1955a, 207 and 229). It is scarcely surprising, therefore, that both writers use the Oedipus myth as a metaphor of their respective discoveries: as Anzieu has rightly pointed out, Freud identified with Oedipus, "who resolved the dark enigma" (Freud 1900, 263), while Lévi-Strauss chose the Oedipus myth as the object of his model structural analysis because he could thereby take his place in an illustrious tradition and, at the same time, surpass it. "Therefore not only Sophocles, but Freud himself, should be included among the recorded versions of the Oedipus myth" (Lévi-Strauss 1955a, 217). Like Freud, he wanted to be the ultimate authority.

The subject cannot control the meaning of his dreams. "In the case of two consecutive dreams it can often be observed that one takes as its central point something that is only on the periphery of the other and *vice versa*, so that their interpretations too are mutually complementary" (Freud 1900, 525). The same is true of mythology: "How are we going to explain the fact that myths throughout the world are so similar?" (Lévi-Strauss 1955a, 208). Only by bringing them together and comparing them is it possible to discover their deep meaning. "The true constituent units of a myth are not the isolated relations but *bundles of such relations*, and it is only as bundles that these relations can be put to use and combined so as to produce a meaning" (ibid., 211).

The features common to both theories need to be compared. It is not the individual who dreams but his unconscious; it is not the teller of the myth who speaks but the universal structure: "It can thus be seen how the elimination of the subject represents what might be called a methodological need: it corresponds to the scrupulous desire to explain no part of the myth except by the myth, and consequently to exclude the point of view of an arbiter looking at the myth from outside and therefore inclined to propose extrinsic causes for it" (Lévi-Strauss 1971, 628).

In the twentieth century it was Freud who provoked the death of the subject: it is no longer the *I*, or ego, speaking but the unconscious. Hence the rejection, by both writers, of historical contingencies. Freud was fascinated by archaeology, which evoked the impression for him of a buried age, of underlying, universal depths. Lévi-Strauss, in turn, was enthralled by geology: "Suddenly time and space become one: the living diversity of the moment juxtaposes and perpetuates the ages" (Lévi-Strauss 1955b, 69). It amuses both writers to dream of a history that is, as it were, vertical, a history of man that can be reduced to its bedrock. In the case of Lévi-Strauss, this dream takes the form of the concept of transformation that returns, significantly, in Foucault's writings in the framework of what he terms "archaeology":

> Linear successions, which for so long had been the object of research, have given way to discoveries in depth. . . . Behind the rapidly changing history of governments, wars, and famines, there emerge other, apparently *unmoving histories.*[13] . . . The problem . . . is no longer one of lasting foundations, but one of transformations that serve as new foundations, the rebuilding of foundations. (Foucault 1969, 3–5)

Here is a dream of immobile history, the utopian vision of an inert history that can be compressed into the dimensions of a synchronic approach. The denial of time and history is fundamental to Lévi-Strauss's thinking. According to Saussure, language is divided into *parole* (which belongs to nonreversible time) and *langue* (which belongs to the realm of reversible time) (Lévi-Strauss 1955a, 209). "What gives the myth an operational value is that the specific pattern described is timeless; it explains the present and the past as well as the future" (ibid.), as in the Norns' scene that opens *Götterdämmerung*.

The same is true of music inasmuch as myth and the work of music share a common characteristic: both are

> languages which, in their different ways, transcend articulate expression, while at the same time—like articulate speech, but unlike painting—requiring a temporal dimension in which to unfold. But this relation to time is of a rather special nature: it is as if music and mythology needed time only in order to deny it. *Both, indeed, are instruments for the obliteration of time.*[14] Below the level of sounds and rhythms, music acts upon a primitive terrain, which is the psychological time of the listener; this time is irreversible and therefore irredeemably diachronic, yet music transmutes the segment de-

> voted to listening to it into a synchronic totality, enclosed within itself. Because of the internal organization of the musical work, the act of listening to it immobilizes passing time; it catches and enfolds it as one catches and enfolds a cloth flapping in the wind. It follows that, by listening to music, and while we are listening to it, we enter into a kind of immortality. (Lévi-Strauss 1964, 15–16)

This is a crucial passage that, beyond its intrinsic beauty, reveals the quasi-metaphysical foundations of the structuralist method. If the structure of a piece of music, like that of myth, displays unities between which we can establish analogous relations on the level of either listening (in the case of music) or the construction of semantic relationships (in the case of myth)—in a word, if we can reduce the syntagmatic unities that obey the laws of time to paradigmatic families that regroup them "outside time"—it is possible for the structuralist, by virtue of the analytical technique that he employs, to imitate that sense of being torn from time's inexorable passage which we may experience when listening to a piece of music or a mythic narrative.

There is an extensive literature on the epistemological merits and difficulties of paradigmatic analysis in musicology and mythography. To rehearse them here would prolong the debate unduly. Suffice it only to recall that for Lévi-Strauss, history is not only tortuous but empty, and a Hellenist as eminent as Jean-Pierre Vernant, notwithstanding his sympathies with structuralism, has no hesitation in describing Lévi-Strauss's paradigmatic analysis of the Oedipus myth as arbitrary (Vernant 1974, 240) and to ask, inter alia: "What is the link between the semantic space cleared by structural analysis as an intellectual framework for the myth and the sociohistorical context in which that myth was produced?" (ibid., 249–50). In the second part of the present study, I tried to show that Wagner's "myth" of androgyny, as manifest in the various stages of his conception of the relationship between poetry and music, acquired various semantic layers according to its contextualization.

With Lévi-Strauss, an apparently technical method has quasi-metaphysical implications. By freezing time, it is possible to achieve the sense of totality that is expressed in its briefest form in the binary relationships of nature/culture, raw/cooked, boiled/roasted, hot/cold, and so on. The same feature is also found in Freud, even though it is less frequently associated with him. As Anzieu has written:

> His hypotheses are often presented in the form of pairs of opposites: psychic quantity/quality, representation of things/words, latent/manifest content, primary/secondary process, experience of satisfaction/test of suffering, displacement/condensation, primary/secondary benefit of an illness, first/second censorship, hallucinations/discharges (or perception/motricity), autoeroticism/

alloeroticism, activity/passivity, masculine/feminine (an opposition implicit in the notion of "bisexuality"), to name only the most important. (Anzieu 1959, 2.730)

The most adaptable of all these binary systems is the last-named. It is scarcely surprising that both writers are so passionate about incest—in Freud's case it is at the basis of the Oedipus complex in its heterosexual and homosexual form, while Lévi-Strauss sees it as a way of transgressing the opposition of nature/culture. In both cases the ultimate opposition is overturned and the binary categories transferred or merged with the One.

In this way the fundamental androgyny of Freud and Lévi-Strauss allows them to deny all sense of time, abolish history, evade the question of interrelationships, and reduce the world's diversity to an endless series of binary opposites.

The androgyne has neither father nor descendants. In the various religious systems in which he appears, he figures at both the beginning and the end of history. By plunging into intemporal depths, psychoanalysis and structuralism present themselves as the end of science. In the case of Lévi-Strauss, the whole idea behind the structuralist approach stems from his contemplation of a sunset (Lévi-Strauss 1955b, 75–84), while the final volume of his *Mythologies* culminates in an apocalypse, in which the different pairs of opposites dissolve into nothingness (Lévi-Strauss 1971, 695).

Above all, however, androgyny, as an allegory of totality and suspended time, signifies the reversibility of opposites. If *A* is equal to *B*, "+" equal to "−," masculine equal to feminine, and if, as the world's cryptographer and textual exegete, I take the place of God, every interpretative licence will be permissible.

Psychoanalytic exegesis emerged at a time of antipositivist reaction. J. Le Rider (1982) has demonstrated this in the case of Otto Weininger, whose sexual metaphysics now tends to raise a smile when it does not provoke outright irritation. There is a striking parallel with Freud in that Weininger lays down laws "so plausible as to need no demonstration" (Weininger 1903, 42) and seeks proof of his theories in the biology and pseudosciences of his day. Throughout his life Freud remained nostalgic about the biological explanation of bisexuality but, from a strictly epistemological point of view, his conceptual edifice is the result of nothing more than a do-it-yourself approach to human behavior, as he realized only too well. In a letter to Fließ of 1 February 1900, long suppressed from their published correspondence, he confided: "I am actually not at all a man of science, not an observer, not an experimenter, not a thinker. I am by temperament nothing but a conquistador—an adventurer, if you want it translated—with all the curiosity, daring, and tenacity characteristic of a man of this sort" (Freud 1985, 398). Lévi-Strauss, too, would have us believe that biology is at the basis of binary structuralism: "As early as 1945 . . . I applied transformational rules to sociological data and artistic works, with the conviction that I was respecting the teachings of structural linguistics, the same form of linguistics as is now declared to be out of date by people who do not even realize that it has been given a natural and objective status through the discovery and the cracking of the genetic code" (Lévi-Strauss 1971, 684). Clearly one can believe what one likes, but these allusions to science remain a precautionary—or cautionary—measure within his oeuvre.

As with Freud and Jung, androgyny and the denial of time serve to bolster up the liberty and laxity of interpretation. This is not a feature that figures in Wagner, who, as a creative artist, did not have to be accountable to the truth. Quite the opposite: as Leach recognizes, the freedom of every structuralist construction suggests that "the pleasure which can be derived from structural analysis is aesthetic" (1966, 70).

Conversely, Freud and Lévi-Strauss share with Wagner the search for totality (in this case explicative) and the desire for immortality. Umberto Eco is quite right when he claims that "structural models could be instruments for a mystic initiation, ways toward a contemplation of the Absolute" (1968, 367). The charismatic paradigms of the twentieth century are not only androgynous: they also appear as a present-day extension of Romantic patterns of thought and aspirations. By far the most striking of their common features is their passion for analogy, which is the starting point for the whole technique of binary analysis.

If further proof be needed of the fact that the game of "structural" analogies is well anchored in Romantic thought, it comes from the "Brazilian" text with which this chapter began, a gambit for which I must now ask the forgiveness not only of my readers but also of Lévi-Strauss himself, for the text in question is not by him but by Wagner (1871t, *GS* 6.267–68). Is such audience manipulation forgivable? It was the most eloquent way I had of showing that Wagner was not a precursor of structuralism but that Lévi-Strauss is a late Romantic.

Nor is he alone in that.

Chapter Eleven

MARXISM, FEMINISM, AND ROMANTICISM

Social Utopias and Androgyny

It is impossible to emphasize often enough to what extent today's human sciences are close to Romantic thought—so much so, indeed, that it is possible to confuse the discourse of Lévi-Strauss with that of Wagner. After psychoanalysis and structuralism, we need to consider *social* paradigms, in particular Marxism, in our survey of androgynous hermeneutics.

The myth of the androgyne and Marx's historico-social vision rest upon an analogous model: there was once an original unity, that of primitive communism, which was destroyed by the emergence of private property and feudalism and which will be restored by the revolution that ushers in a classless society. The clearest exposition of this model is to be found in Friedrich Engels's *Origin of the Family, Private Property, and State*, in which the androgyne appears not as a metaphor of primitive social unity and of the unity to come but, in keeping with the model of original unity/lost unity/rediscovered unity, in the narrower sense of the relationship between men and women, as was the case in the *Ring*. Taking Lewis Henry Morgan as his starting point (and it is worth recalling in the context of this chapter that Lévi-Strauss dedicated his *Elementary Structures of Kinship* to Morgan's memory), Engels goes back to a "primitive stage at which promiscuous intercourse prevailed within a tribe, so that every woman belonged equally to every man and every man to every woman" (1884, 142). The most primitive form of the family was "group marriage" in which "whole groups of men and whole groups of women belong to one another, and which leaves but little scope for jealousy" (ibid., 145). Brother and sister originally lived together as man and wife (ibid., 146). It is worth noting, on the subject of incest, that in a footnote to this passage Engels cites a letter from Marx of 1882, reproaching Wagner for his "utter falsification of primitive times" in his depiction of Siegmund and Sieglinde. "In primeval times the sister *was* the wife, *and that was moral*" (ibid., 147). In his haste to condemn Wagner's luxury-loving gods and turn the composer into a bourgeois artist, Marx has failed to understand that in the *Ring*, incest is viewed as something preeminently positive: Siegmund and Sieglinde are the only couple to produce a hero even if the overall perspective, which looks beyond the solitary virtues of incest, means that the relationship ends in catastrophe.

Engels sees the earliest form of communist community in the primitive family, whereas marriage among civilized societies coincides with "the first class oppression . . . of the female sex by the male" (ibid., 173). In a spirit not far removed from Feuerbach and, hence, from Wagner, Engels writes:

> In the family, [the man] is the bourgeois; the wife represents the proletariat. . . . It will then become evident that the first precondition for the emancipation of women is the reintroduction of the entire female sex into public industry; and that this again demands that the quality possessed by the individual family of being the economic unit of society be eliminated. . . . We are now approaching a social revolution in which the hitherto existing economic foundations of monogamy will disappear just as certainly as those of its complement—prostitution. (Ibid., 181–82)

In his "Economic and Philosophic Manuscripts of 1844" Karl Marx had suggested that in the communist society of the future, the relationship between men and women would no longer be the same and that, as with other contradictions, the opposition between the sexes would be resolved: "The relation of man to woman is the *most natural* relation of human being to human being. . . . *Communism* as the *positive* transcendence of *private property* as *human self-estrangement*, and therefore as the real *appropriation* of the *human* essence by and for man, . . . is the *genuine* resolution of the conflict between man and nature and between man and man" (Marx 1844, 296).

Although the figure of androgyny remains latent in the writings of Marx and Engels, various currents in mystical French socialism draw on it explicitly as a symbol of social unity. In these constructs it is synonymous both with social equality and, in consequence of women's future emancipation, with the equality of men and women. This type of androgyny is less well known, or at all events less evident, than the androgyny of Freud and Lévi-Strauss, since it is the preserve of authors who are now read only by students of nineteenth-century thought. Indeed, it is only thanks to A.J.L. Busst's outstanding study "The Image of the Androgyne in the Nineteenth Century" (1967) that the following examples are available.

It must not be forgotten that Marxism is far from enjoying the monopoly of a collective vision of humanity. The Orientalist and occultist Antoine Fabre d'Olivet dreamed of "collective man," "Man formed abstractly by an assemblage of all men" (1815–16, 2.58), "Man in general, universal Man" (1822, 22). Lamennais declared: "Man alone is but a fragment of being: the true being is the collective being, Humanity" (Lamennais 1850, 9), while Balzac anthropomorphized humanity as "that vast being," "the whole of humanity, coming to life as a single being, reasoning as a single mind, acting as with a single arm in carrying out its actions."[1] This position is very similar to the one adopted by Jules Michelet, who conceived of the people as an androgynous being: "Genius, that inventive and generative power, supposes that . . . one and the same man . . . combines within himself what can be called the two sexes of the mind, the instinct of the foolish and the reflection of the wise. He is, to some extent, man and woman, childlike and mature, barbarian and civilized, common people and aristocracy" (Michelet 1846, 215).

Fabre d'Olivet was no doubt the first writer to advance an androgynous vision of universal history. In *La Langue hébraïque restituée* (1815–16), he explains how the first man and woman form universal Man and constitute a single androgynous individual. The original unity has been split not into two sexual halves but into three entities: destiny, providence, and will. But the day will come when time will stand still, space will cease to exist, and universal Man will return to his primeval state of "indivisible and immortal unity" (Fabre d'Olivet 1823, 196). This eschatological vision frames a social concept inasmuch as the ills that beset the majority of societies are said to derive from the fact that a single force dominates all others, thereby preventing the restoration of harmony and the primal androgynous unity.

It is in the writings of Pierre-Simon Ballanche, especially his *Vision d'Hébal* of 1831, that the figure of the androgyne becomes an eloquent symbol of social equality. Humanity is divided into two sexes but in this case the male embodies the will that, as such, is responsible for the Fall. In other words, the division between the sexes symbolizes humanity's cosmological division, which, in turn, is embodied in the distinction between East and West. In the East are the Sethites, active, full of initiative, and male; in the West are the Cainites, passive, voluntaristic, "initiable," and feminine. The same distinction exists between plebeians and patricians, with the latter initiating the former into their ways; and the same is true of class divisions, which is why the active and passive principles embodied in male and female must be reunited before human unity can be reestablished. Such reunification will be possible, Ballanche concludes, when woman, as the embodiment of male will, ceases to be man's slave. Only then will man be rehabilitated, and the whole of humanity will act as a single being.

More or less contemporaneous with Ballanche's blueprint for a new society is the social vision of the Saint-Simonians, with its program of women's emancipation and universal industrialization, and its image of androgyny. What mattered for the Saint-Simonians was to give equal weight to body and intellect, matter and spirit, man and woman. The industrious citizen is a couple; the woman embodies matter and flesh, the man mind and intelligence. Similar ideas—with minor shifts of emphasis—may be found in the writings of Barthélemy-Prosper Enfantin and Pierre Leroux, for whom humanity was "held to form a single collective being" (Leroux 1840, 504). Leroux's model was an androgynous Adam, the return to unity being made possible through knowledge. In the case of Ganneau (who in 1838 created an "Evadist" religion based on the fusion of Eve and Adam) and his disciple Caillaux, the androgyne symbolizes the ideals of the French Revolution: the virginal figure of Liberty will appear at the side of Adam, who, seen as the incomplete male principle, is reincarnated in Christ (the equally incomplete Redeemer); as such, she will be the new Eve of the Revolution, thereby achieving true redemption: "In Christ and in liberty, the final stage in the evocation of Genesis, the final symbol of divine unity, of unity in duality! Amen! *Hosannah*!" (quoted in Yriarte 1864, 124).

Finally, the ex-abbé Alphonse-Louis Constant drew an even closer link between social criticism, women's emancipation, and androgyny: for him, it was money that prevented a return to androgyny, since it corrupted love, turning marriage into a form of prostitution, and keeping women in a position of inferiority. The advent of the androgyne will put an end, therefore, to the division between rich and poor: "The two sexes will be no more than one, in accord with Christ's teaching; the great androgyne will be created, humanity will be man and woman" (quoted in Tristan 1845).

There is no doubt, however, that it is the positivism of Auguste Comte that provides the finest example of the reconciliation of social issues and androgyny within a coherent and elaborate philosophical system. In his *Système de politique positive, ou Traité de sociologie, instituant la religion de l'humanité* of 1851–54, he imagines that the "great being" of his religion will be androgynous, thanks in particular to the androgyny of the woman who, being essentially love, feeling, and matter, will assimilate the man's intelligence and spirit. "Since positivism represents the synthesis of the spiritual and the material, of theology and science, the hermaphrodite resumes Comte's philosophy," Busst writes (1967, 4). There seems little doubt that the painter Paul Chenavard was inspired by this androgynous conception of the "great being": his painting, *The Divine Tragedy*, exhibited at the 1869 Salon, depicts Reason—shown as a hermaphrodite, with a woman's breasts and male attributes, wearing a Phrygian cap and seated on a chimera—triumphing over the world's religions. Represented here are the starting point and culmination of humanity, the reintegration of sexual divisions, the overthrow of illusory religions, and the republican symbol of liberty. Busst sees "the statue of deified humanity on God's ancient altar" (ibid., 24) in the thrust of Comte's philosophy, an eloquent image in which androgyny, political eschatology, and a secular version of religious myth find compelling expression.

The Biological Androgyny of Elisabeth Badinter

It was inevitable that the final twitches of the neo-Marxist social utopia, combined with the immense hopes of greater equality between the sexes that have been raised by the feminist movement, should have given birth, in the modern age, to a myth or, more exactly, to the return to an existing myth. Since androgynous ambivalence allows one to say what one likes, it is under the auspices of androgyny that today's human sciences have produced a new mythic vision of past and future humanity, as embodied by Elisabeth Badinter's *Man/Woman: The One Is the Other* (1986).

Anyone reading this highly successful study will be struck by the author's return to a way of thinking to which I have already drawn attention in Wagner's writings. And if one accepts that Engels's monograph *The Origin of the Family* presupposes the development from original unity to the loss of that unity and finally to its rediscovery (even if the figure of the androgyne does not appear here as such), it will be seen that Badinter's vision, slipping into the very same mold, fills the "silence" left by Marxism's founding fathers.

In the case of Badinter, the social and biological equality of men and women replaces primitive egalitarian society and the classless society of the Marxist model. Nonetheless, the *political* question of the relations between men and women provides the framework for her study. "Equality being their principle [i.e., the principle on which Western democracies are based], they have constantly striven to impose it, and to put an end to power systems founded on the idea of a natural hierarchy among human beings" (ibid., xii). In *Man/Woman*, we are witnessing the birth of an androgynous neo-Marxism.

The first section is headed "The One and the Other." In ancient times it was the "original complementarity of the sexes" that predominated. "There is no reason to think," the author writes, "that the men of this era exercised tyrannical power over the women—nor the women over the men" (ibid., 17). Of course, Badinter is conscious of the hypothetical nature of her views: "In our turn, we would like to suggest the idea that, in Palaeolithic societies, control and power may well have been exercised by both men and women" (ibid., 59). Her claim can be sustained, however, only at the cost of an unprecedented epistemological somersault. Opining that historians and anthropologists have hitherto merely projected their own aspirations onto the past (a debatable point at best), she believes herself entitled to proceed in an identical manner: "The hypothesis we are going to suggest is no doubt in its turn influenced by our observation of the present-day evolution of our societies" (ibid., 19). Badinter is not afraid, however, of going into historical detail, suggesting that during the period from the tenth to the second millennium the androgyny of the Mother Goddess in India, Persia, and eastern Europe was an important indication of the nature of everyday relationships: "The Goddess's bisexuality is the clearest way of saying that she is All, the Whole who does not need to call on any outside contribution in order to procreate. She engenders the universe by parthenogenesis, exactly like God the Father, who succeeded her in the male monotheistic religions" (ibid., 38). For Badinter, the original androgyne was a woman. "And it does seem that the Neolithic period comes under the sign of the reign of the mother, and leaves masculine powers in the relative shade" (ibid., 40). "From the Palaeolithic to the Iron Age, men and women shared the tasks with varying degrees of equity, but without ever giving the impression that the One was no more than the pale reflection of the Other, or, worse still, the evil to guard against" (ibid., 52).

The second part of Badinter's study, "The One without the Other," is clearly the least subject to historical caution, since it describes the position of dominance held by men in modern society, from the masculine representation of God and the transition to a male androgynous god to patriarchal domination, the institution of the family, the war of the sexes, and sexist stereotypes. It is not without interest in the present context to note that, starting out from her feminist point of view, Badinter links up neo-Marxism and structuralism. Relying on the writings of Françoise Héritier, Lévi-Strauss's successor at the Collège de France, she writes that in patriarchal societies "creation myths and their many philosophical systems are built on a system of binary categories which opposes masculine to feminine as superior to inferior" (ibid., 88). And she adds a note: "The principal categories are those of hot and cold, dry and wet, each related to the masculine or the feminine, and assigned a positive or negative value" (ibid., 240). But whereas Lévi-Strauss imagined an androgynous complementarity of opposites under the mythologist's leadership, Elisabeth Badinter announces the advent of what the American essayist Marc Feigen Fasteau had already described as a future androgynous society (1974). But whereas Fasteau's feminist study, like many of the writings of this period, had been content with a "revision" of sexual roles in everyday life (a revision that has effectively changed for the better the relations between men and women in our society), Badinter replaces the utopia of a classless society with the utopia of a biological *coup d'état*.

In the third part of her study, "The One Is the Other," Badinter describes the death throes of patriarchy before going on to envisage a state beyond the control of fertility that has come from women's emancipation, beyond the reestablishment of the principle of equality between "the one and the other," and the "blurring of traditional sexual roles" (Badinter 1986, 159), a state, in short, when it will be possible to cross the ultimate biological barrier. At this juncture, the author appeals to Freud for support, drawing on his notion of "unconscious bisexuality" (ibid., 171). The individual, she claims, blossoms on recognizing his or her bisexuality. We no longer know where the difference between masculine and feminine lies, she maintains. "In actual fact, we are all androgynous, because human beings are bisexual, on several levels and to different degrees" (ibid., 167). The way is open to drive back the frontiers of nature and usher in an age when it will be possible to question the predominance of biology. "Feminine destiny is no longer linked to motherhood" (ibid., 185). The day will come when our "androgynous mutation" will allow men to bring children into the world. "This is the possibility of a pregnant man. Delirium? Science fiction? Perhaps not" (ibid., 218). And here Freudian thinking serves as the basis for a spectacular biological upheaval: "The male unconscious has for so long been haunted by fantasies of pregnancy that some men may indeed try to put an end to that longing and powerlessness, that they now discuss more and more openly" (ibid., 219).

This is not the place to examine the scientific basis of Elisabeth Badinter's analyses and propositions, whether they be the historico-anthropological considerations of the first part of her study or the biological ones of the final part. These chapters were in any case extensively criticized at the time of their first publication. But it seems to me that at the time, writers failed to notice the contribution that Badinter's study made to the development and transformation of the myth of the androgyne, simply because they failed to see that in terms of its form and content, her book was none other than a myth itself.

In the first place, Badinter produces a synthesis of psychoanalysis, structuralism, and Marxism, and she does so, moreover, on the basis of total fantasy: whereas the myth of the androgyne has appeared hitherto as an imaginative response not only to the impossibility of being or knowing the opposite sex but also to our biological destiny, which is imposed on us at birth, Badinter seriously envisages men's biological transformation, thereby capping the Freudian myth of the equivalence of the sexes that is currently fashionable.

It cannot be denied that this myth has left a deep and lasting impression on our lives in the sense that it can truthfully be said that certain generations have lived through the myth of Brigitte Bardot, Marilyn Monroe, and James Dean. Androgyny is everywhere: from unisex boutiques to successful films such as *Tootsie* and *Victor/Victoria*, from David Bowie and Annie Lennox to Klaus Nomi, Boy George, and Michael Jackson. And today's artists are not afraid to declare their feelings of androgyneity. Maurice Béjart admits, "I am androgynous when I create" (1979, 175). Jean-Luc Godard has said, "For me, women are my 'other' self, my true double, though I never manage to find myself in agreement with them."[2] Carole Laure confesses, "There are times I no longer know whether I'm a girl or a boy. I then wake up in the morning and scream. There are times, when I'm having sex, when I don't know if I'm penetrating my partner or being penetrated myself."[3] And Gérard Depardieu claims, "What I most like about men is their femininity."[4]

Androgyny has entered into our lives. All it still has to do is to change those lives for us. It is not surprising, therefore, that Elisabeth Badinter has inserted the myth of the biological equality of the two sexes into the mold—itself mythological—that has been used by reformers in their attempts to change society. Like so many writers before her, she has shown that androgyny allows us to say whatever we want, but she has done so within the framework of late twentieth-century thoughts, aspirations, and dreams, thereby revitalizing the Romantic myth of the androgyne.

Androgynous Hermeneutics and Romanticism

Elisabeth Badinter is not the only writer to attest to the continuation of Romantic ideas into the twentieth century. Even if Althusser falls back on thought processes in vogue in 1968 to distinguish a pre-Marxist Marx from an antihumanist and scientific Marx (a "postrevolutionary" Marx), the links between Marxism and Romanticism are worth picking up in an attempt to explain whether there is still any interest in the subject following the debacle surrounding those governments in which a whole generation placed its hopes. Some of the elements in this analysis were set out at the beginning of the present chapter. As for the Modern Age, suffice it to recall the typical "Romantic hero" embodied in Che Guevara and his influence at that time. In the previous chapter we saw where the analogy between Wagner and Lévi-Strauss could lead. Only the fear of taxing my reader's patience discourages me from looking in greater detail at the Romantic aspects of Lévi-Strauss's thinking, although I cannot resist listing them as the Romantic love of opposites and binary structures, reasoning by analogy, recourse to rash etymologies which do duty for factual demonstrations, the organic character of the concept of structure, the distinction (as with Marx) between a hidden and unconscious "infrastructure" (in Lévi-Strauss's case, the universal structure of the human mind) and its surface manifestations, the search for totality, and a nostalgic longing for the absolute.

Writers on Freud have shown an increasing interest in the Romantic roots of psychoanalytic concepts. It is too little known that Freud changed his first name from Sigismund to Sigmund following the first

Viennese performance of *Die Walküre* on 5 March 1877, and when one knows the importance of proper names in both psychoanalysis and Jewish thought, one's wish is not so much to explain psychoanalysis by reference to Wagner (which would be an absurdity) as to have at one's disposal sufficient philological evidence to sort out to what extent a work described by Groddeck as a "manual of psychoanalysis" has contributed to the formation of Freud's conceptual edifice. In the meantime, other writers—notably Thomas Mann (1936)[5]—have already drawn attention to some of the important influences of Romantic thought on Freud. Before being integrated into a coherent theory, the concept of the unconscious had left its mark on Western thought long before Freud, finding expression, for example, in the writings of Goethe, Hegel, Schelling, Schopenhauer, and Nietzsche (see Whyte 1960), even if these writers give it another name. (One thinks in particular of Schopenhauer's concept of the will.)

> The key to an understanding of the nature of the conscious life of the soul must be sought in the realm of the unconscious. Hence the difficulty, if not the impossibility of understanding fully the secret life of the soul. If it were completely impossible to rediscover the unconscious in the conscious, man would be left feeling nothing but despair at the hopelessness of ever arriving at an understanding of his soul, in other words, an understanding of himself. But if this impossibility is merely apparent, the first task of a science of the soul will be to establish how the mind of man can fathom these depths.

These lines could have been written by Freud but were in fact penned by Carl Gustav Carus in 1846.[6] It is the influence of writings such as Carus's *Psyche*, Schubert's *The Symbolism of Dreams* (1814), and Hartmann's *Philosophy of the Unconscious* (1869) that needs to be studied in the context of Freud and Jung.[7] Nor should it be necessary to insist on the role of night and dreams in Romantic art, a role that has been examined in detail by Albert Béguin (1937). I have already mentioned the 421 dreams of Wagner himself, recorded by Cosima in her diaries, together with the fact that his heroes and heroines, often on the brink of hysteria, dream a great deal (one thinks here of Senta, Elsa, Sieglinde, and Tristan), to say nothing of the oneiric worlds of the Venusberg and Klingsor's magic garden that are presented on stage as though they were real.

A study of twentieth-century Romanticism would run to more than a single volume.[8] But, having reached the present stage, we may perhaps be in a better position to understand why the androgynous hermeneutics of the twentieth century are unsuited to explaining Wagner's androgyny: taking their place in a long line of development stretching back to Romanticism, they can be explained only by Romanticism itself.

Chapter Twelve

DECONSTRUCTION OR RESTORATION OF MEANING?

TO DATE, our own generation has been confronted with three major approaches—both theoretical and practical—to the interpretation of literary texts and works of art.

We do not need to linger over the first of them, described around 1965 as "university criticism" by its detractors among adherents of the New Criticism. What was involved was the whole exegetical tradition from Lanson onward, a tradition that argued that in order to reveal the meaning of a text, it was necessary not only to establish the exact letter and reconstruct the history of its different versions according to the principles of philology but also to explain its significance in terms of the writer's life, be it biographical, social, or historical. We may conveniently recall the explicit words of Raymond Picard, who was at the heart of the "quarrel of the New Criticism," an updated version of the *querelle des anciens et des modernes* between the Gluckists and Piccinnists: for Picard, it was possible for the "patient and unassuming seeker" to "rely on the *certainties* of language, on the *implications* of psychological coherency, and on the *imperatives* of the structure of the genre to disentangle *evidence*[1] that would, to some extent, define the areas of objectivity: on the basis of this, one can attempt, very cautiously, to venture an interpretation" (Picard 1965, 69). Castigating Roland Barthes, he had no hesitation in asserting: "There is *one*[2] truth concerning Racine and everyone can reach agreement on that point" (ibid.). Since this hermeneutical tradition is based, essentially, on a reconstruction of categories of thought and of a semantic world unique to the author, I have chosen to describe it—borrowing from the language of semiotic tripartition that governs my other writings[3]—as *poietic*, inasmuch as it is directed toward the world of the author.

During the 1960s, reaction set in against the univocity of meaning extolled by "university criticism"[4] and a new type of exegesis came into fashion, founded on total freedom of interpretation. For that reason, I describe it as *esthesic* because it rests on the perception of the critic and is independent of the writer's intentions and world, which are considered unattainable or obsolete. By way of illustration, it is worth stating the positions held not only by Roland Barthes, who was one of the chief representatives of the New Criticism, but also by Jacques Derrida, a leading advocate of "deconstruction."

It was with a firm emphasis on androgyny that Barthes inaugurated his career as a critic with *Michelet* in 1954. The study opens with an epigraph borrowed from the historian's writings: "I am a complete man having the two sexes of the mind." "Michelet turned himself into a hero," Barthes comments, "in other words, of double sex, the progenitor of Justice at the breast of female Grace" (1954, 52). "History is male, Syria female. But erotically, there is only one spectator and his spectacle; Michelet himself is no longer either man or woman, he is only the expression in his eye" (ibid., 130). And he goes on, "Michelet's heroes are, by definition, androgynous beings" (ibid., 155). Barthes returned to androgyny fifteen years later in his famous study *S/Z*, a work that needs to be seen as a metaphor for total freedom of interpretation.

It is worth recalling what Barthes wrote here. One must

> forgo establishing a deep and ultimate structure for the text and in reconstituting the paradigm of each code aim at multiple structures; prefer structuring to structure; seek out the play of the codes, not the plan of the work. . . . Analysis provides material for various criticisms. This does not imply liberality, conceding some truth to each form of criticism, but observance of the plurality of meanings as being, not as deduction or tolerance. . . . The code as an anonymous voice. (1970b, 261)

Expressed in Barthes' quintessential style, which transforms his explanation of the "method" into a literary text, this is all perfectly clear:

> Let us first posit the image of a triumphant plural, unimpoverished by any constraint of representation (of imitation). In this ideal text, the networks are many and interact, without any one of them being able to surpass the rest; this text is a galaxy of signifiers, not a structure of signifieds; it has no beginning; it is reversible; we gain access to it by several entrances, none of which can be authoritatively declared to be the main one; the codes it mobilizes extend as far *as the eye can reach*, they are *indeterminable*[5] (meaning here is never subject to a principle of determination, unless by throwing dice); the systems of meaning can take over this absolutely plural text, but their number is never closed, based as it is on the infinity of language. . . . It is a question, against all in-difference, of asserting the very existence of plurality, which is not that of the true, the probable, or even the possible. . . . All of which comes down to saying that for the plural text, there cannot be a narrative structure, a grammar, or a logic. (Ibid., 5–6)

What Barthes is saying—and a paraphrase must inevitably trivialize his meaning—is that there is no longer a hierarchy of value or validity between the commentaries on a text: one can say whatever one wants.

In what way is androgyny the symbol of this vast hermeneutical *laissez-faire*? The answer is provided by an article significantly entitled "Masculine, Feminine, Neuter" (Barthes 1970a), in which Barthes subjects Balzac's *Sarrasine* to his critical scrutiny, a short story that he has chosen to gloss because the world of sexual ambiguity that reigns here can be interpreted as a symbol of exegetical freedom: "Balzac feels a constant need for a third sex, or for an absence of sex" (Barthes 1970a: 900). Why? It is because he has to transcend the opposition between masculine and feminine in order to "say" castrato. French, however, has no neuter gender, so that Barthes is obliged to replace the contrast between masculine and feminine with that between animate and inanimate, in other words—according to the well-tried binary logic of structuralism—with the contrast between life and death, and hot and cold. "The whole of the novella is dominated by an initial antithesis, which installs its symbolic level from the outset. . . . As the poet, [the narrator] possesses the integral paradigm" (ibid., 900–901). In order to achieve this, Balzac is obliged to merge masculine and feminine as an animate object according to his schematic model (ibid.):

Animate (Masculine/Feminine) / Inanimate (Neuter)

"On a formal level, art consists in an operation involving the reassembly of existing parts; faced by his art, the real world of Sarrasine is divided, he shares a major guilt" (ibid., 901). On the other hand, "Zambinella is an *objet d'art* for Sarrasine, . . . *her perfection stems from her unity*"[6] (ibid., 902). In *S/Z* Barthes passes from the delightful confusion provoked by sexual ambiguity to what he later calls "the pleasure of the text," that is, the infinite proliferation of meanings that can be assigned to it: "Sarrasine passionately kisses a castrato (or a boy in drag); the castration is transposed onto Sarrasine's own body and *we ourselves, second readers, receive the shock*.[7] Thus it would be wrong to say that if we undertake to reread the text we do so for some intellectual advantage (to understand better, to analyze on good grounds): it is actually and invariably for a ludic advantage: *to multiply the signifiers, not to reach some ultimate signified*"[8] (1970b, 165).

Twenty years later, in his attempt at a "remake" of Barthes' essay, Michel Serres is even more specific. For the author of *L'Hermaphrodite*, the opening of Balzac's novella is a metaphor for every kind of exegetical and critical work on literature:

> A parasitical crowd flits around at the ball at the Hôtel Lanty, asking real questions: "Why? How? Where has he come from? Who are they? What is it? What has she done?" Balzac articulates the canonical program of what will later be called the human sciences[9] and uses laughter to castigate the

> customs of the inquisitive race that is the actual cause of it. . . . The parasites become policemen in order to put their hosts to death. Honoré de Balzac foretells the ways of critics who live off other people's works. . . . The inquisitive searcher, prying, annoying, discourteous, lacking in reserve and self-control, is shown here as an ill-mannered oaf, a boor who reads other people's letters, digging and prying into their private lives, probing the secrets of their childhood and bedrooms, incessantly striking below the belt and hitting out at their bank accounts. He is happy if he discovers a skeleton in the family cupboard. Detective, customs officer, and voyeur, he needs the right to ask questions. Do not answer him, distrust inquisitive people. (Serres 1987, 62–63)

All this, it must be emphasized once again, is written against a background of androgyny, for Serres sees a paradox in Balzac's novella: this study in castration reveals a plenitude of meaning. "*Sarrasine* excludes exclusion" (ibid., 81). "To exclude exclusion or to eradicate the dominant phallic law is the deeper meaning behind castration" (ibid., 82). As was the case with Barthes, structuralist philosophy precludes the possibility of explaining the novella's meaning by reference to the "externals" of the work. With Zambinella, the existence of androgyny within her breast is the very image of what she is: "Set out from the idea of antithesis and you will end up with castration. Set out from the enantiomorph left/right or the superimposition of images, set out from symmetry and you will create the hermaphrodite, a consummate expression of inclusion. How long did Hermes spend looking for Aphrodite? Overwhelmed at rediscovering her, . . . *Sarrasine* revives Hermaphrodite as the champion of inclusion and the condition of the work, which is born of the additional plenitude of meaning. *Sarrasine* or the superabundant androgyne: Hermes must be imagined as overwhelmed" (ibid., 86–88). There is no doubt that Serres, too, is overwhelmed. But we must be grateful to him, at least, for having denounced the obscurity of the interpretation of androgyny in the writings of his predecessors. "The sexual explanation is certainly exciting, but the clarity that it brings is in inverse proportion to the interest that it produces. While one's attention is transfixed by this one point, one can say or do whatever one wants, protected by the heat and glow of this fire" (ibid., 123). The danger is that Serres himself does not escape unsinged. With Barthes, Sarrasine is contaminated by the castration of the castrato; with Serres, it is Sarrasine himself who is the castrator, inasmuch as he "brandishes the scissors, the instrument of castration" (ibid., 130–31). One can certainly say whatever one wants.

It was left to Jacques Derrida to attempt to raise the principles of hermeneutical freedom to the level of a philosophy, to which he gave the name "deconstruction." Perhaps one can risk a definition:

> Invoking the commonplace but cardinal verity that in all interpretation, in all statements of understanding, language is simply being used about language in an infinitely self-multiplying series (the mirror arcade), the deconstructive reader defines the act of reading as follows. The ascription of sense, the preference of one possible reading over another, the choice of this explication, and paraphrase and not that, is no more than the playful, unstable, undemonstrable option or fiction of a subjective scanner who constructs and deconstructs purely semiotic markers as his own momentary pleasures, politics, psychic needs or self-deceptions bid him do. There are no rational or falsifiable decision-procedures as between a multitude of differing interpretations or "constructs of proposal." At best, we will select (for a time, at least) the one which strikes us as the more ingenious, the richer in surprise, the more powerfully decompositional and re-creative of the original or *pre-text*. (Steiner 1988, 80)

By borrowing this definition from a critic of deconstruction and not quoting directly from Derrida's text, we no doubt risk incurring his wrath.[10] But it is difficult to find a definition of deconstruction in Derrida's own writings. "If I had to risk a single definition of deconstruction, one as brief, elliptical, and economical as a password, I would say simply and without overstatement: *plus d'une langue*—both more of a language and no more of *a* language. In fact it is neither a statement nor a sentence. It is sententious, it makes no sense if, at least as Austin would have it, words in isolation have no meaning. What makes sense is the sentence. How many sentences can be made with 'deconstruction'?" (Derrida 1988, 15). How can the reader be expected to know? "Deconstruction—*if there be such a thing*"[11] (ibid., 73 and 83–84). "In the same way we could have asked: what does the word 'deconstruction' signify?" (ibid., 112).

> This is because everything depends upon *contexts which are always open*,[12] non-saturable, because a single word (for example, a word in a title) begins to bear the meaning of all the potential phrases in which it is to be inscribed . . . and because, inversely, no phrase has an absolutely determinable "meaning": it is always in the situation of the word or title in relation to the text which borders it and which carries it away, in relation to the always more open context which always promises it more meaning. What I am saying here goes for the words "mémoire" or "deconstruction." (Ibid., 115–16)

Nothing has a decidable meaning. With Derrida and de Man, hermeneutics has entered into a phase characterized by the headlong flight of meaning. "On the level of thought," de Man asserts, "it is difficult to distinguish between a proposition and its opposite" (de Man 1979, 225).

Once again, it is symptomatic of the situation under review that in order to explain the apparent complete plasticity of meaning, writers have recourse to the notion of androgyny. Derrida's study, from which we have just quoted, is called *Mémoires*. The title is not an accident. Just as one of the greatest pleasures of deconstruction consists in treating as the object of discourse the very discourse with which I myself discuss discourse, Derrida glosses this title as follows: "The deleted article and mark of the plural lend to this noun, 'Mémoires,' within the contextual wilderness which surrounds a title, its greatest potential for equivocation. The perversion of language is at its peak here." Much the same could be said of Derrida. "In French, *mémoire* is hybrid or androgynous"[13] (1988, 102). The symbol is clear: "If I have left the title, *Mémoires*, to its destiny as an untranslatable idiom, it is no doubt in order to say all of this, but also, and above all, in order to welcome what the signature of a promise keeps untranslatable" (ibid., 105).

Derrida is perfectly at liberty to state that the description of "nihilist," when applied to students of deconstruction, constitutes "the sinister ineptitude of an accusation" (ibid., 21). We are not obliged to believe him, especially when he describes as "destroyers" three thinkers (Nietzsche, Freud, and Heidegger) whom deconstructionists refer to as their predecessors (Derrida 1966, 280–81). If Derrida ends by denying what he himself has written, if he expends so much effort in failing to provide a clear definition of what he himself wants others to understand, and if, as he himself admits, his discourse "is sometimes unmistakably similar to negative theology" (Derrida 1968, 44), it is no doubt because deconstruction is essentially a form of escapism. "Difference is what ensures that the movement of meaning is possible only if each element described as 'present,' appearing on the scene of presence, relates to something other than itself, retaining within itself the mark of the past element and already allowing itself to be eaten into by the mark of its relationship with the future element" (ibid., 51). Meaning is no longer firmly anchored to anything; it lacks a "point of a being-present" (ibid., 53). "Difference does not exist" (ibid., 60); meaning is always movement, "the game played by a trace . . . which has no sense and which does not exist" (ibid., 61). From this point of view, the unconscious, too, constitutes a form of difference, "definitively removed from every process of presentation by which we could call on it to appear in person" (ibid., 59).

From now on, philosophical texts are "convoked" less for what they have to say in themselves than because they "deconstruct themselves" (Derrida 1988, 123), and if Derrida glosses Mallarmé's *Mimique*, it is because he believes he can discover here a metaphor for deconstructive processes. We can trace a line back from Mallarmé's text to one by Paul Margueritte, cited by Mallarmé himself, and thence to Théophile Gautier.

"An eye graft, a text extending far out of sight" (Derrida 1970, 203): every form of writing is dissemination.

> One could go on at great length in order to find out where this Pierrot had read the exemplary story of this husband who tickled his wife and thus made her laughingly give up her life. With all the threads provided by the *commedia dell' arte*, one would find oneself caught in an interminable network. Bibliographical research, source studies, the archeology of all Pierrots would be at once endless and useless. (Ibid., 205)

We are caught in "points of infinite pivoting" (ibid., 221). "This undecidability is marked and re-marked in *writing*" (ibid., 222). Deconstruction is not a form of criticism, since criticism is "linked . . . to the possibility of decidability" (ibid., 236–37). There is no point, therefore, in seeking "a theme or an overall meaning in an imaginary, intentional, or lived domain beyond all textual instances" (ibid., 251). In consequence, "whatever might have been going on in Mallarmé's head, in his consciousness or in his unconscious, does not matter to us here" (ibid., 225). "There is no essence of literature, no truth of literature, no literary-being or being-literary of literature" (ibid., 223). There is no longer any truth, no originality, no stability: all that remains are traces or "grammes" with which the deconstructionist can play indefinitely.

But, as George Steiner rightly says: "The summons of nihilism demands an answer" (Steiner 1988, 82). The position he adopts in his splendid lecture, "Real Presences,"[14] justifies a final detour before we return to Wagner, not least because it expresses the idea that, after the age of suspicion, we have now entered the age of doubt.

Steiner sets out from the "university criticism" mentioned at the beginning of this chapter and sums up its principles as follows:

> The determination of a true or most probable meaning in a text has, in contrast, been held to be the reasonable aim and merit of informed reading or philology. . . . The process of textual interpretation is cumulative. . . . At any given point in the long history of disciplined understanding, a decision as to the better reading, as to the more plausible paraphrase, as to the more reasonable grasp of the author's purpose, will be a rational and demonstrable one. At the end of the philological road, now and tomorrow, there *is* a best reading, there is a meaning or constellations of meanings to be perceived, analysed and chosen over others. (Ibid., 77–78)

Curiously, however, Steiner invokes the experience of deconstruction to admit that "no *auctoritas* external to the game can legislate between these alternatives" (ibid., 80). "I do not perceive any adequate logical or epistemological refutation of deconstructive semiotics" (ibid.). Nonetheless, common sense shows us that consensuses and coherent interpretations are possible, in spite of differences. "The serious scholar, editor and critic will get on, as they always have, with the work in hand, with the elucidation of what is taken to be the authentic, though often polysemic and even ambiguous sense, and will enunciate what are taken to be informed, rationally arguable, though always provisional and self-questioning, preferences and value-judgements" (ibid., 81). Interpretation, therefore, is possible. On what is it based? And what guarantees its meaning?

"We must read *as if*," Steiner replies. "We must read as if the text before us had meaning" (ibid., 85). Clearly, his position is relatively close to that of Hans-Georg Gadamer, for whom truth can be grasped in an act of interpretative disclosure that depends on the historicity of the interpreter. "This will not be a single meaning," Steiner goes on, "if the text is a serious one, if it makes us answerable to its force of life. . . . The true understanding(s) of the text or music or painting may, during a briefer or longer time-spell, be in the custody of a few, indeed of one witness and respondent" (ibid., 85–86). There is no overall sense.

> We must read as if the temporal and executive setting of a text do matter. The historical surroundings, the cultural and formal circumstances, the biographical stratum, what we can construe or conjecture of an author's intentions, constitute vulnerable aids. We know that they ought to be stringently ironised and examined for what there is in them of subjective hazard. They matter nonetheless. They enrich the levels of awareness and enjoyment; they generate constraints on the complacencies and licence of interpretative anarchy. (Ibid., 86)

In this way Steiner returns to the methods of "university criticism," having thrown in the towel when confronted by the radical undecidability that Derrida posits as a matter of principle: "I do not see how a secular, statistically based theory of meaning and of value can, over time, withstand either the deconstructionist challenge or its own fragmentation into liberal eclecticism" (ibid., 90).

A sudden shift in Steiner's argument suggests the workings of an act of faith:

> Where we read truly, where the experience is to be that of meaning,[15] we do so as if the text (the piece of music, the work of art) *incarnates* (the notion is grounded in the sacramental) *a real presence of significant being*. This real presence, as in an icon, as in the enacted metaphor of the sacramental bread and wine, is finally irreducible to any other formal articulation, to any analytic deconstruction or paraphrase. It is a *singularity* in which concept and form constitute a tautology. (Ibid., 86–87)

Steiner is no doubt right to remind us that, historically, "the disciplines of reading, the very idea of close commentary and interpretation, textual criticism as we know it, derive from the study of Holy Scripture" (ibid., 87–88). But is the exegete inspired by the Holy Ghost in his search for the one and only Truth? "We have borrowed, traded upon, made small change of the reserves of transcendent authority. Very few of us have made any return deposit. At its key points of discourse and inference, hermeneutics and aesthetics in our secular, agnostic civilisation are a more or less conscious, a more or less embarrassed act of larceny" (ibid., 88).

But in order to feel the constraint of having to pay for something, we must first be convinced that an epiphany of meaning exists, which we have only to be sufficiently inspired to grasp in the fullness of its revelation. "To be 'indwelt' by music, art, literature, to be made responsible, answerable to such habitation as a host is to a guest—perhaps unknown, unexpected—at evening, is to experience the *commonplace mystery of a real presence*" (ibid., 87). But is this meaning revealed in a single presence? By approaching the question from the angle of "as if," Steiner is saying that it is. There is a hypostatis of meaning here that assumes the aspect of "metaphysics," to quote his own description (ibid., 90). What he is saying essentially is that in order to interpret a text we need to *believe*. It is no accident that Steiner cites Gerard Manley Hopkins in this context: "Reception and validation lay with Christ, 'the only true critic'" (ibid., 89). In an earlier series of lectures, *The Nostalgia for the Absolute* (1974), Steiner had rightly denounced the transcendental character of the hermeneutics of Marx, Freud, and Lévi-Strauss but in "Real Presences" he dispenses with the methods used by this particular criticism. Should the interpreter turn himself into a theologian just because the artist sometimes has the impression of vying with the deity (Steiner 1988, 89)? Even if Marxist, analytical, and structuralist hermeneutics are atheistic, they are still based on an apodictic faith in class consciousness, the unconscious, and the universal structure of the human mind. With Steiner, there is a difference of substance but not of kind. And all these exegetical paradigms are based on faith in a form of transcendence, be it secular or sacred.

Critics influenced by Barthes and Derrida would have no difficulty in showing that this return to univocity of meaning is part of a wider reactionary ideological trend. By his own admission, Steiner is looking for an interpretative authority (ibid., 82). By giving his series of lectures, *In Bluebeard's Castle*, a subtitle that alludes to the title of Eliot's essay, "Notes Towards the Definition of Culture," Steiner pins his colors to the mast from the very outset: "Throughout my essay, I will be returning to issues posed in Eliot's plea for order" (Steiner 1971, 13).

For the purposes of the present discussion, it will be enough to single out the author's observations on the question of sexuality:

> The typologies of women's liberation, of the new politically, socially ostentatious homosexuality (notably in the United States) and of "unisex," point to a deep re-ordering or dis-ordering of long-established frontiers. "So loosly disally'd," in Milton's telling phrase, men and women are not only manoeuvring in a neutral terrain of indistinction, but exchanging roles—sartorially, psychologically, in regard to economic and erotic functions which were formerly set apart. . . . A common formlessness or search for new forms has all but undermined classic age-lines, sexual divisions, class structures and hierarchic gradients of mind and power. (Ibid., 66–67)

Our earlier analyses have already revealed the close connection between androgyny, the denial of history, and freedom of interpretation. Steiner draws an explicit link between the return to sexual austerity, reliance on historical tradition, and the restoration of meaning.

Three major hermeneutical families have been revealed: the hermeneutics of the Letter (or Truth), the hermeneutics of Undecidability, and the hermeneutics of Transcendence. It will be clear that I agree with only individual aspects of each of these three positions and that the basis of my own approach needs to be sought elsewhere.

Adherents of what I have termed the hermeneutics of the Letter were wrong to argue that it was possible to reduce a work to a single meaning, but they were perfectly right, in my own opinion, to seek not *the* meaning of the work but part of the network of meanings associated with it by virtue of the writer's own context. The author is not dead. He has merely been put to sleep by certain critics. As was pointed out at the beginning of Part Two of the present study, the linguist Leonard Bloomfield had established as long ago as 1933 that the meaning of a word is not the same as its dictionary definition but that its meanings (!) depend on the contexts—textual and extratextual—in which the word appears. The author's individual, social, and historical lived experience, and the formal, stylistic, and generic antecedents on the basis of which he creates something new constitute the *poietics* of the work and a by no means negligible number of its possible meanings.

Advocates of the hermeneutics of Undecidability were certainly right to recognize that the processes of meaning also involved the reader or listener but, anxious to contrast total liberty of interpretation with the hermeneutics of the Letter, they considered only the esthesic processes and were wrong, therefore, to conclude on the basis of the very real difficulties involved in reconstructing poietic meanings that such methods were useless. They had the merit of reminding us that, overall, meaning is plural, that there is an infinite number of other texts behind any given text, and that, as the history of interpretation clearly shows, all attempts to grasp these meanings are all too often relative. But such writers were overhasty in leaping to the conclusion that the infinity of possible views justifies us in saying *what we like* on any given subject. It would be easy to "deconstruct" Derrida from this point of view, not least because the verbal associations he permits himself both by way of exegesis and in the name of an endless game of cross-references from one sign to another are a demonstration less of the undecidability of the meanings concerned than of the surreal and often whimsical character of a mode of discourse that can convince only believers.[16]

It remains a fact, nonetheless, that Derrida has based what he considers the total undecidability of meaning on the same notion of semiology as my own (see Nattiez 1975, 57; 1990, 6)—on Peirce's definition of the sign as an infinite chain of interpretants (see Derrida 1967, 71–72). It is important, therefore, to respond to this epistemological challenge, not only because the identical reference obliges me to define my own position but also because, if there is no longer any safety-catch on the processes of meaning, how is it that—in spite of all Derrida's efforts to the contrary—it is still possible to understand what he means by deconstruction?[17] We come up against the congenital problem of all absolute relativisms, as Paul Veyne discovered for himself (1983, 136): if I state that there is never any such thing as truth, I believe at least in the truth that there is no truth—which seems to prove that for the relativists, there is still an intuitive belief, however slight, in the decidability of discourse and the truth of interpretations.

It is precisely for this reason that, *pace* Steiner, it seems possible to reply to the "challenge" of deconstruction by drawing on epistemological arguments rather than by laying bets against transcendence. Relying on Austin for his evidence, Derrida states that a word takes on meaning only within a phrase (Derrida 1988, 114) but that since the number of possible phrases into which it may be inserted is infinite, it is impossible to assign decidable meanings either to the word or to the phrases (ibid., 116). It is not difficult to refute this in theory: if it is possible, after all, to understand Derrida and if the concepts of unconscious and contradiction are not wholly metaphysical, it is because when a word appears, it is not in the infinite set of all its possible contexts but in one or more phrases and in contexts that it is possible to delimit and define. There is no doubt that Margueritte is behind Mallarmé's *Mimique* and that Gautier is behind Margueritte, but does this mean that one has to go back to Gautier to interpret Mallarmé? The chain of genetic relations that leads from one text to another is not necessarily *transitive* from the point of view of the meaning of the text at which the chain ends. Of course, there is in this world of ours an infinity of possible contexts for words, phrases, and events, but it is entirely possible for us to *explain* the contexts by reference to which we *construct* our explanatory and exegetical plots, and, by comparing them, to base our choices, when faced with several possible explanations and interpretations, on discussable, verifiable, and falsifiable criteria, just as we did in the second part of this study. It will then be seen that if, in certain cases, several explanations are possible and if the work can bear a network of meanings, certain interpretations are nonetheless excluded. We have the choice, therefore, between two attitudes: we can either raise our hands in despair in the face of an infinitude of possible contexts and spend the rest of our lives signifying that signification is insignificant, or we can base our interpretations on explicit criteria while acknowledging that the search for truth is always asymptotic and that if Absolute Knowledge is not of this world, an understanding, however fragmentary, that is based on close study and human works is still better than the masturbatory self-satisfaction provoked by the headlong flight of meaning.

The hermeneutics of Transcendence need not detain us long. There is no point in repeating my sympathy either for Steiner's definition of the hermeneutics of the Letter or for his criticisms of deconstruction[18] and his way of circumscribing the contradiction that is felt by all men and women of good sense when faced by the possibility of assigning networks of meaning to a work and by the existence of exegetical fluctuations in its interpretation. It is plainly impossible to discuss the transcendental basis of Steiner's discourse, since faith is not open to discussion. But it is perfectly legitimate to observe (and this does not contradict his underlying transcendentalism) that he confines himself to an *immanent* conception of the works he interprets: for him, there is a "real presence" of *the* meaning of a text. In both cases he has bypassed the *symbolic dimension* of the works and their interpretations. On the one hand, the set of meanings associated with a text is made up not only of its immanent configurations but also of the poietic processes that result from them and the esthesic processes they produce. On the other hand, what I can say both about these configurations and these processes is still the result of a *construction*, and the only question that really matters is to know how I went about establishing them and whether my conclusions have a modicum of plausibility.

There is, therefore, a fourth way that it is now important to define by returning to our analyses of Wagner. Having taken it upon myself to give names to the three major hermeneutical families that seem to coexist today, I may perhaps be allowed to add a fourth and, on the basis of Jean Molino's works and reflections,[19] describe my own approach as the "hermeneutics of Construction."

INTERPRETING WAGNER IN THE AGE OF DOUBT

> The text does not have a single meaning but, no doubt, a multiplicity of irreconcilable meanings. All one can do is propose partial and local models which take account of certain aspects of the text without claiming to exhaust its meaning.
> —Jean Molino

Is There a Single Wagnerian Androgyny?

To sum up the position reached so far: it is not possible to reduce any work, whatever it may be, to a single network of meanings. It has more than one meaning, but that does not mean that the interpreter can say what he or she likes. There is more than one type of Wagnerian androgyny.

There are three reasons for this. First, as the second section of our study showed, the theme of androgyny recurs at various stages in Wagner's life and works and, in consequence, is modified semantically at each of its manifestations.

Second, the figure of androgyny is a symbolic fact at each separate stage of Wagner's development and its articulations may be the object, therefore, of three families of analysis:

1. an immanent and descriptive analysis of the manifestations of androgyny;
2. an esthesic analysis that describes the way in which Wagner's brand of androgyny is perceived and interpreted; and
3. a poietic analysis that attempts to reconstruct the meaning that androgyny had for Wagner at any given time.

However (and this is the third point), the symbol under review is not univocal, since none of these analyses can claim to speak the definitive truth about Wagner's androgyny: the semantic configurations that are exhibited here are the result of plots, explanatory strategies, and a selective approach to relevant data that vary according to the theories, interpreters, and contingencies of the research. Is this not tantamount to putting weapons into the hands of the partisans of deconstruction? I shall attempt to show that this is not the case.

Wagner's Androgyny from a Diachronic Point of View

At the time of his Zurich essays, Wagner was still under the influence of Feuerbach's anthropocentric philosophy, so that the figure of androgyny had a metaphysical significance for him that can be summarized as follows:

> In seeking androgynous union in love and death, male and female rediscover the natural character of their loving relationship under a sexual angle, seeking to exorcise the drama of individuation by merging the *I* with the vast All. Their self-sacrifice constitutes a fundamental renunciation of egoism and prepares the way for a society that is metaphysically freed from divine idols. In parallel to this development, the union of music and poetry in an androgynous whole prepares the way for a communist society in which art and genius will be shared by all, and the work of art will be the product of the people.

At the time of *Tristan und Isolde* Wagner had succumbed to the influence of Arthur Schopenhauer, with the result that androgyny now takes on a different philosophical significance:

> Only in death can Tristan and Isolde guarantee the eternity of their love. Androgynous union is achieved through renunciation of the will or the will to live, for only in this way can the lovers attain to a state of nirvana or pure contemplation. The androgyny of *Tristan und Isolde* is an androgyny of the night dominated by woman, just as music is now the dominant partner in the union of poetry and music.

The semantic context has changed completely. Abandoning Feuerbach for Schopenhauer and Novalis, we are no longer in the presence of a luminous androgyny in which self-sacrifice prepares the way for a blissfully happy society. Brünnhilde had greeted the sun when she awoke, whereas Wagner's later lovers long for night's protective mantle, a prefiguration of the death that, from the outset, Isolde had planned for Tristan and herself.

The shift from Feuerbachian "optimism" to Schopenhauerian "pessimism" was effected without undue difficulty. A change of sign is all that was needed to transform the same elements in the equation from positive to negative. Moreover, Wagner was already waiting to be converted, as is clear from his letter to August Röckel of 25/26 January 1854, written only months before he read Schopenhauer's magnum opus: "We must learn *to die* . . . . Wotan rises to the tragic heights of *willing* his own destruction. This is all that we need to learn from the history of mankind: *to will what is necessary* and to bring it about ourselves."[1]

It is worth asking whether, at the time that he reinterpreted the *Ring* from a Schopenhauerian point of view, Wagner also reread the love duet for Siegfried and Brünnhilde from a perspective analogous to that of *Tristan*. As I have shown elsewhere (Nattiez 1983: 47), Wagner's letter to Röckel of 23 August 1856 bears witness to a shift of interest away from Siegfried and in the direction of Wotan. And in the letter he wrote to Röckel from London in 1855, he reinterprets Feuerbach's drama of individuation as one that ought to evoke compassion rather than a desire to be absorbed into the vast universe: for this to be possible, he writes, we must deny our individual *will*, an act of denial that will constitute the authentic form of redemption. It is through pity that we are united with all that lives. But it is not pity that drives Siegfried and Brünnhilde into each other's arms. Rather, this is the attitude adopted by Parsifal toward Kundry, who embodies that "Judaic optimism" and sense of affirmation that Wagner denounces in 1855. It should not be forgotten in this context that, according to Wagner's own account, the earliest prose sketch for *Parsifal* dates from 1857. In his letter to Röckel of 23 August 1856, in which he adopts one of those retrospective readings with which he was past master,[2] the underlying theme of *Der fliegende Holländer*, *Tannhäuser*, and *Lohengrin* is said to be resignation.[3]

There is no commentary, therefore, on androgyny as such, even though it occupied a by no means negligible place in Wagner's "Feuerbachian" interpretation of the *Ring* in his letter to Röckel of 25/26 January 1854. To the extent that the libretto of the *Ring* is essentially a contradictory text, it is difficult to maintain that at the time of *Tristan*, for example, the composer saw the relationship between Siegfried and Brünnhilde as in any way analogous to that between Tristan and Isolde.

What we *can* say for certain, by contrast, is that, in the letter of 23 August 1856, Wagner places considerable emphasis on the difference between intuitions and conceptions: "We cannot accept a thing conceptually if we have not already grasped it intuitively."[4] Now, we know that, starting with the essays of 1848–51, Wagner had begun to identify the rational world with the masculine universe and that of intuition with the feminine universe. Brünnhilde's insight, which guides the action of the *Ring*, is based on intuitive understanding. This becomes even clearer in *Tristan und Isolde*. In forsaking the androgyny of the earlier period, in which poetry had been the dominant force, Wagner adopts a form of androgyny dominated by intuition, music, and Isolde—in short, an androgyny whose essential component is *woman*. By the date of the *Beethoven* essay of 1870, Wagner had even come to assimilate the heroine with the spirit of music.

It remains to be asked whether Wagner maintained this vision when it came to the musical setting of the *Ring* and, in particular, of *Götter-*

dämmerung. There is clearly a return to a certain form of optimism, as Deathridge points out in his comments on the final pages of the tetralogy. In the end, Wagner chose not to set either the Feuerbach ending or the Schopenhauer ending, but, as Deathridge reminds us, concluded the work with a motif that Wagner himself described not as that of redemption but as "the glorification of Brünnhilde": "It is as if Wagner were inviting us to break the circle of history. If we do, he could be saying, there may still be a glimmer of hope" (Deathridge 1988, 48). If this suggests a return to optimism, it is certainly not the optimism of 1848, but nor is it the metaphysical pessimism of 1856.

There remains the androgyny of Wagner's final years, which, as noted, is clearly anti-Semitic in its thrust—an anti-Semitism of purity and regeneration, from which womankind has been banished in favor of the asexual saint. The world of the Flower-maidens crumbles away and Parsifal repulses Kundry. The chorus that praises the Redeemer is a mixed chorus, Wagner tells us, because Christ is "neither man nor woman." As such, the work represents the triumph of the androgyny of angelism.

How Is Wagner's Androgyny to Be Interpreted?

The fact that Wagner changed his philosophical and aesthetic conceptions in the course of his life is scarcely revolutionary in terms of the semiological status of meaning. Saussure taught us long ago that synchronism should be distinguished from diachronicism, an important point that needs to be borne in mind since there is understandably a danger of interpreting Wagner's androgyny in a global manner, in other words, from an ahistorical, decontextualized point of view—the very attitude adopted by psychoanalytic and structuralist schools of thought that, as we have seen, are characterized by their denial of time.

An interpretation of the *Ring* on the basis of "androgynous hermeneutics" comes under the heading of what I earlier termed *esthesics*. It may perhaps be objected that these families of exegesis have been treated as forms of perception. That Wagner's works reveal his suppressed desire for his mother's breast, that they are shot through with the double archetype of animus and anima or that they reveal the workings of the universal structures of the human mind—all these are *poietic* explanations. I have tried to show that their starting point is in fact an analytical grid that, strictly speaking, molds the data in such a way as to conform with the transcendental postulates that govern the theory. In the third part of our study, however, we encountered too many contradictions between interpretations and given facts, too many examples of whole sections of the corpus being either forgotten or manipulated in favor of an a priori explanational model, not to see in these paradigms evidence of the way in which Wagner's works are *perceived* and *understood* by a particular category of specialist readers.

When one notes that the relationship between Siegfried and Brünnhilde is of a totally different nature from that between Parsifal and Kundry even if, in both cases, the image of the mother is implied, one can only observe that psychoanalysis is powerless to explain the change in the symbolic configuration since distinctive configurations in both works ought in fact to be explained by the same relationship with the mother, a relationship experienced by Wagner in the course of his early infancy. In the same way, it may be argued that if, as textual evidence appears to indicate, the Wood Bird acts as intermediary between Siegfried and Brünnhilde and if Brünnhilde reveals herself as Siegfried's surrogate mother, Wagner would have found some way to indicate that Fafner represents the "Terrible Mother," as Jung has proposed: after all, Wagner has found other ways, where necessary, of suggesting the allegorical significance of his characters. And is it really necessary to go hunting for a meaning to the forbidden question in *Lohengrin* other than the one that Wagner himself advances, plausibly enough, in *A Communication to My Friends*, namely, that Lohengrin embodies the drama of the lonely artist and that one must trust the artist's intuition?

The reader will of course object that although this is no doubt true, these are conscious meanings and that what interests the student of depth psychology are "the unconscious and actual drive motives" (Rank 1911, 265). But what is a meaning of which the author is unaware? Is this not merely the meaning that the decoder imputes to the work rather than that of the subject himself? My own position is as follows: *on the metaphorical level intended by Wagner himself*, the network of meanings implicit in the music dramas is in itself sufficiently complex and difficult to unravel without further obscuring the interpretation by projecting reductive and a priori theories onto it.

One would no doubt be more indulgent if the practitioners of the "hermeneutics of Undecidability" had based their interpretations on an initial level of reconstruction of the tautegorical significance of the work, as I tried to do in the first part of the present study. These hermeneutics fail, in principle, to include each of their partial observations within a global plot that takes account of the meaning of each symbol within the logical and syntactical chain of the narrative as a whole.

Mutatis mutandis, my own position is very similar to that of Clifford Geertz, which he himself defines as follows within the context of cultural anthropology:

> The anthropological study of religion is therefore a two-stage operation: first, an analysis of the system of meanings embodied in the symbols which

> make up the religion proper, and, second, the relating of these systems to social-structural and psychological processes. My dissatisfaction with so much of contemporary social anthropological work in religion is not that it concerns itself with the second stage, but that it neglects the first, and in doing so takes for granted what most needs to be elucidated. (1973, 125)

I hope I have followed this preliminary stage and that I have embarked on an analysis that allows us to see that, in the *Ring*, androgyny, for Wagner, is a particularly complex symbol in which we can make out at least three different levels:

1. as I tried to demonstrate in the first part of the present study,[5] there are links between the *Ring* and Wagner's theory of the relationship between poetry and music;
2. the Feuerbachian significance of androgyny as a social and metaphysical response to the drama of individuation was established, I hope, in the Introduction to Part Two; and
3. these two levels of meaning come together in the story of *Siegfried*, which, before reflecting Wagner's relationship with his mother, his sisters, his uncle, and his stepfather, tells of the sexual awakening of Siegfried and Brünnhilde in the context of hominization, in other words, the collapse of the old world of the gods and the advent of humanity.

The function of the mother is interpreted first and foremost within the context of the individual work, an approach that is more tautegorical (in the sense understood by Schelling) than that of psychoanalytic interpretations. Wotan desires the birth of a hero capable of expunging his original error—he has traduced the laws that the runes on his spear are intended to guarantee—and, as a prisoner of these same laws, is forced to order Siegmund's death. As the female incarnation of Wotan's deepest desires, Brünnhilde rescues Sieglinde in order for this hero to be born. In this sense, she is Siegfried's symbolic mother (hence the role of the Wood Bird as intermediary). Siegfried is the sun and, as such, the antithesis of chaos, the night, and ignorance. The fear he has sought in vain to know is the fear of his other half, a fear that he must feel in order to rediscover the joyful sensation of quintessential unity and to escape the drama of individuation. But Siegfried never knew his mother and has not yet met a representative of the female sex. In one and the same person he now discovers the woman who "invented" him in Wotan's name and who embodies that other half of humanity of which he has lived in ignorance hitherto. As the grandson of Wotan (of whom Brünnhilde represents both the feminine aspect and the intuitive authenticity of feelings and of knowledge), Siegfried seeks to rediscover the original sense of androgynous unity with her, inasmuch as she is the image of the woman who gave him birth. But what he discovers, at the moment of kissing her, is that this unity is attainable only in death—that is, when he renounces his egoistical individuality in favor of the Other, when all movement ceases, and time is definitively suspended. For Siegfried, Brünnhilde embodies both the beginning and end of his personal history, the woman who introduces him to life at the same time as awakening his sexuality, sexuality in this case implying the promise of death.

On this basis it seems possible to suggest a global interpretation of Wagner's androgyny that, far from destroying the three earlier levels of meaning, rests on them and deepens them: for Wagner, recourse to the figure of androgyny is a magical attempt to deny time—an attempt, moreover, that is bound up organically with his search for totality and his identification with God.

The sense of nostalgic longing for primitive androgyny, the search for an androgyny that can be reinstated, and the attempt to reduce the two (and, beyond it, multiples of two) to one are all aspects of Wagner's fundamental search for totality, of his desire to reduce the whole to something unique. On the level of family relationships, this manifests itself in the predominance in the *Ring* of incestuous relationships, not only between Siegmund and Sieglinde, of course, but also, if less frequently noticed, between Siegfried and his half-aunt, Brünnhilde. With Wagner, exogamy is regarded as evil (Alberich and Grimhilde, Siegfried and Gutrune, Gunther and Brünnhilde). Indeed, Siegfried dies for the "crime" of exogamy. As with the androgynous relationship between Siegfried and Brünnhilde, Wagner favors the closest possible sexual relationships.

Totality signifies proximity, therefore, but also fulfillment and achievement. If it is possible to say of the Jena Romantics that the fragment is one of the manifestations of the search for the absolute and for totality (see Lacoue-Labarthe and Nancy 1978, 63, 64, 79, 80), then Wagner aspires to that totality through the completed work of art. Throughout his life he was obsessed by the fantasy of the finished work: he arranged his theoretical writings in such a way as to decide which should be passed down to posterity; on no fewer than three occasions he set about reworking *Tannhäuser*, a work that, two months before his death, he announced with his customary modesty that he still owed the world; and even if it required twenty-six years to do so, he still managed to complete the *Ring*: "What characterizes Wagner and constitutes his greatness," Pierre Boulez maintains, "is the will to build and complete a total universe within a single existence" (in Liébert 1976, 149).

This work—total and complete—is also self-contained: the *Ring* tells the story of sexual awakening, a story of life and death, and, metaphorically, the history of opera from its beginnings to its ultimate end. The cycle aims to reduce the history of both gods and men to a single, clearly circumscribed moment in time—sixteen hours of spectacle for a whole history of the world—so that the *Ring* has to represent a fusion of all the possible arts, and it is in order to express the nature of the *Gesamtkunstwerk* that Wagner has recourse to the metaphor of sexual union: the work of total art—the work of art of the future—also has to be the one that, by restoring our original androgyny, will complete the history of music.

In his irrepressible longing for totality, the androgyne cannot admit to temporal limitations: he existed at the beginning of human history—since the world was born of the one—and will also be found at the end, in the whole that will then be synonymous with nothingness. Wagner uses the figure of androgyny to give symbolic expression to his desire to stem the irresistible tide of time.

Throughout his life Wagner was obsessed by time: he dated the beginning and end of his manuscripts, sometimes even to the hour; he was literally obsessed by autobiography, by means of which he attempted to fix his passage through history—not only *Mein Leben*, of course, but also the Red Pocketbook, the "Autobiographical Sketch," *A Communication to My Friends*, the "Venice Diary" for Mathilde Wesendonck, the annals, *The Brown Book*, and Cosima Wagner's diaries. He evidently felt the need to salvage every least gesture, every least word, every least dream from potential oblivion. Siegfried loses his memory, then recovers it: in the *Ring* the crime of forgetting is punished by death.

From this point of view, it is scarcely surprising that the Norns' scene, which brings together past, present, and future in the prologue to *Götterdämmerung*, occupied an important place in Wagner's life. It was with this scene that he began setting *Siegfrieds Tod* to music in August 1850; and it was the Norns' scene that, toward the end of his life, he would play on the piano whenever he could, as Cosima's diaries attest.

His treatment of his musical material reveals the same obsession. Infinite melody is a way of suggesting that it is possible to freeze eternity in a single favored moment. The leitmotifs, at least in the *Ring*, derive in the main from the E♭-major triad and its transformations. Indeed, Wagner wanted all the motifs to be interrelated, at least in *Das Rheingold*: "There is scarcely a bar in the orchestra that does not develop out of preceding motifs," he told Röckel in his letter of 25/26 January 1854.[6] The leitmotif is the best possible means of controlling time: incessantly varied and transformed thanks to its plastic pliability, it remains forever the same.

Wagner the androgyne is thus in search of a timeless eternity that will allow him to flee the contingencies of human events. This is the choice he made in his career as a creative artist, passing from history to legend and finally to myth.

The refusal to acknowledge time, which is synonymous with the refusal to acknowledge history, necessarily signifies the refusal to acknowledge life. When Siegfried and Brünnhilde finally achieve androgynous orgasm, the shadow of death already hovers over them, just as it hovered over the whole of Wagner's life—which did not prevent him from treating it indulgently. He contemplated suicide after his failure in Vienna and before his rescue by Ludwig II, suicide being yet another means by which to gain control of time and bring his work to an end. What is more "total" than eternity? Death holds out a positive prospect when it seals the love of two lovers forever, as it does in *Tristan und Isolde*, preserving it from time's brutal distraint.

Androgyny is thus one of the manifestations of that fantastical dream of immortality that runs through Wagner's life, a dream that he sought to realize through his work. He would be the first—and also the last—to create the work of total art: "A further series [of performances of the *Ring*] is a matter of as much indifference to me as it is bound to appear superfluous," he wrote in *A Communication to My Friends* (1851h, *GS* 4.343). In his search for the permanence of time, Wagner identifies with God.

God is androgynous by nature. It is through God that human beings were divided into men and women. And it is in God that their primordial unity will be restored at the end of time. At the same time, God evades time, which is why the androgyne has difficulty in admitting to antecedents. Wagner rarely cites those to whom he is indebted, preferring instead to fabricate a mythology of distant and untouchable ancestors. The poet who redeems the world must appear to be a being out of the ordinary. What is there that has not been written on Wagnerian "religion"? The Sacred Hill, the mystic abyss—not for nothing did Wagner call *Parsifal* a "Bühnen*weih*festspiel," that is, a festival drama for "consecrating" the Bayreuth stage. Through the agency of art he wanted to found a new religion in which, like a latter-day Parsifal, he would have sat enthroned as Deus Androgynus.

With Wagner the figure of androgyny is one of the most striking forms of the Romantic search for totality.

Superimposition, Plurality, and Modifications to Interpretations of Androgyny

A symbolic figure has a plurality of meanings, therefore, not only because its author changes his conception in the course of his life but also because it is not possible to take account of it on the basis of a single semantic layer. In the preceding section I distinguished three such layers before adding a fourth one of my own, a broader, more global layer, which interprets androgyny in the widest context of Wagner's personality and the Romantic age in general.

But the plurality of networks of meaning does not stop there. The whole history of hermeneutics shows that the interpretation of a single work changes each time that the discovery of new facts modifies an earlier interpretation and leads to the formulation of a new plot.

One example of this is provided by recent analysis of the article "Pasticcio." As soon as Wagner's authorship is denied, the incoherence that Stein[7] noted in Wagner's early writings disappears. I should like to propose a further illustration of this point. It is more hypothetical but, if confirmed, would substantially modify our conception of the relationship between Siegfried and Brünnhilde.

In the second part of my study, I quoted Jakob Böhme among the sources of the Romantics' interest in androgyny. Now, it turns out that Böhme's complete works, in Schiebler's edition, formed part of Wagner's library at Wahnfried. Was he already familiar with their contents when he drafted the libretto of the *Ring*? If there had been contact between the composer and the Sage of Görlitz, it would be legitimate to see Brünnhilde as the incarnation of Hagia Sophia, who, also mentioned in Baader, appears in Böhme's *Mysterium Magnum* of 1618–23 not only as the embodiment of wisdom (this, after all, is how Brünnhilde is presented at the end of the *Ring*, where she attains to understanding and becomes "all-knowing" [*GS* 6.252]) but also as the image of the mother contained within man and, in Böhme's conception, constitutive of man's primal androgyneity. Clearly, this throws new light on Siegfried's cry "Mutter! Mutter! / Gedenke mein'!" (Mother! Mother! Remember me!), which cannot be reduced to a psychoanalytic explanation (*GS* 6.165). The story of *Siegfried* would therefore be that of an originally asexual being who, confronted by the revelations of nature, abandons his primitive Adamicality and rediscovers in Brünnhilde that lost image of his Sophic mother that every man carries within him.

I use the conditional tense advisedly since, so far as I am aware, there is no evidence that Wagner had access to Böhme in 1851. Cosima records only one reference to Böhme, on 16 June 1871. (There is an error in the index of the German edition of her diaries: the "Herr Böhme" who wrote Wagner an "impertinent letter" on 9 February 1875 is unlikely to have been the seventeenth-century German mystic.) It would be gratifying to think that even though Böhme's works were missing from Wagner's Dresden library, he obtained them soon after his arrival in Switzerland. But this is bound to remain an indirect assumption, however plausible it may be.

It appears from *Mein Leben* that in September 1852 Wagner read a two-volume edition of the works of the Persian poet Hafiz, an edition that found its way into his library in Wahnfried, where he took up residence on 28 April 1874. It is not out of the question, therefore, that he acquired books during the early years of his exile in Switzerland that were lodged in Wahnfried twenty years later. Equally, he may have bought new copies of works that he read twenty years previously, in 1852. Nothing is certain. If I insist on this point—even at the risk of seeming an obtuse positivist—it is because, whatever may have been said in recent years, factual proof of Wagner's firsthand acquaintance with Böhme is a sine qua non of any attempt to advance a reasoned reappraisal of the character of Brünnhilde.

Such a reinterpretation would not shake the foundations of the Feuerbachian explanation but would deepen it, making it richer, denser, and more complex. One point at least must be stressed: the error of "university criticism" was to forget that on the surface of the text there is not just one signifier, expressing the author's intentions, but the result of diverse poietic strategies.

From the point of view of classical hermeneutics, two claims advanced in the first part of the present study might be open to question. It is worth recalling Erwin Panofsky's summation of one of the fundamental principles of such an approach:

> Whether we deal with historical or natural phenomena, the individual observation of phenomena assumes the character of a "fact" only when it can be related to other, analogous observations in such a way that the whole series "makes sense." This "sense" is, therefore, fully capable of being applied, as a control, to the interpretation of a new individual observation within the same range of phenomena. If, however, this new individual observation definitely refuses to be interpreted according to the "sense" of the series, and if an error proves to be impossible, the "sense" of the series will have to be reformulated to include the new individual observation. (1939, 35)

What Panofsky is describing here was later termed *seriation* by Molino—a procedure that allows the observer to regulate the relevance of particular facts within an overall interpretation.[8]

My analyses may be called into question by certain "dissonant" facts. My interpretation of the *Ring* was based, in part, on an analogy between the music of *Das Rheingold* and a passage in Auber. But it may reasonably be objected that I have neglected to mention the striking reminiscence of Mendelssohn's overture to *Die schöne Melusine* in the prelude to *Das Rheingold*. How can this be integrated into my plot?

One of Wagner's strategies, which sometimes brings him perilously close to plagiarism, consists in seizing hold of an unfinished or badly executed musical idea in the works of earlier composers and in bringing it to a pitch of perfection that surpasses and transcends the original. It was this "urge to improve" that persuaded him to revise Gluck's *Iphigénie en Aulide* in 1846–47 (*WWV*, 77); the melodic sweep of the opening phrase of

Tristan und Isolde was inspired by Berlioz's *Roméo et Juliette* (Chailley 1962, 43–44; Bernstein 1976, 227); and a passage in Cosima Wagner's diaries reveals the extent to which he felt the need to check that he had not plagiarized Liszt in writing *Parsifal*.[9] The same is true, in the present case, of Mendelssohn.

Another dissonant fact could be used to refute my analysis of the duet between Alberich and Floßhilde, where I pointed out that the doubling of voice and orchestra is a feature of French operatic style. This same procedure is also found in another passage in the *Ring*, the love duet for Siegfried and Brünnhilde in Act III of *Siegfried* (bars 1486ff.). This is not a stumbling block, however, since it is the result of another poietic strategy on Wagner's part, whereby he has used a passage for four string instruments in his *Siegfried Idyll*, a work closely bound up with the private lives of himself and his second wife. It is not impossible that in making Brünnhilde sing in unison with the orchestra Wagner was attempting, on a wholly private level, to give musical expression to the closeness of his relationship with Cosima. Certainly, Wagner was keen to break down the barriers between life and art, as is clear from the names he gave to his children—Isolde, Eva, and Siegfried.

I would propose a subtle shift of emphasis in the exegetical principles so clearly presented by Erwin Panofsky: *a heterogeneous fact in a series is an obstacle to the coherence of an interpretation only if it can be shown to be the result of the same family of poietic strategies*. This coexistence of diverse poietic strategies explains why it is necessary, if we are to do justice to the semiological richness of a work, to propose several plots in order to take account of them all and, hence, to admit to the plurality of its levels of meaning.

It is precisely because, in its search for an immanent logic to its semantic configurations, structuralism has obscured the role of poietic strategies behind the surface of a text that we are disturbed by its incoherencies. But creative processes are not homogeneous, a point admirably made by Carolyn Abbate in her discussion of another problem of Wagnerian hermeneutics: "Wagner in the end composed with many different voices, the voice that ignores poetry, the voice that hears poetry, the banal voice, the excessively formal voice, the anarchic voice, the diatonic voice, the chromatic voice" (Abbate 1989a, 56).

There is another motif that can both lead to a modification of the explanatory plots and add to the diversity of meanings uncoverable in a work, and this is the modification of those referential paradigms that govern the various interpretations of a single object. If we admit that the hermeneutics of Freud, Jung, and Lévi-Strauss are epistemologically admissible, it is because they do not interpret the same facts on the basis of the same premises and that androgyny, the mother, and incest take on different meanings as a result. If we have so much difficulty explaining Wagnerian androgyny, it is partly because we do not have a clear theory of what it is.

In an extremely revealing study of the "third sex" in Inuit symbolism, the anthropologist Bernard Saladin d'Anglure has pointedly denounced the confusion that exists between "sexual orientation, identity, sexual roles, and symbolic representation" (Saladin d'Anglure 1986, 36). Certainly, the concept of androgyny soon becomes a catch-all, encompassing realities that need to be kept apart.

1. When Freud speaks of bisexuality, he means a fundamental biological constitution that, for him (in his *Three Essays on the Theory of Sexuality*), explains a latent homosexuality present in human beings of both sexes. The sexual ambivalance that is found in the so-called complete version of the Oedipus complex is similarly explained by a physical substratum. As with Marx, the symbolism has no autonomous reality even if Freud does not feel equipped to explain the causal relationship between the two levels. There is an explanation that I have deliberately ignored here, even if there is no shortage nowadays of speculations on the "sex of the brain" (see, for example, Durden-Smith and De Simone 1983): this is the influence that biology could have had on Wagner's *ideas*. Although it is not yet possible to establish a link between levels of *X* and *Y* chromosomes and mental activity, we know that one day we shall be able to read in the interplay of neurons in the brain the reasons for that complex combinatorial ability that we call "thought."

2. Is there a link between homosexuality and androgyny? In terms of sexual activity, the former is physically directed toward the Other, while androgyny is more akin to onanism and erotic autosatisfaction.[10] To paraphrase a celebrated remark, albeit one in doubtful taste, we do not know—even assuming the answer is of any interest—what Wagner was doing with his left hand while composing the *Ring* with his right hand. Perhaps he needed both hands at once.

3. Nor should sexual orientation be confused with the *idea* that one can have of human bisexuality. Although it may be tempting to draw a parallel between Virginia Woolf's sexual orientation and the contents of her novel *Orlando*, it is questionable whether any such link exists between Théophile Gautier's private life and *Mademoiselle de Maupin* or between that of Balzac and *Séraphita*.

At the beginning of the third part of the present study, I quoted two letters from Wagner on the subject of Peter Cornelius that might lead one to think that he felt homosexually attracted to the younger man. But even if we are right to interpret it in this sense (though one must also take account of Romantic effusiveness), it is scarcely sufficient grounds for turning the Knights of the Grail into a gay community. Pseudodeterminisms must be mistrusted in this particular field. Was Mozart homosexual because he wrote *Apollo et Hyacinthus*? Was Flaubert gay because he claimed that "Madame Bovary, c'est moi"? And was Wagner a friend of Dorothy because he conceived of music as a woman?

4. Just as we need to distinguish between *phallus* and *penis*, so we must avoid confusing androgyny as a symbol of the union of man and woman with the strictly biological forms of hermaphroditism. What I hope to have shown in the course of my study is that androgyny, like a number of metaphors used in science such as Descartes's model of the "animal-machine," electricity, language, computers, and so on, is a symbolic *representation* that helps us to understand and take account of the complexity of the world.

The question of sexual identity—do I feel, fundamentally, that I am a man or a woman?—depends, therefore, on the framework given to this symbolic characterization and on the traits by which I define the concepts of masculine and feminine. But the whole contemporary discussion on the nature of sexual roles in everyday life should have taught us that it is impossible to speak of an essential masculinity as opposed to an essential femininity—categories that, in terms of social customs, prove to be culturally determined.

Wagner's is not the only theory to appeal to the figure of androgyny as a model of the representation of the world. Ethnomusicologists have cataloged the sexual characteristics attributed to instruments all around the world (Sachs 1961, 94). The yin and yang have been discovered in a science as pragmatic as physics,[11] and in the reflections of at least one archaeologist on the dualism of understanding (Gardin 1979, 296), while an eminent representative of American "music criticism," Leo Treitler, has even sought to explain the semiological fusion of the signifier and signified in music by reference to the androgynous complementarity of the sexes (Treitler 1989, 14–18). But the metaphor of androgyny explains nothing on its own. It seems to be based on a simple, universal formula:

X is to *Y* as man is to woman

However, this formula takes on a meaning only as a result of the specific features with which each theoretician invests masculinity and femininity. Although it is possible to observe the universal *existence* of androgyny throughout different ages, cultures, and fields of application, androgyny itself is a symbolic figure that per se has *no universal significance*.

5. It is for this reason that—even on the level of symbolic representation—we find such different forms of androgyny from one age to another and even within the works of a single author. In the case of Wagner, for example, it was possible to distinguish a male-dominated androgyny during his Swiss period, a female-dominated androgyny during the *Tristan* years, and an asexual androgyny in *Parsifal*.

Moreover, the dominant androgyny changes its meaning from one age to another, with the androgyneity of totality in Wagner and the Romantics contrasted with the androgyneity of ambiguity of such fin-de-siècle artists as Sâr Péladan, Gustave Moreau, and the pre-Raphaelites. To these two categories of Mircea Eliade (1962) and Jean Molino (1981), I should like to add a third, the androgyneity of equality, which, in our own day, has led us, under the influence of feminism, to reconsider our own sexual roles.

And—since nothing is simple—these major categories certainly do not imply the homogeneity of the conception of androgyneity at any given period. After all, Jean Broc's *La mort de Hyacinthe*, a detail of which appears on the front of this book, dates from 1801, whereas Gautier's *Mademoiselle de Maupin* was written in 1835–36: both these works bespeak an androgyneity of ambiguity at a time when the category of totality seems otherwise to be predominant. The French Saint-Simonians illustrate ideas associated with the androgyneity of equality, while Lévi-Strauss's structuralist androgyneity is more reminiscent of the Romantic androgyneity of totality—a similarity that should no longer seem surprising. It is impossible to reduce all the symbolic manifestations of a particular age to a uniform epistemological level.

All this explains why it is difficult, especially from a psychoanalytic point of view, to establish a satisfactory etiology of androgyny as a symbolic representation, since no clear determinist link can be established between this representation and the events in an artist's life. By contrast, it is possible to define the constitutive elements at various stages in the artist's thinking—and if, in the course of the foregoing study, I have been able to point out the links between those elements and recognizable forms of philosophical and religious thought, it is because a connection was established, representation by representation. Every thought comes from somewhere, notably from earlier forms of thinking.

There is no general theory of androgyny, since such a theory is impossible to establish. All that we can and *must* do is to draw up an inventory of the intrinsic content of its manifestations—an inventory that, however laborious it may be to compile, is all the more deeply instructive for that. Only on that basis can we advance a cautious interpretation and explanation.

La querelle des intrigues (*conclusion*)

It might be thought that in advancing the foregoing arguments I am offering ammunition to the partisans of deconstruction. But this is not the case, for two reasons. In the first place, the infinite appeal to interpretants on which Derrida relies is certainly no justification for the most outrageous interpretations: one cannot say whatever one wants. Second, plurality of meaning, far from sanctioning a general de(con)structive approach, invites us to *construct* interpretations on the basis of explicit, reproducible, and contestable criteria.

Not all interpretations are admissible, as is clear from the conception of Parsifalian androgyny proposed by Hans Jürgen Syberberg both in his film of the work and in his book of the film (1982), which is often clearer than the opaque symbolism of his images.

Of course, Syberberg has seen the angelic side of Parsifal qua androgyne: "In Parsifal, man and woman complement each other in the idea of Paradisal man" (ibid., 54). But in transforming Parsifal into a woman after Kundry's kiss, he suggests that the character is feminized, whereas it is clear from Wagner's own remarks, as transmitted by Cosima, that the Christian Parsifal "must appear entirely sexless, neither man nor woman" (*CT*, 27 June 1880). In spite of what Syberberg suggests, womankind perishes so that Parsifal's sanctity is not corrupted by the female element. Parsifal is asexual, and it is he who saves Kundry. Nothing in his book, moreover, indicates that Syberberg has attempted or even felt the wish to rediscover Wagner's concept of androgyny. Quite the opposite; one has the impression that he wants to save Wagner from himself: "The film comes to Wagner's assistance" (ibid., 21).

> By becoming a woman in the second part, Parsifal allows the problem to be divorced from the traditional dialectic of evil woman and male redeemer. What is involved, however, is an idea of redemption that can—and must—be carried out by a woman to the advantage of the better part of herself. Transferred to the field of the Jewish problem, it is not the Jew, as an image of dread and as the myth of Christian malediction, who needs a redeemer in order to be purified: no, this development now takes place of its own accord until the end of time. It is no longer a form of racism but a development that takes each of us as its starting point if we are ready to accept it. (Ibid., 56)

The idea of Paradisal angelism, as attested by Cosima's diaries, is sidetracked here and its primary meaning subverted: "This idea provided an entirely natural solution to all the problems of antifeminism and anti-Semitism" (ibid., 161).

Of course, the director has the right to hijack the work he is producing, a right I myself have endorsed elsewhere (Nattiez 1983). By denouncing Wagner's anti-Semitism, Chéreau, for example, succeeded in revealing its existence on a second level. But it is far from certain whether the change that Syberberg has made is as clear-cut as this since the meaning of the work becomes totally contradictory if a female Parsifal redeems Kundry and if she dies nonetheless. If this is Syberberg's way of showing that he has understood Wagner's underlying significance, it is at the price of a hermeneutical detour that, in contradistinction to Chéreau's powerful and immediate images, strikes the spectator as being altogether opaque. In his attempt to rescue Wagner, Syberberg has projected onto the end of the nineteenth century ideas that are familiar to us through the androgyny of equality, including the equality of race, culture, and sex. By investing the work with this particular meaning, he is no longer staging Wagner's *Parsifal* but a *Parsifal* by Syberberg *about* Wagner.

There are plots, therefore, which the constraints of the text oblige us not to accept. Specifically, they lack poietic relevance. Like the hermeneutics of psychoanalysis and structuralism, their relevance is purely esthesic: Syberberg's *Parsifal* tells us what the director "reads" into Wagner's work or, more exactly, what he projects onto it.

It is possible, then, to prove that an interpretation is *false*. But this does not mean that, even with carefully substantiated interpretations, we can put our finger on *the* truth in all its dazzling certainty. As was pointed out above, the search for the truth is asymptotic. But if the relativism that I seem to advocate differs from the relativism that is integral to deconstruction, it is because I believe it possible to establish a *hierarchy* between different possible interpretations of one and the same object. A particular exegesis is never totally false or totally true. As already indicated, Syberberg was right to see the interdependence of misogyny and anti-Semitism in *Parsifal* and to draw attention to the hero's angelic nature. Glass has advanced our understanding of Wagner's theoretical writings by treating the concept of the "poetic intent" as a theme in its own right. For my own part, I have approached these writings and Wagner's stage works by examining the theme of androgyny, which Stein, Glass, and all other writers on Wagner's theoretical essays have generally left untouched. In introducing a new theme into the interpretation, I have challenged the analysis proposed by Glass, who sees only unimportant and superficial accidents in the variations to Wagner's theory. This does not mean that I have written off the important role he ascribes to the "poetic intent." Quite the opposite. In a word, there has been a cumulative advance in knowledge.

This is not a new idea, but in an age when doubt might lead one to despair of gaining a stable understanding of the world, this is perhaps as good a time as any to remind ourselves of its existence—and of doing so, moreover, dispassionately, to the extent that in proposing what I believe to be a new interpretation, I am perfectly well aware that others will come after me and perhaps point out that certain facts and claims are incorrect. They may even modify my conception of the relationship between poetry and music in Wagner on the basis of an entirely new set of data. It is already possible to guess from which direction this upheaval might come: the study of Wagner's sketches, meticulously cataloged in the *Wagner Werk-Verzeichnis*, is one I have chosen to ignore since we are still some distance away from a transcription and detailed analysis of these sketches, a task that will take years of specialized study. But even if developments in this particular area of knowledge were to affect the interpretations that I have proposed, it is doubtful whether they would undermine the entire edifice: what would remain is the demonstrable *fact*—and it still seems necessary to insist on the distinction between facts and interpretations, in spite of recent assertions by Veyne (1983, 117) and Meyer (1989, 71)—that androgyny is an integral part not only of Wagner's operas (which we already knew) but also of his theoretical conceptions (which was less widely known) and that it is possible to establish a close link between these two orders of symbolic construction.

If rebuttal of my work proves possible in the future, it is—I believe—because at every stage of my interpretations I have expressly furnished the facts on which I was building those interpretations and thereby provided the evidence on which to base such a rebuttal. As Popper has already said, scientific work is not work that says what is true but work that can be proved to be false. It was in the name of this principle that he challenged the scientific nature of the psychoanalytic approach. When we speak of the cumulative nature of knowledge, we think above all of the exact sciences. I should like to show that this principle can also be applied to the hermeneutics of aesthetics by drawing on an interpretative problem directly bound up with the subject of Wagner's androgyny.

Is The Tristan Chord an Androgynous Chord?

This is not the place to reexamine the various interpretations to which the Tristan Chord has been subjected. Gut (1981) has studied a number of them, and I myself have already looked into the question at some length (Nattiez 1977; reprinted in Nattiez 1987, 217–29). It will be sufficient, therefore, to recall Gut's central argument.

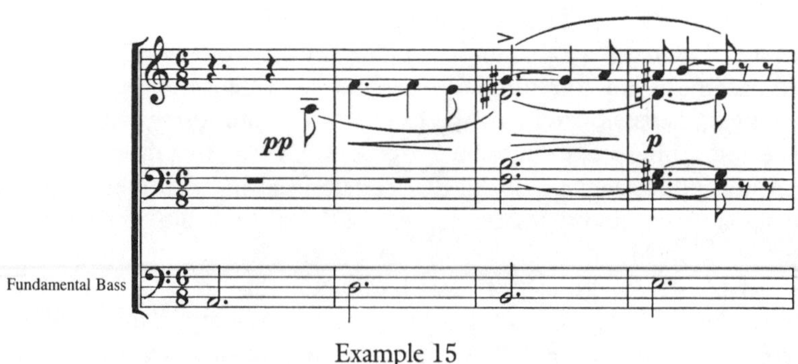

Example 15

On the one hand, the ambiguity of the chord derives from the fact that it belongs potentially to two tonalities, E and A. The opening bars of the work are clearly in A minor and can be interpreted either as I–IV–V (taking the D♮ as the root of the chord) or as I–II–V (treating the chord as a French sixth). In both cases the G♯ is considered as an appoggiatura. However, the repetition of the descending figure from F to E gives the note E the value of a fixed polarity, which is reinforced by the D♯. This was stressed by one of the chord's earliest analysts, Karl Mayrberger (1881a, 1881b, 1881c), who reconstructed an imaginary bass line for the first three bars, A–D–B–E (see Example 15), and who therefore described the chord as a *Zwitterakkord*, literally a "hybrid or androgynous chord." As a result of the G♯, the chord belongs to the key of A, whereas the D♯ belongs to the key of E. According to Gut,

> It seems likely that within this tonal dualism the world of E minor is that of Isolde, from which we can deduce that the world of A minor belongs to Tristan. In fact, when this ambivalent chord makes its final appearance

Example 16

> Tristan is already dead and Isolde is on the point of death as she merges with the universe. [The Desire motif] is no longer androgyous: Isolde alone is involved here. And so the chord—although acoustically and notationally the same—can no longer be analyzed in the way that it was at the outset: the F is no longer the real note and D♯ the altered note. Rather the opposite is the case: the D♯ is the real note (we are in B major with a temporary borrowing from E minor), while the F♮ is the altered fifth below it. The D♯ no longer moves toward D♮, as it did at the beginning, but rises to E, just as the F descends to E. This marks the definitive victory of E over A in this androgynous chord, which initially had tended more toward A. (1981, 151)

Gut goes on to ask whether we should see here the victory of the "eternal feminine." "Although E is a fifth higher than A, it is difficult to confirm this. Truth to tell, this final question is no doubt superfluous" (ibid.).

In fact, the question is not superfluous at all, and Gut shows very clearly that after this passing chord of E minor, the work ends on the perfect chord of B major (where the same interval of a fifth is involved). "Thus one sees the fundamental framework of the drama, which, through the ascending fifth, achieves transfiguration by suppressing desire: from A, the world of Tristan, we pass to E, the world of Isolde, and thence to B, the realm of nirvana" (ibid.).

I should stress at the outset that it is not mere perversity that leads me to criticize the work of a colleague whose writings I have long admired. Quite the opposite. It is because Gut uses a precise method in order to propose a symbolic interpretation of the chord that his work may be described as scientific (does the word have to instill such a sense of fear?) and that it is possible, therefore, to challenge certain aspects of it, thereby adding greater depth to our own analysis.

Gut's interpretation is based on a thesis that certainly deserves to be taken seriously: tonality in Wagner's operas, he believes, is related to individual characters on a one-to-one basis. Anyone reading *Opera and Drama* would be right to think that Wagner assigns a symbolic dimension to the key signatures that he chooses: "Starting out from the musical sound of the vowel in the spoken language, feeling is raised to the point where it governs all further communication to the senses, so that musical feeling alone now determines the choice and significance of the secondary and primary keys and does so, moreover, on the basis of those tonal relationships whose particular member is decided by the necessary emotional expression of the phrase" (1851a, *GS* 4.141). But is it only in the case of Wagner's characters that we can establish a symbolic dimension to his choice of tonality? Bailey questions this idea (1977, 53). Gut, it has to be said, uses a very limited corpus to suggest this relationship, referring only to the final bars of the work, while he merely "infers" that the tonality of A is attributed to Tristan.

There is a "simple" technique that allows us to check the validity of this proposition, and this consists in examining the sequence of tonalities and their context within the work as a whole. In short, we have to attempt a systematic "seriation"[12] of the symbolic associations of the various tonalities. It is not without a certain sense of irony that I use quotation marks around the word "simple," since establishing the tonality of any given passage in *Tristan und Isolde* presents the analyst with a highly complex problem, as emerges from a comparison between the two existing attempts to provide an overall tonal and harmonic interpretation of the work (Lorenz 1926; Scharschuch 1963): their description of the tonalities changes completely depending on the size of the units used to characterize those tonalities.[13] By confining his attention to the surface of the work, the analyst sinks without trace into the unfathomable abyss of endless modulation. Can one—at the other extreme—claim, as Lorenz does (1926, 173), that *Tristan* is in E major, with the beginning in the subdominant (A) and the end in the dominant (B)? Little would be gained by rehearsing the feats of mental gymnastics that Lorenz is required to perform in his attempt to show that the tonalities pivot around the key of E, for which we have to wait until Act III ("Mäßig langsam," leading into Tristan's passage, "Und drauf Isolde, wie sie winkt"). It is clear that Lorenz is anxious at all costs to rediscover Riemann's sacrosanct trinity, I–IV–V.

A solution to the problem may be found in the writings of Robert Bailey (Bailey 1977) and Patrick McCreless (McCreless 1982). We must admit that beyond the surface harmonies, there are at least two further levels that are hierarchically broader: those that characterize acts and scenes and, within the individual scenes, a series of intermediary subdivisions (McCreless 1982, 89). If we want to test Gut's proposition, we need to remain on the widest level of characterization.

Is it possible, against this background, to claim that the tonality of A is associated with the character of Isolde? In the opening act—at least in the scenes in which she herself is present—it is the key of C (major and minor) that predominates and on which the act ends. Especially noteworthy is the phrase with which Isolde gives her orders to Brangäne (bars 374–79). Brangäne herself repeats the formula when addressing Kurwenal a moment later (bars 481–85). A variant of it occurs somewhat later (bars 1059–63), still in C, and again when she addresses Kurwenal directly (bars 1176–79). The phrase expresses authority, confirmation, a decision that has been taken, and it returns to accompany the lovers from the time they drink the potion until the end of the act: Brangäne, as her mistress's double, has carried out Isolde's innermost wish.

Example 17

The keys of C major and C minor return in the love duet in Act II, but this section is dominated above all by the key of A and its chromatic neighbor A♭. In all these contexts it is difficult to say whether the key of A is related more to Tristan or to Isolde. Now, this tonality—which, with the obvious exception of the scene in which the lovers drink the potion, is absent from virtually the whole of the opening act and does not return at all in Act III—is one that we have already heard: it is the tonality of the prelude. Since Bailey published his critical edition of the beginning and end of the work (1985), it has been no secret that when Wagner performed the prelude on its own (with a specially composed conclusion), he called it the *Liebestod*, reserving the term *Verklärung* (transfiguration) for the orchestral version of Isolde's death (traditionally known as the *Liebestod*; see Wagner 1863f). This is no accident, since Isolde has already chosen to die of love even before the action begins, as the substitution of the potions makes clear in the course of the opening act.

So far as the tonality of E is concerned, we noted earlier, in the context of Lorenz's analysis of the work, that Wagner systematically exploits this key in the third act, where Tristan succumbs to a paroxysm of frenzy. Musically speaking, it appears to be a development of the motif from the prelude to Act I, G♯–A–A♯–B, traditionally labeled the Desire motif. In his letter to Mathilde Wesendonck of 3 March 1860, Wagner describes the way in which the theme "swells and grows denser, until finally the whole world stands before me again in all its impenetrable solidity,"[14] a description that may also refer to the orchestral "swell" that seizes hold of the composer and to which these four notes give rise.

As for B major, this is clearly the key of the Transfiguration, as Gut recognized: not only does the Tristan Chord resolve onto B major at the end of the work (a resolution we have been waiting for since the beginning of the prelude), it is also the key on which the love duet culminates in Act II.

It is tempting to deal with the other keys along similar lines. That of G is associated with the acceptance of death in Act II (bars 801–52), and it is on a suspension on the dominant of C that Tristan dies, while Isolde grieves over his body in G minor (bars 1325ff.).

This seems to me to obey a particular logic. A is the key of the Love-Death, which has been presented from the outset as the drama's fundamental fact of life. C is the tonality of Isolde's initiative and of the decision to die. E is the key of Tristan's desire, G that of his death, and B that of the lovers' reunion in death. It is no accident that this symbolic sequence involves a circle of thirds (not fifths), since a close study of the score reveals that this circle largely controls the system of modulations. Two keys—F and D—are relegated to the edges of the system, and not without good reason. They are heard in Act I, when Isolde invites Tristan to enter her circle (bars 326–428), and when Kurwenal and Isolde evoke Cornwall, the kingdom that will take Tristan from Isolde (bars 491–509 and 711–66). D minor is the tonality of Marke's grief. It is in F that Act III opens, with Tristan injured and once again separated from Isolde at Kareol. F is also used for the scene in which Marke and Melot irrupt onto the stage, before Isolde's final transfiguration. D and F symbolize the separation of Tristan and Isolde. They are also the two keys farthest apart on the circle of thirds that starts at A.

Is the Tristan Chord an androgynous chord? The answer is yes, even if the foregoing seriation requires us to modify Gut's exegesis. The Tristan Chord in A (the key of Isolde's death wish) is clouded by the key of E, expressive of Tristan's desire, and resolves only onto the key of B, which is that of Isolde's transfiguration. In this sense, these three bars—the essential notes of which are the initial A, the final E in the bass, and the final suspended B—sum up the whole of the drama and confirm the suggestion in Part Two that the androgyny of *Tristan und Isolde* is a female-dominated androgyny.

The progression from Gut's interpretation to my own provides a good example of the cumulative process of knowledge. His work is in fact far from being invalidated. Gut saw that the opening of the work summed up the piece's overall symbolism, and his interpretation of the key of B has proved to be correct. He had the crucial idea of relating an apparently technical problem of harmonic analysis to the far wider question of Wagnerian androgyny. One of his ideas in particular is reinforced by my own extension of his line of thinking: reexamined in the light of the global significance of androgyny in *Tristan*, Mayrberger's analysis acquires the poietic relevance that it otherwise lacks, a lack that it shares with all the other analyses of this chord. Gut is the only writer, apart from Tittel (1966, 86), to point out that, according to Wolzogen, Wagner had given an enthusiastic welcome to this approach and that he saw in Mayrberger "the theorist whom he had long been awaiting" (Gut 1981, 149).[15] If we accept this testimony,[16] we shall also have to accept in future that from Wagner's point of view this "androgynous" chord is based on two tonalities and that in the key of A it rests on the second degree of B, without the appoggiatura G♯.[17]

It is tempting at this juncture to return to our starting point, the love duet for Siegfried and Brünnhilde, and ask whether the androgyny of these two characters finds its equivalent in the music of *Siegfried*.

Analyzing Opera

The specificity and difficulty of analyzing opera as a genre derives from the fact that whereas, in the instrumental field, a "technical" analysis can ignore the emotive and semantic connotations aroused by the work, the action and psychology of the characters in opera are so intimately bound up with the piece as part of its global reality that it is hard to imagine an analysis of its "purely" musical dimension that disregards its links with the unfolding drama. But, however obvious this fact, it immediately raises a particular problem: if in opera it is not only the characters who sing but also the composer who "speaks" to us through his music, there are bound nonetheless to be aspects of the musical material that, from the point of view of the story being treated, demand to be tackled as though we were dealing with pure music. Put more simply, what is there in the score of an opera that proves to be relevant in terms of its subject matter?

The previous section was inspired by the approach adopted by McCreless in his analysis of *Siegfried* and sought to establish the symbolism of Wagner's use of tonality in *Tristan* on a very general level. The subject was examined in only the broadest outline, not least because an exhaustive study of the use of tonality in *Tristan* would require a volume in itself—but what this means, in accordance with the epistemological principle that I have adopted (construction, critique, reconstruction – cumulative character of knowledge), is that it is perfectly clear that other writers will come along who will refine or dispute the interpretations offered here. At the same time, it must be admitted that the function of sequences of tonality is not justified simply by the symbolism that can be attached to them. It must be admitted, therefore, that—as was suggested earlier in the context of Panofsky—tonal organization in Wagner, from the time of *Tristan* onward, is the result of at least two distinct families of poietic strategies: a strategy that is symbolic in nature and one that, purely syntactical, obeys various other principles, be they the circle of fifths, circle of thirds, confusion between major and minor, associative tonality, structural progressions in whole tones or semitones, and so on (see McCreless 1982, 94–95), all of which it is for the analyst to untangle.

Beyond all the changes of tonality patiently cataloged by him, McCreless also manages to show (ibid., 101) that in *Siegfried*, C is the tonality of Wotan, and that Siegfried's quest leads him from B♭ (Act I, scene 1), through C and D, to E, which is associated first with his mother (Act II, scene 2) and then with Brünnhilde (Act III, scene 3). The act ends in C, which, as mentioned, is Wotan's key and also the tonality of the sword from *Das Rheingold* onward. In explaining why this is so, McCreless argues that "it is in the union of Siegfried and Brünnhilde that the god's plans come closest to realization" (ibid., 97).

In other words, C major is the tonality of androgyny in *Siegfried*. Brünnhilde and Siegfried are in fact the two sexually dissociated halves of Wotan: he envisioned Siegfried at the end of *Das Rheingold*, while Brünnhilde embodies the feminine expression of his real desires when she attempts to save Siegmund and rescue Sieglinde, an act of compassion that allows Siegfried to be born. If this is accepted, it follows that Wotan—the "father" of Siegfried qua poet and Brünnhilde qua music—must be a reflection of Wagner himself, of Wagner the androgyne, poet, composer, and creator of the *Ring*.[18]

The musical setting of Act III of *Siegfried* dates from 1869 to 1871. (The libretto, it will be recalled, had been written between May 1851 and

December 1852.) One has the impression that musically Wagner was more than capable of sorting out the various poietic strategies through which he had passed.

> The importance of third-relationships is clearly evident in Act III. The tonal level of G for Wotan's *peripeteia*, for example, is determined neither associatively (although G is, of course, the dominant of the Wanderer's associative key of C) nor "expressively" but through a more abstract musical relationship: G can connect by the interval of a third to the associatively determined E of the critical moments of the entire opera—Siegfried's *cognitio* and his waking of Brünnhilde—and by a further third relationship, to C, the associatively determined goal of the work. (Ibid., 103)

In writing the music for the third act of *Siegfried*, Wagner continues the technique of symbolic tonal associations that he had already used in *Das Rheingold*, *Die Walküre*, and the first two acts of *Siegfried*, but, following the experience of *Tristan* and *Die Meistersinger*, he adds a further technique in Act III, as well as in *Götterdämmerung* and *Parsifal*, which is based on the circle of thirds and on chromaticism (Bailey 1969, 146–48; McCreless 1982, 103). Specific tonalities are even less likely to find a symbolic equivalent here in that this is the period when music emerges triumphant in Wagnerian theory and practice.

At the same time, however, it appears that as a composer Wagner has not forgotten the optimistic significance that, following his reading of Feuerbach, he had imputed to the union of Siegfried and Brünnhilde during his first encounter with androgyny. It is sufficient to compare the music that characterizes Isolde's transfiguration, resigned and serene in mood, with the ringing, jubilant sounds that accompany the final words of *Siegfried* ("lachender Tod," or laughing death) to realize that through music Wagner has been able to rediscover the philosophical thrust of the work's original conception.

It is impossible, therefore, to deny that "behind" the musical and literary text of this act there is a complex web of diverse poietic strategies. This is particularly true of an androgynous genre such as opera, which, by combining not only words and music but also gesture, scenery, and lighting, brings together discrete symbolic forms that obey autonomous principles of operation. And it is also, no doubt, because any given work, no matter what that work may be, is always the result of several poietic strategies that it is never possible to reduce it to a single global meaning that would succeed, as though by magic, in distilling its essence and taking account of it as a whole.

At the end of this voyage of exploration, the final scene of *Siegfried* assumes an allegorical significance for us, subjectively, which Wagner certainly did not foresee. As soon as he has to take account of androgyny—

that symbol par excellence of unity and totality—the analyst is confronted by a variety of layers of meaning. The history of modern hermeneutics bears witness to this well-nigh desperate search for global explanations that might provide us not only with the key to humanity but to the ultimate meaning of a work. But if, like ourselves, interpreters have found androgyny along their way, it is because androgyny allows us a brief glimpse of the perfect image of unity while at the same time telling us that this unity does not exist and that, unless we lapse into masturbatory monomania, we shall find only multiplicity in this world.

The Question of Androgyny Today

By its very nature, human knowledge aims at total understanding of humanity and the universe, but, as Veyne remarks, "we have complete knowledge of nothing" (Veyne 1971, 309). In the wake of Romanticism, the great paradigms of twentieth-century human sciences—Freud, Jung, Lévi-Strauss, and the contemporary derivatives of Marxism—have tried to provide a unitary and definitive response to the enigmas of the human race. More than that, all of them (with the possible exception of structuralism, which is not a pragmatic theory) have attempted to increase the happiness of the human race. The Marxist myth hoped for the advent of a classless society; the Freudian myth aimed at ridding human beings of the causes of their neuroses and psychoses; and the feminist myth envisages, at least in certain of its manifestations, a redefinition of biological boundaries between the sexes.

If we have believed in Marx, Freud, or Lévi-Strauss and if, perhaps, we like Wagner, it is because the artist, like the theoreticians (or vice versa), has given us the reassuring illusion that, by continuing to evolve as it has done, humanity could reach a stable point at which contradictions no longer exist and time can be arrested. But we can no more prevent the inexorable march of time than we can abolish the difference between the sexes. It is no doubt for this reason that androgyny and death so often appear together, that social utopias end in massacres, and that the structuralist utopia of an all-embracing explanation of mankind reducible to torrents of binary opposites issues, in the case of Lévi-Strauss, in "nothingness" and in the sense of cosmic collapse reflected in the final pages of *The Naked Man*.

The various myths of androgyny are dominated by the notion of an absolute utopia. If we can dream of a just society, of human beings rid of their neuroses, and of harmonious relationships between men and women, and if human progress is not possible without our first ensuring that injustices are wiped out and suffering reduced in our collective and individual actions, it is still difficult to share Elisabeth Badinter's vision of a radical change to the biological order of the world, which is to create the One on the basis of the Two, rather than the other way around. After all, the idea of *difference* is an inescapable part of our lives.

Against this background, it is worth asking why there has been a return in recent years to the question of androgyny. The final manifestation of Romantic and post-Romantic utopias, today's androgyny certainly reveals their utopian nature, and it is surely not irrelevant that it has arisen at the very time when the credibility of androgynous hermeneutics—from Marx to Freud and Lévi-Strauss—has begun to be eroded.

Clearly this does not mean the end of the human sciences as we know them and, equally clearly, humanity will never renounce its search for the absolute, since we can never enter the realm of ultimate ends. But, deprived of the possibility of providing unitarian and all-embracing explanations, and condemned to *construct* interpretations while knowing that one day they will be disputed and superseded, we are reduced to that fragmentation of reality from which the androgyneity of totality has sought to save us from the Romantic period onward. In consequence, we are obliged to content ourselves with lacunary interpretations that are only partially true. This in turn is a result of the fact that, whatever its aspirations to totality and timelessness, androgyneity remains an unstable figure. Aiming at an image of totality by merging the two sexes, it always presents itself to us with the features of an effeminate man or a woman endowed with male characteristics. Even the asexual Parsifal remains a man. There is an irreducible difference between the sexes, and one that no androgyne will ever succeed in transcending.

It is not surprising, therefore, that the theme of androgyny has resurfaced at a time when what has long been the great illusion of interpretation (and what remains so in many eyes)—the belief that human works of art have a unique and global meaning, which it is possible to define—is beginning to be undermined. At the same time, however, and in spite of the ambiguity of possible networks of meaning, it requires only a certain amount of patience to make out harder and clearer kernels of meaning alongside undeniably shadowy areas. It is here, perhaps, that our hope resides: following the era of unique truths and of the triumph of a single, all-embracing meaning, after the age of prophets of doom reveling in the void and in no matter what, we may now be entering an age of greyness, an age of doubts and hesitations, but possibly also an age of certainties.

We must imagine androgynes as happy creatures.

CATALOG OF WAGNER'S WRITINGS

THE FOLLOWING LIST of Wagner's writings is a simplified version of a detailed catalog running to around one hundred pages, which I plan to publish at a later date and which will contain a description of the manuscript, where known, together with a note of its location and details of its first publication.

The present list of 301 titles is the first to attempt a chronological classification of Wagner's writings. The list published in vol. 20 of *The New Grove* and in Deathridge and Dahlhaus 1984 (which derives in part from the *Grove* article on Wagner) does not lay claim to exhaustiveness (Deathridge and Dahlhaus 1984, 188). The article by Jürgen Kühnel, published in the *Wagner Handbuch* (1986; English trans. 1992), provides a survey of some 240 items but suffers the drawback of grouping the texts generically within six chronological sections, which makes it difficult to use, especially for anyone undertaking a genetic study like my own.

The first edition of Wagner's *Gesammelte Schriften* (Collected writings) appeared between 1871 and 1883, the second—differently paginated—between 1887 and 1888. This ten-volume edition was reprinted by Georg Olms Verlag in 1976. The initials *GS*, followed by the volume and page number, refer to this edition. Wagner's *Sämtliche Schriften* (Complete writings) were published between 1911 and 1916: to the ten volumes of the *Gesammelte Schriften*, the new editors added Wagner's previously unpublished libretti and sketches (vol. 11), *Mein Leben* (vols. 13–15), and two volumes of writings that Wagner had not seen fit to include in the edition that he superintended during his lifetime or that were not available to him at that time. The initials *SS* are used to refer to these later volumes.

William Ashton Ellis's eight-volume edition of Wagner's prose works appeared between 1892 and 1899, and was reprinted in 1972. References to this edition (*PW*) are included for the sake of convenience, although Ellis's translation has not been used.

If no initials are given, the document is previously unpublished.

German titles are the ones used in *GS*, *SS*, or the catalog in the Wagner archives at Bayreuth. French titles are used for articles that first appeared in French. The date of composition (where known) is followed by that of the first publication.

Dated Texts

1834a "Die deutsche Oper" (German opera). In *Die Zeitung für die elegante Welt*, 10 June 1834 (published anonymously); *SS* 12.1–4; *PW* 8.55–58.

1834b "Pasticcio." In *Neue Zeitschrift für Musik*, 6 and 10 November 1834 (published under the pseudonym "Canto Spianato"; attribution uncertain); *SS* 12.5–11; *PW* 8.59–66.

1835a *Die Rote Brieftasche* (The red pocketbook), begun mid-August 1835. In *Allgemeine Musik-Zeitung* 63 (1936): 196; *SB* 1.81–84.

1835b "Eine Kritik aus Magdeburg" (A review from Magdeburg). In *Magdeburger Zeitung*, 7 November 1835 (signed "—r"); *SS* 16.57–58.

1836a "Aus Magdeburg. (Die Verschwörungen.—Die Oper.)" (From Magdeburg [The conspiracies.—the opera.]). In *Neue Zeitschrift für Musik*, 3 May 1836 (anonymous); *SS* 12.12–14.

1836b "Berliner Kunstchronik von Wilhelm Drach" (Chronicle of Berlin's artistic life by Wilhelm Drach [= Richard Wagner]). Sent to Schumann on 28 May 1836 but not published (cf. *SB* 1.274–75); lost.

1837a "Der dramatische Gesang" (Dramatic singing), dated 1837 by its first editor, Otto Lessmann. In *Musik-Zeitung* 15 (1888): 97; *SS* 12.15–18.

1837b "Zum ersten Male: Norma, von Bellini" (For the first time: Bellini's *Norma*), March 1837; Friedrich Lippmann, "Ein neu entdecktes Autograph Richard Wagners." In *Musicae scientiae collectanea: Festschrift Karl Gustav Fellerer* (Cologne: Arno-Volk-Verlag, 1973), pp. 373–79.

1837c Handwritten note relating to concert in Riga on 13 November 1837; 12 November 1837.

1837d "Bellini: Ein Wort zu seiner Zeit" (Bellini: a word in season). In *Der Zuschauer*, 7 December 1837 (signed "O."); *SS* 12.19–21; *PW* 8.67–69.

1837e "Theater-Anzeige" (Theater announcement). In *Der Zuschauer*, 8 December 1837; *SS* 16.3.

1838 "Concert-Anzeige" (announcement of concert in Riga on 19 March 1838). In *Der Zuschauer*, 14 March 1838.

1839a "Konzertanzeige" (Concert announcement). In *Der Zuschauer*, 8 March 1839; *SS* 16.4.

1839b Manuscript program for Wagner's concert on 14 March 1839.

1840a "Ein Tagebuch aus Paris" (A Paris diary), 23, 29, and 30 June 1840. In *Richard Wagner-Jahrbuch*, ed. Joseph Kürschner (Stuttgart [privately published], 1886), pp. 289–92; *SS* 16.4–6.

1840b "De la musique allemande." In *Revue et Gazette musicale*, 12 July 1840; published as "Über deutsches Musikwesen" (On German music) in *GS* 1.149–66; *PW* 7.83–101.

1840c "Über Meyerbeers 'Hugenotten'" (On Meyerbeer's *Les Huguenots*), 1837 or 1840; *SS* 12.22–30.

1840d "'Stabat Mater' de Pergolèse, arrangé pour grand orchestre avec choeurs par Alexis Lvoff, membre des Académies de Bologne et de Saint-Pétersbourg." In *Revue et Gazette musicale*, 11 October 1840; *SS* 12.401–5; *PW* 7.102–7.

1840e "Du métier de virtuose et de l'indépendance des compositeurs" (On the profession of virtuoso and the independence of composers). In *Revue et Gazette musicale*, 18 October 1840; published as "Der Virtuos und der Künstler" in *GS* 1.167–80; *PW* 7.108–22 (in a note to his translation, Ellis points out that the French and German versions of this essay amount to two independent pieces).

1840f "Une visite à Beethoven: Épisode de la vie d'un musicien allemand" (A visit to Beethoven: episode in the life of a German musician). In *Revue et Gazette musicale*, 19, 22, 29 November, 3 December 1840; published as "Eine Pilgerfahrt zu Beethoven" (A pilgrimage to Beethoven) in *Abend-Zeitung*, 30 July—5 August 1841; *GS* 1.90–114; *PW* 7.21–45.

1840g "Wie ein armer Musiker in Paris starb" (How a poor musician died in Paris), sketch for 1841b, late 1840; Glasenapp 1.394; *SS* 16.235.

1841a "De l'ouverture" (On the overture). In *Revue et Gazette musicale*, 10, 14, 17 January 1841; published as "Über die Ouvertüre" in *GS* 1.194–206; *PW* 7.151–65.

1841b "Un musicien étranger à Paris" (A foreign musician in Paris). In *Revue et Gazette musicale*, 31 January, 7, 11 February 1841; published as "Das Ende in Paris" in *Abend-Zeitung*, 6–11 August 1841, and as "Ein Ende in Paris" in *GS* 1.114–36; *PW* 7.46–68.

1841c "Pariser Bericht für die Dresdener Abendzeitung" (Paris report for the Dresden *Abend-Zeitung*), first report of 23 February 1841. In *Abend-Zeitung*, 19, 20, 22 March 1841; *SS* 12.65–73; *PW* 8.108–18.

1841d "Caprices esthétiques: Extraits du journal d'un musicien défunt. Le musicien et la publicité" (Aesthetic caprices: excerpts from the diary of a dead musician. The musician and his public). In *Revue et Gazette musicale*, 1 April 1841; published as "Der Künstler und die Öffentlichkeit" (The artist and his public) in *GS* 1.180–86; *PW* 7.134–41; as with 1840e, the French and German versions differ considerably.

1841e "Pariser Amüsements." In *Europa*, part 2 (1841): 577–91 (published under the pseudonym "V. Freudenfeuer"); *GS* 12.31–45; *PW* 8.70–86.

1841f "Pariser Bericht für die Dresdener Abendzeitung," second report of 6 April 1841. In *Abend-Zeitung*, 24–28 May 1841; *SS* 12.74–86; *PW* 8.118–31.

1841g "Pariser Bericht für die Dresdener Abendzeitung," third report of 5 May 1841. In *Abend-Zeitung*, 14–17 June 1841; *SS* 12.87–95; *PW* 8.131–41.

1841h "Une soirée heureuse" (A happy evening), completed 12 May 1841. In *Revue et Gazette musicale*, 24 October, 7 November 1841; published as "Ein glücklicher Abend" in *GS* 1.136–49; *PW* 7.69–81.

1841i "Le Freischütz." In *Revue et Gazette musicale*, 23, 30 May 1841; published as "Der Freischütz: An das Pariser Publikum" (*Der Freischütz*: to Paris audiences) in *GS* 1.207–19; *PW* 7.167–82.

1841j "Le Freischutz: Bericht nach Deutschland" ("Le Freischutz": Report to Germany), letter of 20 June 1841. In *Abend-Zeitung*, 16, 17, 19, 20, 21 July 1841; *GS* 1.220–40; *PW* 7.183–204.

1841k "Pariser Bericht für die Dresdener Abendzeitung," fourth report of 6 July 1841. In *Abend-Zeitung*, 2–4 August 1841; *SS* 12.96–103; *PW* 8.141–48.

1841l "Pariser Bericht für die Dresdener Abendzeitung," fifth report of 1 August 1841 ("Sunday Impressions"). In *Abend-Zeitung*, 23 August 1841; *SS* 12.104–6 (incomplete, unsigned, and not included in Ellis's translation).

1841m "Pariser Fatalitäten für Deutsche" (Parisian fatalities for Germans). In *Europa*, part 3 (1841): 433–50; *SS* 12.46–64; *PW* 8.87–107.

1841n "Pariser Bericht für die Dresdener Abendzeitung," sixth report of 8 September 1841. In *Abend-Zeitung*, 1–2 October 1841; *SS* 12.107–11; *PW* 8.149–53.

1841o "Pariser Bericht für die Dresdener Abendzeitung," seventh report of 5 November 1841. In *Abend-Zeitung*, 4–8 December 1841; *SS* 12.112–22; *PW* 8.154–64.

1841p "Pariser Bericht für die Dresdener Abendzeitung," eighth report of 1 December 1841. In *Abend-Zeitung*, 25 December 1841; *SS* 12.123–26; *PW* 8.164–67.

1841q "Pariser Bericht für die Dresdener Abendzeitung," ninth report of 23 December 1841. In *Abend-Zeitung*, 10–11 January 1842; *SS* 12.127–30; *PW* 8.167–71.

1841r "Rossinis 'Stabat mater,'" letter of 15 December 1841. In *Neue Zeitschrift für Musik*, 28 December 1841 (published under the pseudonym "H. Valentino"); *GS* 1.186–93; *PW* 7.142–49.

1841s "Bericht über eine neue Pariser Oper ('La Reine de Chypre' von Halévy.)" (Report on a new French opera: Halévy's *La Reine de Chypre*), letter of 31 December 1841. In *Abend-Zeitung*, 26–29 January 1842; *GS* 1.241–57; *PW* 7.205–22.

1842a "Ein Pariser Bericht für Robert Schumanns *Neue Zeitschrift für Musik*," letter of 5 [February] 1842. In *Neue Zeitschrift für Musik*, 22 February 1842 (published under the pseudonym "H. V."); *SS* 16.58–60; *PW* 8.172–74.

1842b "Halévy et la Reine de Chypre." In *Revue et Gazette musicale*, 27 February, 13 March, 24 April, 1 May 1842; *SS* 12.131–48 and 406–13 (only the first part of Wagner's original manuscript has survived and is published in *SS* 12.131–48 under the title "Halévy und die Französische Oper," the ending of the piece being supplemented from the French first edition); *PW* 8.175–200.

1843a "Autobiographische Skizze" (Autobiographical sketch). In *Zeitung für die elegante Welt*, 1, 8 February 1843; *GS* 1.4–19; *PW* 1.1–19.

1843b "Das Oratorium 'Paulus' von Felix Mendelssohn-Bartholdy," written for the 1843 Palm Sunday concert in Dresden. In *Bayreuther Blätter* 20 (1899): 4; *SS* 12.149–50.

1843c "An die Dresdener Liedertafel: Anruf" (Appeal to the Dresden Liedertafel), 20 April 1843. In *Festschrift zum 50jährigen Bestehen der Dresdener Liedertafel* (Dresden, 1889), p. 9; *SS* 16.6–7.

1843d and e "Zwei Erklärungen über die Verdeutschung des Textes 'Les deux grenadiers'" (Two clarifications concerning the German translation of *Les deux grenadiers*). In *Neue Zeitschrift für Musik*, 15 May, 19 June 1843; *SS* 16.10–11.

1844 "Rede an Weber's letzter Ruhestätte" (Speech at Weber's final resting place), 15 December 1844; *GS* 2.46–48; *PW* 7.235–37.

1845 "An die Dresdener Liedertafel: Niederlegung der Leitung" (To the Dresden Liedertafel: letter of resignation), 14 November 1845. *Festschrift zum 50jährigen Bestehen der Dresdener Liedertafel* (Dresden, 1889), p. 15; *SS* 16.8–10.

1846a "Die königliche Kapelle betreffend" (Concerning the royal orchestra), completed 1 March 1846. In *Der junge Wagner*, pp. 335–419; *SS* 12.151–204.

1846b "Zu Beethovens Neunter Symphonie" (On Beethoven's Ninth Symphony); program note for concert on 5 April 1846. In *Dresdener Anzeiger*, 24, 31 March, 2 April 1846; *SS* 12.205–7; *PW* 8.201–3.

1846c "Programm zur 9. Symphonie von Beethoven," program for concert on 5 April 1846; *GS* 2.56–64; *PW* 7.247–55.

1846d "Künstler und Kritiker, mit Bezug auf einen besonderen Fall" (Artist and critic, with reference to a particular case), letter of 11 August 1846. In *Dresdener Anzeiger*, 14 August 1846; *SS* 12.208–19; *PW* 8.204–14.

1846e "Eine Rede auf Friedrich Schneider" (Speech relating to Friedrich Schneider), speech delivered on 7 November 1846. In *Der Merker*, 15 October 1913; *SS* 16.61–62.

1848a Untitled manuscript of 20 April 1848 relating to concerts in Dresden during the 1847–48 season.

1848b "Entwurf zur Organisation eines deutschen National-Theaters für das Königreich Sachsen" (Plan for the organization of a German national theater for the Kingdom of Saxony), completed 11 May 1848; *GS* 2.233–73; *PW* 7.319–60.

1848c "Wie verhalten sich republikanische Bestrebungen dem Königthume gegenüber?" (How do Republican aspirations stand in relation to the monarchy?), Wagner's *Vaterlandsverein* speech of 14 June 1848. Published anonymously in *Dresdener Anzeiger* of 16 June 1848; *SS* 12.220–29; *PW* 4.136–45.

1848d and e "Zeitungs-Erklärungen" (two newspaper articles clarifying points in 1848c). In *Dresdener Anzeiger*, 20, 22 June 1848; *SS* 16.27.

1848f "Trinkspruch am Gedenktage des 300jährigen Bestehens der königlichen musikalischen Kapelle in Dresden" (Toast on the tercentenary of the Dresden Royal Orchestra), speech delivered on 22 September 1848; *GS* 2.229–32; *PW* 7.313–18.

1848g "Die Nibelungensage (Mythus)" (The Nibelung legend [Myth]), completed 4 October 1848. Published as "Der Nibelungen-Mythus. Als Entwurf zu einem Drama" (The Nibelung myth: as draft for a drama) in *GS* 2.156–66; *PW* 7.299–311.

1848h "Deutschland und seine Fürsten" (Germany and her princes). In *Volksblätter*, 15 October 1848 (published anonymously); *SS* 12.414–19.

1849a *Die Wibelungen: Weltgeschichte aus der Sage* (The Wibelungs: world history from legend), February 1849 [?], revised August–September 1849. Published Leipzig early 1850; *GS* 2.115–55; *PW* 7.257–98.

1849b "Die Wibelungen: Schlußworte" (The Wibelungs: closing words), conclusion of 1849a. Suppressed from *GS*; *SS* 12.229.

1849c "Über Eduard Devrients 'Geschichte der deutschen Schauspielkunst'" (On Eduard Devrient's *History of German Acting*), submitted to Augsburg *Allgemeine Zeitung* on 8 January 1849 but not published. In *Der junge Wagner*, pp. 459–64; *SS* 12.230–32; *PW* 8.218–21.

1849d "Theater-Reform," *Dresdener Anzeiger*, 16 January 1849 (published under the pseudonym "J.P.-Fr.R."); *SS* 12.233–36; *PW* 8.222–25.

1849e "Nochmals Theater-Reform." In *Dresdener Anzeiger*, 18 January 1849 (published under the pseudonym "J. P.-Fr. R."); *SS* 12.237–39.

1849f "Der Mensch und die bestehende Gesellschaft" (Man and existing society). In *Volksblätter*, 10 February 1849 (published anonymously); *SS* 12.240–44; *PW* 8.227–31.

1849g "Die Revolution." In *Volksblätter*, 8 April 1849 (published anonymously); *SS* 12.245–51; *PW* 8.232–38.

1849h *Die Kunst und die Revolution* (Art and revolution), completed late July 1849; published Leipzig 1849; *GS* 3.8–41; *PW* 1.21–65.

1849i "Zu 'Die Kunst und die Revolution'" (marginalia relating to *Art and Revolution*); *Entwürfe, Gedanken, Fragmente aus nachgelassenen Papieren zusammengestellt*, pp. 49–50; *SS* 12.252–53; *PW* 8.362 (incomplete).

1849j "Das Künstlertum der Zukunft" (The artists of the future), random jottings from 1849–50 for a projected article on the artists of the future; *Entwürfe, Gedanken, Fragmente aus nachgelassenen Papieren zusammengestellt*, pp. 11–33; *SS* 12.254–65; *PW* 8.343–55.

1849k "Das Genie der Gemeinsamkeit" (Communal genius), random jottings, 1849–50; *Entwürfe, Gedanken, Fragmente aus nachgelassenen Papieren zusammengestellt*, pp. 34–45; *SS* 12.266–71; *PW* 8.355–61.

1849l "Aphorismen zu den Kunstschriften der Jahre 1849–51" (Aphorisms relating to the aesthetic essays of 1849–51); *Entwürfe, Gedanken, Fragmente aus nachgelassenen Papieren zusammengestellt*, pp. 51–70; *SS* 12.272–80 and 283; *PW* 8.363–75.

1849m *Das Kunstwerk der Zukunft* (The art-work of the future), completed 4 November 1849; published Leipzig 1850; *GS* 3.42–177; *PW* 1.67–213.

1850a "Kunst und Klima" (Art and climate), begun 23 February 1850. In *Deutsche Monatsschrift für Politik, Wissenschaft, Kunst und Leben*, April 1850; *GS* 3.207–21; *PW* 1.249–65.

1850b "Vorwort zu einer 1850 beabsichtigten Herausgabe von Siegfrieds Tod" (Preface to an edition of *Siegfrieds Tod* planned for 1850), May 1850. In *Die Musik* 12 (1910): 15–23; *SS* 16.84–85.

1850c "Das Judenthum in der Musik" (Judaism in music), completed before 22 August 1850. In *Neue Zeitschrift für Musik*, 3 and 6 September 1850 (published under the pseudonym "R. Freigedank"); revised 1869; *GS* 5.66–85 (1869 version, although dated 1850); *PW* 3.79–100.

1850d "Vorwort zu der 1850 beabsichtigten Veröffentlichung des Entwurfs von 1848 'Zur Organisation eines deutschen Nationaltheaters für das Königreich Sachsen'" (Preface to the planned publication, in 1850, of the 1848 draft "On the Organization of a German National Theatre for the Kingdom of Saxony"), letter of 18 September 1850. Published incomplete in *Neue*

Zeitschrift für Musik, 3 January, 7 February, and 7 March 1851; published complete in *Richard Wagner's Briefe an Theodor Uhlig, Wilhelm Fischer, Ferdinand Heine* (Leipzig: Breitkopf und Härtel, 1888), pp. 51–58; *SS* 16.86–92.

1850e "Über die musikalische Direktion der Züricher Oper" (On the musical direction of the Zurich opera). In *Eidgenössische Zeitung*, 17 October 1850; *SS* 16.16–18.

1851a *Oper und Drama* (Opera and drama), begun after August 1850, completed 10 January 1851; published Leipzig 1852; revised 1868; *GS* 3.222–320 and 4.1–229; *PW* 2.1–376.

1851b "Nachruf an Spontini" (Obituary of Spontini). In *Eidgenössische Zeitung*, 25 January 1851; *GS* 5.86–8; *PW* 123–27; see also 1872h.

1851c "Zur Empfehlung Gottfried Sempers" (In recommendation of Gottfried Semper). In *Eidgenössische Zeitung*, 6 February 1851; *SS* 16.18–19.

1851d "Über die musikalische Berichterstattung in der Eidgenössischen Zeitung" (On the *Eidgenössische Zeitung*'s reporting of musical events). In *Eidgenössische Zeitung*, 7 February 1851; *SS* 16.19–20.

1851e "Beethoven's 'heroische Symphonie'" (Beethoven's *Eroica* Symphony), written for concert in Zurich on 26 February 1851. In *Neue Zeitschrift für Musik*, 15 October 1852; *GS* 5.169–72; *PW* 3.221–24.

1851f *Ein Theater in Zürich* (A Theater in Zurich), completed 17 April 1851; published Zurich 1851; *GS* 5.20–52; *PW* 3.23–57.

1851g "Über die 'Goethestiftung': Brief an Franz Liszt" ("On the Goethe foundation": letter to Franz Liszt), letter of 8 May 1851. In *Neue Zeitschrift für Musik*, 5 March 1852; *GS* 5.5–19; *PW* 3.5–22.

1851h *Eine Mittheilung an meine Freunde* (A communication to my friends), July–August 1851; published Leipzig 1851; *GS* 4.230–344; *PW* 1.267–392.

1852a "Über musikalische Kritik: Brief an den Herausgeber der 'Neuen Zeitschrift für Musik'" (On music criticism: letter to the editor of the *Neue Zeitschrift für Musik*), letter of 25 January 1852. In *Neue Zeitschrift für Musik*, 6 February 1852; *GS* 5.53–65; *PW* 3.59–74.

1852b "Wilhelm Baumgartners Lieder." In *Eidgenössische Zeitung*, 7 February 1852; *SS* 12.286–88.

1852c "Beethoven's Ouvertüre zu 'Koriolan,'" program note for concert in Zurich on 17 February 1852. In *Neue Zeitschrift für Musik*, 5 November 1852; *GS* 5.173–76; *PW* 3.225–28.

1852d "Ouvertüre zu 'Tannhäuser,'" program note for concert in Zurich on 16 March 1852. In *Neue Zeitschrift für Musik*, 14 January 1853; *GS* 5.177–79; *PW* 3.229–31.

1852e *Über die Aufführung des "Tannhäuser": Eine Mittheilung an die Dirigenten und Darsteller dieser Oper* (On performing *Tannhäuser*: an address to the conductors and performers of this opera), completed on 23 August 1852; privately printed 1852; *GS* 5.123–59; *PW* 3.167–205.

1852f "Vieuxtemps." In *Eidgenössische Zeitung*, 20 September 1852; *SS* 16.20.

1852g "Über die Aufführung der 'Tannhäuser'-Ouvertüre" (On performing the *Tannhäuser* overture), 30 October 1852. In *Neue Zeitschrift für Musik*, 5 November 1852; *SS* 16.20.

1852h "Bemerkungen zur Aufführung der Oper 'Der fliegende Holländer'"

(Remarks on performing the opera *The Flying Dutchman*), completed 22 December 1852; *GS* 5.160–68; *PW* 3.207–17.

1853a "Vorlesung der Dichtung des 'Ring des Nibelungen'" (Invitation to a public reading of the poem of *Der Ring des Nibelungen*). In *Eidgenössische Zeitung*, 12 February 1853; *SS* 16.21.

1853b "Vorwort zu der Veröffentlichung der als Manuskript gedruckten Dichtung des 'Ringes des Nibelungen'" (Preface to the first printed edition of *Der Ring des Nibelungen*), privately printed 1853; *SS* 12.289–90.

1853c "Ankündigung der im Mai 1853 zu veranstaltenden Konzerte" (Preliminary announcement of concerts to be held in May 1853). In *Eidgenössische Zeitung*, 2 April 1853; *SS* 16.21–22.

1853d "Ouvertüre zum 'fliegenden Holländer,'" program note written for concerts on 18, 20, 22 May 1853; *GS* 5.176–77; *PW* 3.228–29.

1853e "'Tannhäuser': I. Einzug der Gäste auf Wartburg; II. Tannhäusers Romfahrt" (I. Entry of the guests to the Wartburg; II. Tannhäuser's journey to Rome), program notes written for concerts on 18, 20, 22 May 1853; *SS* 16.167–69.

1853f "Vorspiel zu 'Lohengrin'" (Prelude to *Lohengrin*), program note for concerts on 18, 20, 22 May 1853; *GS* 5.179–81; PW 3.231–33.

1853g "'Lohengrin': I. Männerszene und Brautzug; II. Hochzeitsmusik und Brautlied" (I. Men's chorus and bridal procession; II. Wedding music and bridal chorus), program notes for concerts on 18, 20, 22 May 1853; *SS* 16.170.

1853h "Über die programmatischen Erklärungen zu den Konzerten im Mai 1853" (On the programmatical explanations to the concerts in May 1853); *SS* 16.22–23.

1854a "Gluck's Ouvertüre zu 'Iphigenie in Aulis': Eine Mittheilung an den Redakteur der 'Neuen Zeitschrift für Musik'" (Gluck's overture to *Iphigénie en Aulide*: a communication to the editor of the *Neue Zeitschrift für Musik*), letter of 17 June 1854. In *Neue Zeitschrift für Musik*, 1 July 1854; *GS* 5.111–22; *PW* 3.153–66.

1854b "Empfehlung einer Streichquartett-Vereinigung" (Recommendation of a string quartet), *Eidgenössische Zeitung*, 3 October 1853; *SS* 16.23.

1854c "Beethovens Cis moll-Quartett (Op. 131)" (Beethoven's C♯-minor string quartet, Op. 131), program note for concert in Zurich on 12 December 1854; *Entwürfe, Gedanken, Fragmente aus nachgelassenen Papieren zusammengestellt*, p. 100; *SS* 12.350; *PW* 8.350.

1855 "Bemerkung zu einer angeblichen Äußerung Rossinis" (Comment on an alleged remark of Rossini's), 1855; *Entwürfe, Gedanken, Fragmente aus nachgelassenen Papieren zusammengestellt*, pp. 79–80; *SS* 12.313.

1856 "Über die Leitung einer Mozart-Feier" (On the administration of a Mozart festival). In *Eidgenössische Zeitung*, 15 February 1856; *SS* 16.23–24.

1857 "Über Franz Liszt's Symphonische Dichtungen. (Brief an M.W.)" (On Franz Liszt's symphonic poems: letter to M[arie] W[ittgenstein]), completed 15 February 1857. In *Neue Zeitschrift für Musik*, 10 April 1857; *GS* 5.182–98; *PW* 3.235–54.

1859a "Nachruf an L. Spohr und Chordirektor W. Fischer. (Brieflich an einen älteren Freund in Dresden. Paris 1860)" (Obituary of Ludwig Spohr and chorus-master Wilhelm Fischer. [Written communication to a longstanding friend in Dresden. Paris 1860]). In *Neue Zeitschrift für Musik*, 2 December 1859; *GS* 5.105–10; *PW* 3.145–52.

1859b "Aus der 'Europe Artiste,'" newspaper correction. In *Europe Artiste*, November 1859; German original in *Signale für die musikalische Welt*, 8 December 1859; *SS* 16.28.

1859c "'Tristan und Isolde': Vorspiel," program note for concert on 25 January 1860, written before 19 December 1859; *Entwürfe, Gedanken, Fragmente aus nachgelassenen Papieren zusammengestellt*, pp. 101–3; *SS* 12.346–47; *PW* 8.386–87.

1860a "Concert Richard Wagner," program booklet for concerts in Paris on 25 January, 1, 8 February 1860; published Paris 1860.

1860b "Ein Brief an Hector Berlioz" (A letter to Hector Berlioz). In *Journal des débats*, 22 February 1860; German original in *Neue Zeitschrift für Musik*, 2 March 1860; *GS* 7.82–86; *PW* 3.285–91.

1860c *Quatre Poèmes d'opéra traduits en prose français précédés d'une Lettre sur la musique par Richard Wagner*, published Paris 1861, more familiar under its German title, *"Zukunftsmusik." An einen französischen Freund (Fr. Villot) als Vorwort zu einer Prosa-Übersetzung meiner Operndichtungen* ("The Music of the Future": letter to a French friend [Frédéric Villot] by way of a preface to a prose translation of my opera poems), completed by 13[?] September 1860; published Leipzig 1861; *GS* 7.87–137; *PW* 3.293–345.

1861a "Bericht über die Aufführung des 'Tannhäuser' in Paris. (Brieflich.)" (Report on the performance of *Tannhäuser* in Paris. [Written communication.]), letter of 27 March 1861. In *Deutsche Allgemeine Zeitung*, 7 April 1861; *GS* 7.138–49; *PW* 3.347–60.

1861b "Vom Wiener Hofopertheater" (On the Vienna court opera). In *Österreichische Zeitung*, 8 October 1861 (published under the pseudonym "P. C."); *SS* 12.292–96.

1861c "Aus der 'Ostdeutschen Post,'" newspaper correction. In *Ostdeutsche Post*, November 1861; *SS* 16.28.

1862 "An die Direktion der philharmonischen Gesellschaft in St. Petersburg" (To the directors of the Philharmonic Society of St. Petersburg), letter of 12 December 1862; *SS* 16.29–30.

1863a "Vorwort zur Herausgabe der Dichtung des Bühnenfestspieles 'Der Ring des Nibelungen'" (Preface to an edition of the poem of *Der Ring des Nibelungen*), January 1863; published with complete libretto, Leipzig 1863; *GS* 6.272–81; *PW* 3.274–83.

1863b "An die Direktion der philharmonischen Gesellschaft in St. Petersburg," letter of 30 March 1863; *SS* 16.30–31.

1863c "Richard Wagner über die ungarische Musik," letter of 8 August 1863 to Cornel Abrányi. In *Pesther Lloyd*, No. 188, and *Niederrheinische Musik-Zeitung*, 29 August 1863, pp. 279–80.

1863d "Das Wiener Hof-Operntheater" (The Vienna Court Opera). In *Der Botschafter*, October 1863; *GS* 7.272–95; *PW* 3.361–86.

1863e "'Die Meistersinger von Nürnberg': Vorspiel," program note for performance of the prelude on 2 December 1863. In *Bayreuther Blätter* 25 (1902): 168; *SS* 12.347–48.

1863f "'Tristan und Isolde.' Vorspiel (Liebestod) und Schlußsatz (Verklärung)" (Prelude [Love-Death] and final section [transfiguration]), program note for concert on 27 December 1863. In *Bayreuther Blätter* 25 (1902): 167; *SS* 12.347.

1864a "Grabschrift für sich selbst" (Epitaph for Wagner), 25 March 1864; *ML*, 786.

1864b "Buddha—Luther," April 1864; *Entwürfe, Gedanken, Fragmente aus nachgelassenen Papieren zusammengestellt*, p. 99; *SS* 12.282; *PW* 8.386.

1864c "Über Staat und Religion" (On state and religion), completed 16 July 1864; *GS* 8.3–29; *PW* 4.3–34.

1865a "Zur Erwiderung des Aufsatzes 'Richard Wagner und die öffentliche Meinung'" (By way of a reply to the article "Richard Wagner and Public Opinion"). In Augsburg *Allgemeine Zeitung*, 22 February 1865; *SS* 12.297–303.

1865b *Bericht an Seine Majestät den König Ludwig II. von Bayern über eine in München zu errichtende deutsche Musikschule* (Report to his majesty King Ludwig II of Bavaria on a German school of music to be established in Munich), completed 23 March 1865; published Munich 1865; *GS* 8.125–76; *PW* 4.171–224.

1865c "Einladung zur ersten Aufführung von 'Tristan und Isolde'" (Invitation to the first performance of *Tristan und Isolde*), dated 18 April 1865. In *Der Botschafter*, 21 April 1865; *SS* 16.32–41; *PW* 8.239–48.

1865d "Ansprache an das Hoforchester in München vor der Hauptprobe zu 'Tristan' am Vormittag des 11. Mai 1865" (Address to the court orchestra in Munich before the dress rehearsal of *Tristan und Isolde* on the morning of 11 May 1865). In *Bayrische Zeitung*, 15 May 1865; *SS* 16.42–43.

1865e "Dankschreiben an das Münchener Hoforchester" (Letter of thanks to the Munich Court Orchestra), letter of 19 July 1865; Altmann No. 1878; *SS* 16.43–44.

1865f *Mein Leben* (My life), dictated between 17 July 1865 and 25 July 1880; published privately in four volumes 1870, 1872, 1875, 1880; first authentic edition Munich 1963; English trans. 1983.

1865g *Das Braune Buch: Tagebuchaufzeichnungen 1865 bis 1882* (The brown book: diary entries 1865–1882), private journal for period 10 August 1865 to 9 April 1882; first complete edition Zurich 1975; English trans. 1980.

1865h "Was ist deutsch?" (What is German?), 14–27 September 1865; incompletely published in *GS* 10.36–53; *PW* 4.149–69; published complete in *König Ludwig II. und Richard Wagner: Briefwechsel*, ed. Otto Strobel (Karlsruhe: G. Braun, Verlag, 1936), 4.3–34.

1865i "Ein Artikel der Münchener 'Neuesten Nachrichten' vom 29. November 1865." In *Neueste Nachrichten*, 29 November 1865 (published under the pseudonym "fr."); *SS* 16.44–47.

1866a "Preußen und Österreich" (Prussia and Austria), Wagner's "political program" of June 1866. In *König Ludwig II. und Richard Wagner: Briefwechsel* (see 1865h), 4.147–50.

1866b "Erklärung im 'Berner Bund'" (Declaration in the *Berner Bund*). In *Berner Bund*, 10 June 1866; *SS* 16.47–48.

1866c "An die Direktion der philharmonischen Gesellschaft in St. Petersburg," letter of 8 November 1866; *SS* 16.31–32.

1867a *Deutsche Kunst und deutsche Politik* (German art and German politics), incompletely published in twelve installments in *Süddeutsche Presse*, 24 September–19 December 1867; published complete in pamphlet form, Leipzig 1868; *GS* 8.30–124; *PW* 4.35–135.

1867b "Censuren I: W. H. Riehl. ('Neues Novellenbuch.')" (Review of Wilhelm Heinrich Riehl's *Neues Novellenbuch*). In *Süddeutsche Presse*, November 1867 (published anonymously); *GS* 8.205–13; *PW* 4.253–60.

1867c "Censuren II: Ferdinand Hiller. ('Aus dem Tonleben unserer Zeit.')." In *Süddeutsche Presse*, November 1867 (published anonymously); *GS* 8.213–20; *PW* 4.261–68.

1868a "Annalen" (Annals for 1846 to 1868), transcribed into *Das Braune Buch* (1865g) in February 1868 and January 1869. In *Das Braune Buch*, pp. 111–47 and 197–201; English trans., pp. 93–124 and 166–69.

1868b "Vorwort zu der Buchausgabe der Aufsätze 'Deutsche Kunst und deutsche Politik'" (Foreword to the publication of the essays "German Art and German Politics"), 16 March 1868; published with 1867a; *SS* 16.92–93.

1868c "Zur Widmung der zweiten Auflage von 'Oper und Drama' (An Constantin Frantz)" (Dedication of the second edition of *Opera and Drama* to Constantin Frantz), 26 April 1868; published Leipzig 1869; *GS* 8.195–99; *PW* 2.3–7.

1868d "Inhaltsverzeichnis einer ursprünglich geplanten Ausgabe der Schriften und Dichtungen in sechs Bänden" (List of contents of an edition of writings and poems originally planned in six volumes), 1868[?]; manuscript.

1868e "Anordnung der Gesammtausgabe meiner Schriften" (Arrangement for a complete edition of my writings), 26 April 1868. In *Das Braune Buch* (1865g), pp. 156–58; English trans., pp. 131–33.

1868f "Meine Erinnerungen an Ludwig Schnorr von Carolsfeld" (My recollections of Ludwig Schnorr von Carolsfeld), completed 3 May 1868. In *Neue Zeitschrift für Musik*, 12 June 1868; *GS* 8.177–94; *PW* 4.225–43.

1868g "Censuren III: Eine Erinnerung an Rossini" (A memoir of Rossini), completed 7 December 1868. In Augsburg *Allgemeine Zeitung*, 17 December 1868; *GS* 8.220–25; *PW* 4.269–74.

1869a "Censuren V: Aufklärungen über das Judenthum in der Musik. (An Frau Marie Muchanoff, geborene Gräfin Nesselrode.)" (Some explanations concerning "Judaism in Music"), January 1869; published Leipzig 1869; *GS* 8.238–60; *PW* 3.77–78 and 101–22.

1869b *Herr Eduard Devrient und sein Styl*, written 10–15 February 1869; published under the pseudonym "Wilhelm Drach," Munich 1869; republished as "Censuren IV: Eduard Devrient. 'Meine Erinnerungen an Felix Mendelssohn-Bartholdy'" in *GS* 8.226–38; *PW* 4.275–88.

1869c "Erklärung in den 'Signalen für die musikalische Welt,'" *Signale für die musikalische Welt*, 23 January 1869; *SS* 16.49.

1869d "Fragment eines Aufsatzes über Hector Berlioz" (Fragment of an essay on Hector Berlioz), after 11 March 1869; *Entwürfe, Gedanken, Fragmente aus nachgelassenen Papieren zusammengestellt*, pp. 77–78; *SS* 12.312.

1869e "Erklärung in den 'Signalen für die musikalische Welt.'" In *Signale für die musikalische Welt*, 19 March 1869; *SS* 16.49.

1869f "Erklärung im 'Berner Bund.'" In *Berner Bund*, 16 September 1869; *SS* 16.48 (where it is incorrectly dated 1866).

1869g "Das Münchener Hoftheater. (Zur Berichtigung.)" (The Munich Court Theater: by way of a correction). In Augsburg *Allgemeine Zeitung*, 16 September 1869; *SS* 12.304–8.

1869h *Über das Dirigiren* (On conducting), begun 31 October 1869; published Leipzig 1869; *GS* 8.261–337; *PW* 4.289–364.

1869i "Warum ich den zahllosen Angriffen auf mich und meine Kunstansichten nichts erwidere" (Why I do not reply to the countless attacks on me and my artistic views); *Entwürfe, Gedanken, Fragmente aus nachgelassenen Papieren zusammengestellt*, pp. 89–93; *SS* 12.309–11.

1869j "Zur Walküre (I. Siegmunds Liebesgesang; 2. Der Ritt der Walküren; 3. Wotans Abschied und Feuerzauber)," program notes for concert in Munich on 11 December 1869; *SS* 16.171–72.

1869k "Gedanken über die Bedeutung der deutschen Kunst für das Ausland" (Thoughts on the significance of German art for foreign countries), 1869[?]; *Entwürfe, Gedanken, Fragmente aus nachgelassenen Papieren zusammengestellt*, pp. 81–85; *SS* 12.314–16.

1870a "Erklärung in den 'Signalen für die musikalische Welt.'" In *Signale für die musikalische Welt*, 20 June 1870; *SS* 16.50.

1870b Draft of an unpublished reply to the Augsburg *Allgemeine Zeitung*, after 26 June 1870.

1870c "Beethoven und die deutsche Nation" (Beethoven and the German nation), between 3 and 19 July 1870. In *Das Braune Buch* (1865g), pp. 210–11; English trans., pp. 176–77.

1870d *Beethoven*, 20 July—11 September 1870; published Leipzig 1870; *GS* 9.61–126; *PW* 5.57–126.

1870e "Ein nicht veröffentlichter Schluß der Schrift 'Beethoven'" (An unpublished ending to the *Beethoven* essay), 11 September 1870. In *Musikalisches Wochenblatt*, 1906; *SS* 16.108–10.

1870f "Zum Journalismus" (On journalism), 21 September 1870. In *Das Braune Buch* (1865g), p. 214; English trans., pp. 179–80.

1870g "Vorwort zu 'Mein Leben'" (Foreword to *Mein Leben*), November[?] 1870; *ML*, ix.

1870h "Offener Brief an Dr. phil. Friedrich Stade" (Open letter to Dr. Friedrich Stade), letter of 31 December 1870. In *Musikalisches Wochenblatt*, 13 January 1871; *SS* 16.103–8.

1871a *Über die Bestimmung der Oper* (On the destiny of opera), lecture written March–April 1871 and delivered to the Berlin Academy of Arts on 28 April 1871; published Leipzig 1871; *GS* 9.127–56; *PW* 5.127–55.

1871b "Rede anläßlich des Banketts im Hôtel de Rome in Berlin" (Speech on the occasion of a banquet in the Hotel de Rome in Berlin on 29 April 1871), 24 April 1871; manuscript.

1871c "Ansprache an das Orchester in der Singakademie" (Address to the orchestra at the Singakademie on 30 April 1871), April 1871; manuscript.

1871d "Über die Aufführung des Bühnenfestspieles: 'Der Ring des Nibelungen' und Memorandum über Aufführung des 'Ring' im markgräflichen Opernhaus Bayreuth" (On the performance of the stage festival drama *Der Ring des Nibelungen* and memorandum on performance of the *Ring* in Margraves' Opera House, Bayreuth), April 1871; manuscript.

1871e "Ankündigung der Festspiele" (Announcement of the festival), 12 May 1871. In *Bayreuther Blätter* 9 (1886): 6; *SS* 16.131–32.

1871f "Aufforderung zur Erwerbung von Patronatsscheinen" (Invitation to acquire patrons' certificates), 18 May 1871; *SS* 16.132–33.

1871g "Inhaltsverzeichnis aller 9 Bände der Gesammelten Schriften und Dichtungen" (Table of contents of all nine volumes of collected writings and poems), 1871; manuscript.

1871h "Vorwort zur Gesammtherausgabe" (Foreword to complete edition), dated 22 May 1871; *GS* 1.iii–vii; *PW* 1.xv–xviii.

1871i "Inhaltsverzeichnis des 1. Bandes der Gesammelten Schriften und Dichtungen" (Table of contents of vol. 1 of collected writings and poems), 1871; manuscript.

1871j "Einleitung" (Introduction to vol. 1 of collected writings), 1871; *GS* 1.1–3; *PW* 7.1–3.

1871k "'Das Liebesverbot.' Bericht über eine erste Opernaufführung" (*Das Liebesverbot*: account of a first operatic performance), 1871[?]; *GS* 1.20–31; *PW* 7.5–18; see also *ML*, 111–18.

1871l "Bericht über die Heimbringung der sterblichen Überreste Karl Maria von Weber's aus London nach Dresden. Aus meinen Lebenserinnerungen ausgezogen" (Report on the bringing home of Carl Maria von Weber's mortal remains from London to Dresden: from my memoirs), 1871[?]; *GS* 2.41–46; *PW* 7.229–34; see also *ML*, 296–99.

1871m "Ein deutscher Musiker in Paris. Novellen und Aufsätze. (1840 und 1841.)" (A German musician in Paris: short stories and essays), 1871; *GS* 1.90 and 193; *PW* 7.20 and 150.

1871n "Einleitung" (Introduction to vol. 2 of collected writings), 1871; *GS* 2.1–2; *PW* 7.223–26.

1871o "Bericht über die Aufführung der neunten Symphonie von Beethoven im Jahre 1846 in Dresden (aus meinen Lebenserinnerungen ausgezogen) nebst Programm dazu" (Report on the performance of Beethoven's ninth symphony in Dresden in 1846 [from my memoirs], together with program for same), 1871[?]; *GS* 2.50–56; *PW* 7.239–46; see also *ML*, 328–33.

1871p "Einleitung zum dritten und vierten Bande" (Introduction to vols. 3 and 4 of collected writings), *GS* 3.1–7; *PW* 1.23–29.

1871q "Erinnerungen an Auber" (Reminiscences of Auber), completed 31 October 1871. In *Musikalisches Wochenblatt*, 10, 17, 24 November 1871; *GS* 9.42–60; *PW* 5.35–55.

1871r "Brief an einen italienischen Freund über die Aufführung des 'Lohengrin' in Bologna" (Letter to an Italian friend concerning the performance of *Lohengrin* in Bologna), letter of 7 November 1871; *GS* 9.287–91; *PW* 5.285–88.

1871s "Erklärung in den 'Signalen für die musikalische Welt.'" In *Signale für die musikalische Welt*, 12 November 1871; *SS* 16.50–51.

1871t "Bericht an den Deutschen Wagner-Verein über die Umstände und Schicksale, welche die Ausführung des Bühnenfestspieles 'Der Ring des Nibelungen' begleiteten" (Report to the German Wagner Society of the circumstances and vicissitudes that attended the realization of the stage festival drama *Der Ring des Nibelungen*), completed 7 December 1871; published Leipzig 1872; *GS* 6.257–72 and 9.311–22; *PW* 3.255–73 and 5.309–19.

1871u "Ein später fortgelassener Schluß des Berichtes an den deutschen Wagner-Verein" (A conclusion later discarded from the report to the German Wagner Society), 7 December 1871; *SS* 16.110–11.

1871v "Rede, gehalten in Mannheim am 20. Dezember 1871" (Speech held in Mannheim on 20 December 1871), privately printed.

1872a "Eine Mitteilung an die deutschen Wagner-Vereine" (A communication to the German Wagner Societies), 1 January 1872. In *Musikalisches Wochenblatt*, 1872; *SS* 16.134–40.

1872b "Patronatschein" (Patron's certificate), 1 February 1872; manuscript and printed versions.

1872c "Ankündigung für den 22. Mai 1872" (Announcement for 22 May 1872), 1 February 1872. In *Bayreuther Blätter* 9 (1886): 9; *SS* 16.141–42.

1872d "Ankündigung der Aufführung der Neunten Symphonie für den 22. Mai 1872" (Announcement of performance of Ninth Symphony for 22 May 1872), 16 March 1872. In *Bayreuther Blätter* 9 (1886): 10; *SS* 16.142–43.

1872e "An die Patrone" (To the patrons), 16 March 1872; manuscript.

1872f "Zirkular an die Patrone über ihre Anwesenheit bei der Grundsteinlegung" (Circular to the patrons concerning their presence at the foundation stone–laying ceremony), April 1872; *Bayreuther Blätter* 9 (1886): 10–11; *SS* 16.143–44.

1872g "Instruction," 1872[?]; manuscript.

1872h "Erinnerungen an Spontini" (Reminiscences of Spontini), 1872; *GS* 5.86–104; *PW* 3.127–43; see also 1851c.

1872i "Einleitung zum fünften und sechsten Bande" (Introduction to vols. 5 and 6 of collected writings), 1872; *GS* 5.1–4; *PW* 3.1–4.

1872j "Censuren. Vorbericht" (Reviews: preliminary report), *Musikalisches Wochenblatt*, 19 April 1872; *GS* 8.200–205; *PW* 4.247–52.

1872k "Rede zur Grundsteinlegung" (Speech on the laying of the foundation stone), completed on 21 April and delivered on 22 May 1872; published Bayreuth 1872; *GS* 9.326–30; *PW* 5.324–28.

1872l "Dank an die Bürger von Bayreuth nach der Grundsteinlegung am 22. Mai 1872" (Letter of thanks to the townspeople of Bayreuth following the laying of the foundation stone on 22 May 1872), 24 May 1872. In *Bayreuther Blätter* 9 (1886): 12–13; *SS* 16.144–45.

1872m "Bruchstück einer Danksagung" (Fragment of an expression of thanks), May 1872. In *Bayreuther Blätter* 9 (1886): 13; *SS* 16.145–46.

1872n "Erklärung in der 'Augsburger Allgemeinen Zeitung' über die Oper 'Theodor Körner' von Wendelin Weißheimer: Berichtigung" (Declaration in the Augsburg *Allgemeine Zeitung* concerning Wendelin Weißheimer's opera *Theodor Körner*: correction). In *Allgemeine Zeitung*, 1 June 1872; *SS* 16.51–52.

1872o "Erklärung in der 'Augsburger Allgemeinen Zeitung' über die Oper 'Theodor Körner' von Wendelin Weißheimer: In Sachen Herrn Weißheimers" (Declaration in the Augsburg *Allgemeine Zeitung* concerning Wendelin Weißheimer's opera *Theodor Körner*: in Herr Weißheimer's cause). In *Allgemeine Zeitung*, 10 June 1872; *SS* 16.52.

1872p "An Friedrich Nietzsche, ordentl. Professor der klassischen Philologie an der Universität Basel" (Letter to Friedrich Nietzsche, professor of classical philology at Basel University), letter of 12 June 1872. In *Norddeutsche Allgemeine Zeitung*, 23 June 1872; *GS* 9.295–302; *PW* 5.292–98.

1872q "Berichtigung" (Correction), 29 July 1872. In *Musikalisches Wochenblatt*, 9 August 1872; *SS* 16.52–54.

1872r *Über Schauspieler und Sänger* (On actors and singers), completed 14 September 1872; published Leipzig 1872; *GS* 9.157–230; *PW* 5.157–228.

1872s "Schreiben an den Bürgermeister von Bologna" (Letter to the mayor of Bologna), 1 October 1872. In *Musikalisches Wochenblatt*, 11 October 1872; *GS* 9.291–94; *PW* 5.289–91.

1872t "Über die Benennung 'Musikdrama'" (On the term *Music Drama*), 26 October 1872. In *Musikalisches Wochenblatt*, 8 November 1872; *GS* 9.302–8; *PW* 5.299–304.

1872u "Brief über das Schauspielerwesen an einen Schauspieler" (Letter to an actor on acting), letter of 9 November 1872. In *Almanach der Bühnengenossenschaft*, 1873; *GS* 9.258–64; *PW* 5.257–62.

1872v "Unter Gott sucht sich der Mensch" (Man seeks himself in God), 1872; *Entwürfe, Gedanken, Fragmente aus nachgelassenen Papieren zusammengestellt*, p. 114; *SS* 12.338; *PW* 8.392.

1872w "Ein Einblick in das heutige deutsche Opernwesen" (A glance at the operatic stage in Germany today), December 1872—January 1873. In *Musikalisches Wochenblatt*, 3, 10, 17 January 1873; *GS* 9.264–87; *PW* 5.263–84.

1873a "Zwei Reden gehalten anläßlich eines Banketts auf der Brühlschen Terrasse in Dresden am 14. Januar 1873" (Two speeches held at a banquet on the Brühlsche Terrasse in Dresden on 14 January 1873); manuscript.

1873b "Einleitung zu einer Vorlesung der 'Götterdämmerung' vor einem ausgewählten Zuhörerkreise in Berlin" (Introduction to a reading of *Götterdämmerung* before a select audience in Berlin), 17 January 1873. In *Musikalisches Wochenblatt*, 7 March 1873; *GS* 9.308–10; *PW* 5.305–6.

1873c "An den Vorstand des Wagner-Vereins Berlin" (To the committee of the Berlin Wagner Society), 18 March 1873; *SS* 16.111–14.

1873d "Berichtigung im 'Musikalischen Wochenblatt': Protest" (Correction in *Musikalisches Wochenblatt*: protest), *Musikalisches Wochenblatt*, 25 March 1873; *SS* 16.54.

1873e "Zum Vortrag der neunten Symphonie Beethoven's" (On performing Beethoven's Ninth Symphony). In *Musikalisches Wochenblatt*, 4, 11 April 1873; *GS* 9.231–57; *PW* 5.229–53.

1873f "Zu: was ist deutsch?" (On "What is German?"), April 1873. In *Das Braune Buch* (1865g), p. 232; English trans., p. 194.

1873g "Das Bühnenfestspielhaus zu Bayreuth. Nebst einem Berichte über die Grundsteinlegung desselben" (The festival theater in Bayreuth, with a report on the laying of the foundation stone of the same), 22 May 1872 and 1 May 1873; Leipzig 1873; *GS* 9.322–44; *PW* 5.320–40; see also 1872k.

1873h "An die Patrone der Bühnenfestspiele in Bayreuth" (To the patrons of the Bayreuth Festival), letter of 30 August 1873; privately printed; *SS* 12.317–23.

1873i "An die Patrone der Bühnenfestspiele in Bayreuth" (To the patrons of the Bayreuth Festival), letter of 15 September 1873. In *Bayreuther Blätter* 9 (1886): 18; *SS* 16.146–47.

1873j *Gesammelte Schriften und Dichtungen* (Collected writings and poems), vols. 7, 8, 9, published (without introductory matter) Leipzig 1873; *GS* 7, 8, 9; *PW* 2, 3, 4, 5.

1874a "Notgedrungene Erklärung" (Necessary declaration), 16 February 1874. In *Bayreuther Blätter* 9 (1886): 21–22; *SS* 12.323–24.

1874b "Über eine Opernaufführung in Leipzig. Brief an den Herausgeber des 'Musikalischen Wochenblattes'" (On an opera performance in Leipzig: letter to the editor of the *Musikalisches Wochenblatt*), letter of 28 December 1874. In *Musikalisches Wochenblatt*, January 1875; *GS* 10.1–10; *PW* 6.1–11.

1875a "Einladungsschreiben an die Sänger für Proben und Aufführungen des Bühnenfestspiels 'Der Ring des Nibelungen'" (Invitation to the singers for rehearsals and performances of the stage festival drama *Der Ring des Nibelungen*), letter of 14/15 January 1875. In *Bayreuther Blätter* 9 (1886): 22–24; *SS* 16.147–50.

1875b "An die Orchester-Mitglieder" (To members of the orchestra), January 1875. In *Bayreuther Blätter* 9 (1886): 24–25; *SS* 16.150–52.

1875c "Zur Götterdämmerung: I. Vorspiel; II. Hagens Wacht; III. Siegfrieds Tod; IV. Schluß des letzten Aktes" (On *Götterdämmerung*: I. prelude; II. Hagen's Watch; III. Siegfried's Death; IV. end of the final act), program notes for concert in Vienna on 1 March 1875; *SS* 16.173–75.

1875d "Die 'Presse' zu den 'Proben'" (The "press" on "rehearsals"), 1875. In *Bayreuther Blätter* 9 (1886): 26; *SS* 12.324.

1875e "Ankündigung der Festspiele für 1876" (Announcement of the festival for 1876), letter of 28 August 1875. In *Bayreuther Blätter* 9 (1886): 26–27; *SS* 16.153–54.

1875f "Über Bewerbungen zu den Festspielen" (On applications for the festival), 4 October 1875. In *Musikalisches Wochenblatt*, 8 October 1875; *SS* 16.154–55.

1875g "An die Künstler" (To the artists), letter of 1 November 1875. In *Bayreuther Blätter* 9 (1886): 28; *SS* 16.155–56.

1876a "Austeilung der Rollen" (Distribution of roles), 1876; manuscript.

1876b "Voranschlag der 'Entschädigungen'" (Estimate of "compensation"), 1876; manuscript.

1876c "Skizzierung der Proben und Aufführungen 1876" (Draft schedule of rehearsals and performances 1876), 1876; manuscript.

1876d "An die Orchestermitglieder (Einladung)" (To the members of the orchestra [Invitation]), 6 April 1876. In *Bayreuther Blätter* 9 (1886): 29; *SS* 16.156–57.

1876e "An die Sänger (Einladung)" (To the singers [invitation]), 9 April 1876. In *Bayreuther Blätter* 9 (1886): 29–30; *SS* 16.157–58.

1876f "Für die Patrone" (For the patrons), 18 April 1876; *Bayreuther Blätter* 9 (1886): 30; *SS* 16.159.

1876g "An die Ehrenpatrone" (To the patrons of honor), 22 May 1876; manuscript.

1876h "Verzeichnis der Ehrenpatrone und Freikarten-Empfänger" (List of patrons of honor and those in receipt of complimentary tickets), 1876; manuscript.

1876i "Circular, die 'Costümproben auf der beleuchteten Bühne' betreffend" (Circular relating to dress rehearsals on the lit stage), 22 July 1876; manuscript.

1876j "Anordnung der Proben zu den Aufführungen des Bühnenfestspieles 'Der Ring des Nibelungen' in Bayreuth im Jahre 1876" (Timetable of rehearsals for the performances of the stage festival drama *Der Ring des Nibelungen* in Bayreuth in 1876), 1876. Privately printed, Bayreuth 1876.

1876k "Über den Gebrauch des Textbuches" (On the use of the libretto), 1876. In *Bayreuther Blätter* 9 (1886): 32; *SS* 16.160.

1876l "Über den Hervorruf (Zum ersten Festspiel)" (On curtain calls [for the first festival]), 1876. In *Bayreuther Blätter* 9 (1886): 32; *SS* 16.160.

1876m "Für das Orchester" (For the orchestra), 1876. In Glasenapp 5.287; *SS* 16.161.

1876n "Letzte Bitte an meine lieben Genossen. Letzter Wunsch (Zum ersten Festspiel)" (Final entreaty to my dear associates. Final request [for the first festival]), 13 August 1876. In Glasenapp 5.287; *SS* 16.160.

1876o "Ansprache nach Schluß der 'Götterdämmerung'" (Address at the end of *Götterdämmerung*), of uncertain authenticity, 17 August 1876. In Glasenapp 5.294; *SS* 16.161.

1876p "Abschiedswort an die Künstler (Zum ersten Festspiel)" (Parting words to the artists [for the first festival]), of uncertain authenticity, 30 August 1876. In Glasenapp 5.294; *SS* 16.161.

1876q "Gedanken über Zahlung des Defizits und Fortführung der Festspiele" (Thoughts on paying off the deficit and continuing the festival), 1876; manuscript.

1876r "An die geehrten Patrone der Bühnenfestspiele von 1876" (To the honored patrons of the 1876 Festival), 11 October 1876. In *Bayreuther Blätter* 9 (1886): 33; *SS* 12.324–25 (wrongly dated).

1877a "An die geehrten Vorstände der Richard Wagner-Vereine" (To the honored presidents of the Richard Wagner Societies), 1 January 1877. Privately printed; *GS* 10.11–15; *PW* 6.15–18.

1877b "Entwürfe und Notizen zu den Programmen der (1.) 6 Konzerte in London" (Sketches and notes for the programs of the [first] six concerts in London), 7–19 May 1877; manuscript.

1877c "Entwurf veröffentlicht mit den Statuten des Patronatvereines" (Prospectus published with the statutes of the Patrons' Society), 15 September 1877; *GS* 10.16–18; *PW* 6.19–21.

1877d "Ansprache an die Abgesandten des Bayreuther Patronats" (Address to the delegates of the Bayreuth Patronage Scheme), 15 September 1877. In *Richard Wagner-Jahrbuch*, ed. Joseph Kürschner (Stuttgart [privately published], 1886), pp. 200–208; *SS* 12.326–34.

1877e "Aufforderung zur Anmeldung für die Stilbildungsschule" (Letter inviting applications for the Bayreuth School of Stylistic Training), 1 October 1877; manuscript.

1877f "Ankündigung der Aufführung des 'Parsifal'" (Announcement of the performance of *Parsifal*), 8 December 1877. In *Bayreuther Blätter* 1 (1878): 15–17; *SS* 12.334–36.

1878a "Zur Einführung. (Bayreuther Blätter, Erstes Stück.)" (By way of an introduction [*Bayreuther Blätter*, first issue]), 8 January 1878. In *Bayreuther Blätter* 1 (1878): 1–5; *GS* 10.19–24; *PW* 6.22–27.

1878b "An die geehrten Vorstände der noch bestehenden lokalen Wagner-Vereine" (To the honored presidents of such local Wagner societies as still exist), 15 January 1878. In *Bayreuther Blätter* 1 (1878): 23–24; *SS* 16.162–63.

1878c "Modern," completed 12 March 1878. In *Bayreuther Blätter* 1 (1878): 59–63; *GS* 10.54–60; *PW* 6.41–49.

1878d "Erläuterung des 'Siegfried-Idylls' für S. M. den König" (Note on the *Siegfried Idyll* for His Majesty the King), April[?] 1878; manuscript.

1878e "Publikum und Popularität" (Public and popularity), completed 1 May 1878. In *Bayreuther Blätter* 1 (1878): 85–92, 171–77, 213–22; *GS* 10.61–90; *PW* 6.51–81.

1878f "Das Publikum in Zeit und Raum" (The public in time and space), completed 11 October 1878. In *Bayreuther Blätter* 1 (1878): 277–85; *GS* 10.91–102; *PW* 6.83–94.

1878g "Ein Rückblick auf die Bühnenfestspiele des Jahres 1876" (A retrospective glance at the 1876 festival), completed 19 December 1878. In *Bayreuther Blätter* 1 (1878): 341–51; *GS* 10.103–17; *PW* 6.95–109.

1879a "Ein Wort zur Einführung der Arbeit Hans von Wolzogen's 'Über Verrottung und Errettung der deutschen Sprache'" (A word of introduction to Hans von Wolzogen's study *On the Decay and Rescue of the German Tongue*), February 1878. In *Bayreuther Blätter* 2 (1879): 33; *GS* 10.24–26; *PW* 6.28–29.

1879b "Wollen wir hoffen?" (Shall we hope?), completed 13 May 1879. In *Bayreuther Blätter* 2 (1879): 121–35; *GS* 10.118–36; *PW* 6.111–30.

1879c "Über das Dichten und Komponiren" (On poetry and composition), completed 28 June 1878. In *Bayreuther Blätter* 2 (1879): 185–96; *GS* 10.137–51; *PW* 6.131–47.

1879d "Erklärung an die Mitglieder des Patronatvereines" (Declaration to the members of the Patrons' Society), 15 July 1879. Privately printed; *GS* 10.26; *PW* 6.30.

1879e "Über das Opern-Dichten und Komponiren im Besonderen" (On opera poetry and composition in particular), completed 29 July 1879. In *Bayreuther Blätter* 2 (1879): 249–66; *GS* 10.152–75; *PW* 6.149–72.

1879f "Über die Anwendung der Musik auf das Drama" (On the application of music to the drama), October 1879. In *Bayreuther Blätter* 2 (1879): 313–25; *GS* 10.176–93; *PW* 6.173–91.

1879g "Offenes Schreiben an Herrn Ernst von Weber, Verfasser der Schrift: 'Die Folterkammern der Wissenschaft'" (Open letter to Herr Ernst von

Weber, author of the essay *The Torture Chambers of Science*), completed 9 October 1879. In *Bayreuther Blätter* 2 (1879): 299–310; *GS* 10.194–210; *PW* 6.193–210.

1879h "Zur Einführung in das Jahr 1880" (By way of an introduction to 1880), December 1879. In *Bayreuther Blätter* 3 (1880): 1–5; *GS* 10.27–32; *PW* 6.31–35.

1880a "Religion und Kunst" (Religion and art), completed 19 July 1880. In *Bayreuther Blätter* 3 (1880): 269–300; *GS* 10.211–53; *PW* 6.211–52.

1880b "'Was nützt diese Erkenntniß?' Ein Nachtrag zu: Religion und Kunst" (What use is this knowledge? A supplement to "Religion and Art"), completed 25 October 1880. In *Bayreuther Blätter* 3 (1880): 333–41; *GS* 10.253–63; *PW* 6.253–63.

1880c "*Parsifal*: Vorspiel" (*Parsifal*: prelude), written for concert performance of prelude on 12 November 1880; *EGF*, 106–7; *SS* 12.349 (wrongly dated).

1880d "Zur Mittheilung an die geehrten Patrone der Bühnenfestspiele in Bayreuth" (Communication to the honored patrons of the festival in Bayreuth), letter of 1 December 1880. Privately printed; *GS* 10.32–33; *PW* 6.36–37.

1880e "Gedanken zur Fortführung der Festspiele" (Thoughts on continuing the festival), 1880; manuscript.

1881a "Ausführungen zu 'Religion und Kunst'. 1. 'Erkenne dich selbst'" (Continuations of "Religion and Art." 1. "Know Yourself"), February 1881. In *Bayreuther Blätter* 4 (1881): 33–41; *GS* 10.263–74; *PW* 6.264–74.

1881b "Zur Einführung der Arbeit des Grafen Gobineau 'Ein Urtheil über die jetzige Weltlage'" (Introduction to Count Gobineau's study *A Critique of the Present State of the World*), 25 April 1881. In *Bayreuther Blätter* 4 (1881): 121–23; *GS* 10.33–35; *PW* 6.38–40.

1881c "Ausführungen zu 'Religion und Kunst.' 2. 'Heldenthum und Christenthum'" (Continuations of "Religion and Art." 2. "Heroism and Christianity"), completed 4 September 1881. In *Bayreuther Blätter* 4 (1881): 249–58; *GS* 10.275–85; *PW* 6.275–84.

1882a "Einladung der Sänger" (Invitation to the singers), 1882; manuscript.

1882b "Austheilung der Partien" (Distribution of roles), 1882; manuscript.

1882c "Begleitschreiben zur 'Austheilung' der Partien sowie Plan der Proben und Aufführungen" (Letter accompanying distribution of roles and timetable of rehearsals and performances), 1882; manuscript.

1882d "Proben-Plan. Entwurf" (Rehearsal schedule. Draft), 1882; manuscript.

1882e "Brief an H. v. Wolzogen" (Letter to Hans von Wolzogen), letter of 13 March 1882. In *Bayreuther Blätter* 5 (1882): 97–100; *GS* 10.286–90; *PW* 6.285–91.

1882f "Über das Männliche u. Weibliche in Kultur u. Kunst" (On the masculine and feminine in culture and art), written between 21 March and 9 April 1882. In *Das Braune Buch* (1865g), pp. 245–46; English trans., p. 204.

1882g "Offenes Schreiben an Herrn Friedrich Schön in Worms" (Open letter to Herr Friedrich Schön in Worms), letter of 16 June 1882. In *Bayreuther Blätter* 5 (1882): 193–97; *GS* 10.291–96; *PW* 6.293–300.

1882h "Rede, gehalten in Wahnfried anläßlich der Hochzeit Blandine von Bülows" (Speech held in Wahnfried on the occasion of Blandine von Bülow's wedding), 25 August 1882. The accuracy of the transcription has been called into question; manuscript.

1882i "Danksagung an die Bayreuther Bürgerschaft" (Letter of thanks to the Bayreuth citizenry), letter of 3 September 1882. In *Bayreuther Tagblatt*, 5 September 1882; *SS* 16.164.

1882j "Das Bühnenweihfestspiel in Bayreuth 1882" (The stage consecration festival in Bayreuth in 1882), completed 1 November 1882. In *Bayreuther Blätter* 5 (1882): 321–29; *GS* 10.297–308; *PW* 6.301–12.

1882k "Bericht über die Wiederaufführung eines Jugendwerkes. An den Herausgeber des 'Musikalischen Wochenblattes'" (Report on the revival of an early work. To the editor of the *Musikalisches Wochenblatt*), letter of 31 December 1882. In *Musikalisches Wochenblatt*, 11 January 1883; *GS* 10.309–15; *PW* 6.313–21.

1883a "Brief an H. v. Stein" (Letter to Heinrich von Stein), letter of 31 January 1883. In *Bayreuther Blätter* 6 (1883): 5–10; *GS* 10.316–23; *PW* 6.323–32.

1883b "Über das Weibliche im Menschlichen" (On the womanly in the human), written 11–13 February 1883; *Entwürfe, Gedanken, Fragmente aus nachgelassenen Papieren zusammengestellt*, pp. 125–29; *SS* 12.343–45; *PW* 6.333–37.

Texts of Uncertain Date

a "Aphorismen über Farben und Töne, über Modulation und über Styl" (Aphorisms on colors and sounds, on modulation and style); *Entwürfe, Gedanken, Fragmente aus nachgelassenen Papieren zusammengestellt*, pp. 73–74; *SS* 12.280–81; *PW* 8.375.

b "Beethoven und Schumann: Gegenüberstellungen" (Beethoven and Schumann: comparisons); *Entwürfe, Gedanken, Fragmente aus nachgelassenen Papieren zusammengestellt*, p. 86; *SS* 12.281; *PW* 8.380.

c "Goethe und Schiller: Gegenüberstellungen"; *Entwürfe, Gedanken, Fragmente aus nachgelassenen Papieren zusammengestellt*, p. 86; *SS* 12.281; *PW* 8.380.

d "Bemerkungen über den letzten Satz von Beethovens VII. Symphonie" (Remarks on the final movement of Beethoven's Seventh Symphony); manuscript.

e "Bemerkungen, die Kostüme und Attribute der Götter im 'Ring' und der Hauptgestalten des 'Tristan' betreffend" (Remarks concerning the costumes and attributes of the gods in the *Ring* and of the principal characters in *Tristan*); manuscript.

f "Metaphysik. Kunst und Religion. Moral. Christenthum" (Metaphysics. Art and Religion. Morality. Christianity); *Entwürfe, Gedanken, Fragmente aus nachgelassenen Papieren zusammengestellt*, pp. 110–21; *SS* 12.337–42; *PW* 8.390–95.

g "Programmatische Erläuterung zu Beethovens IX. Symphonie" (Programnote on Beethoven's Ninth Symphony); manuscript.

NOTES

Preface

1. The conventions that I have adopted when referring to the texts from which I have quoted are spelled out in the Bibliographical Note.

2. It is claimed that more has been written about Wagner than about any other historical figure, with the possible exceptions of Jesus Christ and Napoleon. Whether or not there is any truth in this claim, the library at the Wagner Archives in Bayreuth is every bit as impressive as that of a faculty library, even though it does not contain a systematic collection of all the *articles* that have been written on Wagner. By the date of the composer's death in 1883, his bibliography already ran to no fewer than 10,180 titles (Oesterlein 1882–95).

3. I shall return to this point in a study currently in preparation, *Analyse musicale et sémiologie*; but see also *Tétralogies (Wagner, Boulez, Chéreau)*, especially the conclusion (Nattiez 1983).

4. To date, only seven volumes of the *Sämtliche Briefe* (Collected letters) have appeared, although there are numerous collections for the later period.

5. I have already had recourse to this idea both in my earlier work on Pierre Boulez's and Patrice Chéreau's conception of the *Ring* (Nattiez 1983, 260–65) and in my semiological study of the way in which musical analyses are *constructed* (Nattiez 1985, 218).

Introduction to Part One

1. The reader familiar with the plot of the *Ring* may omit this section and go straight to the second part of the introduction, on p. 8.

2. On this new dating of *The Wibelungs*, see *WWV*, 329.

3. See, for example, the chronological table published by Werner Breig and Hartmut Fladt in their collection of documents relating to the genesis of the *Ring* (Breig and Fladt 1976, 12–13).

Chapter One

1. The last of these texts will be examined in detail at the beginning of Part Two of the present study.

2. See also Wagner's letter to Theodor Uhlig of 16 September 1849; *SB* 3.121–27.

3. It was originally intended as an article, as is clear from Wagner's letter to Uhlig of 20 September 1850; *SB* 3.423–30.

4. "I confess that if one of my pupils were to bring me such an example of counterpoint, I would beg him not to produce anything as awful in the future" (Schumann 1837, 323).

5. In August 1850 Wagner jotted down two musical sketches for the opening scene of *Siegfrieds Tod*, the first of which ends with the words "Brünnhilde zu erwecken" in the love duet between Siegfried and Brünnhilde. These sketches al-

ready contain a number of themes that were to be taken up into the future tetralogy, although Wagner appears to have forgotten about them by the time he came to write *Götterdämmerung*. They have been examined more recently by a number of writers on Wagner: Newman 1933, 2.159–61; 1949, 435–37; Westernhagen 1962, 38–54; 1963; and 1973, 13–15; Bailey 1968; and Breig 1973.

6. See *Über die Bestimmung der Oper* (On the destiny of opera [1871a]) and *Über Schauspieler und Sänger* (On actors and singers [1872r]).

7. It is on this expression that Frank Glass (1981) has based his conception of the relationship between poetry and music in Wagner's works, a conception that has led him to modify earlier "plots." I shall return to the problems raised by Glass's interpretation in the second part of this study.

8. As Jean Molino has pointed out to me, Wagner is no doubt referring here to the neo-Spinozistic conception of conscious necessity, which allows the notions of determinism and liberty to be reconciled. In *The Art-Work of the Future*, necessity is what drives "the solitary figure of Shakespeare" (1849m, *GS* 3.110) or the common people to act: "The folk is the embodiment of all those *who feel a common need*" (ibid., 3.48). Wagnerian necessity is an irresistible force that drives mankind to action and creativity: "True *need* alone is the mother of all invention" (ibid., 3.129).

9. *SB* 3.467.

10. Ibid., 3.477.

11. Emphasis added.

Chapter Two

1. On the concept of necessity, see chap. 1, n. 8. Wagner appears to use the words *Noth*, *Nothwendigkeit*, and *Bedürfniß* interchangeably (see *GS* 3.43, 44, 48, 49), although he prefers the term *Noth* in the final pages of *The Art-Work of the Future* and in the *Wieland* prose draft quoted on pp. 43–45. The word *Noth* has a far wider semantic field in German than its cognate form in English, *need*, since it includes such concepts as poverty, distress, affliction, and necessity. In his translation of the *Wieland* draft, Ashton Ellis uses the term *want*.

2. Emphasis added.

3. The first sketch is unpublished in German (Nationalarchiv der Richard-Wagner-Stiftung, Bayreuth, B I a 4). A French translation of it was included in the French edition of the present volume. The second draft appears in *GS* 3.178–206 and is placed, significantly, immediately after *The Art-Work of the Future*, just as the résumé of the fictional narrative comes at the end of the theoretical text.

4. *SB* 3.251.

5. The subject seems to have remained close to Wagner's heart: on two occasions he suggested that Liszt might set the libretto to music (see his letters to Carolyne Sayn-Wittgenstein of 9 October 1850 and to Liszt of 25 November 1850), but on both occasions Liszt refused (18 October 1850 and 3 January 1851). Some eighteen months later, however, we find Wagner asking Liszt to show the draft to Berlioz (8 September 1852), while even later he tried to interest both August Röckel and Wendelin Weißheimer in the poem (see *WWV*, 343).

Toward the end of his life, he toyed with the idea of basing an overture on the subject (*CT*, 10–16 February 1874; see also *WWV*, 520).

6. *SB* 3.330. It is striking that within the same breath Wagner moves from one abandoned artistic project to its theoretical counterpart, a counterpart that is its exact equivalent from the point of view of its content.

7. See chap. 1, n. 5.

Chapter Three

1. Emphasis added.
2. Emphasis added.
3. Emphasis added.
4. Emphasis added.
5. Emphasis added.
6. Emphasis added.
7. Emphasis added.
8. *SB* 4.151.
9. Emphasis added.
10. Emphasis added.
11. Emphasis added.
12. Emphasis added.
13. Emphasis added.
14. Emphasis added.
15. Emphasis added.
16. Emphasis added.
17. Wagner is entirely consistent on this point. In Act III of *Götterdämmerung*, for example, Siegfried bids the Rhine daughters: "So singet, was ihr wißt" (Then sing of what you know [*GS* 6.237]). (It may be added that this line is already present in the forerunner of *Götterdämmerung*: *Siegfrieds Tod*, written in 1848 [*GS* 2.213].)
18. Emphasis added.
19. Emphasis added.
20. Emphasis added.
21. Emphasis added.
22. Emphasis added.
23. *Richard Wagner an Mathilde Maier (1862–1878)*, ed. Hans Scholz (Leipzig: Theodor Weicher, 1930), p. 53.
24. In this passage Wagner is replying to the criticism leveled at him by Eduard Hanslick, namely, that his art is lacking in form. Typically, Wagner does not mention Hanslick by name. Equally typically, he pours fun on Mime and Hanslick by availing himself of identical images.
25. Emphasis added.
26. Emphasis added.
27. Emphasis added.
28. Wagner also alludes to the assimilation of Siegfried and the sun in *Opera and Drama* (1851a, *GS* 4.38).

29. *SB* 4.95.
30. Emphasis added.
31. *SB* 6.63.
32. Ibid., 6.68.
33. Emphases added.
34. *SB* 3.467; emphasis added.
35. Emphasis added.
36. When Shaw writes in his commentary on Act III of *Siegfried*, "The only faith which any reasonable disciple can gain from The Ring is not in love, but in life itself" (1898, 76), he is certainly guilty of playing fast and loose with the text.
37. Boulez's remarks relate to Act I, scene 1 of *Götterdämmerung*, where he draws a contrast between Gutrune's musical style and that of Hagen and Gunther. Boulez was quoting from memory and no doubt alluding to Porges' account of the 1876 rehearsals, the quoted excerpt from which relates, in fact, to Act II. Boulez returns to this point a few pages later: "When Gutrune reappears in the scene of Siegfried's return, we have a recurrence of that parody of *opéra comique* à la Auber that Wagner had indulged in ironically in the opening act, a style that is light, brilliant, and superficial" (1980, 38).
38. Wagner's relations with French grand opera deserve to be treated in a separate, systematic study. His Wahnfried library contained copies of the scores of several of Auber's works, including *La Muette de Portici*, *Fra Diavolo*, *Lestocq*, *Le Maçon*, and *Le Cheval de bronze*. Certain aspects of this last-named work are not unrelated to Wagner's operatic world: one of its heroes flies through the air on a winged stallion and is forbidden to reply to a certain question. In *La Muette de Portici*, Masaniello bears a certain similarity to Rienzi, inasmuch as both are repudiated by the common people in whom they place their trust; and, following her brother's death, Fenella throws herself into an erupting Mount Vesuvius. The tale of *Tristan* is retold at the beginning of Auber's and Scribe's *Le Philtre* (1831), the libretto of which was later used by Donizetti in his *L'elisir d'amore* (1832).
39. Emphasis added.
40. Emphasis added.
41. In other words, *Siegfrieds Tod*, the precursor of *Götterdämmerung*.
42. *SB* 4.426.

Chapter Four

1. Nothing will be lost by noting here that this model also governs the relationship between Siegfried and Brünnhilde. Brünnhilde embodies the actual will of Wotan, who willed the "invention" of Siegfried at the end of *Das Rheingold*; having rescued the pregnant Sieglinde, Brünnhilde is thus Siegfried's spiritual mother. Hence the following diagram:

Brünnhilde
↓
Siegfried + Brünnhilde
↓
The art-work
of the future

2. Emphasis added.

3. The published text (*SS* 11.125–35) is a conflation of these two sketches and this is the one rendered into English by the present translator in *Wagner* 6 (1985): 99–107. A critical edition of both sketches is in preparation and will be published in vol. 31 of the *Sämtliche Werke*.

4. Emphasis added.

5. The joins between the work of art and the theoretical discourse are so airtight with Wagner that they have perplexed the editors of the *Wagner Werk-Verzeichnis*. Wagner's plans to write a three-act drama on the life of Achilles were elaborated in Dresden in early 1849 and again in Paris and Zurich between February and June 1850. They are attested by different documents, including several letters of the period (see *WWV*, 340). The first catalog of Wagner's works (Kastner 1878) includes the drama under no. 81. The manuscript of a "sketch" of *Achilleus* has disappeared, but a series of jottings was published posthumously under the title "Bruchstücke eines Dramas 'Achilleus'" (Fragments of an "Achilles" drama) in vol. 12 of Wagner's complete writings (*SS* 12.283). However, the editors of the *Wagner Werk-Verzeichnis* hesitate to see a sketch in these "fragments": "It is impossible to decide whether the published notes on the classical Achilles have anything to do with the plan to write a stage play or whether they are connected, rather, with Wagner's theoretical writings of 1849–50" (*WWV*, 340). It is evidently the third of the four paragraphs that causes the problems: "Man is God perfected. The eternal gods are only the elements that create Man. Creation finds its ultimate conclusion in Man. Achilles is higher and more perfect than the elemental Thetis." Achilles is mentioned briefly in *Opera and Drama* (1851a, *GS* 4.88). It is difficult to decide the status of these four paragraphs. Perhaps more extensive notes have been lost. But it is so self-evident that Wagner's philosophical or pseudo-philosophical ideas are illustrated by his works for the theater that there is nothing abnormal about a theoretical note turning up in the middle of three other paragraphs that, for their part, seem very much concerned with a dramatic project. After all, the sketch for *Jesus of Nazareth* (*SS* 11.273–324) begins with a résumé of the five-act scenario before developing into a commentary, often philosophical in nature, that is freely based on Feuerbach.

6. Emphasis added.

7. It is not clear which article Cosima is referring to here.

Chapter Five

1. Between 1834 and 1840 Wagner wrote no fewer than twenty-two essays (see the Catalog of Wagner's Writings in the present volume).

2. The reader will recall my earlier interpretation of the prelude to *Das Rheingold*.

3. Emphasis added.

4. *SB* 2.358–59.

5. Ibid., 2.437.

6. Ibid., 2.511–15.

7. Ibid., 2.536.

8. See Stein 1960 for examples of the relationship between words and music

in Wagner's stage works. The following is a résumé of those of his conclusions that bear on the present discussion.

9. Emphasis added.

10. Emphasis added.

11. See Gliese 1919; Huch 1933, 1.63, 124, 134, 160, 165, and 2.54, 74, 81, 194, 195, 237; Eliade 1962, 124–27; Busst 1967; Molino 1980, 1981; Gusdorf 1982, 372–73; 1984, 220–37.

12. "In the interest of the progress of culture, one partner must be superior to the other in a heterogeneous way. The man must be superior to the woman in respect to his physical strength and courage, while woman must be superior to the man in respect to her natural talent for mastering his desire for her. . . . Feminine traits are called weaknesses. People joke about them; fools ridicule them; but reasonable persons see very well that those traits are just the tools for the management of men, and for the use of men for female designs. . . . The inclination to dominate is the real goal, while public gratification, by which the field of their charm is extended, is only the means for providing the effect for that inclination" (Kant 1798, 216–19).

13. In the present study I have reserved the term *androgyny* for the *symbolic* representation of the union of the two sexes; the term *hermaphrodite* is used to describe a real *biological* being with attributes of both sexes. The distinction is similar to the one drawn between the phallus and the penis. I shall return to the ambiguity of the term *androgyne* in the Epilogue to the present volume.

14. Baader's writings are not available in English and are quoted here from Franz von Baader, *Über Liebe, Ehe und Kunst: Aus den Schriften, Briefen und Tagebüchern* (Munich: Kösel-Verlag, 1953). See also Susini 1942a, 1942b, and 1967; and Faivre 1977, 1981, 1983, 1986.

15. The reader will recognize an allusion to the famous quarrel among supporters of the New Criticism surrounding Barthes' *Sur Racine* (1963), a quarrel sparked by Raymond Picard's 1965 pamphlet and further fueled by Barthes' rejoinder the following year.

16. See Molino 1981, 27 (cited on p. 42).

17. D'Indy was in error when he claimed that these terms existed in Beethoven's day.

18. Plato, *The Symposium*, trans. W. Hamilton (Harmondsworth: Penguin Books, 1951), pp. 59–62.

19. *SB* 3.105.

20. Ibid., 3.161.

21. But see ibid., 3.371.

22. Ibid., 3.427.

23. See ibid., 3.163–64.

24. *Röckel-Briefe*, p. 16.

25. Emphasis added.

26. Emphasis added.

27. *SB* 6.63.

28. Ibid., 6.64.

29. Ibid.

30. Ibid., 6.65.

31. Ibid., 6.68.
32. Ibid., 6.67.
33. Ibid., 6.68.

Chapter Six

1. Emphasis added.
2. The first of these quotations, italicized by Wagner, concludes part 2 of *Opera and Drama*; the second is again italicized by Wagner, and the third appears in bold type at the end of chap. 6 of part 1.
3. Glass continues: "The poet . . . had to make sure that the verses he wrote had been compressed and refined enough to be capable of emotional expression in music" (1981, 55). A glance at the passages quoted in his résumé of *Opera and Drama* (1851a, *GS* 4.195–96) makes it difficult to accept so radical an assertion as his insistence that "poetry may provide the seed that fertilizes music and leads to its growth, but the fruit that grows after fertilization forms and ripens by music's own individual powers" (Glass 1981, 45). It seems that Glass is interpreting the 1851 text retrospectively from the standpoint of Wagner's later writings.
4. Emphasis added.
5. Emphasis added.
6. *SB* 4.285.
7. Ibid., 4.289.
8. Ibid., 4.459.
9. Ibid., 4.71–72.
10. *Liszt-Briefe*, p. 492.
11. Ibid., pp. 425–26.
12. Emphasis added.
13. It is worth recalling that with the exception of two musical sketches for *Siegfrieds Tod*, both of which date from August 1850, Wagner did not write a note of music between the completion of *Lohengrin* on 28 April 1848 and the start of *Das Rheingold* on 1 November 1853—an unprecedented compositional silence in Wagner's career. Instead, he devoted his energies to libretti and operatic projects, including *Friedrich I.* (October 1846 and winter 1848–49), *Jesus of Nazareth* (early 1849), *Achilleus* (early 1849 and February–June 1850), *Wieland the Smith* (December 1849–March 1850), *Siegfrieds Tod* (October 1848 and November–December 1852), and the whole of the *Ring* (October 1851–December 1852).
14. Péladan is of particular interest in the present context as the author of *L'Androgyne* (Paris: E. Dentu, 1891); on the subject of Péladan's androgyny, see Busst 1967, 42–57.
15. Brangäne's identity as a double is underscored by the fact that the two women not only share the same vocal tessitura but, often enough, launch their respective vocal lines on the very same note.
16. In his commentary on *Tristan und Isolde*, Jean Matter (1977, 268) suggests that in Isolde's final lines, "breath, as a preeminently masculine symbol," joins with "the sea, the waves, the flood tide, as a preeminently feminine symbol"—which, if true, would serve only to reinforce the work's androgynous interpretation.

17. "Whether the decline of our culture could be reversed by means of a violent expulsion of that foreign element which is the cause of its fragmentation is something I cannot judge, since it would require forces whose existence is unknown to me" (1869a, *GS* 8.259).

18. "The influence exerted on the French musician by the Italian school . . . is admirable to the extent that music is understandable to him only through song: to be able to play an instrument well means being able to sing well on it. And this excellent orchestra [that of the Paris Conservatoire] *sang* this symphony. But in order to be able to 'sing' it, the *right tempo* first has to be discovered" (1869h, *GS* 8.273).

19. Emphasis added.

20. Emphasis added.

21. Emphasis added.

22. I am immensely grateful to my Italian colleague Francesco Giannatasio for drawing my attention to the fact that this gondolier's song, to words by Tasso, was published in 1842 in a collection of popular melodies. I intend to show elsewhere the true nature of the analogies between this melody and Wagner's cor anglais solo. It will also be noted, however, that this same melody is used by Liszt as the principal theme of his symphonic poem *Tasso: lamento e trionfo* of 1849–54. Liszt points out its Venetian origins in his preface to the score. It is difficult to establish whether Wagner—who plagiarized Liszt on other occasions—took his inspiration from the melody that he heard in Venice or, rather, from his friend's symphonic poem. What matters here, however, is the philosophical and metaphysical use to which he put it.

23. The word *mächtig* (mighty) in the published text (*GS* 9.68) appears to be a misprint for *nächtig* (nocturnal).

24. Emphasis added.

25. These same words were set to music by Liszt at the end of his *Faust* Symphony. It is worth mentioning parenthetically that Wagner's own *Faust* Overture, written in 1839–40 and revised in 1855 (*WWV*, 59), was described by its composer as "Faust in solitude" in letters to Liszt and Uhlig of November 1852. In his own letter of 7 October 1852, Liszt had observed that he "would have welcomed a second central section, or a calmer and more agreeably colored treatment of the existing central section:" in other words, what was missing was a delicate, tender melodic phrase corresponding with the character of Gretchen. Wagner replied on 9 November: "You caught me out quite splendidly when I tried to delude myself into thinking I had written an 'Overture to Faust'! You were quite right to feel that something was missing here—and what was missing is womankind! . . . I wanted to write a complete Faust Symphony. . . . Only in the second movement was Gretchen—the woman—to be introduced" (*Liszt-Briefe*, 241–48). For his own part, Liszt had begun sketching his *Faust* Symphony in the mid-1840s, not completing the work until the summer of 1854. Three years later he added the final chorus with Goethe's apostrophe of the Eternal Feminine. The opening movement is a portrait of Faust, the second a portrait of Gretchen, and the third a portrait of Mephistopheles, with motifs borrowed from the two previous movements. In chap. 4 of his recent study, *Music as Cultural Practice* (1990), Lawrence Kramer offers a brilliant demonstration of the patriarchal conception of

the relationship between the sexes and of the way in which that conception is reflected in Liszt's musical treatment of the characters. It is nonetheless permissible, from our present perspective, to extend Kramer's analysis. Kramer pays unduly scant attention to the fact that in the third movement Faust's themes are ironically transformed to become Mephistopheles' motifs. In this way Liszt suggests that, just as Alberich and Wotan are complementary opposites, the Devil is Faust's dark shadow. Thus he demonstrates that "coincidentia oppositorum" of which Mircea Eliade speaks in his well-known study, with its significant title, *Méphistophélès et l'androgyne* (1962, chap. 2). Eliade points out the parallelism between the union of good and evil on the one hand and male and female on the other. For him, the theme of androgyny, in both myth and religion, is another manifestation of the magian attempt to achieve a union of opposites. The same may be true of the *Faust* Symphony. After all, the Chorus Mysticus is based on Gretchen's theme and even if this theme is penetrated by Faust's characteristic motif (C–E–G♯), it is still worth asking whether—notwithstanding the fact that it is the male element, embodied in the tenor soloist and male-voice chorus, which predominates here—we are not in fact assisting at the *ultima unio* of male and female, much as the thematic analogies invite us to assist at the union of good and evil.

26. The chronology established by Colli and Montinari (Nietzsche 1988, 15.10–18) also mentions visits on 22 May, 21–22 September, and late October to early November 1869, but Cosima Wagner's diaries are silent on the subject. See also the chronology in Hollinrake (1982, 206–11).

27. Emphasis added.

28. Emphasis added.

29. *Nietzsche-Briefe*, 2.2.493–94.

30. I am grateful to my colleague Georges Leroux for drawing my attention to these conceptual links between Wagner and Nietzsche.

Chapter Seven

1. Emphasis added.

2. Nationalarchiv der Richard-Wagner-Stiftung der Stadt Bayreuth B II d 25.

3. Wagner read Gobineau's *Essai sur l'inégalité des races humaines* in February 1881, by which time he had already completed the poem of *Parsifal*. He emerged from this exposure to Gobineau's brand of racism with his own ideas reinforced and with a new vocabulary of invective to color his final essays.

4. There is no doubt that Wagner was influenced by Darwin in his reflections on race. He read *On the Origin of Species* (see *CT*, 29 June, 21 July 1872, 10 February 1873) and later began *The Descent of Man* (*CT*, 28 September, 23, 24 October 1877). In between he wrote the text of *Parsifal*, working first on the prose draft (25[?] January–23 February 1877) and then on the poem (14 March–19 April 1877). From Darwin he took over the idea that only the strongest can bring about salvation (*CT*, 24 January 1878).

5. Emphasis added.

6. It is not impossible that Wagner found the idea of an androgynous Christ in August Friedrich Gfrörer's *Geschichte des Urchristentums*: "R. tells me a lot more

about what he is reading in Gfrörer's book, which he finds of endless interest; among other things, for example, the definition of the Trinity made shortly before Christ's birth—God the Father, masculine; the Holy Ghost, feminine; the Redeemer as the world stemming from them; will, idea, and world, the world emerging from the division of the sexes" (*CT*, 6 January 1875).

7. Emphasis added.

8. One could object, of course, that Lohengrin is Parsifal's son, but *Lohengrin* was written thirty years earlier.

9. On the distinction between the androgyny of totality and that of ambiguity, see Eliade 1962, 121–27, repeated in Molino 1981.

Chapter Eight

1. *SB* 2.155–60.

2. See, for example, her diary entry of 24 January 1869: "Unfortunately R.'s passion for silk materials brought forth a remark from me which I should have done better to leave unsaid, for it produced a bit of ill feeling."

3. *Freunde und Zeitgenossen*, p. 292.

4. *Wille-Briefe*, p. 130.

5. *Familienbriefe*, pp. 276–77; emphasis added.

6. Emphasis added.

7. *Nietzsche-Briefe*, 2.2.117–18.

8. It is this resemblance that is important here, not the fact that Wagner uses the word *father* in referring to Ludwig Geyer. If he had described Geyer as his father from an early age, it was to explain the role that Geyer played in the family, not necessarily to indicate any blood relationship.

9. For an analogous psychoanalytic explanation of Wagner's androgyny, see Rattner 1986, 780.

10. Other examples of this anxiety deserve to be quoted here: "I opened a recently published book by Janet, *Hystérie et idées fixes*, with a pounding heart and put it aside again with my pulse calmed. He has no inkling of the key" (letter of 10 March 1898; Freud 1985, 302); "No other work of mine has been so completely my own" (letter of 28 May 1899; ibid., 353); "I am swamped with psychological literature—it has a depressing effect on me, giving me a feeling that I know nothing when I had thought I had grasped something new" (letter of 9 June 1899; ibid., 354); "Next month I shall start the last, philosophical chapter, which I dread and for which I shall again have to do more reading" (letter of 20 August 1899; ibid., 367).

11. On Freud's other intellectual and philosophical antecedents, see Whyte (1960), Ellenberger (1970, esp. chap. 4), and Assoun (1976).

12. Later in the same letter of 4 January 1898, Freud blames his own latent bisexuality for the resistance that he feels toward the idea of bisexuality ("which, after all, we hold responsible for the inclination to repression"; Freud 1985, 292). Always blame the unconscious!

13. Emphasis added.

14. The case in question is that of Dora, which Freud refused to publish immediately for reasons of professional ethics. It appeared in 1905 under the title

"Fragment of an Analysis of a Case of Hysteria" and was republished in vol. 7 of the standard edition of Freud's writings (1905b).

15. For an account of the later relationship between Freud and Fließ and the question of priority, see Jones 1953–57, 1.346–47; Anzieu 1959, 2.715; and Sulloway 1979.

16. It may be added that in his letter of 4 January 1898 and in *Three Essays on the Theory of Sexuality*, Freud attributes repression of homosexual desire to the man rather than to the woman.

17. Emphasis added.

18. Emphasis added.

19. See lines 774–75, 874–77, 966–67, 984–85, 990, 995, 1001, 1015, 1017, and 1021.

20. See, for example, Rank (1911, chap. 8) and Rattner (1986, 782).

21. Quoted from Pourtalès 1932, 210.

22. The concept of latent homosexuality allows one to say whatever one wants and seems to justify the most scandalous travesty of the facts. Philippe Olivier, for example, interprets this same dream of 1 January 1882 as follows: "During his sleep, [Wagner] saw himself firmly bound to the King's feet. The latter had been spanking him at length with an impressively large, half-molten candle" (1979, 46). This might be called quoting from memory. Olivier has the effrontery to claim that "this fantasy needs no further comment." It comes as no surprise, therefore, to find that Tristan is twice said to have been King Marke's lover (ibid., 48–49), that "there is nothing understated" about the relationship between Tristan and Kurwenal (ibid., 49), and that Melot "seeks revenge for having failed to retain the knight's favors" (ibid., 52). If Tristan refuses to speak to Isolde, it is "because the presence of this woman would destroy the harmony of an exclusively male society" (ibid., 47).

23. See, in particular, Groddeck 1933.

24. "In the depths of the female soul the desire for vengeance is kindled, and it smolders until the end. It is women's fate to have a false ideal of the hero, not to understand what the hero has that is better—his little boy's aspect—and not to accept it openly. Woman always reawakens the hero in man; yet she reproaches him for the fact that the hero dies in her and through her, and that he has to die at all" (1927, 224).

25. It is worth pursuing Groddeck's critique here to show the curious idea he has of feminine psychology in accounting for human nature: "For the woman, the hero is the man who thinks, who foresees, who takes care, and in whom one can place one's trust" (ibid., 226).

26. Emphasis added.

27. See his 1935 study, *Richard Wagners Kampf gegen seelische Fremdherrschaft* (Wagner's struggle against foreign intellectual domination), from which Hartmut Zelinsky (1983, 234) reproduces a compromising section.

28. This appears to be confirmed by the later publication of Cosima Wagner's diaries: on 24 December 1869 she reports that conversation turned on Geyer's stage play, *The Massacre of the Innocents*.

29. The caricature published here appeared in the Viennese satirical magazine *Der Floh* in 1879. Wagner is shown as a Jew surrounded by Jewish children, one

of whom offers him the latest quotations on the stock exchange. On the piano is a bust of Offenbach, with a score of *La belle Hélène* lying open on the music rack. Newman (1933–47, 2.612–13) includes a list of all the writings that allude to Wagner's alleged Jewishness: all are later than 1869.

30. Unfortunately, Katz is ill-served by his American translator, who has rendered this crucial sentence as "the name Geyer, unlike Adler, scarcely ever appears among Jews" (p. 121). The German original ("der Name Geyer, im Gegensatz zu Adler, kommt bei Juden überhaupt nicht vor," p. 195) is unequivocal.

Chapter Nine

1. On this point, see Caïn 1982.
2. In his 1976 staging of the *Ring* at Bayreuth, Patrice Chéreau dressed Loge in a cloak of white voile, which, in this particular production, clearly symbolized the character's femininity.
3. On the relationship between *persona* and anima, see Jung's 1933 essay "The Relations between the Ego and the Unconscious."
4. Emphasis added.
5. "They have in fact constructed a winged dragon, which makes R. ask why, if it could fly, it has laboriously to crawl up, and anyway it is nowhere called a dragon but a *serpent*" (*CT*, 3 April 1878).
6. It may be pointed out at this juncture that in the Epilogue to the present volume an additional layer of interpretation will be added to this quotation, thereby giving it greater depth.
7. *SB* 4.43.
8. This also explains Jung's fascination with alchemy and the fact that Jungians dabble in areas such as esotericism and astrology, which are located at the very edge of objective knowledge.
9. Emphasis added.

Chapter Ten

1. I am particularly grateful to Señora Maria da Paz Gueria Guerreira for drawing my attention to this text, buried away as it was in an out-of-the-way journal in a language unfamiliar to me, and for having provided a translation of it.
2. Emphasis added.
3. Emphasis added.
4. Emphasis added.
5. For a critique, see Nattiez 1973.
6. Lévi-Strauss believes that he can identify "a sort of fugue, 'unpicked and laid out flat'" in *Boléro*, a piece in which the different parts, arranged in linear sequence, are placed end to end rather than overlapping (Lévi-Strauss 1971, 660).
7. A great deal has been written about the status of women in psychoanalysis. One should also consider the role of "loose change" that Lévi-Strauss attributes to women both in *The Elementary Structures of Kinship* and in *Tristes tropiques*.
8. Emphasis added.

9. Emphasis added.
10. Emphases added.
11. Emphasis added.
12. It remains to explain the problem raised by Lévi-Strauss. The Renunciation of Love motif does not occur at semantically coherent moments. It is the question itself that needs to be questioned, just as we need to remind ourselves—as Carolyn Abbate does in the context of this very motif (1991)—that the leitmotifs (which Wagner himself described as *Grundthemen*) have a morphological and syntactic function that may make the unequivocal labels attached to them in the past seem positively irrelevant.
13. Emphasis added.
14. Emphasis added.

Chapter Eleven

1. This passage from Balzac is quoted without a source reference in Busst 1967, 12.
2. In an interview with *Marie-Claire*, no. 340, December 1980.
3. In a performance given with Lewis Furey in Montreal at the end of the 1970s.
4. In a television interview with Radio-Canada, Montreal, February 1989.
5. See also Scheler 1929 and Cassirer 1946, both of whom are quoted in Ellenberger 1970, 177.
6. Quoted in Ellenberger 1970, 175.
7. See ibid., pp. 173–74 and 177–78.
8. As far as music is concerned, it is worth drawing attention here to the similarity between my own point of view and that advanced by Leonard B. Meyer in his latest book, *Music and Style* (1989), which ends with a chapter devoted to the contemporary period and headed, significantly, "The Persistence of Romanticism."

Chapter Twelve

1. Emphases added.
2. Emphasis added.
3. The tripartite theory of semiology was proposed by Jean Molino (1975) and distinguishes three levels in human works and praxis: the neutral or immanent level, the poietic level (the process of production), and the esthesic level (the process of perception). For a detailed presentation of this thesis, see Nattiez 1987, chap. 1.
4. There is all the greater need to place the term "university criticism" in quotation marks since the supporters of the New Criticism and, latterly, of deconstruction are not the last to aspire to and, in certain cases, obtain university posts from the École Pratique des Hautes (!) Études to the Collège de France—the highest positions in the hierarchy of the French university system.
5. Emphasis added.
6. Emphasis added.

7. Emphasis added.

8. Emphasis added.

9. By his own admission, Serres has learned more about fetishism from Hergé's *L'Oreille cassée* "than from Freud, Marx, and Auguste Comte. . . . Hergé wrote extraordinary treatises without realizing it" (*Le Monde*, 6/7 March 1983, p. 18). With the same degree of seriousness, he claims at the end of his study of *Sarrasine* that Balzac "wrote a critique of judgment" (Serres 1987, 150). Well, why not indeed?

10. See Derrida's admonitions of those writers who do not cite his own texts (Derrida 1988, 35).

11. Emphasis added.

12. Emphasis added.

13. A systematic critical study of Derrida would draw attention to and examine the fate he metes out to androgyny in his different texts. In *Glas*, for example, he has the following to say on the subject of the union of the sexes in the context of Hegel's *Philosophy of Right*: "Each is like an absorbing part, both a fraction and the whole; this general structure recuts them both, passes *like* [emphasis added] bisexuality in each of them. . . . The *Aufhebung* of sexual differences is, manifests, and expresses *stricto sensu Aufhebung* itself and in general" (Derrida 1974, 155–56). Expressed more clearly, Hegelian *Aufhebung* or supersession is synonymous with androgynous union: "Everything must happen as though the partners were of the same sex, as though both were bisexual or asexual. *Aufhebung* has taken place" (ibid., 176). Here we see the perils of Derridian speculations on the meaning of "difference" (see also ibid., 328–29).

14. This lecture, "Real Presences," was published in French, English, and German under the general title *Le Sens du sens* (Steiner 1988) and should not be confused with the study published in English the following year under the same title, *Real Presences*. The same ideas are developed here, but in a less concise manner.

15. Note the singular.

16. Examples abound. To quote only one: it is still a source of bemusement to me that readers could reasonably (but reason has been banished by deconstruction) take seriously Derrida's exegetical jokes about the word *entre* (between) and its homonym *antre* (cave or antrum) in Mallarmé's *Mimique*: "The hymen enters into the antre. *Entre* can just as easily be written with an *a* . . . . Indeed, are the two *(e)(a)ntres* not really the same?" (Derrida 1970, 212). One would have no difficulty ridiculing Derrida by quoting the whimsical uses to which he puts his dictionary and the free-and-easy manner with which he refers to Mallarmé's various texts. I leave the reader, armed only with that redoubtable and much-despised commodity, good sense, to judge for him- or herself.

17. Also worth mentioning here are the hesitations of Houdebine, who, in *Positions*, has difficulty in reconciling his sympathy for deconstruction with the need that he nonetheless feels to base any discussion of Freud and Marx on concepts that "elude metaphysical reduction" à la Derrida (Derrida 1972, 98).

18. "The carnival and saturnalia of poststructuralism, of Barthes' *jouissance*, or Lacan's and Derrida's endless punning and willful etymologizing, will pass as have so many other rhetorics of reading. 'Fashion,' as Leopardi reassures us, 'is

the mother of death'" (Steiner 1988, 81). "The bark and ironies of deconstruction resound in the night but the caravan of 'good sense' passes on" (ibid., 82).

19. For the problems that concern us here, see Molino 1989.

Epilogue

1. *SB* 6.67–68.

2. Here is an additional source for a plurality of interpretations, a fine example of which is Cosima's Gobineau-inspired interpretation of *Tristan und Isolde*. It is no doubt for this reason that in "*Zukunftsmusik*," Wagner is able to advance a new, music-based explanation of the forbidden question in *Lohengrin*.

3. *Röckel-Briefe*, pp. 65–72.

4. Ibid., p. 68.

5. The poietic relevance of my analysis of the role of androgyny in terms of the relationship between poetry and music is induced from a paradigmatic analysis of the Zurich essays. (On the concept of inductive poiesis, see Nattiez 1987, 87–88.) To the extent that I have used this paradigmatic technique in the first part of this study (a technique that I owe to Lévi-Strauss, through the intermediary of Ruwet [1966, 101]), while criticizing Lévi-Strauss's structuralism in the third part, it seems to me necessary to spell out the essential point on which our approaches differ. In the case of Lévi-Strauss, the primary aim of the paradigmatic technique is to isolate main lines corresponding to universal semantic categories such as raw, cooked, boiled, and roasted. My own aim, by contrast, was to construct a level of meaning in the *Ring* that remains unique to the tetralogy and to Wagner's thinking, since I believe it is necessary to establish this before undertaking any kind of broader interpretation. It is for this reason that I have not attempted to consider the model of original unity—lost unity—rediscovered unity extrapolated from Wagner's theoretical writings against the wider background of universal structures of religious or mythic thinking, but, rather, to use that model to advance a new and specific interpretation of the tetralogy itself. It is this that makes my own conception of symbolic exegesis tautegorical rather than allegorical, in the sense understood by Schelling.

6. *SB* 6.72.

7. "The statement is significant in so far as it is the first indication of Wagner's recognition of the dramatic authenticity of opera, but it is an isolated remark, not developed until a later period" (Stein 1960, 14).

8. For a concrete example, see his analysis of Verlaine's poem "Walcourt" in Molino and Gardes-Tamine 1988, chap. 4, and, for its theoretical implications, ibid., 172.

9. "R. works on the 'Holy Grail March,' he has cut out the crystal bells; he looked again at my father's 'Die Glocken von Strassburg' to make sure he has not committed a *plagiarism*" (*CT*, 28 December 1877). Again: "My father's indescribable modesty about his works touches R. very much—he says with splendid high spirits that he has himself 'stolen' so much from the symphonic poems" (*CT*, 27 August 1878).

10. Like Sarotte (1976, xiii, xiv), one can also distinguish homoeroticism, a mode of behavior that reveals a desire for physical contact without engaging in the act itself, an attitude for which he proposes the term *homogenitalism*.

11. "When Bohr was awarded the Danish Order of the Elephant in 1947, he had to supervise the design of a coat of arms for placement in the church of the Fredericksborg Castle at Hillerød. The device presents the idea of complementarity: above the central insignia, the legend says 'Contraria sunt complementa,' and at the center Bohr placed the symbol for Yin and Yang" (Holton 1970, 1020).

12. For an example of seriation in literature, see n. 8; for the concept of seriation in musicology, see Nattiez 1985.

13. This seems to show that in musical analysis it is impossible to get by without explicit criteria of segmentation of musical units by reference to which the features in question are considered.

14. *Wesendonck-Briefe*, p. 260.

15. It is important to establish the source of Tittel's information. He must have taken it either from Friedrich Eckstein's book on Bruckner (1923, 33), which repeats it without citing a reference, or, directly, from the offprint of Mayrberger's complete analysis (1881c), published by the Bayreuth Patrons' Society and prefaced with a note by Hans von Wolzogen attesting Wagner's "enthusiastic approval." The incomplete publication of this analysis in the *Bayreuther Blätter* (1881b) is devoid of commentary. I am grateful to John Deathridge for drawing my attention to Eckstein's monograph and the Mayrberger offprint, and to Robert Bailey for pointing out the existence of the article in the *Bayreuther Blätter*.

16. This is the nub of the problem, since Wagner's remarks, as reported by Wolzogen, do not make it clear exactly what the object of Wagner's "enthusiastic approval" was. It is doubtful, nonetheless, whether Wolzogen would have reported the Master's approval in such an official publication without the composer's consent. It may also be noted that as early as 1874 Wolzogen himself had proposed an interpretation of *Tristan und Isolde* that is indebted to Plato's concept of androgyny: see "Die Moral des 'Tristan,'" reprinted in Wolzogen 1888.

17. In his technical analysis, Gut relies on Wagner's alleged approval of Mayrberger's analysis to support his thesis that the G♯ is an appoggiatura (Gut 1981, 149), but, in arguing that the chord is based on the subdominant, he seems to forget on the following page that if Wagner accepts this analysis, he must also accept that we are dealing with a chord on the second degree of A, as Mayrberger suggested.

18. Carolyn Abbate reaches the same conclusion, albeit by a different route, when she argues that it is Wotan who has written the *Ring* (Abbate 1991).

REFERENCES

Abbate, Carolyn. 1989a. "Wagner, 'On Modulation,' and *Tristan*." *Cambridge Opera Journal* 1 (1989): 33–58.

———. 1989b. "Opera as Symphony: A Wagnerian Myth." *Analyzing Opera: Verdi and Wagner*, ed. Carolyn Abbate and Roger Parker, pp. 92–124. Berkeley and Los Angeles: University of California Press.

———. 1991. *Unsung Voices: Opera and Musical Narration in the Nineteenth Century*. Princeton: Princeton University Press.

Adorno, Theodor Wiesengrund. 1952. *Versuch über Wagner*. Frankfurt am Main: Suhrkamp. English trans. by Rodney Livingstone, *In Search of Wagner*. London: NLB, 1981.

Altmann, Wilhelm. 1905. *Richard Wagners Briefe nach Zeitfolge und Inhalt: Ein Beitrag zur Lebensgeschichte des Meisters*. Leipzig: Breitkopf und Härtel.

Anzieu, Didier. 1959. *L'Auto-analyse de Freud et la découverte de la psychanalyse*. 2 vols. Paris: Presses Universitaires de France.

Assoun, Pierre-Laurent. 1980. *Freud et Nietzsche*. Paris: Presses Universitaires de France.

Azouvi, Jean. 1977. "Siegfried ou la quête de l'unité." *L'Avant-Scène Opéra*, no. 12 (*Siegfried*), pp. 114–18.

Baader, Franz von. 1822–25. *Fermenta Cognitionis*. Berlin: Reimer.

Bachelard, Gaston. 1960. *Poétique de la rêverie*. Paris: Presses Universitaires de France.

Badinter, Élisabeth. 1986. *L'Un est l'autre*. Paris: Éditions Odile Jacob. English trans. by Barbara Wright, *Man/Woman: The One Is the Other*. London: Collins Harvill, 1989.

Bailey, Robert. 1968. "Wagner's Musical Sketches for *Siegfrieds Tod*." *Studies in Music History: Essays for Oliver Strunk*, pp. 459–94. Princeton: Princeton University Press.

———. 1969. *The Genesis of "Tristan und Isolde" and a Study of Wagner's Sketches and Drafts for the First Act*. Ph.D. dissertation, Princeton University.

———. 1977. "The Structure of the *Ring* and Its Evolution." *19th-Century Music* 1 (1977): 48–61.

———, ed. 1985. *Wagner: Prelude and Transfiguration from "Tristan and Isolde."* New York: Norton.

Ballanche, Pierre-Simon. 1831. *La Vision d'Hébal*. Paris.

Barthes, Roland. 1954. *Michelet*. Paris: Seuil.

———. 1970a. "Masculin, féminin, neutre." *Échanges et Communications: Mélanges offerts à Claude Lévi-Strauss à l'occasion de son soixantième anniversaire*, ed. Jean Pouillon and Pierre Maranda, pp. 893–907. Paris: Mouton.

———. 1970b. *S/Z*. Paris: Seuil. English trans. by Richard Miller. London, 1975.

Baudelaire, Charles. 1861. "Richard Wagner et *Tannhäuser* à Paris." *Oeuvres complètes*, ed. Claude Pichois, pp. 779–815. Paris: Gallimard, 1976.

Béguin, Albert. 1937. *L'âme romantique et le rêve: Essai sur le romantisme allemand et la poésie française*. Marseilles.

Béjart, Maurice. 1979. *Un instant dans la vie d'autrui*. Paris: Flammarion.

Bellour, Raymond, and Cathérine Clément, eds. 1979. *Claude Lévi-Strauss*. Paris: Gallimard.

Bernstein, Leonard. 1976. *The Unanswered Question: Six Talks at Harvard*. Cambridge: Harvard University Press.

Bloom, Peter. 1974. "Communication." *Journal of the American Musicological Society* 27 (1974): 161–62.

Bloomfield, Leonard. 1933. *Language*. New York: H. Holt.

Borchmeyer, Dieter. 1986. "Richard Wagner und Nietzsche." *Richard-Wagner-Handbuch*, ed. Ulrich Müller and Peter Wapnewski, pp. 114–36. Stuttgart: Kröner Verlag. English trans. Cambridge: Harvard University Press, 1992, pp. 327–42.

Boulez, Pierre. 1980. "A partir du présent, le passé." *Histoire d'un "Ring,"* by Pierre Boulez, Patrice Chéreau, Richard Peduzzi, and Jacques Schmidt, pp. 13–36. Paris: Diapason-Laffont.

Brailoiu, Constantin. 1953. "Sur une mélodie russe." In vol. 1 of *Opere*, pp. 305–99. Bucharest: Éditions musicales de l'union des compositeurs de la République socialiste de Roumanie.

Breig, Werner. 1973. *Studien zur Entstehungsgeschichte von Wagners "Ring des Nibelungen."* Ph.D. dissertation, University of Freiberg.

Breig, Werner, and Hartmut Fladt, eds. 1976. *Richard Wagner: Sämtliche Werke*, vol. 29, part 1: *Dokumente zur Entstehungsgeschichte des Bühnenfestspiels Der Ring des Nibelungen*. Mainz: B. Schott's Söhne.

Burghold, Julius, ed. 1980. *Richard Wagner: Der Ring des Nibelungen. Vollständiger Text mit Notentafeln der Leitmotive*. Mainz: B. Schott's Söhne.

Busst, A.J.L. 1967. "The Image of the Androgyne in the Nineteenth Century." *Romantic Mythologies*, ed. I. Fletcher, pp. 1–95. London: Routledge and Kegan Paul.

Caïn, Jacques and Anne Caïn. 1982. "Freud, 'absolument pas musicien . . .' (18.1.1928)." *Psychanalyse et musique*, pp. 91–137. Paris: Les belles lettres.

Carus, Carl Gustav. 1846. *Psyche: Zur Entwicklungsgeschichte der Seele*. Pforzheim: Flammer und Hoffmann.

Cassirer, Ernst. 1946. *The Myth of the State*. New Haven: Yale University Press.

Chailley, Jacques. 1954–55. *Formation et transformation du langage musical*, vol. 1: *Intervalles et échelles*. Paris: Centre de documentation universitaire.

———. 1963. *Tristan et Isolde de Richard Wagner*. 2 vols. Paris: Centre de documentation universitaire.

Comte, Auguste. 1851–54. *Système de politique positive, ou traité de sociologie, instituant la religion de l'humanité*. Paris. English trans. by J. H. Bridges, Frederic Harrison, et al. as *System of Positive Polity*. London: Longman, Green, 1875–77.

Cone, Edward. 1974. *The Composer's Voice*. Berkeley and Los Angeles: University of California Press.

Cooke, Deryck. 1959. *The Language of Music*. Oxford: Oxford University Press.

———. 1979. *I Saw the World End: A Study of Wagner's "Ring."* Oxford: Oxford University Press.

———. N.d. *An Introduction to Wagner's "Der Ring des Nibelungen"* (analysis of the *Ring* on records, accompanying the Decca recording).

Dahlhaus, Carl. 1971. *Richard Wagners Musikdramen*. Velber: Friedrich Verlag. English trans. by Mary Whittall, *Richard Wagner's Music Dramas*. Cambridge: Cambridge University Press. 1979.

———. 1984. "Theoretical Writings and Works." *The New Grove Wagner*, by John Deathridge and Carl Dahlhaus, pp. 68–87 and 111–64. London: Macmillan.

Deathridge, John. 1984. "Life." *The New Grove Wagner*, pp. 1–67.

———. 1988. "The *Ring*: An Introduction." (booklet accompanying James Levine's recording of *Die Walküre*, DGG), pp. 41–48.

De Man, Paul. 1979. *Allegories of Reading*. New Haven: Yale University Press.

Derrida, Jacques. 1966. "La structure, le signe et le jeu dans le discours des sciences humaines." *L'écriture et la différence*, pp. 409–28. Paris: Seuil. English trans. by Alan Bass, *Writing and Difference*. London, 1978.

———. 1967. *De la grammatologie*. Paris: Minuit.

———. 1968. "La différance." *Théorie d'ensemble*, pp. 41–66. Paris: Seuil.

———. 1970. "La double séance." *La dissémination*. pp. 199–317. Paris: Seuil. English trans. by Barbara Johnson. London: Athlone Press, pp. 173–285.

———. 1972. *Positions*. Paris: Minuit.

———. 1974. *Glas*. Paris: Éditions Galilée. All quotations from 1981 ed., 2 vols. Paris: Gonthier.

———. 1988. *Mémoires pour Paul de Man*. Paris: Galilée. English trans. by Cecile Lindsay, Jonathan Culler, and Eduardo Cadava, *Memoirs for Paul de Man*. New York: Columbia University Press, 1986.

Donington, Robert. 1963. *Wagner's "Ring" and Its Symbols*. London: Faber and Faber.

Durand, Gilbert. 1960. *Les structures anthropologiques de l'imaginaire*. Paris: Dunod. All quotations from the 10th ed. of 1983.

———. 1964. *L'imagination symbolique*. Paris: Presses Universitaires de France. Quotations from the 3d ed. of 1976.

Durden-Smith, Jo, and D. Desimone. 1983. *Le sexe et le cerveau*. French trans. by Annick Duchâtel-Bussière. Montréal: La Presse.

Eckstein, Friedrich. 1923. *Erinnerungen an Anton Bruckner*. Vienna: Universal.

Eco, Umberto. 1968. *La struttura assente*. Milano: Bompiani. French trans. by Uccio Esposito-Torrigiani, *La structure absente*. Paris: Mercure de France, 1972.

Einstein, Alfred. 1947. *Music in the Romantic Era*. London: J. M. Dent.

Eliade, Mircea. 1962. *Méphistophélès et l'androgyne*. Paris: Gallimard.

Ellenberger, Henri Frederic. 1970. *The Discovery of the Unconscious: The History and Evolution of Dynamic Psychiatry*. New York: Basic Books.

Engels, Friedrich. 1884. *Der Ursprung der Familie, des Privateigentums und des Staats*. Stuttgart. English trans., *Origin of the Family, Private Property, and State*, vol. 26 of Karl Marx and Frederick Engels, *Collected Works*. London: Lawrence and Wishart, 1990.

Fabre d'Olivet, Antoine. 1815. *La langue hébraïque restituée, et le véritable sens des mots Hébreux rétabli et prouvé par leur analyse radicale*. Paris. English trans. by Nayán Louise Redfield, *The Hebraic Tongue Restored*. New York: G. P. Putnam's Sons, 1921.

———. 1822. *De l'état social de l'homme; ou vues philosophiques sur l'histoire du genre humain*. Paris. English trans. by Nazán Louise Redfield, *Hermeneutic Interpretation of the Social State of Man and of the Destiny of the Adamic Race*. New York: G. P. Putnam's Sons, 1915.

———. 1823. *Baron Byron: Cain, mystère dramatique traduit en vers français par F. d'O.* Paris.

Faivre, Antoine. 1977. "Foi et savoir chez Franz von Baader et dans la gnose moderne." *Les études philosophiques*, no. 1. Paris: Presses Universitaires de France.

———. 1981. "Ténèbre, Éclair et Lumière chez Franz von Baader." *Lumière et cosmos*, pp. 265–306. Paris: Albin Michel, "Cahiers de l'Hermétisme."

———. 1983. "Ame du Monde et Divine Sophia chez Franz von Baader." *Sophia et l'âme du monde*, pp. 243–88. Paris: Albin Michel, "Cahiers de l'Hermétisme."

———. 1986. "Amour et androgynie chez Franz von Baader." *Accès de l'ésotérisme occidental*, pp. 235–326. Paris: Gallimard.

Feuerbach, Ludwig. 1830. *Gedanken über Tod und Unsterblichkeit*. Nuremberg. Quotations from Ludwig Feuerbach in vol. 1 of *Werke in sechs Bänden*, ed. Erich Thies, pp. 77–349. Frankfurt am Main: Suhrkamp, 1975.

———. 1841. *Das Wesen des Christenthums*. Leipzig: Otto Wigand. Quotations from Ludwig Feuerbach in vol. 2 of *Sämmtliche Werke*, ed. Wilhelm Bolin and Friedrich Jodl. Stuttgart, 1903.

———. 1843. *Grundsätze der Philosophie der Zukunft*. Leipzig: Otto Wigand. Quotations from Ludwig Feuerbach in vol. 3 of *Werke in sechs Bänden*, pp. 247–322. English trans. by Manfred H. Vogel, *Principles of the Philosophy of the Future*. Indianapolis: Hackett Publishing Company, 1986.

Fließ, Wilhelm. 1897. *Die Beziehungen zwischen Nase und weiblichen Geschlechtsorganen*. Leipzig and Vienna.

Foucault, Michel. 1969. *L'archéologie du savoir*. Paris: Gallimard. English trans. by A. M. Sheridan Smith, *The Archaeology of Knowledge*. London: Tavistock Publications, 1972.

Freud, Sigmund. 1900. *The Interpretation of Dreams*. Vols. 4 and 5 of *The Standard Edition of the Complete Psychological Works of Sigmund Freud*. London: Hogarth Press, 1955.

———. 1901. *The Psychopathology of Everyday Life*. Vol. 6 of *The Standard Edition of the Complete Psychological Works of Sigmund Freud*. 1960.

———. 1905a. *Three Essays on the Theory of Sexuality*. In vol. 7 of *The Penguin Freud Library*, pp. 31–169. 1977.

———. 1905b. "Fragment of an Analysis of a Case of Hysteria." In vol. 7 of *The Standard Edition of the Complete Psychological Works of Sigmund Freud*, pp. 3–122. 1953.

———. 1910a. "Leonardo da Vinci and a Memory of His Childhood." In vol. 11 of *The Standard Edition of the Complete Psychological Works of Sigmund Freud*, pp. 57–137. 1960.

———. 1910b. "Five Lectures on Psycho-Analysis." In vol. 11 of *The Standard Edition of the Complete Psychological Works of Sigmund Freud*, pp. 57–137. 1957.

———. 1910c. "A Special Type of Choice of Object Made By Men." In vol. 7 of *The Penguin Freud Library*, pp. 227–42. 1977.

———. 1913. "The Disposition to Obsessional Neurosis." In vol. 10 of *The Penguin Freud Library*, pp. 129–44. 1979.

———. 1914. "On the History of the Psycho-Analytic Movement." In vol. 14 of *The Standard Edition of the Complete Psychological Works of Sigmund Freud*, pp. 3–66. 1957.

———. 1919. "A Child Is Being Beaten." In vol. 10 of *The Penguin Freud Library*. pp. 159–93. 1979.

———. 1920. "Beyond the Pleasure Principle." In vol. 18 of *The Standard Edition of the Complete Psychological Works of Sigmund Freud*, pp. 3–64. 1955.

———. 1923. "The Ego and the Id." In vol. 19 of *The Standard Edition of the Complete Psychological Works of Sigmund Freud*, pp. 3–66. 1962.

———. 1927. "The Future of an Illusion." In vol. 21 of *The Standard Edition of the Complete Psychological Works of Sigmund Freud*, pp. 3–56. 1961.

———. 1974. *The Freud-Jung Letters: The Correspondence between Sigmund Freud and C. G. Jung*. Ed. William McGuire. Trans. Ralph Manheim and R.F.C. Hull. Princeton: Princeton University Press.

———. 1985. *The Complete Letters of Sigmund Freud to Wilhelm Fliess, 1887–1904*. Trans. and ed. Jeffrey Moussaieff Masson. Cambridge: Harvard University Press.

Fuchs, Hanns. 1903. *Richard Wagner und die Homosexualität: Unter besonderer Berücksichtigung der sexuellen Anomalien seiner Gestalten*. Berlin.

Gardin, Jean-Claude. 1979. *Une archéologie théorique*. Paris: Hachette.

Geertz, Clifford. 1973. *The Interpretation of Cultures*. New York: Basic Books.

Giese, Fritz. 1919. *Der romantische Charakter*, vol. 1: *Die Entwicklung des Androgynenproblems in der Frühromantik*. Langensalza: Wendt und Klauwell.

Glasenapp, Carl Friedrich. 1905–12. *Das Leben Richard Wagners in sechs Büchern dargestellt*. 4th ed. Leipzig: Breitkopf und Härtel.

Glass, Frank W. 1981. *The Fertilizing Seed: Wagner's Concept of the Poetic Intent*. Ann Arbor: UMI Research Press.

Gregor-Dellin, Martin. 1972. *Wagner-Chronik: Daten zu Leben und Werk*. Munich: Carl Hanser Verlag. 2d ed., Munich: Deutscher Taschenbuchverlag, 1983.

———. 1980. *Richard Wagner: Sein Leben, sein Werk, sein Jahrhundert*. Munich: R. Piper. English trans. by J. Maxwell Brownjohn, *Richard Wagner: His Life, His Work, His Century*. London: William Collins Sons, 1983; all references to the German edition rather than to the incomplete English translation.

Grimm, Jacob and Wilhelm. 1819–22. "Märchen von einem, der auszog das Fürchten zu lernen." *Kinder- und Hausmärchen*. Berlin. Quoted from 10th ed., pp. 13–24. Berlin: Franz Duncker, 1858.

Groddeck, Georg. 1927. "Der Ring." *Die Arche* 3, no. 11 (11 November 1927): 11–31; reprinted in *Psychoanalytische Schriften zur Literatur und Kunst*, ed. Egenolf Roeder von Diersburg. Wiesbaden, 1964. Quoted from the French trans. by Roger Lewinter, *La maladie, l'art et le symbole*, pp. 218–36. Paris: Gallimard, 1969.

Groddeck, Georg. 1933. "Du vivre et du mourir." *La maladie, l'art et le symbole*, pp. 290–309.

Gusdorf, Georges. 1984. *L'homme romantique*. Paris: Payot.

Gut, Serge. 1981. "Encore et toujours: 'L'accord de Tristan.'" *L'Avant-Scène Opéra*, nos. 34 and 35 (*Tristan und Isolde*), pp. 148–51.

Gutman, Robert W. 1968. *Richard Wagner: The Man, His Mind, and His Music*. London: Secker and Warburg.

Hagège, Claude. 1982. *La structure des langues*. Paris: Presses Universitaires de France.

Halévy, Daniel. 1945. *Nietzsche*. Paris: Grasset. Quoted from the 1977 ed., Paris: Librairie Générale Française.

Hanslick, Eduard. 1854. *The Beautiful in Music*. Trans. Gustav Cohen. Indianopolis: Bobbs-Merrill Educational Publishing, 1957.

Hartmann, Carl Robert Eduard von. 1869. *Philosophie des Unbewußten*. Berlin: Franz Duncker. English trans. by W. C. Coupland, *Philosophy of the Unconscious*. London: Kegan Paul, 1931.

Hoffmann, Ernst Theodor Amadeus. 1819–21. *Die Serapions-Brüder*. Ed. Hartmut Steinecke. 4 vols. Frankfurt am Main: Insel, 1983.

Hollinrake, Roger. 1982. *Nietzsche, Wagner, and the Philosophy of Pessimism*. London: George Allen and Unwin.

Holton, Gerald. "The Roots of Complementarity." *Daedalus* 99 (1970): 1015–55.

Huch, Ricarda. 1908. *Die Romantik*. 2 vols. Leipzig.

Jakobson, Roman, and Claude Lévi-Strauss. 1962. "'Les Chats' de Charles Baudelaire." *L'homme* 2 (1962): 5–21.

Jones, Ernest. 1953–57. *Sigmund Freud: Life and Work*. 3 vols. London: Hogarth Press.

Juliard, Jean-Pierre. 1979. "Le Tondichter et l'Androgyne." *Obliques* (special Wagner issue): 57–66.

Jung, Carl Gustav. 1912. *Symbols of Transformation*. Trans. R.F.C. Hull. London: Routledge and Kegan Paul, 1956.

———. 1913. *Psychological Types*. Trans. R.F.C. Hull. London: Routledge and Kegan Paul, 1971.

———. 1922. "On the Relation of Analytical Psychology to the Poetic Art." *The Spirit in Man, Art, and Literature*, trans. R.F.C. Hull, pp. 65–83. London: Routledge and Kegan Paul, 1971.

———. 1930. "Psychology and Literature." *The Spirit in Man, Art, and Literature*, pp. 84–105.

———. 1933. "The Relations between the Ego and the Unconscious." *Two Essays on Analytical Psychology*, trans. R.F.C. Hull, pp. 121–241. London: Routledge and Kegan Paul, 1953.

———. 1946. "The Psychology of the Transference." *The Practice of Psychotherapy*, pp. 163–323. London: Routledge and Kegan Paul, 1954.

Kant, Immanuel. 1798. *Anthropology from a Pragmatic Point of View*. Trans. Victor Lyle Dowdell. Carbondale: Southern Illinois University Press, n.d.

Kapp, Julius. 1910. *Der junge Wagner*. Berlin and Leipzig: Schuster und Loeffler.

Katz, Jacob. 1985. *Richard Wagner: Vorbote des Antisemitismus*. Königstein:

Athenäum Verlag. English trans. by Allan Arkush, *The Darker Side of Genius: Richard Wagner's Anti-Semitism*, Hanover: Brandeis University Press, 1986.

Kerman, Joseph. 1956. *Opera as Drama*. New York: Knopf. Quoted from revised ed., Berkeley and Los Angeles: University of California Press, 1988.

Kneif, Tibor. 1969. "Zur Deutung der Rheintöchter in Wagners *Ring*." *Archiv für Musikwissenschaft* 26 (1969): 297–306. English trans. by Stewart Spencer, "On the Meaning of the Rhinemaidens in Wagner's *Ring*." *Wagner* 10 (1989): 21–28.

Konrad, Ulrich. 1987. "Robert Schumann und Richard Wagner: Studien und Dokumente." *Augsburger Jahrbuch für Musikwissenschaft*.

Kramer, Lawrence. 1990. *Music as Cultural Practice: 1800–1900*. Berkeley and Los Angeles: University of California Press.

Kühnel, Jürgen. 1986. "Wagners Schriften." *Richard-Wagner-Handbuch*, ed. Ulrich Müller and Peter Wapnewski, pp. 471–588. Stuttgart: Alfred Kröner Verlag. English trans. by Simon Nye. Cambridge: Harvard University Press, 1992, pp. 565–651.

Lacoue-Labarthe, Philippe, and Jean-Luc Nancy. 1978. *L'absolu littéraire*. Paris: Seuil.

Lavignac, Albert. 1897. *Le voyage artistique à Bayreuth*. Paris: Delagrave. Quoted from 1951 ed.

Lamennais, Félicité-Robert de. 1850. *De la société première et de ses lois ou de la religion*. 4th ed. Paris.

Leach, Edmund. 1966. "The Legitimacy of Solomon." *Archives Européennes de Sociologie* 7 (1966): 58–101.

———. 1972. "The Influence of Cultural Context on Non-Verbal Communication in Man." *Non-Verbal Communication*, ed. R. A. Hinde, pp. 315–44. Cambridge: Cambridge University Press.

Le Rider, J. 1982. *Le cas Otto Weininger: Racines de l'antiféminisme et de antisémitisme*. Paris: Presses Universitaires de France.

Leroux, Pierre. 1840. *De l'humanité*. Paris.

Lévi-Strauss, Claude. 1949. *The Elementary Structures of Kinship*. Trans. James Harle Bell and John Richard von Sturmer. Boston: Beacon Press, 1969.

———. 1955a. "The Structural Study of Myth." In vol. 1 of *Structural Anthropology*, trans. Claire Jacobson and Brooke Grundfest Schoepf, pp. 206–31. Harmondsworth: Penguin Books, 1977.

———. 1955b. *Tristes Tropiques*. Trans. John and Doreen Weightman. Harmondsworth: Penguin Books, 1976.

———. 1964. *The Raw and the Cooked*. Trans. John and Doreen Weightman. London: Jonathan Cape, 1970.

———. 1967. "The Sex of the Sun and Moon." In vol. 2 of *Structural Anthropology*, trans. Monique Layton, pp. 211–21. London: Allen Lane.

———. 1971. *The Naked Man*. Trans. John and Doreen Weightman. London: Jonathan Cape, 1981.

———. 1983. *The View from Afar*. Trans. Joachim Neugroschel and Phoebe Hoss. Oxford: Blackwell, 1985.

Lévy, Albert. 1904. *La philosophie de Feuerbach et son influence sur la littérature allemande*. Paris: Alcan.

Libis, Jean. 1980. *Le mythe de l'androgyne*. Paris: Berg International.

Lichtenberger, Henri. 1898. *Richard Wagner: Poète et penseur*. Paris: Alcan.

Liébert, Georges. "Entretien avec Pierre Boulez." *L'Avant-Scène Opéra*, nos. 6 and 7 (*L'Or du Rhin*), pp. 144–58.

Lindau, Paul. 1882. "*Parsifal* von Richard Wagner." *Kölnische Zeitung*, nos. 208, 210, 212 (29, 31 July, 2 August); reprinted in vol. 2 of Susanna Großmann-Vendrey, *Bayreuth in der deutschen Presse: Dokumentenband*, pp. 30–40. Regensburg: Gustav Bosse, 1977.

Lindenberg, Édouard. 1974. Thematic Analysis of *Tristan und Isolde* in booklet accompanying Furtwängler's 1952 recording, EMI C 153–00899/903.

Lorenz, Alfred. 1924. *Der musikalische Aufbau des Bühnenfestspieles Der Ring des Nibelungen*. Berlin: Max Hesses Verlag.

———. 1926. *Der musikalische Aufbau von Richard Wagners "Tristan und Isolde."* Berlin: Max Hesses Verlag.

McCreless, Patrick. 1982. *Wagner's "Siegfried": Its Drama, History, and Music*. Ann Arbor: UMI Research Press.

McDougall, J. 1973. "L'idéal hermaphrodite et ses avatars." *Nouvelle Revue de Psychanalyse* 7 (1973): 263–75.

Magee, Bryan. 1968. *Aspects of Wagner*. London: Alan Ross. Rev. ed., Oxford: Oxford University Press, 1988.

Mann, Thomas. 1933. "Leiden und Größe Richard Wagners." *Wagner und unsere Zeit: Aufsätze, Betrachtungen, Briefe*, ed. Erika Mann, pp. 63–121. Frankfurt am Main: Fischer, 1983. English trans. by Allan Blunden, "The Sorrows and Grandeur of Richard Wagner." *Pro and Contra Wagner*, pp. 91–148. London: Faber and Faber, 1985.

———. 1936. *Freud und die Zukunft*. Vienna: Bormann-Fischer.

———. 1937. "Richard Wagner und *Der Ring des Nibelungen*." *Wagner und unsere Zeit: Aufsätze, Betrachtungen, Briefe*, ed. Erika Mann, pp. 127–50. Frankfurt am Main: Fischer, 1983. English trans. by Allan Blunden, "Richard Wagner and *Der Ring des Nibelungen*." *Pro and Contra Wagner*, pp. 171–94.

Marx, Adolf Bernhard. 1845. *Die Lehre von der musikalischen Komposition*, part 3. Leipzig: Breitkopf und Härtel.

Marx, Karl. 1844. *Economic and Philosophic Manuscripts of 1844*. Karl Marx and Frederick Engels, *Collected Works*. London: Lawrence and Wishart, 1975.

Matter, Anne-Marie. 1959. *Richard Wagner éducateur: Une méditation pédagogique sur les rapports de la poésie et de l'éducation*. Lausanne: Imprimeries réunies.

Matter, Jean. 1968. *Wagner l'enchanteur*. Neuchâtel: La Baconnière.

———. 1977. *Traduction et commentaires de Richard Wagner, "Tristan et Isolde."* Lausanne: L'âge de l'homme.

Mauron, Charles. 1963. *Des métaphores obsédantes au mythe personnel*. Paris: Corti.

Mayrberger, Karl. 1881a. *Lehrbuch der musikalischen Harmonik*. Pressburg.

———. 1881b. "Die Harmonik Richard Wagner's an den Leitmotiven des Vorspieles zu *Tristan und Isolde* erläutert." *Bayreuther Blätter* 4 (1881): 169–80.

———. 1881c. *Die Harmonik Richard Wagner's an den Leitmotiven des Vorspieles aus "Tristan und Isolde" erläutert*. Bayreuth: Burger.

Meyer, Leonard B. 1989. *Style and Music*. Chicago: University of Chicago Press.

Michel, André. 1951. *Psychanalyse de la musique*. Paris: Presses Universitaires de France.

Michelet, Jules. 1846. *Le Peuple*. Paris: Hachette et Paulin.

Molino, Jean. 1975. "Fait musical et sémiologie de la musique." *Musique en Jeu* 17 (1975): 37–62. English trans. by J. A. Underwood, "Musical Fact and the Semiology of Music." *Music Analysis* 9 (1990): 105–56.

———. 1980. "Le mythe de l'androgyne." In vol. 2 of *Aimer en France, 1760–1860*, ed. Paul Viallaneix and Jean Ehrard, pp. 401–11. Clermont-Ferrand.

———. 1981. "L'androgyne." In vol. 1 of *Dictionnaire des poétiques*, ed. Yves Bonnefoy, pp. 27–29. Paris: Flammarion.

———. 1988. "Balzac et la technique du portrait: Autour de *Sarrasine*." *Mélanges offerts à Henri Coulet*, pp. 247–83. Aix-en-Provence: Publications de l'Université de Provence.

———. 1989. "Interpréter." *L'interprétation des textes*, ed. C. Reichler, pp. 9–52. Paris: Minuit.

Molino, Jean, and Joëlle Gardes-Tamine, 1988. *Introduction à l'analyse de la poésie*, vol. 2: *De la strophe à la construction du poème*. Paris: Presses Universitaires de France.

Mounin, Georges. 1969. *La communication poétique*. Paris: Gallimard.

Muller, Philippe. 1981. *Wagner par ses rêves*. Brussels: Pierre Mardaga éditeur.

Nattiez, Jean-Jacques. 1973. "Analyse musicale et sémiologie: Le structuralisme de Lévi-Strauss." *Musique en Jeu* 12 (1973): 59–79.

———. 1977. "Armonia." In vol. 1 of *Enciclopedia Einaudi*, pp. 841–67. Torino: Einaudi.

———. 1983. *Tétralogies (Wagner, Boulez, Chéreau): Essai sur l'infidélité*. Paris: Christian Bourgois éditeur.

———. 1984. *Proust musicien*. Paris: Christian Bourgois éditeur. English trans. by Derrick Puffett, *Proust as Musician*. Cambridge: Cambridge University Press, 1989.

———. 1985. "Les concepts de mise en série et d'intrigue dans l'analyse musicale." *Analytica: Studies in the Description and Analysis of Music in Honour of Ingmar Bengtsson*, pp. 35–46. Stockholm: Publications issued by the Swedish Academy of Music, no. 47.

———. 1987. *Musicologie générale et sémiologie*. Paris: Christian Bourgois éditeur. English trans. by Carolyn Abbate, *Music and Discourse: Toward a Semiology of Music*. Princeton: Princeton University Press, 1990.

Newman, Ernest. 1933–47. *The Life of Richard Wagner*. 4 vols. London: Cassell. All quotations from 1976 ed., Cambridge: Cambridge University Press.

———. 1949. *Wagner Nights*. London: Putnam.

Nietzsche, Friedrich. 1870a. "Das griechische Musikdrama." In vol. 1 of *Kritische Studienausgabe in 15 Bänden*, ed. Giorgio Colli and Mazzino Montinari, pp. 515–32. Munich: Deutscher Taschenbuchverlag, 1988.

———. 1870b. "Socrates und die Tragödie." In vol. 1 of *Kritische Studienausgabe in 15 Bänden*, pp. 533–49.

———. 1872. "Die Geburt der Tragödie." In vol. 1 of *Kritische Studienausgabe in 15 Bänden*, pp. 9–156. English trans. by Walter Kaufmann, *Basic Writings of Nietzsche*, pp. 15–144. New York: Modern Library, 1968.

———. 1887. "Zur Genealogie der Moral." In vol. 5 of *Kritische Studienausgabe in 15 Bänden*, pp. 245–412. English trans. by Walter Kaufmann, *Basic Writings of Nietzsche*, pp. 449–599.

Nietzsche, Friedrich. 1888. "Der Fall Wagner." In vol. 6 of *Kritische Studienausgabe in 15 Bänden*, pp. 9–53. English trans. by Walter Kaufmann, *Basic Writings of Nietzsche*, pp. 609–48.

———. 1988. *Friedrich Nietzsche: Sämtliche Werke. Kritische Studienausgabe in 15 Bänden*, ed. Giorgio Colli and Mazzino Montinari. 15 vols. Munich: Deutscher Taschenbuchverlag.

Novalis. 1800a. "Geistliche Lieder." In vol. 1 of *Schriften*, ed. Paul Kluckhohn and Richard Samuel, pp. 159–79. 5 vols. Stuttgart: W. Kohlhammer, 1960–88.

———. 1800b. "Hymnen an die Nacht." In vol. 1 of *Schriften*, pp. 130–58.

———. 1802. "Heinrich von Ofterdingen." In vol. 1 of *Schriften*, pp. 181–369.

Nunberg, H. 1973. "Tentatives de rejet de la circoncision." *Nouvelle Revue de Psychanalyse* 7 (1973): 205–28.

Oesterlein, Nikolaus. 1882–95. *Katalog einer Richard Wagner-Bibliothek*. 4 vols. Leipzig: Breitkopf und Härtel. Reprint, Wiesbaden: Sandig, 1970.

Olivier, Philippe. 1979. "Le Roi Marke, Kurwenal et Melot, ou trois évangiles de l'homosexualité wagnérienne." *Obliques* (special Wagner issue): 45–52.

Panofsky, Erwin. 1939. *Meaning in the Visual Arts*. Woodstock: Overlook Press.

Péladan, Sâr. 1911. *Amphithéâtre des sciences mortes: La science de l'amour*. Paris.

Picard, Raymond. 1965. *Nouvelle critique ou nouvelle imposture?* Paris: J.-J. Pauvert éditeur.

Porges, Heinrich. 1881–96. *Die Bühnenproben zu den Bayreuther Festspielen des Jahres 1876*. Chemnitz: Ernst Schmeitzner; and Leipzig: Verlag von Siegismund und Volkening. English trans. by Robert L. Jacobs, *Wagner Rehearsing the "Ring": An Eye-Witness Account of the Stage Rehearsals of the First Festival*. Cambridge: Cambridge University Press, 1983.

Pourtalès, Guy. 1932. *Wagner: Histoire d'un artiste*. Paris: Gallimard.

Prüfer, Arthur. 1906. "Novalis *Hymnen an die Nacht* in ihren Beziehungen zu Wagners *Tristan und Isolde*." In vol. 1 of *Richard Wagner-Jahrbuch*, ed. Ludwig Frankenstein, pp. 290–304. Leipzig: Deutsche Verlagsactiengesellschaft.

Rank, Otto. 1911. *Die Lohengrinsage: Ein Beitrag zu ihrer Motivgestaltung und Deutung*. Leipzig and Vienna.

Rattner, Josef. 1986. "Richard Wagner im Lichte der Tiefenpsychologie." *Richard-Wagner-Handbuch*, ed. Ulrich Müller and Peter Wapnewski, pp. 777–91. Stuttgart: Alfred Kröner Verlag.

Ritter, Johann Wilhelm. 1810. *Fragmente aus dem Nachlasse eines jungen Physikers*. 2 vols. Heidelberg: Mohr und Zimmer.

Ruwet, Nicolas. 1966. "Méthodes d'analyse en musicologie." *Revue belge de musicologie* 20 (1966): 65–90. Reprinted in *Langage, musique, poésie*, pp. 110–34. Paris: Seuil, 1972. English trans. by Mark Everist, *Music Analysis* 6 (1987): 3–36.

Sachs, Curt. 1961. *The Wellsprings of Music*. New York: McGraw Hill.

Saladin d'Anglure, Bernard. 1986. "Le troisième sexe Inuit." *Études Inuit Studies* 10 (1986): 25–113.

Sans, Édouard. 1969. *Richard Wagner et la pensée schopenhauerienne*. Paris: Klincksieck.

Sarotte, Georges-Michel. 1976. *Comme un frère: comme un amant. L'homosexualité masculine dans le roman et le théâtre américain de Herman Melville à James Baldwin*. Paris: Flammarion. English trans., *Like a Brother, Like a Lover*. Garden City: Anchor Press–Doubleday, 1978.

Scharschuch, Horst. 1963. *Gesamtanalyse der Harmonik von Richard Wagners Musikdrama "Tristan und Isolde."* Regensburg: Gustav Bosse.

Scheler, Max. 1929. *Mensch und Gesellschaft*. Zurich: Verlag der Neuen Rundschau.

Schelling, Friedrich Wilhelm Joseph von. 1802–3. "Philosophie der Kunst." In vol. 3 of *Schellings Werke*, ed. Manfred Schröter, pp. 135–387. Munich: C. H. Beck und R. Oldenbourg, 1959.

Schlegel, Friedrich. 1798. "Athenäums-Fragmente." In vol. 2 of *Kritische Schriften und Fragmente*, ed. Ernst Behler and Hans Eichner, pp. 105–56. 6 vols. Paderborn: Ferdinand Schöningh, 1988.

———. 1799a. *Lucinde*. Facsimile of 1799 ed., ed. Rudolf Frank. Leipzig: Insel, 1907.

———. 1799b. "Über die Philosophie [1799]: An Dorothea." In vol. 2 of *Kritische Schriften und Fragmente*, pp. 170–85.

———. 1800. "Gespräch über die Poesie." In vol. 2 of *Kritische Schriften und Fragmente*, pp. 186–222.

———. 1804. "Vom kombinatorischen Geist." In vol. 3 of *Kritische Schriften und Fragmente*, pp. 64–68.

Schubert, Gotthilf Heinrich von. 1814. *Die Symbolik des Traumes*. Leipzig: Brockhaus.

Schumann, Robert. 1837. "Giacomo Meyerbeer." In vol. 1 of *Gesammelte Schriften über Musik und Musiker*, pp. 323–27. 2 vols. 3d ed. Leipzig: Georg Wigand's Verlag.

Seidl, Anton. 1912. "Analogien-Parallelen-Harmonien." In vol. 4 of *Richard-Wagner-Jahrbuch*, ed. Ludwig Frankenstein, pp. 73–101. Berlin: Hausbücher-Verlag Hans Schippel.

Serrès, Michel. 1987. *L'hermaphrodite*. Paris: Flammarion.

Shaw, Bernard. 1898. *The Perfect Wagnerite: A Commentary on the Ring of the Niblungs*. London: Grant Richards.

Stein, Jack M. 1960: *Richard Wagner and the Synthesis of the Arts*. Detroit: Wayne State University Press.

Steiner, George. 1971. *In Bluebeard's Castle: Some Notes Towards the Re-definition of Culture*. London: Faber and Faber.

———. 1974. *The Nostalgia for the Absolute*. Toronto: Canadian Broadcasting Corporation Publications (CBC Massey Lectures).

———. 1988. *Le sens du sens*. Paris: Vrin.

———. 1989. *Real Presences*. Chicago: University of Chicago Press.

Strobel, Otto, ed. 1930. *Richard Wagner: Skizzen und Entwürfe zur Ring-Dichtung*. Munich: Verlag der F. Bruckmann A.G.

Sulloway, Frank J. 1980. *Freud, Biologist of the Mind: Beyond the Psychoanalytic Legend*. London: Fontana.

Susini, Eugène. 1942a. *Franz von Baader et le romantisme mystique*. 2 vols. Paris: Vrin.

———. 1942b. *Lettres inédites de Franz von Baader*. Paris: Vrin.

———. 1967. *Notes et commentaires aux lettres inédites de Franz von Baader*. Paris: Presses Universitaires de France.

Syberberg, Hans Jürgen. 1982. *Parsifal: Ein Filmessay*. Munich: Wilhelm Heyne Verlag. French trans. by Claude Porcell, *Parsifal: Notes sur un film*. Paris: Cahiers du cinéma and Gallimard.

Tittel, Ernst. 1966. "Wiener Musiktheorie von Fux bis Schönberg." *Beiträge zur Musiktheorie des 19. Jahrhunderts*, ed. Martin Vogel, pp. 163–201. Regensburg: Gustav Bosse.

Treitler, Leo. 1989. *Music and the Historical Imagination*. Cambridge: Harvard University Press.

Tristan, Flora. 1845. *L'émancipation de la femme ou le testament de la Paria: Ouvrage posthume de Mme Flora Tristan, complété d'après ses notes et publié par A. Constant*. Paris.

Vernant, Jean-Pierre. 1967. "Oedipe sans complexe." Reprinted in *Mythe et tragédie en Grèce ancienne*, ed. Jean-Pierre Vernant and Pierre Vidal-Naquet, pp. 75–98. Paris: Maspéro, 1981.

———. 1974. "Raisons du mythe." *Mythe et société en Grèce ancienne*, pp. 195–250. Paris: Maspéro.

Veyne, Paul. 1971. *Comment on écrit l'histoire*. Paris: Seuil. English trans. by Mina Moore-Rinvolucri. Middletown: Wesleyan University Press, 1984.

———. 1983. *Les Grecs ont-ils cru à leurs mythes?* Paris: Seuil.

Wagner, Richard. 1885. *Entwürfe, Gedanken, Fragmente aus nachgelassenen Papieren zusammengestellt*. Leipzig: Breitkopf und Härtel.

———. 1887–88. *Gesammelte Schriften und Dichtungen*. 10 vols. 2d ed. Leipzig: E. W. Fritzsch.

———. 1892–99. *Richard Wagner's Prose Works*. Trans. William Ashton Ellis. 8 vols. London: Kegan Paul, Trench, Trübner.

———. 1911–16. *Sämtliche Schriften und Dichtungen*. Ed. Richard Sternfeld and Hans von Wolzogen. 16 vols. Leipzig: Breitkopf und Härtel.

———. 1963. *Mein Leben*. Ed. Martin Gregor-Dellin. Munich: List Verlag. English trans. by Andrew Gray. Cambridge: Cambridge University Press, 1983.

———. 1967–. *Sämtliche Briefe*. Ed. Gertrud Strobel, Werner Wolf, Hans-Joachim Bauer, and Johannes Forner. Leipzig: VEB Deutscher Verlag für Musik.

Weininger, Otto. 1903. *Geschlecht und Charakter: Eine prinzipielle Untersuchung*. Vienna and Leipzig. English trans. from 6th German ed., *Sex and Character*. London: William Heinemann, 1906.

Westernhagen, Curt von. 1962. *Vom Holländer zum Parsifal: Neue Wagner-Studien*. Zurich: Atlantis.

———. 1963. "Die Kompositions-Skizze zu *Siegfrieds Tod*." *Neue Zeitschrift für Musik* 124 (1963): 178–82.

———. 1966. *Richard Wagners Dresdener Bibliothek, 1842–1849*. Wiesbaden: F. A. Brockhaus.

———. 1968. *Wagner*. Zurich: Atlantis. English trans. of 2d revised ed. by Mary Whittall, *Wagner: A Biography*. Cambridge: Cambridge University Press, 1978.

Whyte, Lancelot Law. 1967. *The Unconscious before Freud*. London: Social Science Paperbacks, in association with Tavistock Publications.

Wolzogen, Hans von. 1888. *Wagneriana*. Leipzig: Freund.

Yriarte, Charles. 1864. *Paris grotesque: Les célébrités de la rue*. Paris.

Zelinsky, Hartmut. 1976. *Richard Wagner: Ein deutsches Thema*. 2d ed., Berlin: Medusa, 1983.

INDEX